SLAVERY & RACE
IN AMERICAN
POPULAR CULTURE

SLAVERY & RACE IN AMERICAN POPULAR CULTURE

William L. Van Deburg

THE UNIVERSITY OF WISCONSIN PRESS

Published 1984

The University of Wisconsin Press
114 North Murray Street
Madison, Wisconsin 53715

The University of Wisconsin Press, Ltd.
1 Gower Street
London WC1E 6HA, England

First printing

Printed in the United States of America

For LC CIP information see the colophon

ISBN 0-299-09630-0 cloth
ISBN 0-299-09634-3 paper

To Alice

CONTENTS

ACKNOWLEDGMENTS

While conducting the research for this book, I came to realize that prevailing cultural images of a particular social group can be more important than reality in determining both individual and societal responses to that group. I also learned that the progress of my research depended to a great extent upon cooperative responses from individuals and groups who were asked to share their knowledge, opinions, or resources with me. The following people and organizations are owed a debt of gratitude for their contributions to and encouragement of this study: my congenial editor, Mary Wyer; professors Raymond Arsenault, Dominic Capeci, Darlene Hine, Ronald Lewis, Randall Miller, Carolyn Sylvander, and Harold Woodman; my able colleagues in the Department of Afro-American Studies at the University of Wisconsin–Madison; the staff members of the Wisconsin Center for Film and Theater Research, the State Historical Society Library, and the Memorial Library Interlibrary Loan Office; the members of the Graduate School Research and Kemper K. Knapp Bequest Committees; and the trustees of the Spencer Foundation. Finally, I offer typically inadequate, but sincere thanks to my wife Alice — a self-directed woman of rare good sense and tolerance.

INTRODUCTION

> No man can quite emancipate himself from his
> age and country, or produce a model in which
> the education, the religion, the politics, usages
> and arts of his times shall have no share.
>   Ralph Waldo Emerson, 1841

Slavery and Race in American Popular Culture is not a traditional text
on black slavery. Instead of detailing the operational mechanisms of the
Old South plantation society, the behavioral characteristics of its inhabi-
tants, or its place within the nation's political and economic structure, this
study describes how American novelists, historians, dramatists, poets, filmmakers, and songwriters have *perceived* and *interpreted* the Afro-American
slave experience from the seventeenth century to contemporary times. Although less easily ascertained than the beliefs of platform politicians, newspaper editors, or civil rights leaders, the interpretive views expressed in
period novels, poetry, short fiction, history texts, playscripts, songsheets,
and feature films reveal and record a great deal about the cultural underpinnings of American opinion on matters of race and slavery.[1]

For black Americans, the character and the overall effect of these opinions have been especially important. Subjected to a lengthy period of
bondage during the nation's formative years, Afro-Americans long were
confined by the chains of prejudice. As outcasts in a white-dominated
society, blacks alternately were portrayed as feeble-willed noble savages,
comically musical minstrel figures, and dehumanized brutes. Even their
white sympathizers, the antislavery spokespersons, were not free from
entrapment in a culture which seemed determined to forward slave images derogating black humanity while soothing majoritarian fears of a
black rebellion.

In response to the creation of these stereotypes, Afro-American historians, poets, and playwrights used the various modes of cultural expression
in a purposeful manner. Black historians wrote of slave achievement and
invention. Black poets told of the beauty inherent in blackness and spoke
often of racial consciousness. Black dramatists spoke more frequently of
white hypocrisy than they did of Uncle Tom and Tambo.

In ways such as these, black and white interpretations of chattel slavery
have conflicted with and challenged one another even to the present day.
The slave experience, both mental and physical, sociological and intellectual, has been the root cause of American sociocultural divergence, but
the images forwarded by writers of fiction, history, and drama also have

xi

served to divide and antagonize. Characterizations of slavery, as presented for popular consumption, tell us much about white anxieties and the continuing black desire to achieve equality through group strength, self-definition, and racial pride.

Slavery and Race in American Popular Culture does not presume to end once and for all the ancient controversy over how well art imitates life or vice versa. After all, the exact relationship of the creative artist to the social order has been debated in western society since the days of Plato's *Republic.*[2] The work does, however, proceed upon two basic and interrelated assumptions: that creative expression is a reflection of the author's beliefs, perspectives, and attitudes; and that this creative expression not only symbolizes society's values, but also to some variable degree creates, shapes, confirms, and strengthens them. In some sense then, all writers are cultural historians, and American authors thus have recorded the shifts and developments of national values through the centuries. *Slavery and Race in American Popular Culture* examines this archive of public opinion regarding black bondage and thereby offers a unique overview of the history, role, and progress of the Afro-American people in American society.[3]

I had hoped to write a book comparable to Thomas J. Pressly's *Americans Interpret Their Civil War* (1954). For better or for worse, the work now before you is proof that I strayed from my original plan to focus on shifting historiographical trends. Russel Nye's memorable graduate school lectures on early nineteenth-century literature and popular culture, John Blassingame's 1977 Mid-America Conference on History paper, entitled "Black Literary Images of Slavery," the poetry colloquia of former colleagues Eugene Redmond and Sarah Fabio, and fresh, innovative studies in popular and folk culture penned by Robert Toll, Thomas Cripps, and Lawrence Levine all served to expand the focus of my research to include literature and drama.

Lest innocent readers be led to believe that they are about to enter upon an epic journey in search of the American National Character, it must be noted that *Slavery and Race in American Popular Culture* seeks only to examine a limited schedule of questions and to offer a modest amount of interpretation and suggestive commentary. Nevertheless, a wide variety of viewpoints from a fairly extensive selection of published sources has been considered. My commentary on these sources is organized chronologically and by discipline. Individual sections treating a particular field are not meant to be exhaustive bibliographical essays, but when combined with associated sections provide a general review of the era's sociocultural opinion on questions of slavery and race.

Throughout the study I have attempted to present an honest interpretation of American cultural history. Nevertheless, this book should not be the final statement on the topic. All readers are encouraged to construct alternative formulations and interpretations; the selected bibliography contains a listing of reference works and secondary sources that will aid in such endeavors.

SLAVERY & RACE
IN AMERICAN
POPULAR CULTURE

CHAPTER 1

From African to Slave, 1619–1830

Look o'er your fields, and see them black with
slaves,
Where freedom's flag in boasted triumph waves
Anonymous poet, 1797

"No man is an island, entire of itself; every man is a piece of the continent, a part of the main." By 1830, these words from John Donne's *Devo-
tions* had acquired a far more complex meaning than his seventeenth-
century world could have imagined. In the United States, a new nation
was out of its dependence on the mother country and into budding ado-
lescence. The youthful society of early nineteenth-century America already
had begun to question imported values and structures of institutional organization. Within the new republic, men and women of ideas greatly
influenced national events and were, in turn, strongly affected by the developing culture in which they lived.

Black slavery gradually was becoming a fundamental of American sociopolitical life. During the years 1619–1830, the use and importance of African
labor had expanded to the extent that it was impossible to speak of black
bondage solely as an economic tool for the agricultural development of
frontier America. Long before the nineteenth-century's third decade, slavery had become a significant determinant of southern social values and
an important ingredient in interregional political relationships. Moreover,
while politicians were engaged in vigorous debate over the slave question —
constructing tentative solutions to immediate problems by designing the
three-fifths compromise, the 1793 fugitive slave law, the slave trade act
of 1807, and the 1820 Missouri Compromise — contributors to a unique
United States culture were examining and judging black bondage. As a
result, images of masters and slaves entered into the intellectual and cultural
fabric of the new nation.

In a period of beginnings, it is understandable that characterizations of
slavery forwarded by America's first dramatists, novelists, and historians
often would be vague, incomplete, or internally contradictory. What is remarkable, however, is the degree to which early impressions of the slave
institution approximated later, more fully considered and more heavily

textured descriptions. The relatively rapid development of images of blacks as natural slaves, noble savages, and comic minstrels tells us something about both the long-term importance of first impressions in human history and early Americans' deep-seated psychological need for an orderly universe. Seemingly, this world where perception and reality, word and deed were well matched could be created only by offering reasonable explanations for the continued existence of slavery in a God-fearing, liberty-loving, rapidly modernizing country.

That these initial descriptions of black slaves had tragic consequences for the earliest generations of African laborers is far more apparent than the fact that these same interpretations of slavery continued to affect later generations. When white writers first viewed what came to be called "the peculiar institution," they made vital decisions about the mode, means, and manner of expressing their initial response to black bondage. In offering possible explanations for their society's actions during the early colonial and post-Revolution years, they offered an easily modified, adaptable, and open-ended rationale for the slaveholders' perspective. In part, the result of this contribution to American ideas and popular culture has been to deny black Americans their place on the continent. In many respects, Afro-Americans today remain on a cultural and historical island within a predominantly white-oriented society. An explanation for this long-term segregation cannot be found solely in the history of labor regimentation, in the tracing of economic and demographic forces, or in the tallying of congressional votes. Images created by early historians, novelists, and dramatists also must be examined in seeking to uncover the genesis of today's cultural attitudes and intellectual assumptions.

Tory Villainy and the Black Victim

As interpreters of the black past, modern day American historians have found the colonial origins of slavery to be a decidedly compelling, but endlessly perplexing topic. Most contemporary scholarship on this particular historiographical problem has focused on the interrelationship of black bondage with white racism. Like the time-honored chicken-or-egg conundrum, the question of the slavery-racism interface has generated a wide variety of responses; but recent studies, influenced by the progressive evolution of American race relations during the last twenty-five years, generally agree that race prejudice preceded and contributed greatly to the establishment of racial slavery in the colonies.[1]

Just as these scholars reflect contemporary values by their identification of proscriptive racial attitudes in individual and institutional behavior, the first generation of American writers recorded white attitudes toward blacks-as-slaves even as they penned the first histories of the colonies. If we accept the main thrust of historian Winthrop Jordan's proposition that Anglo-American colonists were possessed of a seldom articulated but apparently preconceived notion of African difference and inferiority — and that this contributed to an "unthinking decision" to enslave blacks — it becomes possible to explain certain judgments made by seventeenth-, eighteenth-, and early nineteenth-century writers regarding the slaves' place in history.[2]

The most striking characteristic of the early histories was the sketchy nature of the accounts of slavery. The reader could learn little more of bondsmen than that a Dutch ship deposited twenty Negroes on the banks of the James River sometime in 1619 or 1620. The problem of the origins of slavery seemed to bother few writers. Following the lead of Captain John Smith — whose *Generall Historie* (1624) contained the terse statement, "About the last of August came in a dutch man of warre that sold us twenty Negars" — later chroniclers of colonial Virginia assumed that the blacks were purchased and put to work as slaves. With status options for Afro-Americans thus eliminated, most early writers rushed on to other matters. Missing from such accounts was the questioning attitude which in more recent times has led historians to seek out cause-and-effect relationships between slavery, prejudice, and economics.[3]

That colonial writers were not ready to entertain historiographical complexities of this nature can be explained in various ways. First of all, during the eighteenth century hereditary black bondage was not as tenaciously embedded within the nation's economic or social systems as it was to be in later years. This relative lack of institutional development could explain why at least one early history devoted more text and considerably more invective to the "stinking, nauseous, and unpalatable Weed" tobacco than it did to the situation of the laborers who were employed to produce that major cash crop. Nevertheless, the claim of Boston physician-historian William Douglass that Virginia and Maryland were importing some 4,000 black slaves annually during the mid-eighteenth century, and that one Maryland planter owned as many as 1,300 chattels, seemingly should have spurred others to investigate the roots of this developing system of labor mobilization.[4]

A second explanation for the exclusion of slavery from early analyses lies in the nature of the historical profession prior to 1830. The most prolific writers of history in colonial America were, for the most part, New England clerics who modeled their works on traditional methods and ideas. In the writing of history, as in all study, piety came first. To Puritan historians such as Edward Johnson, author of *The Wonder-working Providence of Sion's Saviour in New England* (1653), the acts of men and the purposes of God were merely two aspects of a single morality play. History, as he saw it, was a record of the Creator acting through human events which were deemed important insofar as they revealed the divine. Such a book was useful only when it served as a testimony to God's providential power, as a memorial to the pious, or as an incentive to righteousness. To the degree that Puritan scholars wrote of their own recent past in order to emphasize their ties with the scholarly and religious traditions of the Old World, they slighted other areas of colonial history. Even when not engaged in writing in the filiopietistic tradition, New England clerics more often were concerned about their Indian neighbors than about the less threatening black slave system.[5]

Pietistic usage and focus aside, the colonial histories were affected by another societal obstacle which served to limit their concern with the details of Afro-American bondage: the miniscule role accorded New World history in seventeenth- and eighteenth-century higher education. While the course of study in colonial colleges was intended to be a liberal education equally suitable for future ministers, physicians, or governors, the curriculum was stolidly traditional. As such, students underwent a course of study very similar to that which had been offered at Old Cambridge. Harvard College undergraduates, for instance, took a prescribed course in the Liberal Arts (grammar, logic, rhetoric, arithmetic, geometry, and astronomy), in the Three Philosophies (metaphysics, ethics, and natural science), and in Greek, Hebrew, and Ancient History.[6] While Harvard's first history course, Historia Civis, was offered to seniors in 1643, it was not until 1839 that the institution endowed its first professorship in history. Jared Sparks, biographer of George Washington and first holder of the McLean Professorship of Ancient and Modern History, finally nudged postsecondary historical studies from their classical foundations through his lectures on the American Revolution.[7]

Influenced by institutional and intellectual ties to England, recipients of colonial higher education did not attempt to divorce themselves from that tradition until events of the Revolution made such a separation desirable. Thus, American printers produced works which expressed the everyday concerns and preoccupations of the reading public. Books on the history of slavery were not well represented in their list of titles. Of the total colonial publishing output for the period 1639–1763, thirty-seven percent consisted of theological writings, about thirty-nine percent were either legal or literary works, and only about four percent were histories. Most popular of the pre-Revolutionary secular history books were William Robertson's *History of Scotland* (1759) and David Hume's *History of Great Britain* (1759) — two lengthy works little concerned with recalling the recent American colonial past or the role of nonwhite peoples in that past.[8]

Eventually, during the second half of the eighteenth century, the American colonists were stirred to both political and intellectual rebellion against their British cousins. Nationalistic tendencies so tellingly evident in the colonies' representative assemblies could also be seen in the histories of the day. As they changed their orientation toward England, the patriots reshaped their understanding of the origins of black bondage. The consensus which emerged from this examination of slavery's roots held that the British had forced unwilling African laborers on unwilling New World settlers. Great Britain's merchants, magistrates, and ministers were assailed by American writers for engaging in conspiratorial machinations which "baffled the voice of humanity" emanating from colonial assemblies. Unlike the patriots who tried to arrest the progress of slavery through restrictive importation laws, British officials not only yielded to traders in "the abominable traffic," they "persisted with criminal obstinacy" in withholding their assent to restrictive legislation. Thus was the historiography of slavery revised and the "unthinking decision" made more purposeful in the minds of the post-Revolution readers.[9]

As they verbally flogged the Tory villain, historical writers of the late eighteenth and early nineteenth century demonstrated an increased willingness to express their feelings about slavery and the slave trade. Influenced by the same sociopolitical trends which encouraged the growth of early antislavery sentiment, many historians concluded that it was a moral wrong to hold blacks in chains while declaring their own national liberation from George III. Acting upon this belief, writers now condemned England and slavery in the same breath; the British had introduced "an evil of the most serious and afflicting nature" which had resulted in a blot on the American character. In this manner, the historians expressed both their nationalism and their morality—two components of human belief and experience which have not always rested easily in the same frail, mortal body.[10]

While historians of the post-Revolutionary War era assured their readers that slavery's blot would soon be wiped away by the humanitarian efforts of recently liberated white Americans, and while they wrote that "negroes in general, have experienced a favourable change in their condition, since the Revolution," this optimism would prove to be short-lived. Patriotism and anti-British sentiment were not going to free the entire slave population. As recorded in histories of the era, late eighteenth-century nationalism was a flawed and unstable combination of war-borne attitudes, local attachments, and lingering colonial influences. Though they may have recognized the basic character of this national feeling, historians failed to act upon their analysis of the situation in a manner which would have freed their writings from the lingering influence of the "unthinking decision."[11]

Histories written in this country after the war were not for the most part national histories. Most of the volumes produced between 1783 and 1830 dealt with individual states rather than the nation as a whole. The War of 1812 helped to solidify American nationalism, but history writers continued to echo Charleston physician and historian David Ramsay to the effect that in new nations or states composed of settlers from diverse backgrounds "a considerable period must elapse, before the people amalgamate into a mass possessing an uniform national character."[12] At the same time, a need to promote and encourage feelings of national unity prompted historians to place the first American heroes before the reading public with rhapsodic descriptions of the "religion, patriotism, and valour, supported by industry and economy, joined to resolution, perseverance, and enterprise" of the Founding Fathers. Surely, wrote one such eulogist, virtues such as these "made this wilderness blossom like the rose, and this savage desert become vocal with the praises of our God."[13]

Even as they were awakened to the slaves' plight by the rhetoric of 1776 and stirred by the possibilities of a new national spirit, writers of this generation realized that slavery and its related evils had survived the British exodus. It became increasingly apparent that black bondage in America was not a temporary arrangement supported solely by aristocratic, liberty-usurping Tories; instead it was a growing, institutionalized economic system sanctioning the use of an unpaid labor force. As such, the question of the origins of slavery had to be reexamined. But this time the answers would be formulated in a vastly different social atmosphere.

By the early nineteenth century, influential national leaders joined historians in condemning chattel slavery as immoral. Since British avarice could not be blamed for post-Revolution government support, an explanation for slavery had to be found within the context of America's developing national identity. Criticizing American leaders would endanger the national spirit, so the historiographical compromise for some was, in effect, a modified version of Revolutionary War ideals. Slavery was still seen as a fait accompli, a long established method of labor regimentation. Once before these modifications had included an element of blame — British merchants and officials were said to have foisted the bond system on the colonies. In the same manner historians again shifted the onus of slavery's origins onto someone else — the Afro-American bondsmen themselves.

During the early years of the nineteenth century, a number of histories appeared which proposed that African descent "fitted [blacks] peculiarly for the indurance of labor in hot climates." As Hugh McCall recounted in his *History of Georgia* (1811), the most promising source of wealth in the early days of that colony had been the cultivation of rice, farming which "could not be carried on successfully without the assistance of Africans, whose constitutions seemed formed by nature to bear the heat and exposure of a climate, most favorable for its production." David Ramsay's *History of the United States* (1818) noted that much of the southern sea coast would have remained uncultivated were it not for black slaves. Plagued by disease-breeding marshes and low lying acreage, the entire region was deemed fatal to white laborers. Slavery, then, "seemed to be forced on the southern provinces" by nature.[14]

While such accounts of southern agriculture were by no means universally proslavery and some were even highly critical of black bondage, this plausible physiological answer to the question of slavery's genesis was not soon forgotten by American historians.[15] If histories of early America record concern for the plight of those denied an equitable portion of the Revolution's gains, they also contain the seeds of the proslavery argument that African-Americans were admirably suited by both strength of body and weakness of mind to serve an agricultural apprenticeship of indefinite length. For those white Americans who would follow this line of reasoning, neither racial bias against blacks nor British usurpation of colonial legislative prerogative could explain the origins of the American slave labor system quite as well as the idea that African peoples were natural slaves whose proper status long had been that of servants. Beyond the relatively underdeveloped and unthreatening nature of the era's slave system, beyond scholarly preoccupation with the Founding Fathers, beyond the inadequacies of professional training, it was historians' acceptance of this decision to equate blacks with slaves and slaves with blacks which foreclosed historiographical possibilities that might have served as a liberating force toward ending black bondage before it became embedded in the American past.

The Noble Captive

Like the historians, America's first novelists, poets, and short story writers worked in an intellectual atmosphere which owed much to British precedent and New England piety. Those early American settlers who had both the time and the taste for literature generally favored works that were mannered, didactic, sentimental, and European. For a good number of readers, the messages of such poetry and fiction had to be religiously orthodox as well. While not all would agree with clergyman-educator Timothy Dwight that "between the Bible and novels there is a gulf fixed which few novel readers are willing to pass," Americans tended to shun writings which failed to promote time-tested moral values.[16]

This moralistic sentimentality could be seen in early British fictional treatments of black characters in New World settings. Mrs. Aphra Behn's *Oroonoko* (1688), contributed importantly to the development of a noble savage tradition in English literature. Through the adventures of her hero, an African prince who was kidnapped and forced to labor as a slave in Surinam, Behn described Africans as unspoiled children of nature whose descent into bondage could only serve to awaken humanitarian sympathies. As a literary appeal to view the slave's plight as pitiable, Behn's book worked well — perhaps too well given the influence the novel would have on later depictions of African adaptation to New World life.

A key section of *Oroonoko* describes how the noble African prince, re-named Caesar by his captors, responded to being flogged "like a common Slave." Vowing to kill those who had whipped him, the fallen prince announces that "Oroonoko scorns to live with the Indignity that was put on Caesar"; he plans to kill both himself and his wife, the beautiful Imoinda, as well as his enemies. Discussing his plans with his mate, he tells her that it would be impossible to escape and so they must die. Sharing Caesar's belief that without his protection she would be "ravished by every Brute; expos'd first to their nasty Lusts, and then a shameful Death," Imoinda pleads for an immediate end to her life. Caesar clutched his bride in a final embrace, drew his knife, and "with a hand resolved, and a heart-breaking within, gave the fatal Stroke, first cutting her Throat, and then severing her yet smiling Face from that delicate Body, pregnant as it was with the Fruits of tenderest Love." Burdened with grief, the prince delayed killing his enemies. For more than a week he mourned over Imoinda's body until eventually he could not rise from her side. It was in this morose and physically weakened condition that he was discovered by a search party. Instead of attacking them, the noble Caesar acted the tragic victim as he "cut a piece of Flesh from his own Throat, and threw it at 'em . . . rip'd up his own Belly, and took his Bowels and pull'd 'em out, with what strength he could." Beleaguered by bondage, the noble African sought release from his trials by attempting suicide.[17]

While few writers could surpass the sheer volume of sentimental and moralistic literary devices included in such British works — Daniel Defoe's depiction of slavery in *The History and Remarkable Life of the Truly Honourable Col. Jacque* (1722) included at least two swoonings and thirty-three instances of weeping — American literature further encouraged the notion that African-Americans were either weak-willed or psychologically ill-adapted to the demands of an ordered life.[18] Early American writers created panoramic West African backdrops for their gentle and sensitive noble savages. These settings offered such a stark contrast to New World vistas that it is not at all surprising to find the Africans suicidal once they entered the dark environs of bondage. According to Thomas Branagan's

Avenia (1805), the first American poem of any considerable length devoted to the subject of black slavery, "Afric" was a place:

> Where, fraught with fragrance, crops luxuriant grow,
> Where cornels, blushing on the hawthorn glow.
> Where with soft tendrils the rich clust'ring vine,
> Doth round its friend, the aged elm entwine,
> And tow'ring oaks their shadowy branches spread,
> O'er the fat herds that on their fruit are fed;
> Where stately palm trees form a cool retreat,
> To screen the native from the sultry heat.[19]

As with the original Eden, evil eventually appeared in the midst of this peaceable kingdom. In these poetic accounts, Christian slave-traders transformed the pastoral landscape into a battleground:

> See verdant fields all clotted stiff with gore,
> Which ne'er were stain'd with human blood before;
> Where mortals wounded pil'd on mortals dead,
> Made verdant green be ting'd with crimson red![20]

Defeated in warfare, the heroic but captive African would descend into a melancholy stupor. From the dank hold of a slaving vessel the chattel might wistfully cry:

> Adieu, to my dear native shore,
> To toss on the boisterous wave;
> To enjoy my kindred no more,
> But to weep—the tears of a SLAVE![21]

If the shackled slave was especially eager to escape the uncertainties of life on the New World plantation, he might try to defy his guards—those "armed murderers with smiles on their lips and audacity on their fronts"—while the ship was still at sea. One piece of short fiction published in 1791 describes a group of African captives who were lined up on the deck of a slave ship. A few of the enslaved "fiercely demanded vengeance from Heaven," but more common were the spiritually defeated—slaves who soaked the deck with their tears or who gazed hopelessly into the distance. One young man "driven to raging madness . . . tore out his teeth with gnawing the chains which crushed his father's limbs." A pregnant woman who, unaided and in irons, gave birth to her child on the aft deck was said to have flung both herself and the infant overboard in a desperate act of "dumb ferocity." Such portrayals of the men and women who were torn from their African paradise by the Atlantic slave trade encouraged readers to conclude that black slaves were violently suicidal.[22]

Images of madness and death remained even when the scene shifted to the American South. Rare was the noble savage who could be found alive and well at the end of an early American account of bondage. Those who survived slavery's cruelties the longest might make their final soliloquy especially poignant by comparing life in their homeland with present conditions. As the narrator in *The American in Algiers* (1797) recalled:

> In youth's gay hours, I spent a joyous life,
> Free from contention, care, or feudal strife;
> Nurs'd in the lap of luxury and ease,
> Nocturnal pleasures follow'd days of peace,
> And life was one continued scene of bliss; . . .

Now, however, after enduring a quarter century of enslavement, he summed up a ruined life by noting:

> Suffice to say, 'gainst me all ills combin'd,
> Enerv'd my body, and unhing'd my mind;
> · · · · · · · · · · · · · · ·
> I'm now worn out with servitude and woe,
> And patient wait for death to strike the blow
> That ends each care, each suffering and dread,
> Lets drop the curtain of oblivion's shade,
> And sends me headlong to the silent dead.[23]

Even if they were not old and near death, fictionalized slaves were shown to be noble and contented while in Africa, weak and wretched in America. An anonymous piece of short fiction first published in 1798 featured one such bondsman as its central character. As he took a brief respite from his arduous field work, this "child of sorrow" told a plantation visitor of slavery's burdens — of the constant threat of whippings and of the bitter labors which served only to fatten the masters. Then, in a voice "which misery seemed to have rendered almost inarticulate," the slave described earlier years. In Africa he had been strong and cheerful and had greeted each morning with joy. After a day of pleasant and fruitful work, he would relax by joining a dance in the meadow at sunset. Moreover, in his homeland he had triumphed over all rivals by winning the hand of "the beauteous Yoncha . . . the envy of surrounding virgins." The valiant lover had risked his life to win Yoncha's approval; but now it was fortunate that she could not see his enfeebled form or hear his desperate groans. Changed from hero to slave the broken man felt helpless: "white men are very powerful; for their Gods are stronger than ours. They are not appeased by the sighs of the negro."[24] Characterizations of African-Americans cowed and defeated by bondage left little room for doubting that self-sacrifice was the antidote to pitifully shattered dreams:

> Oh! had we died upon our native plain,
> Stretch'd like brave heroes, by our tyrants slain!
> Oh! had our blood smoak'd on each ruffian spear,
> And thus sav'd us from sin, insult and fear
> But now we meet a shameful shocking fate,
> Unworthy of the brave, the bold, the great.[25]

As the first American historians foreclosed historiographical and sociological possibilities with their "unthinking decision" to equate blacks with slaves and slaves with blacks, authors of fiction and poetry portrayed the black American as, to quote an eighteenth-century bard, "a Man almost unman'd." For those in the reading public who would compare the slaves' weakness and degradation to the bold character and heroic exploits of white American champions of faith and freedom, "almost" must have seemed a somewhat superfluous modifier.[26]

Unable to help themselves when confronted with powerful whites, fictional portraits of slaves were well suited for use as sentimental props in the early antislavery campaign. Founded upon religious and patriotic beliefs in freedom and natural rights, the pre-1830 freedom movement and much of its literature expressed the incomplete egalitarianism of the patriot generation. Though it perpetuated the suspicion that blacks were a different and inferior type of humankind, early antislavery writing nevertheless angered slaveholding interests. After all, literary treatments of the insult of black bondage also pictured whites as greedy exploiters of an agricultural labor system based upon "blood and rapine."[27] Moreover, the idea that important moral differences were developing between sections of the new nation did little to relieve the slaveholder's anxiety. According to one poet, the advantages of living in a freedom-loving state such as Ohio should have been obvious to all:

> Heres no dominereing
> No curseing no swearing
> Nor nocking poor negroes about
>   .   .   .   .
> Ohios fine stream

Has the foremost claim
Of Liberty here upon earth
All coulors are free
In equality
All equal all free from their birth.[28]

The advantages of such a life would be hotly debated in literature discussing sectional and ideological questions.[29]

During the first decades of the nineteenth-century, Virginia political
economist George Tucker and New York's patrician novelist James Fenimore
Cooper not only constructed a series of fictional images which long would
influence American cultural views of slavery, but in addition each contributed importantly to a new modification — the development of a socioeconomic rationale which could support the continued existence of "the
peculiar institution."

Set in Westchester County, New York, during the Revolution, Cooper's
The Spy (1821) benefitted from the postwar generation's willingness to support authors who described American manners, promoted the new national
consciousness, and who located their plots in American settings. A small,
first printing of the book was quickly followed by a larger 3,000 copy issue. Two months later, another 5,000 copies were printed. English, French,
German, and Italian editions followed.[30]

In *The Spy*, Cooper presented his readers with the first detailed portrait
of an Afro-American slave to appear in an American novel.[31] Caesar Whar-
ton was a house servant of some sixty years who had been reared from
infancy in his master's home. Unlike free blacks roaming the countryside
"unfettered by principles, and uninfluenced by attachments," he "identified himself with the welfare of those whom it was his lot to serve." Considering himself a part of the whites' family, Caesar was devoted to his
master's interests. He took pride in his contributions to the smooth func-
tioning of the estate.[32]

Although his presence in the novel served to delineate the social class
and genteel manner of the whites, Caesar's chief function was to provide
comic relief. The elderly slave seemed a born comedian. He possessed a
pair of eyes which "stood at a most formidable distance from each other,"
a nose with "abundantly capacious" nostrils, and a mouth which opened
to reveal a "double row of pearls" stretching from ear to ear. All were contained in a skull so hard and dense that falling on his head could not damage it. Contributing to his comic appeal was a lower body which seemed
to be composed of an "abundance of material injudiciously used." His calves
were placed "neither before nor behind," but rather on "the outer side of
the limb, inclining forward." His feet were so large and abnormally shaped

that it was said to be an occasional matter of dispute "whether he was not walking backwards."[33]

When placed in stressful or dangerous situations, Caesar's body served as a visual barometer of the slave's inner strength. Although naturally endowed with a constitution tolerant of heat "that would have roasted a white man," this trait was of little value when the slave's mind was controlled by the icy fingers of fear. Indeed, Caesar's teeth "chattered with affright" so often that it seemed this was the only response he could offer in a crisis. Uppermost on the list of things which set the faithful servant "shaking in his shoes" was his uncontrollable fear of ghosts. When, on one occasion, he was ordered to make a nighttime ride past the local graveyard, Caesar was seized with a superstitious awe that would have made Ichabod Crane appear intrepid. Imagining that he saw something superhuman coming toward him, the fearful slave abandoned the reins to the coachhorse he was riding, clung tightly to his mount, and let the road fly past like lightning. It was not until he saw the cheerful hearth at his destination that Caesar could calm his fears enough to recall "whither and on what business he was riding in this headlong manner."[34]

In contributing such bits of lightness and humor to *The Spy*'s more serious examination of conflicting Revolutionary era loyalties, Cooper's Caesar walked a fine line between characterization and typecasting. While Caesar possessed the traits of loyalty, comic appearance, and superstition which in later years would form key elements in a rigid formula for depicting black characters, the houseservant was not yet wholly reduced to burlesque. Cooper incompletely stereotyped slave behavior and personality. Though Caesar had been named in the classical manner of later Cooper characters — such as Agamemnon in *The Pioneers*, or Scipio Africanus and Cassandra in *The Red Rover* — he nevertheless insisted upon claiming his own rather than his master's surname. While the elderly slave seemed stereotypically fond of gaudy colors, he possessed enough individual dignity to be offended by the word "nigger" — in one instance tartly responding to the insult by declaring: "A black man so good as white so long as he behaves heself." Caesar often played the buffoon, but he had the presence of mind to construct a philosophical explanation for the low status accorded blacks in the New World. According to the comic slave philosopher, "much mischief come of curiosity. If dere had nebber been a man curious to see Africa, dere would be no color people out of dere own country."[35]

Like *The Spy*, George Tucker's *The Valley of Shenandoah* (1824) — the first American novel to employ a southern plantation setting in any important way — depicted certain aspects of slavery and slave personality which later southern writers, fearful of giving ammunition to abolitionists, would shun as being politically unwise. In tracing the moral and economic decline of a late eighteenth-century Virginia family, Tucker revealed inherent weaknesses in the society of which he was a part.[36]

Treating the negative side of the institution frankly, Tucker criticized the wastefulness of absentee management. At Easton, a secondary plantation owned by the once-proud, but now financially-pressed Grayson family, Edward Grayson discovered how a fine estate could be totally destroyed by careless overseer management. He found the slaves poorly clothed, sick, badly nursed, and without proper medicine or food. Throughout their quarters there was a sense of sadness and discontent. Much of this misery could be traced to the fact that Master Edward was being forced to sell in order to settle debts accumulated by Colonel Grayson, the now deceased Revolutionary War hero and family patriarch. Through the Colonel's bad example, Tucker's novel took planters to task for their extravagant hospitality, inordinate pride, and lack of acumen in business affairs.[37]

In his account of the resulting slave sale, Tucker introduced readers to the shock of seeing "beings of the same species with himself, set up for sale to the highest bidder, like horses or cattle." Hoisted up before a gawking audience of prospective buyers, the bondsmen were anxious over their prospects for the future and humiliated by the buyers' questions about their age, health, and abilities. Although each slave who stood on the auction block was made to feel something of his or her "utter insignificance as a member of civilized society," not all were silent. Some were openly hostile or mounted the platform with "a look of firmness, and of what some might consider sullenness." Incompletely moulded into antebellum stereotypes, Tucker pictured slaves who expressed bitterness and rebellion when they shouted "No!" to the rude questions of prospective white owners.[38]

Despite his willingness to expose certain of the less picturesque aspects of southern life, Tucker made it clear that the benevolence of Virginian planters could compensate for the societal blemishes of slave-trading. If Edward Grayson felt that black bondage was a moral and political evil, he was equally convinced that the situation "admits of no remedy that is not worse than the disease." Since "no good or prudent man" would risk the "waste and butchery" which general emancipation might bring, and since no practical plan for foreign colonization had been devised, the planters were said to have been forced to "set down contented, and endeavor to *mitigate* a disease which admits of *no cure*."[39]

Even when hounded by debt, Tucker's Virginia gentlemen tried their best to be good masters. On most occasions, slaves reciprocated with the expressions of love and respect which in many later fictional works would become their standard response to almost any situation. Successful in their efforts to avoid the auction-day separation of husbands from wives or young children from mothers, the Graysons were rewarded by shouts of "Heaven bless my kind mistress wherever she goes," "Remember me to Miss Louisa," and "God bless my mistress — we never shall get such another!" as the slaves departed for their new and sometimes distant homes. The whites responded to these kind words by parceling out gifts of sugar and molasses to each departing family. Despite his critique of the southern labor system's more noticeable flaws, Tucker tells his readers that the slaves' "simple hearts are very susceptible of warm attachment."[40]

If the works of Tucker and Cooper contained slave imagery which had not yet hardened into stereotype, they nevertheless foreshadowed fictional treatments by both southern and northern authors who would more adamantly forward the view that the nation's bondsmen were "better supplied with the necessaries of life than the labouring class of any country out of America." During the 1830s, the growing controversy over slavery included Cooper's *The American Democrat* (1838), with its hardened defense of an institution "as old as human annals" which was likely to continue "as long as man shall remain under the different degrees of civilization that mark his actual existence."[41] Buffeted by abolitionist invective, novelists of the 1830–60 period would be compelled to abandon their tentative and ambiguous portraits of slave characters — choosing instead to create fictional types suitable for use in either the proslavery or antislavery campaigns. As they completed a process begun by the early poets and short fiction writers, this generation of authors would remove completely the modifying adverb "almost" from the eighteenth-century description of the black American as "a Man almost unman'd."

Whites in Blackface

Just ten weeks after the 1821 publication of *The Spy*, New York businessman Charles Powell Clinch brought the Revolutionary War tale to the Park Theatre stage. The three act play was well received and various theatrical versions of Cooper's novel continued to be presented into the 1850s. While the creation of Caesar served as an important benchmark in American fiction, his comical antics were already familiar to the theatergoing public: Caesar's similarity to certain stage-characterizations of blacks is quite striking.[42]

The first dramatic portrayals of slaves were presented to American audiences at a time when traveling English acting companies dominated stagecraft. Some colonial religious leaders condemned the theatre as "the snare of concupiscence and filthy lusts of wickid whoredom" even though actors were usually seen in conventional romantic plays drawn directly from the

London stage. As late as the mid-nineteenth century leading American actors still maintained their reputations and sustained themselves in Shakespearean roles.[43]

On occasion, the less inhibited English players cavorted on stage in blackface slave roles. In the stage version of *Oroonoko* (1696), for example, the pathos of Mrs. Behn's original storyline was interrupted in Act 2 when an actor playing the part of Stanmore announced: "Hark! the slaves have done their work; And now begins their evening merriment." The scene then quickly changed to a group of slaves dancing and singing a love song in honor of "fair Clemene," a "little queen" who had infatuated the men and had made the women of the slave community exceedingly jealous of her charms.[44] Isaac Bickerstaffe's *The Padlock* (1768), introduced audiences on both sides of the Atlantic to a West Indian slave who frequently took over the stage with his song-and-dance routines. Mungo spoke in a pseudo-Jamaican dialect and liked to drink. One evening when master Don Diego left him in charge of the estate, Mungo took advantage of the lack of supervision to throw a party. Emboldened by good company and the contents of Diego's wine cellar, the imprudent slave burst forth in song:

> Wit de toot, toot, toot,
> Of a merry flute,
> And cymbalo
> And tymbalo
> To boot:
> We dance and we sing,
> Till we make a house ring,
> And tied in his garters old massa may swing.[45]

Not long thereafter, the comically reeling Mungo was discovered by Don Diego — his bragging judged to be evidence of madness.[46]

Upon this British base, America's first playwrights constructed blackface characters who eventually far surpassed Cooper's Caesar in their ability to elicit howls of laughter from white audiences. By portraying slaves as loyal, servile dupes who spoke and sang in broken English while they unsuccessfully mimicked their white owners, early American dramatists contributed key visual images which long would influence other segments of national culture. The development of the stage slave role foreshadowed the rise of Afro-American minstrelsy and previewed the process by which white popular culture labeled blacks as primitive and comical outsiders even as blacks participated in the development of American social and economic institutions.

Toward the close of the eighteenth century, a number of plays penned by American writers contained comic black characters. Although differing in theme and setting, several of these productions portrayed slaves as possessing what seemed an almost universal Negro trait — the unflappable desire to imitate the appearance and demeanor of whites. If such imitation was not exactly the most supreme form of flattery, it did serve to define both the characters' loyalty and the degree to which they willingly separated themselves from their African/Afro-American cultural roots.

The most striking example of the blacks' distorted assimilation appeared in John Murdock's *The Politicians* (1798). In this often satirical depiction of the late eighteenth-century political climate, a group of black servants argue over the comparative virtues and vices of the English and the French. Proud to consider themselves slave citizens of the new republic, Pompey and Caesar both act according to the accepted standards of their respective masters. Upon meeting in the street, the two begin bantering ceremoniously in a way which reveals the ludicrous incongruity between their attempted gentility and their actual station in life.

> *Caesar:* Citizen Pompey, how you do, to-day, Sir?
> *Pompey:* Tank you, citizen Caesar, berry well; I hope you, and
>   you lady, enjoy good health.
> *Caesar:* Bery good, I gib you tank, Sir.[47]

Having dispensed with formalities, the men begin to discuss the possibility of a war with France. Caesar criticizes the French, Pompey berates the English, and their conversation suggests a dependence upon white opinion.

> *Caesar:* What you dam English, for?
> *Pompey:* What e debil you dam French, for?
> *Caesar:* Cause I don't like 'em.
> *Pompey:* Why you no like 'em?
> *Caesar:* Cause massa no like 'em.
> *Pompey:* My massa no like English — I hate 'em too — drom proud
>   — so conceit coxcomb — look like ebery body tunk in e nose.
> *Caesar:* Ten hundred time better den French, drom fribble, buf-
>   foon, ape, monkey. . . . [48]

To stop his friends from arguing, a third slave urges Pompey and Caesar to avoid political quarrels and chastises them for adopting white manners. According to the elderly Cato, "Negro head got quite wrong now-a-day, you must all be gemmen, must dress in fashion, talk high flow, must have cue and wool powder, dat foolish, only make your face look more black."

Even as Cato seems to advocate independent thinking, he, too, mirrors the beliefs of his own aptly named master, Conciliate. Never quarreling over political questions, the slaveholder is said to be friend to all and enemy of none. Indeed, according to Cato, "he so good, he no hurt cockroach." Thus, all three eighteenth-century bondsmen display a genuine lack of critical thinking ability. Their composite portrait shows black slaves to be loyally imitative in matters of mind and manner.[49]

Murdock's play attempted to achieve much of its comic effect through the juxtaposition of crude black characters and refined white manners. In this context Afro-American dialect became one of the elements of characterization most useful for depicting the backward nature of slaves. Black English, as interpreted by early dramatists, made the slaves' striving after respectability and acceptance seem ludicrous. It was simply another outward sign that they belonged to a different and inferior race.

Few eighteenth- or early nineteenth-century playwrights recorded black dialect with any degree of consistency. Even within a single play spelling was often capricious and syntax varied widely.[50] Robert Munford's comedy *The Candidates* (ca. 1775) pokes fun at ambitious Virginia politicians and contains a few lines of dialect words to be spoken by rustic whites, but it reserves the most humorous mispronunciations of the English language for a loyal body servant named Ralpho. In an exclamation of gratitude for a hand-me-down suit of clothes given to him by master Wou'dbe, Ralpho exhibits both his unmerited pomposity and his inability to use multisyllabic words correctly:

> God bless your honour! What a good master! Who would not do every thing to give such a one pleasure? But, e'gad, it's time to think of my new clothes: I'll go and try them on. Gadso! This figure of mine is not reconsiderable in its delurements, and when I'm dressed out like a gentleman, the girls, I'm a thinking, will find me desistible.[51]

Ralpho just had a poor sense of diction. Other stage slaves were cursed with a combination of the ungrammatical foibles of dialect and diction. In A. B. Lindsley's *Love and Friendship* (1809), a South Carolina house slave, though criticizing the dissolute ways of his habitually drunken master, Dick Dashaway, nevertheless seeks partial relief from homesickness in Dashaway's liquor cabinet. Harry resigns himself to separation from Africa in a soliloquy:

> But why me do no happy? he bees be happy I can, now I here poor slave and no can git backa my country gin. So, now massa

Dicky de gone drunk to bed and leava de wine here, I set up chair and sot myself down happy like he, and drink my glass like gemman.[52]

Thus, with English which seems a curious mixture of stage-Indian, Norwegian, and Italian, Lindsley's Harry gave New York audiences a somewhat melancholy picture of black life among the white "buckrat" of Charleston at the turn of the century.[53]

Portrayed as imitative, but incompletely acculturated in speech and thought, early slave characters were easy prey for their quick-witted white counterparts. Slaves fleeing their patriot masters in John Leacock's Revolutionary War play, *The Fall of British Tyranny* (1776), were crude, lacked individuality, and spoke English awkwardly. In joining forces with the British, these blacks became pawns in the Anglo-American struggle rather than freedom fighters in their own right.

As the fugitive slaves climb aboard Lord Kidnapper's man-of-war anchored off the Norfolk coast, the deposed British governor lavishes praise upon them for the cleverness and bravery which they had exhibited in escaping through his enemy's defenses. He promises that they will be armed, trained, and incorporated into his fighting forces. To Cudjo, the apparent leader of the new recruits, Kidnapper makes special promises. Since Cudjo's master had been a Virginia gentleman named Colonel Thompson — or "Cunney Tomsee" as the slave pronounces the name — Lord Kidnapper promotes Cudjo: "You shall be called Major Cudjo Thompson . . . and if you behave well, I'll soon make you a greater man than your master." After hearing the governor further pledge that the black soldiers will be given food, money, clothing, and their freedom, Cudjo can hardly contain his elation. "Tankee, massa, gaw bresse, massa Kidnap," he drools as he promises to kill the American rebels at Kidnapper's first command. Suitably bedazzled by these newfound opportunities, the slaves are ushered off below decks.[54]

With Cudjo and his companions offstage, the white characters now reveal their true estimation of the blacks' wartime prospects. In a dialogue between Kidnapper and the ship's boatswain, it becomes clear that the slave recruits are valuable to the British not because of their especial cleverness or bravery, but because one can "get them for half price, or nothing at all . . . and that will help to lessen poor Owld England's taxes." Moreover, when they have served their military purpose as cannon fodder, Kidnapper could sell them as slaves to British West Indian planters — and that, the boatswain assures his captain, "will be something in your honour's pocket." The English, this playwright claims, would wage war against the Americans even if it meant using gullible slaves "as black as so many devils."[55]

Other early American stage productions used black roles as easily manipulated props in more lighthearted productions. In Samuel Woodworth's play, *The Forest Rose* (1825), a comical house servant named Lid Rose embarrasses mistress Sally's sweetheart — and herself — by participating in a kissing game. When the blindfolded Jonathan discovers he has been embracing Rose instead of his "dear, sweet, kind, good" Sally, the young suitor realizes that he has fallen prey to his sweetheart's impish sense of humor. Unable to shoulder the humiliation, he blames the black servant: "Darnation! If I have not been bussing Lid Rose! Be off with you, garlic-chops! Darn me, if ever I speak to Sal Forest again. . . . Whew! How the wench smelt of onions!" As far as Rose is concerned, such harsh words seem a minor insult compared to the rejection of her love. "You did serve poor negro so, and ax me to lubber you, and now you desert me," she gravely complains.[56]

In *The Forest Rose*, the initial surprise of the victimized lover may have been funny, but Jonathan's insulting description of Rose, as well as her accommodating response to Sally's ruse, perpetuated images of the incomplete black personality. Treated as a prop, a faceless vehicle for generating humor by her mere presence, Lid Rose's fate anticipated that of numerous black characters. By the 1830s, stage slaves characteristically loved singing and dancing, and like Lid Rose they often were placed in comically awkward or incongruous situations. In this way, the early dramatists prepared their stages for the rise of blackface minstrelsy.

The American musical theatre was born in February 1735 when the English ballad opera *Flora* opened at the Charleston, South Carolina, city courthouse. Some thirty years later, British actor Lewis Hallam, playing the role of Mungo in *The Padlock* performed the first "Negro song" to be presented on an American stage. By 1795, when Philadelphia's John Murdock created an Afro-American character named Sambo, blackface musical theater was primed and ready to become a popular form of entertainment in the new nation.[57]

Claiming to be disgusted with plays which were "foreign to the circumstances of a republican people," Murdock hoped to produce a uniquely American drama. Even so, in his *The Triumphs of Love* (1795), Murdock seems to have drawn on already familiar images of blacks.[58]

Murdock's Sambo speaks in dialect, is inordinately vain, and often spontaneously breaks into song and dance. Claiming that he has the "bess massa in e world," he tries to look like the slaveholder by fixing his hair in a style that is "all de fashion among gemmen." Pompous enough to "tink himself handsome" as well as "berry complish'd" in singing, fiddling, and dancing, Sambo describes himself as a good-looking, well-groomed gentleman. He seems to be living proof that blacks "improbe berry much" when they accept white standards of beauty as their own.[59]

In Act 3 of *The Triumphs of Love*, master George Friendly, Jr., overhears Sambo speaking to himself in a somewhat more somber tone. Despite all of his advantages, the pampered slave fears that some unexpected calamity might one day occasion his sale to another white family who would not "gib him fine clothes for dress" or "plenty money for pend." Affected by the "untutored, pathetic soliloquy of that honest creature," Friendly decides to manumit Sambo — giving him the option to stay on at wages or to leave and seek employment elsewhere as a free man. Sambo is dumbfounded by his master's decision. Soon, however, he jumps about, bowing, weeping, and kissing the hem of Friendly's coat with elation. After regaining his composure, the newly freed slave manages to sing:

> Now let Sambo dance and sing,
> He more happy dan a king.
> Now he fly about like bee,
> He enjoy sweet *liberty*.[60]

The remainder of Sambo's first hours of freedom are spent in no less spirited celebration. Like Bickerstaffe's Mungo, who also saw the chains of bondage loosened for a time, his jubilation is accompanied by an overindulgence in strong spirits. Sambo returns to the stage reeling and singing: "Dans sons carmagnole . . . liberty and quality for eber and eber." Although he had promised Friendly that he would save all of his wages in order to purchase freedom for his slave sweetheart, now about all he can do is mumble: "Sambo feel berry sick. Eh, eh, eh — house go round like a wholagig."[61]

While the new freedman clowns drunkenly, George Friendly and his white friend, Bob Careless, take the stage to provide the audience with a bit of contemporary social commentary. Friendly tries to make the best of the embarrassing scene by maintaining that despite their general lack of education there is much to be said in favor of the black slave population. Careless, on the other hand, is less charitable: "I am afraid our friend Sambo, will make a bad use of his liberty. . . . So much for against liberating those people. The greatest number of them, after they are set free, become vicious."[62]

Stage slaves such as Sambo could be considered vicious in the sense of being defective or faulty. The Sambos and Caesars of the early American theatre were incomplete humans, estranged from a common bond with whites due to their lack of success in adopting white ways. Try as they might to mimic the whites, black characters were destined to be inadequate in speech and originality, offensive in smell, and prone to extravagant, undignified displays of musical comedy. At a time when the larger society was becoming increasingly aware of the economic importance of black agricultural labor, the theatrical community created slave characters with an eye on the joke book rather than the account book.

Within the context of early American society images of slaves in drama served several purposes. First of all, the black character's role as outsider functioned as a reference point for more successful white acculturation. Even the most backward European immigrant could hope to establish a more positive sense of belonging — of American identity — than the grossly foreign African. Secondly, the grotesque nature of the comical black characters provided whites with living, breathing reasons for maintaining racial separatism as an American way of life. That individual political expressions of this attitude might be manifested in adherence to proslavery, gradual emancipationist, or colonizationist ideology was less important than the fact that each of these solutions to the so-called Negro problem was grounded in a single, shared belief — the feeling that Afro-Americans could not, in the foreseeable future, transcend their racial and cultural disabilities successfully enough to become an integral part of the American sociocultural mix. Playwrights' characterizations of black slaves forwarded and solidified this attitude. Finally, and most importantly, the early slave images offered white audiences a comforting psychological reassurance. In the real world of eighteenth-century New York City, Santo Domingo, or Stono, South Carolina, rebellious African slaves might conspire and revolt, but on the stage blackface bondsmen were loyally imitative of and greatly dependent upon their masters. Such intellectually inferior clowns posed little threat to white hegemony. Thus, with their anxieties relieved, white theatergoers in early America could respond to the antics of slave characters much as did George Friendly, Jr. With a smile and a chuckle, they could say of the stage Sambo: "I can hardly refrain from embracing [you]. You are a good black."[63]

CHAPTER 2
The Debate Begins,
1830–1861

"Oh! master, I wish I may find everybody as well
off as I am."
A slave named Albert in Caroline Lee
Hentz, *The Planter's Northern Bride* (1854)

In the years between 1830 and the Civil War, the social and psychological tensions surrounding the black slave system intensified and popular culture reaffirmed its role as a forum for debating the controversy. The slave labor system survived the ideological conflicts of the Revolution, but this did not ensure continued, widespread support in an era characterized by increased urbanization, industrialization, regional economic specialization, and national expansion. On the one hand, the rise of new humanitarian reform movements and the popularization of Jacksonian rhetoric seemed to threaten older assumptions about the viability and permanency of certain established institutions. On the other hand, America's continuing dependence upon a slave-based southern economy, the potency of the antebellum states' rights ethic, and the racial and cultural chauvinism of national policies toward Native Americans and western settlement, all discouraged hopes for a speedy and permanent end to black slavery.

Confused by the uncertain ideals of their government, Americans of various ideological perspectives used history text, novel, poem, song, and stage to persuade and to reassure. Armed with images of blacks as natural slaves, feeble exotics, and comical imitators, writers sought to turn the tentative plantation visions of previous years into convincing—and entertaining —human and institutional portraits. In order to do so, they further developed already existing stereotypes of peoples, places, and possibilities. On the eve of the Civil War, it was apparent that even some of the most adamant white antislavery advocates were not prepared to see black people as equals. To these writers, the slave remained more of a cause than a person. To others, black skin signified membership in a childlike race which was still many decades away from adulthood. Still others seemed captivated by the comic and commercial possibilities of black slave portraiture. All of these attitudes discouraged the apathetic antebellum American from risking his life for black equality.

Thus, although in pre-Civil War popular culture images of blacks contributed to the national debate over "the peculiar institution," visions of the plantation South by themselves caused no dramatic confrontation. Politicians, platform polemicists, and public policy decisions were more crucial determinants in the final division than was popular culture. The various pictures of black slavery forwarded by white historians, songwriters, novelists, and playwrights recorded a good deal more about majoritarian fears and beliefs concerning black people than they did about what it was like to be at once a slave and a human being. By 1860, white America saw the black slave labor system through a cultural window which obscured, distorted, and misinformed more than it revealed.

Slavery in the American Canaan

The task of recording the nation's past increasingly was shared by a primarily white, but nonetheless diverse group of individuals. Following in the tradition of Philadelphia printer John McCulloch's pioneering *Introduction to the History of America* (1787), some 113 general United States history texts were published before the end of the antebellum era. Over seventy percent of the titles went to press during the 1830–1860 period. The authors of these editions no longer came predominantly from the ranks of the clergy, but neither were they full-time historians. Almost all could claim a vocation other than history as their primary profession. Among the 145 most prominent American historians writing during the first half of the nineteenth century could be found booksellers, printers, journalists, teachers, physicians, artists, lawyers, politicians, and businessmen. Even though New England produced almost half of these writers, twenty-five percent were from the Middle States and seventeen percent from the South.[1]

Despite their different backgrounds, antebellum historians shared certain common problems and concerns. Those who advocated college-level American history studies criticized the lack of administrative support for contemporary historical work. Some, too, complained about the difficulties of distributing their books. Soured by past experience with book dealers, printers, and traveling peddlers, newcomers might be advised that "an author can sell more of his own labor among his acquaintances . . . in a single week, than a book store would sell in a year."[2]

Writers of history who were tenacious enough to brave these hazards faced an even greater obstacle to fame and fortune in the person of George Bancroft. For nearly twenty-five years, American historiography was dominated by this representative of the Boston Brahmin class. His steadfast faith in the Common Man, in the workings of Divine Providence, and in the inevitability of human progress was shared by many nonhistorians. Unafraid of voicing strong moral judgments, Bancroft proudly contrasted his research with that which had been completed by his predecessors—and by inference with histories written by his contemporaries. He criticized writers who would seize upon "rumors and vague recollections" instead of "authenticated facts" for their documentation. Historical studies produced in such a manner were nothing more than "wanton perversions" of reality. They were uninformed by the belief that "facts faithfully ascertained, and placed in proper contiguity, become of themselves the firm links of a brightly burnished chain, connecting events with their causes, and marking the line along which the electric power of truth is conveyed from generation to generation."[3]

Rhetoric aside, Bancroft did use primary source material more frequently than earlier historians, but it was an expensive undertaking. With the aid of research assistants he examined original documents from both American and foreign, public and private archival collections. In 1869, he estimated that personal expenses incurred in "journeys, time employed in researches, writing, copyists, money paid for examination, etc., etc." had been between $50,000–$75,000. Given his influence among his contemporaries, Bancroft's sense of black history was an important contribution to the development of pre-Civil War public opinion on the role of black slavery in American society.[4]

Bancroft's advanced studies at the University of Göttingen, Germany, imbued him with a view of history which was well suited to America's first era of "Manifest Destiny and Mission." To Bancroft, it seemed that Divine Providence beneficently had selected members of one racial group to serve humankind as apostles of democracy, individualism, and freedom. He believed that antebellum Anglo-Saxon Americans were destined to control the reins of history and thereby to spread liberty and morality throughout the world—even while the American slave system continued. As an antislavery Jacksonian Democrat, Bancroft wrestled with this apparent conflict and provided a twofold approach to resolving it. First, Bancroft declared that Old World peoples and customs were responsible for tainting freedom-loving Americans with the corruptions of chattel slavery; and second, God must have had some good reason for allowing the institution a foothold on United States soil. It was this second line of reasoning which profoundly misinterpreted the character of the African people.[5]

In his *History of the United States* (1834–1875), Bancroft maintained that the British had ignored "the cry of humanity, and the remonstrances of colonial legislation" in regard to the Atlantic slave trade. Like his predecessors, Bancroft accused England's mercantile, manufacturing, and shipping interests—as well as members of the royal family, the ministry, and parliament—of conspiring in the slave trade. Together, without regard to the needs or wishes of emigrant settlers, the English had fastened an "unjust, wasteful and unhappy" system of labor organization upon the "rising institutions" of America. Thus, paradoxically, the world's only true "asylum of liberty" had been built by hereditary bondsmen.[6]

To avoid contradiction, Bancroft then explained how slavery could survive in a liberty-loving nation. His *History* argues that great wealth—the bane of the idealized Jacksonian Common Man—had encouraged the continuation of the slave system because it was supremely "grateful to the pride and to the interests of the large landed proprietors." Thus, saved from extinction by these wealthy benefactors, chattel slavery supported and renewed a "landed aristocracy, closely resembling the feudal nobility."[7]

What were the champions of democracy and individual freedom doing about this situation? According to Bancroft, they were dutifully awaiting further developments in God's plan for the creation of a millennial republic upon the North American continent. He assured readers that distasteful remnants of European medievalism eventually would vanish and that, in the meantime, the blot of slavery could not tarnish America's long-term contribution to world history. After all, the oldest monuments of human labor, the Pyramids, were built by slave labor; slavery had existed in every ancient Greco-Roman republic; and even in the promised land, bond labor had existed alongside "the oracles of God."[8]

Nevertheless, those people headed for the new promised land had far more to do than passively await the rise of universal enlightenment. To Bancroft's mind, the slave-master relationship existed in the United States for some purpose other than to slow progress. As members of "a branch of the human family not yet conscious of its powers, not yet fully possessed of its moral and rational life," African-American slaves were seen as part of both problem and solution. By helping to enlighten and to develop the "limited faculties" of these "uncivilized" immigrants, white American masters could prove themselves able guardians of God's millennial kingdom. If they succeeded where Europeans had failed, they would show, once and for all, that Americans were the only true and worthy inheritors of the resplendent mantle of Anglo-Saxon civilization.[9]

Contemporary readers of the *History of the United States* must have believed that America was on the right track, since the first African slaves were described as "gross and stupid, having memory and physical strength, but undisciplined in the exercise of reason and imagination." Destitute of "common traditions, customs, and laws," each bondsman was "dependent on his master for civilization." This dependence became a necessary part of shedding their native barbarism as blacks were initiated into the ways of western civilization. According to Bancroft, this was no mere man-made scheme. The "guardianship and the education of the colored race" had been entrusted to southern whites by Divine Providence. Thus, "in the midst of the horrors of slavery and the slave trade," the inheritors of the Teutonic tradition were engaged in a historically important act of implementing God's will. Even as the burden of black bondage continued to delay the introduction of a full-fledged millennial kingdom on the American continent, the slaveholders were moving toward that goal by obediently performing "the office of advancing and civilizing the negro."[10]

Bancroft was not firmly abolitionist. His harshest comments on black bondage came in the earliest volumes of his *History*, which appeared before the controversy flared in the North. Correspondence from the early 1830s reveals that he, like a majority of educated New Englanders, was unsympathetic to slavery but unwilling to make a political issue of it. When President Polk appointed him Secretary of the Navy in 1844, Senate confirmation proceedings were halted until his writings could be examined for signs of radicalism. They passed inspection by both northern and southern senators. After assuming his cabinet post, Bancroft continued to distrust the proslavery wing of the Democratic party, while at the same time seeming to support them on the issue of the annexation of Texas. During the Civil War, he supported Lincoln's emancipation plan to compensate slaveholders. Although he viewed the fighting as an "instrument of Divine Providence to root out social slavery," Bancroft thought of the abolition of hereditary servitude primarily as a means to the end of restoring the Union — not necessarily as an end in itself. He meant only to bring the southern states back into the national compact by removing the reason for their secession.[11]

To Bancroft, chattel slavery was not an invention of the white man, but rather an institution older than recorded history. Indeed, in past centuries the African continent had been a place where human life was assigned "an inferior value." In Africa, "humanity did not respect itself" in any of its forms — not in the individual, in the family, or in the nation. Removed from this "direful captivity" by white slavers, barbarous Africans under Providential guidance were being "transformed into an insulated class, living in a state of domesticity, dependent for culture, employment, and support on a superior race." Consequently, blacks did not consider American slavery "a lower condition of being than their former one;" they even could consider it an opportunity. In this manner, Bancroft helped to convert the bucolic African paradise of early British and American literature into a howling wilderness filled with superstition and slavery. If there was to be a second Eden it would be located in the United States — and it would be the product of white American effort.[12]

For many Americans of the pre-Civil war era Bancroft's version of the country's history was the only accurate version, condensed into eight hard-cover volumes; but a few historians thought otherwise. While the *History of the United States* did dominate the era's historiography, there were dissenting books. Not content with Bancroft's romantic and covenantal interpretation of American destiny, his competitors often expressed the sentiments of sectional or ideological interest groups. Contemporaries who demanded bolder commentary on The Slave Question felt that Bancroft "always contrives to agree with and to flatter every sect, party and opinion, except when the adherents of it are too few or too unpopular to make it worth while to court their favor."[13] By openly presenting either a proslavery or abolitionist perspective, however, historians risked the possibility that their histories would degenerate into impassioned polemic.

Whichever position authors took they were sure to criticize the opposition. James Kirke Paulding titled a chapter in his history of *Slavery in the United States* (1835), "Of the Fanaticism of the Abolitionists, and its hostility to Religion, Morals, Liberty, Patriotism, and the Social Virtues." George Bourne, an advocate of "*immediate, unconditional, and universal emancipation,*" claimed that "very few men-stealers . . . are even nominal Christian believers." Moreover, Bourne declared that "no man in the southern states preaches the gospel of Christ in its fulness and truth" and that "to wait for regeneration from the slaveholders themselves, is idiotism."[14]

Despite their differing opinions over the character of southern slaveholders and northern reformers, many pre-Civil War writers shared key beliefs with Bancroft. Along with members of the larger society, these representatives of the historical profession also valued a vision of America's mission in world civilization, and a significant number undervalued the character and intelligence of blacks. Viewing black skin as evidence of a dangerous viciousness, Bancroft and proslavery historians concurred that Afro-American slaves needed tutoring in the ways of the modern world. As they modified the noble savage accordingly, these authors further encouraged an image of blacks as outsiders who could improve their lives by being good American slaves.

Proslavery sympathizers proposed that black slaves required a lengthy period of contact with civilizing influences in order to overcome the degradation of life on the African continent.[15] Like Bancroft, these writers concluded that bondsmen benefitted from their captivity in America. In being "transferred from the slavery of a savage to that of a civilized and Christian master," a chattel's mental and moral development was advanced, not retarded. If the physical, intellectual, and moral development of African-Americans was promoted by a state of slavery — and "their happiness secured to a greater extent than if left at liberty" — then their enslavement was "consistent with the law of nature, and violative of none of its provisions."[16]

Threatening that irrevocable damage could be done to Bancroft's vision of inevitable American progress, proslavery tracts predicted chaotic consequences if abolitionists succeeded in disrupting the mutually beneficial southern system of labor and social organization. If southern blacks were released from bondage before they were prepared for it, the United States would experience a wave of violent killings. Instead of maturing and expanding, American democracy would disappear under strong, state dictators who could levy burdensome taxes in order to support large military machines. Some states would fall prey to stronger and more warlike neighbors. Even if rival states did not engage in open warfare, they would be forced to form "new alliances, combinations, and political intrigues, such as have occupied the nations of Europe for centuries."[17]

Finally, there was the threat that an abrupt extinction of black bondage would result in the "most direful of all alternatives"—the "final amalgamation of the two races." If this taboo was violated, the American people would experience a "universal retrograde from the moral image of God toward the condition of brutes." As a direct result of abolitionist agitation, the "intellectuality of the white race would be destroyed from off the earth, and merged in the thick skulls of the negroes." To many whites of the 1830–60 period, this was an inglorious and terrifying alternative to Bancroft's view of the American future. For a nation to sacrifice the sure prospect of a millennial kingdom for the evils of dictatorship, entangling alliances, and war was a good deal to ask. For a proud Anglo-Saxon people to risk their racial hegemony was an unthinkable request.[18]

Whether interpreted by Bancroft or the proslavery writers, the historical record described slavery as good for African-American peoples, and educable black bondsmen as living proof of the nation's evolution into the American Canaan. Views on the appropriate nature, length, and extent of servitude might differ between interpreters, but most would agree with George Tucker's contention: "the relation between master and slave more often proves a school of virtue than of vice." That black slaves may have felt differently was irrelevant.[19]

Novel Reforms

Refusing to accept fully the implications of Bancroft's *History*, abolitionist writers contested the notion that God sanctioned slavery. Proslavery authors could condemn petitions for abolition as threats to Anglo-Saxon civilization, but other writers built upon the historical arguments of George Bourne, Richard Hildreth, William Goodell, and others who agreed that slavery in no way could be considered either a progressive, divinely ordained, or virtuous institution. They felt that if indeed the United States did have a mission in world history, it could not begin to perform it while encumbered by the burden of chattel slavery.

Those antebellum Americans who would protest against "the peculiar institution" often expressed their views in poetic form. Much of this verse was characterized by a hearing before a heavenly tribunal, where the poet either pleaded the bondsmen's cause or threatened slaveholders and the apathetic with the eventual justice of the Judgment Day. In a manner which most history texts could not duplicate, antislavery poems proclaimed that black bondage was an unprecedented evil:

> "Sum of all villainies," exceeding far
> All other tyrannies of earth combined.[20]

Specifically, reformers lashed out against the harmful effects of slavery upon cherished American social and political institutions such as marriage, the family, democratic government, and the Christian Church. The setting for such protest verse often was the slave auction block:

> The brutal trader, sly and keen,
> The planter with his sunburnt hue,
> The idle townsman, and between,
> With face unwashed, the foreign Jew.[21]

The auction platform provided a graphic symbol of slavery's worst evil:

> Where Slavery rules, the holy marriage rite,
> Is treated by its votaries as trite;
> The Heaven-commanded rite, where Slavery is,
> If used — is for the vilest purposes.
> There, lovely Virtue is but little known,
> But Vice and Passion set upon her throne.[22]

With the auctioneer's gruff cry of "Going! going! gone!" lifetime relationships were severed, marriages were broken, and children were torn from their mothers' breasts:

> My mother, oh! my mother!
> Alas! they've driven her away,
> To labor through the sultry day —
> To suffer for another —
> Gone for aye![23]

Parents were no less affected by the callous slave sale. The *National Anti-Slavery Standard* in 1859 described one such anguishing scene:

> 'Tis quickly done — the man must go far south — away — away —
> His wife to Alabama, the child to Ches'peake bay —
> Oh! wat a fearful shriek arose, it seemed to pierce the sky —
> "For God's sake, give me back my child — one kiss before I die!"[24]

Such scenes were meant to enlist the empathy of white Christian parents and encourage them to think of slaves as people who shared their problems and needed their help.[25]

Antislavery poets challenged the belief that slavery could be a necessary evil by maintaining that key American institutions already suffered from the corrupting influence of the slave system. Slaveholders had "basely wrecked the ship of State," and now,

> Her mildew'd sails droop o'er her side,
> Her hull is drifting with the tide![26]

Moreover, supporters of the southern labor system were charged with profaning the nation's Christian heritage by citing the scriptures as proslavery, thus perverting the gospel and depriving the enslaved African people of a true knowledge of "Him who came to save / The outcast and the poor."[27]

One of the most controversial authors to speak out against slavery's corrupting influence was a Brunswick, Maine, homemaker and short story writer named Harriet Beecher Stowe. Her *Uncle Tom's Cabin* (1852) effectively combined several important contemporary arguments against black bondage. By marshalling some of the most sensational and sentimental elements of previous antislavery writing, she was able to personify the forces of good and evil which fellow reformers claimed were at work in the slave South. In doing so, she created vivid images of slavery and of black people.[28]

Initially published as a serial in the *National Era*, a Washington, D.C., paper supported by the American and Foreign Anti-Slavery Society, Stowe's story was received with enthusiasm. By the time its final installment appeared in March, 1852, the publisher had already announced the book version. Despite the fact that the two-volume set had only limited circulation in the South, some 305,000 copies were sold within a year. Soon thereafter, the book was translated into both German and Welsh for immigrant readers. Pirated editions appeared throughout Europe and a children's condensation, *A Peep into Uncle Tom's Cabin* (1853) spread Stowe's reformist gospel to even the youngest readers. For those less interested in the printed word, a Rhode Island manufacturer sold a card game called "Uncle Tom and Little Eva"—said to involve "the continual separation and reunion of families." Melodramatic stage adaptations of the book transformed Tom-inspired ballads such as "Eliza's Flight" and "Uncle Tom's Glimpse of Glory" into full-blown production numbers. Certainly, *Uncle Tom's Cabin* was the media event of the decade.[29]

Stowe wrote her novel as a personal response to the passage of the 1850 Fugitive Slave Act. Claiming her book to be "a collection and arrangement of real incidents, of actions really performed, of words and expressions really uttered," she professed a deep desire to portray slavery in its *"living dramatic reality."* Today it is generally accepted that Stowe exaggerated the extent of her personal contact with slavery and that her 1853 compilation, *A Key to Uncle Tom's Cabin*, was actually more an afterthought than a guide to her original research. Nevertheless, it is likely that many of her antebellum readers viewed the matter of historical accuracy somewhat differently. Some may even have agreed that *Uncle Tom's Cabin* was an inadequate representation of black bondage only in the sense that southern slavery was "too dreadful for the purposes of art"—a more accurate account would be unreadable.[30]

To Stowe, as to many of her readers, slavery had no saving grace. It was "absolute despotism, of the most unmitigated form." The major difference between slave and free labor was that slavery could be described as "evil, and only evil, and that continually." It destroyed the black family and inhibited the flowering of Christian virtue. In the words of one of Stowe's characters, it was "a bitter, bitter, most accursed thing!—a curse to the master and a curse to the slave!"[31]

Despite the author's intentions, stereotypical images of blacks as slaves found their way into the pages of *Uncle Tom's Cabin*. Although she created a variety of slave personalities, some of her characters were revitalized portrayals of slaves as desperate noble savages. Beset by the psychological tensions of slavery, even the resourceful George Harris could complain to wife Eliza: "it's all misery, misery, misery! My life is bitter as wormwood; the very life is burning out of me. I'm a poor, miserable, forlorn drudge. . . . What's the use of our trying to do anything, trying to know anything, trying to be anything? What's the use of living?" While Harris eventually avoided the fate of the early noble savages, Stowe's *National Era* serial originally was advertised as "Uncle Tom's Cabin or The Man That Was A Thing." To some, slavery was that bad, that corrosive of human personality, and in individual cases, bondsmen were that low on the scale of humanity. Harris managed to survive the demoralizing forces of depression, but others were less fortunate.[32]

Two unforgettably demonic black slave drivers named Sambo and Quimbo personify the antebellum axiom which held that "the slave is always a tyrant, if he can get a chance to be one." These two slaves had been trained to be savage and brutal by cotton planter Simon Legree, who through "long practice in hardness and cruelty," had succeeded in crushing and debasing them. Sambo and Quimbo hated each other and in turn were feared and despised by the rest of the slave community. By continually manipulating this hatred, Legree maintained complete control of plantation affairs.[33]

Co-opted in this manner, the drivers participated in orgies of drunken debauchery with their master, treated the slave women as sexual playthings, and gloated with "fiendish exultation" at the whippings which they meted out to errant field hands. Illustrating Stowe's contention that "brutal men are lower even than animals," Sambo and Quimbo levied unnecessary and sadistic punishments. Antebellum readers must have been severely shaken by one such response to a female slave who had collapsed due to exhaustion:

> "I'll bring her to!" said the driver, with a brutal grin. "I'll give her something better than camphire!" and, taking a pin from his coat-sleeve, he buried it to the head in her flesh. The woman groaned, and half rose. "Get up, you beast, and work, will yer, or I'll show yer a trick more! . . . See that you keep to dat ar," said the man, "or yer'll wish yer's dead to-night, I reckin!"[34]

Modifying previous stereotypes with vivid descriptions of the "unwholesome character" of slave life, Stowe unwittingly completed the picture of black dehumanization. In *Uncle Tom's Cabin*, slavery was seen as being so cruel and debasing that human personality was either perverted or destroyed. According to Stowe, as well as many of those she influenced, enslaved blacks could be wholly "unman'd" and turned into "things" through the normal operation of the slave regime.[35]

The best protection against such a fate was one part gentle innocence and two parts Protestant Christianity. This remedy began with black slaves as members of a race whose ancestors, "born beneath a tropic sun, brought with them, and perpetuated to their descendants, a character so essentially unlike the hard and dominant Anglo-Saxon race, as for many years to have won from it only misunderstanding and contempt." In seeking to diminish the contempt and to dispel the misunderstanding, she told of how a "moral miracle" named Uncle Tom coped with the burdens of slave life. By appropriating the promises of the Anglo-Saxons' Christian religion, he formed an insulating barrier of faith, compassion, and good works between himself and the most brutalizing, spirit-sapping aspects of bondage. Tom's Christianity made him a "good, steady, sensible, pious fellow," who prayed with "child-like earnestness" for those who abused him. His steadfast, "unquestioning faith" had "shamed that of higher and more skilful culture." Uncle Tom was Stowe's proof of the antebellum view that black people were sensitive and impressionable, domestic, and imbued with a "childlike simplicity of affection, and facility of forgiveness."[36]

Because of Stowe's proclivity to this sort of racial typecasting, twentieth-century historian George Fredrickson has called *Uncle Tom's Cabin* "the classic expression of romantic racialism." Stowe imagined blacks to be an exotic race constitutionally prone to innocence, gaiety, and docility, and a natural counterpoint to the bold and enterprising Anglo-Saxon. (Particularly prevalent among pre-Civil War white liberals, this notion was actually a variant of the aggressive Anglo-Saxon chauvinism which appeared in the writings of George Bancroft. See pp. 26–30 herein.)[37] In her novel, both the gentle slave preacher and the brutal slave driver were products of America's bond labor system; but beyond this, both characters were products of romanticized racism. Either case presupposed the Afro-American's impressionable and childlike nature. The only significant question was whether the slave system would shape a saint or sadist from the undeveloped black character.

Most white southerners were hostile toward *Uncle Tom's Cabin* and its author. In addition to numerous proslavery pamphlets and periodical articles, no fewer than fourteen proslavery novels appeared in the three years following the publication of Stowe's book. By 1861, more than thirty such replies had been published. Anti-Tom authors sometimes claimed that it was "painful to have to speak thus of a woman," but lacking more suitable alternatives, they decided to bear the pain rather than let her "filthy negro novel" go uncriticized — even to touch the book was contaminating. Its "dark design — its injustice — its falsehoods" operated to "pervert public taste, and corrupt public morals." Possessed by an "anti-christian spirit; . . . the atheistic spirit of the old French Revolution," the novel was adjudged capable of leading more Americans to infidelity and flagrant atheism than any other publication, "with the single exception of the New York Tribune." Certainly, said the critics, the creator of a book so filled with inaccuracies must, for the good of society, be forever branded a *"false witness."* Thus, Harriet Beecher Stowe was accused of exploiting abolition sentiment for personal financial gain.[38] One of her most vociferous southern critics, William Grayson, specifically named her in his 1854 book, *The Hireling and the Slave:*

> There Stowe, with prostituted pen assails
> One-half her country, in malignant tales;
> Careless, like Trollope, whether truth she tells,
> And anxious only how the libel sells,
> To slander's mart, she furnishes supplies,
> And feeds its morbid appetite for lies.[39]

Proslavery writers also made claims of historical accuracy. Anti-Tom novels were said to be based upon a strict adherence to truth gained through close personal observation. Even if such claims were a trifle overdrawn, they do point to different popular images of black bondage than those forwarded by antislavery authors.[40] According to Stowe's proslavery critics, abolitionist fiction was nearsighted and hypocritical. White northerners and their British sympathizers were said to be exploiting a dehumanizing labor system in their shops and factories. Northern liberals ought to condemn the "wretchedness" of the "serving women, and of the apprentice and bound girl system" with the same hostility which they directed at southern institutions. Thousands of "idlers, trampers, poachers, smugglers, drunkards and thieves" lived in the North, and the greed of industrialists and merchants had impoverished and ruined the health of thousands more. Living in damp cellars, sick from lack of food and clothing, with children who wore a "sad, uncomplaining look of suffering that cuts you to the heart," these "white niggers" of the North were said to be anxious to throw off their burdensome yoke. They were continually "sighing for an equality which exists only in name." Surely, concluded one writer, southern bondsmen were "blest beyond the pallid slaves of Europe, or the anxious, careworn labourers of the North."[41]

The proslavery authors drew an even more foreboding portrait of life for free blacks in the North. According to Arthur Weston, a character in Mary Eastman's *Aunt Phillis's Cabin* (1852), they were "the most miserable class of human beings I ever saw." On plantations, sick or aged bondsmen were "kindly cared for, and are never considered a burden"; — but in northern cities they were "victims of want and suffering." While the plantation world refused to tolerate idleness or pauperism — and thereby assured homes, food and clothing for all — northern ways had created an "indolent, reckless, and impertinent" black subclass. This unsettling situation was especially dangerous since it could undo all of the "civilizing" efforts of southern planters:[42]

> The negro freeman — thrifty while a slave,
> Freed from restraint, becomes a drone or knave,
> Each effort to improve his nature foils,
> Begs, steals, or sleeps and starves, but never toils,
> For savage sloth, mistakes the freedom won,
> And ends, the mere barbarian he begun.[43]

Thus, William Grayson and other authors who thought Stowe had overestimated black potential argued that while slavery might not be "the best system of labour," it certainly was "the best, for the negro, in this country."[44]

Proslavery novels often described the astonishment of the ignorant when they learned the truth about southern slavery through first-hand observation. In Nehemiah Adams' *The Sable Cloud* (1861), the young and sickly Harriet Freeman is cured of more than misinformation as she watches a group of Afro-American worshippers.She had never seen a slave before; she had only read about them in northern newspapers. Harriet was surprized to find them well-dressed — black gentlemen and ladies carrying red moroccan Bibles as they left their Sunday morning church meeting. "Uncle," she said, "what I have seen here in fifteen minutes shows me that at least one half of that which I have learned in the North about the slaves is false. Our novels and newspapers are all the time misleading us. . . . Such a load is gone from my mind since looking upon these colored people that I feel almost well."[45]

If Hattie Freeman's experience was insufficient to convert an individual, proslavery novelists had other witnesses to their truth. On occasion, bondsmen were portrayed testifying in support of the slave labor system. In the 1852 novel, *The Cabin and Parlor,* two Virginia slaves named Aunt Vilet and Uncle Peter were given an abolitionist tract. As they read the handbill, they comment on its illustration of a kneeling, manacled chattel and the caption "Am I not a man and a brother?" Uncle Peter asks, "Did yer ebber see any ting like dat? . . . Nebber seed any ting of it. . . . 'Spec dese abolitioners no more de brodder of de colored man dan a good massa here. . . . 'Pears to Uncle Peter, for all he heerd, dat dey less so." Aunt Vilet agrees. "Dat's de Lord's truth. . . . Nebber heerd of a white man north bein' more willin' to marry a black gal dan a white man here. Dat don't look like bein' a brodder." Such accounts claimed for the South a workable and mutually acceptable social arrangement between blacks and whites. Even the argument that slavery destroyed family values could be dismissed as ill-informed. When asked whether or not the South tolerated the separation of black families, the novel's town doctor replied: "Of course not. We read of such things in novels sometimes. But I have yet to see it in real life."[46]

In terms of its overall popularity and effectiveness, perhaps the most important literary weapon used by proslavery writers was to create a distinctly southern view of "real life." To do so, they combined antiabolitionist rhetoric with a romantic vision of aristocratic chivalry borrowed from Sir Walter Scott. His English baron became the aristocratic Virginia planter; Indians and frontiersmen replaced Scott's outlaws and Highland warriors; faithful slaves were substituted for loyal retainers, vassals, and serfs.[47] In the fiction of writers such as John Pendleton Kennedy, William Alexander Caruthers, and Caroline Lee Hentz, the South was transformed into one great, romantic, jousting field. Turned to proslavery purposes, these panoramas became politically potent inversions of Harriet Beecher Stowe's wicked South.[48]

An historical romance of the Old South usually pictured the plantation as "a second edition of the garden of Eden, only revised and improved," with a lordly mansion, gracious hostess, and a gentleman planter. "Scattered over the slope of a gentle hill" and "embowered under old and majestic trees" the slave cottages completed an "exceedingly picturesque" landscape. Even the rudest of these dwellings "enhanced the attractiveness of the scene."[49]

The slaves could be seen lazily lying around their quarters enjoying the sun like "terrapins luxuriating in the genial warmth of summer, on the logs of a mill-pond." Dependent upon others for "direction even to the procurement of his most indispensable necessaries," a plantation's bondsman was indeed fortunate. Under the protection and guidance of a benevolent planter, the slave would be provided with daily tasks commensurate with the abilities of one who possessed "no natural sensations but those of obedience." It was a measure of the institution's success that blacks under slavery were "a contented race." Having "no desire except that of happiness," they meshed well with a romanticized literary landscape in which the skies were said to have "a deeper blue than common" and where everything wore "a Sunday look."[50]

Similar images of slave life recur in numerous novels of the pre-Civil War era, and all of them deny black slaves the will and ability to direct their own lives. Proslavery authors could justifiably argue that abolitionist novels were unrealistic, but they, too, failed to tell accurately the story of the Afro-American experience. Despite specific differences in political attitudes, northern and southern authors alike practiced a literary paternalism which emphasized the psychological helplessness of black slaves. Thus, in 1835, when William Ellery Channing expressed his belief that slavery's "Moral influence" was "throughout debasing," he could not have realized how thoroughly this influence pervaded the literature of the times.[51]

The Minstrel's Song

Antebellum authors stereotyped the South by either condemning or romanticizing plantation life; but the American minstrel show thrived in the pre-Civil War era by maintaining and elaborating standard characterizations of blacks and compromising on the issue of slavery. Developing out of the comic antics of white "Ethiopian Delineators" who performed for the audiences of traveling circuses, medicine shows, menageries and showboats during the 1820s and '30s, blackfaced song and dance also owed much to early slave roles in plays such as *The Padlock* (1768) and *The Triumphs of Love* (1795). Thus when the first of the full-fledged minstrel shows appeared during the early 1840s, audiences were suitably prepared for this theater of jokes and music. Fantastically popular during the twenty years preceding the Civil War, minstrelsy provided a form of entertainment which was lighthearted, unpretentious, and immediate. Like earlier stage shows which provided blackfaced characters for the white public, minstrelsy more often reinforced than challenged prevailing social attitudes regarding racial identity. In doing so, these shows furthered the development of black images which long would linger upon the American stage.[52]

As minstrelsy matured, characterizations of Afro-American personality and society became standardized within a formulaic program of entertainment. The basic three-part structure — opening dialect humor and song, a variety segment or olio, and the one-act finale skit — made it possible to shape the individual components of each segment to changing audience tastes. For the customers, the well-defined general format was acceptable, in part, because it was so familiar. Knowing what to expect may have insured the public's enjoyment of the minstrel show, but it also limited the show's repertoire of characters to no more than a handful of standard burnt-cork personalities.[53]

Among the most memorable of these minstrel characters were the dandified Zip Coon (sometimes Dandy Jim) and the dilapidated Jim Crow. The nattily attired Zip Coon overdressed relative to his actual status in northern society. Jim Crow most often appeared in ill-fitting clothes with large patches on his trousers and gaping holes in his shoes. The broad-brimmed hat perched atop his head could not shade the wide grin which repeatedly illuminated his expressive face. Apparently addicted to gin, chicken coops, and watermelons, Jim Crow pranced, joked, and sang before backdrops of cotton patches, slave cabins, and levees piled high with cotton bales. These thematic elements became so familiar to northern audiences that many were convinced they saw more reality than fiction in the exaggerated mannerisms and cornball humor of the blackfaced actors.[54] As described by one New York reviewer's account of an 1840 minstrel performance, this learning experience could be quite exhilarating:

> Entering the theatre, we found it crammed from pit to dome, and the best representative of our American negro that we ever saw was stretching every mouth in the house to its utmost tension. Such a natural gait! — *such* a laugh! — and such a twitching-up of the arm and shoulder! It was *the* negro, par excellence. Long live *James Crow*, Esquire![55]

Actually, most "Ethiopian Delineators" showed little interest in trying to create realistic documentaries of southern life. Furthermore, both performers and audiences typically were northern and urban. Many of the popular jokes and gags performed on the minstrel stage had nothing whatsoever to do with black life, North or South, but simply used the black characters' stock obtuseness, love of big words, and habitual mispronunciations to create humorous situations. While certain elements of slave folk entertainment, the cakewalk for example, were incorporated into the stage shows, it is unlikely that a West African griot—the traveling entertainer of that society—would have recognized the minstrel version.[56] The griot might even have been a bit embarrassed to be the butt of a typically demeaning, rapid-fire minstrel joke:

> *Mr. Interlocutor:* Well, Mr. Bones, how do you feel this evening?
> *Mr. Bones:* I feel just like a stovepipe.
> *Mr. Interlocutor:* You feel like a stovepipe? How is that, Mr. Bones?
> *Mr. Bones:* A little sooty![57]

One of minstrelsy's major contributions to American popular culture was in the area of music. Since melodies could go where theaters could not, and since lyrics could survive long after the details of a show had been forgotten, minstrel songs were an important component of the information about black bondage to which antebellum Americans were exposed. Whether passed along through word-of-mouth or preserved on sheet music or in a songbook, these often nonsensical, sometimes melancholy ditties did more than entertain—they also commented on the social and political issues of the times.[58]

With simple melodies drawn from sources as diverse as Methodist camp meetings and New York opera troupes, minstrel songs could be easily remembered and endlessly adapted. Every new minstrel hit was parodied and imitated avidly, and it was not unusual to hear the same popular tune accompanying both proslavery and antislavery lyrics. It is difficult to determine which songs might have had the greatest impact, but general similarities between them suggest some recurring popular themes.[59]

Songs presented on the minstrel stage stressed what could be termed the lighter side of slave life. Rarely using words such as "chains," "whips," or even "slaves," most minstrel songs neither harshly condemned nor systematically defended the southern institution. Instead, they presented the listener with a collection of images which seemed to summarize much of the era's thought on black people and their status. The songs told of white America's ambivalent feelings toward slavery and revealed the widespread, if often implicit belief that blacks were too different to become full-fledged, equal participants in American society. Lacking the commitment to abolish the economic advantages of slavery, and inculcated with an Anglo-Saxon sense of superiority, minstrel songwriters and audiences endorsed compromise as a solution to the threat of civil war.[60]

With an almost pathological proclivity for ridiculing Afro-American physiognomy, songwriters carried certain characterizations seen in earlier novels and stage productions to the grossest of extremes. Comical minstrel skits exaggerated racially distinctive features to the point of reducing the slaves of minstrel song to mere burlesques of real people. Especially favored by white audiences were songs describing slave romances in which the lovers appeared grotesque or awkward. Who would be so stupid as to court a woman who "look'd jis like a charcoal rose, Her face so dark she scar'd de crows"?[61] What kind of man would be attracted to Dinah from Carolina?

> Her lips war white, her eyes war bright,
> Her voice war berry clear,
> Her lips war big, she could sing like a pig,
> Her mouth stretch'd from ear to ear.[62]

In the minstrel show, almost any bondsman would be flattered to meet her. Lubly Fan, whose lips were "like de oyster plant," Kate of Caroline, whose eye resembled "an onion peeled," or Coal Black Rose, who was said to be "black as ten of spades and got a lubly flat nose," were all attractive — according to black standards. Whether she had "de biggist foot, In all de country round" or was born with hair "curled so very tight, she could not shut her mouth," the black slave woman was an ideal mate for male suitors whose taste was supposed to be the biggest joke of all.[63]

According to minstrel songs, the process of wooing and winning a bride was likely to make the male slave's chest swell with vainglorious pride. Black women swooned over their lovers' dance floor ability and banjo-picking agility. When an eminently eligible young man like "Dandy Jim Ob Caroline" attended a plantation hoedown "wid lips comb'd out and wool quite tall" the women looked at him with eyes that glistened "like snowballs."[64] In the chorus of a song called "Black Sam," an especially fat black man is so pleased to find himself surrounded by admiring women that he brags:

> I am de fattest nigga dat eber you did see,
> And all the gals of colour turn dar eye up at me.[65]

The vanity generated by feminine adulation could pale in comparison to that produced by white approval. Dandy Jim takes his master's word for it accordingly:

For my ole massa told me so I's de best lookin nigga in de county O!
I look in de glass an foun it so, Jus what massa told me O![66]

Fat Black Sam, in a similar way, mistakes his master's words of praise for his own best interests:

> Once I say to massa, whar de cane brake grow,
> I pay you for my freedom if you let me go,
> And he tell dis nigga dat it neber can be,
> 'Case dat no sum ob money worth so much as me.
> Den I jump up an holler, even dis ting I hear,
> And I stretch my red mouf across from ear to ear.[67]

To the minstrel show songwriter, and to those in the audience who would believe the sentiments expressed in these verses, black slaves were so obtuse as to exchange the hope of freedom for a few deceptively kind and flattering words. If they contemplated such songs long enough, white listeners could scarcely fail to join the author of the rollicking "Over the Mountain" in the belief that "de biggest fool I eber see, was nigger come from Tennessee."[68]

Deceived by the slaveholders' self-serving flattery, the bondsmen in these songs were convinced that the food, housing, and recreational possibilities of the plantation more than adequately met their needs. The lyrics recorded slaves' supposed satisfaction with "dere hoe cakes" and "dat old roast possum." Even the "tail an' bristle" of "hog meat" were said to "make de nigger whistle" with contentment. On the southern estate, or "the old Kentucky home" as it was popularly known to minstrel audiences, the contented slaves lived in rustic quarters that not only provided warmth and shelter, but also served as the setting for daily rounds of dancing, fiddling, banjo twanging, bones playing, and tambourine shaking.[69] In fact, according to the blackfaced singer of "Come, Niggas Arouse," a slave's life couldn't be better if he'd chosen if for himself:

> And dis am de life for a nig, for a nig,
> For with it great sport you can see,
> An massa may boast tho he eber so big
> But dis am de life for me.[70]

Minstrel songs even portrayed the slave who decided to leave this life of leisure and seek the rewards of freedom. After a period of separation from the estate of his birth, during which time he might have wandered aimlessly, the disillusioned bondsman often came to the conclusion that he would be better off in the South:

> To Canada old John was bound,
> All by de rail-road under ground;
> He's got no clothes — he's got no tin,
> He wishes he was back agin.
>
> Gib me de place called Dixie Land,
> Wid hoe an shubble in my hand;
> Whar fiddles ring an banjos play,
> I'de dance all night an work all day.[71]

Whether he returned to a cabin "way down upon de Swanee ribber" or to "a place call'd Loozyann, dat 'zactly suits de colord man," such accounts of slave-choices seemed "living proof" that northern society had no attractions comparable to the "land where cotton grows," the "land where milk and honey flows."[72]

Abolitionist sympathizers who considered such sentiments harmful to their cause penned musical responses in the hope of clouding this generally agreeable picture of black slavery. Though often using the same melodies as the popular minstrel songs, the reformers' musical compositions were more often performed on the lecture platform than on the minstrel stage. As an adjunct to speeches, abolitionst sentiments sung to the tune of "O Susannah," "Dandy Jim," or "Old Rosin the Beau" enlivened their meetings. One antebellum songbook editor specifically advocated adapting such songs for use "in the domestic circle, the social gathering, the school, the club-room . . . and in short, wherever music is loved and appreciated — Slavery abhorred, and Liberty held sacred." By using well-known tunes, abolitionist composers and lyricists could ease the spread of their ideas while encouraging singers and listeners to concentrate upon the message contained in each new verse.[73]

Images of life in bondage continued to be filled with the horrible scenes of misery recorded in reformers' fiction and poetry:

> . . . the rice-swamp dank and lone,
> Where the slave-whip ceaseless swings,
> Where the noisome insect stings,
> Where the fever demon strews
> Poison with the falling dews. . . .[74]

Weak and helpless, with no hope of a change for the better, the slaves seemed to barely survive. The slave-traders and slaveholders exploited their "feeble, unresisting prey" without mercy.[75] To the dispirited chattel of abolitionist song, the answer to the question posed in "I Am Monarch of Nought I Survey" was all too readily apparent:

> O slavery, where are the charms
> That "patriarchs" have seen in thy face;
> I dwell in the midst of alarms,
> And serve in a horrible place.[76]

As long as these verses remained within the context of abolitionist rhetoric, the images expressed an unequivocal condemnation of slavery. If the songs found their way to the blackfaced performance, as sometimes happened, the minstrel theater's conciliatory influence could transform horror into melancholy. Minstrelsy, once again, provided a vehicle for avoiding the ideological conflicts of slavery.

A slave's sadness in antebellum song could be the result of personal suffering, separation from home or loved ones, plantation disturbances, or even the death of "Ole Massa," but minstrel songs modified harsh images and made the Afro-Americans' grief and suffering appear transient. In a theatrical context, mournful lyrics like those describing the separation of a slave couple in "Darling Nelly Gray," could be brightened by subsequent burnt cork antics:[77]

> *Interlocutor:* Now, Tambo, didn't that song touch you?
> *Tambo:* No, but the fellow that sang it did. He still owes me five.
> *Interlocutor:* Enough! Enough!
> *Tambo:* He sure has got enough from me, I'll say he has.
> *Interlocutor:* I am astonished at you. Why, the idea of a man of
> your mental calibre talking about such sordid matters, right after
> listening to such a beautiful song! Have you no sentiment left?
> *Tambo:* No, I haven't got a cent left.[78]

Certainly, the impact of the tragic scene described in "Nellie Gray" would be diminished greatly if followed by such laughter-producing material.

Some minstrel ballads included a compromise resolution within their verses. Songs like "The Bee-Gum" and "The Dinner Horn" told of the bondman's hard lot—the long hours spent in the fields under a hot sun, the inadequate compensation for work completed, and the trauma of losing family and friends to the interregional slave trade. The same songs tempered this picture of slavery's cruelties by discounting the long-term effects of such suffering. In fact, the slaves in the minstrel songs always seemed able to shrug off their worries for after-hours play. When he heard the

dinner horn or went out to hunt "de big racoon," the ordinarily melancholy field hand became a jolly "Nigger Nabob." As for his daytime troubles,
"pshaw — he soon forgets dem" as he frolicks "by de sunshine ob de moon."
For the songwriter seeking to entertain rather than alienate, compromises
in plantation imagery were essential. When minstrel tunesmiths combined
conflicting cultural visions of the slave South in a single composition, the
resulting song may have entertained, but it did little to stimulate a careful
examination of American values. The lyrics did more than entertain, however; by their easy acceptance of the southern system of race and labor
regimentation these songs implied that such a system worked quite well.
If, on occasion, a slave justifiably could "cuss his tiresome lot," it was
equally evident to minstrel audiences that in general, "niggers are contented as long as they've a home":[79]

> Sometimes de nigga's life is sad, sometimes his life is gay,
> When de work dont come too hard he's singin all de day.[80]

Minstrelsy's conciliatory combination of plantation images had a counter-
part in antebellum drama. Even plays based upon adamantly antislavery
fiction contained music or dialogue which could serve the purpose of ideological compromise. The era's playwrights, if they wanted audiences, wrote
to meet the demands of popular culture. While some Americans seemed
willing to criticize the institution of slavery, the dramas themselves molli-
fied any conflicts arising within their plots, thereby sidestepping once again
the pressing paradox of slavery in a liberty-loving culture.[81]

In 1834, the footlights went up on a short, hunched, curly headed,
blackfaced Bostonian character named Sambo in the stage production of
George Lionel Stevens' drama, *The Patriot*; and he immediately began to
"weel about-turn about-do just so, and eb'ry time weel about jump Sambo."
Possessing this same flair for musical comedy, later burnt cork stage characters could "take de words out of de mouth of de *illustrious* Jim Crow,
and give him Sambo's own pecooliar twist and turn." With one eye fixed
upon past public acceptance of Isaac Bickerstaffe's and John Murdock's
comic creations, and the other scanning recent trends in American minstrelsy, antebellum playwrights gave their audiences a strong dose of "Ethiopian delineation." Plays such as *Horseshoe Robinson* (1856), *Fashions and
Follies of Washington Life* (1857), *Major Jones' Courtship* (1850), and *Self*
(1856) depicted Afro-American bondsmen as exceedingly loyal to their
owners, but generally incapable of pronouncing or understanding even the
simplest multisyllabic words. Thus, the laughable slave role was alternately
played as a good and faithful servant and as a black idiot.[82]

The foolish slave can also be found in plays by or based upon the works of antislavery reformers. John Brougham's stage adaptation of Harriet Beecher Stowe's *Dred* (1856) opens with a scene in which the singing slaves seem to have a carefree life:

> Pretty Carolina rose,
> Won't you hear, won't you hear?
> Pretty Carolina Rose,
> Won't you hear?
> De sun, he igin to shine —
> Dat's a berry lucky sign,—
> Happy days be eber thine,
> Pretty Carolina Rose![83]

Referred to as "cater wauling rascals" by one white character, slaves are the constant target of white folks' jokes throughout the rest of the script. One character, a black youth named Tom Tit, is described as "the curly-headed abomination", a "bellowing black bull of Bashan!", and "a living hoax, an incarnate joke." To earn these epithets he sometimes somersaulted onto stage — at least once while carrying flowers and singing "Camptown Races" — or he might play the banjo gaily. The script's third act underscores that first scene describing the troublefree plantation life by having a slave cheer her despondent husband with a song: "me have no care. . . . me happy, so me sing . . . my heart is light . . . me think not what to-morrow bring." When Tom Tit salutes her attitude by exclaiming, "Oh, golly, glory, a'n't that like 'lasses . . . oh, my, it so good," it is not clear whether he is talking about romance or plantation life.Despite Stowe's antislavery sympathies, this adaptation of her novel suggests that slave life had some advantages.[84]

Stage adaptations of Harriet Beecher Stowe's most famous novel were even more popular than *Dred*. *Uncle Tom's Cabin* never left the boards from 1852 until 1931. Unprotected by copyright, the author of the best-selling novel received no part of the huge profits which others made from the book's dramatization. Neither did she have the satisfaction of seeing her work treated in a wholly serious manner. Burlesques such as *Happy Uncle Tom's Cabin* (1854), *Uncle Tom's Cabin in Louisiana* (1854), and *The Cloud with the Silver Lining* (1854) were advertised as featuring "joyous Negroes," "holiday festivals — Marriages — Congo Dances &c." On one occasion, the promotional ballyhoo which accompanied *Uncle Tom's Cabin* included the lively music of a thirty member brass band, a "Drummond Light" exhibition, and "a grand display of fireworks under the direction of Isaac Edge of Jersey City." Variations of Stowe's novel were further enlivened by the contributions of Thomas D. "Jim Crow" Rice and other blackfaced comedians who performed songs like "Uncle Breve Tells About the Good Time He Had on the Old Plantation," or "Happy Are We, Darkies So Gay." As the threat of civil war became more immediate, minstrel farces and humorous burlesques of *Uncle Tom's Cabin* came to dominate theatrical productions of the novel.[85]

In stage versions of Stowe's novel, her antislavery message as well as her slave characterizations underwent a not-so-subtle metamorphosis. New characters were introduced and old ones transformed into minstrel clones. Before the end of the decade, George Harris' lamentations on the misery of slavery were virtually drowned out by the laugh-producing strains of Topsy's "Oh! I'se So Wicked":

> Black folks can't do naught, they say,
> I guess I'll teach some how to play,
> And dance about dis time ob day,—
> Ching a ring a bang goes de break-down.
>
> . . . .
>
> Eat de cake and hoe de corn,
> I'se de gal dat ne'er was born,
> But 'spects I grow'd up one dark morn,
> Ching a ring a smash goes de break-down.[86]

Even the deeply religious Uncle Tom, in some versions, could be portrayed as a crooner. In an 1854 burlesque of Stowe's novel, blackfaced minstrel Dan Rice played Tom singing a song called "Wait for the Wagon" which told of the slave's misadventures in the North. After discovering that white northerners did not see him as an equal, he summed up his recent experiences by telling the audience:

> I travel'd round de country an' felt dat I was free,
> For I was cold and starvin' from de elbow to de knee,
> But Massa has forgib me, an' I know dat all am right,
> Tho' if it gibs you pleasure, I'll run off eb'ry night.[87]

Indeed, pleasure was the basic idea behind such singing and dancing stage characters. Few observers would have wept for this Uncle Tom —"except from laughing too hard."[88]

While the bulk of these *Uncle Tom's Cabin* bowdlerizations were either minstrel-like or prosouthern variations, Stowe herself contributed to the antebellum theatrical climate of compromise between opposing views of black bondage. Although initially unsympathetic to the adaptation of her work for the worldly American stage, she was said to have been delighted with her first viewing — her "smiles and tears succeeding each other through the whole." Unable to stem the exploitation of her book, she wrote a play based on a portion of the novel and titled it *The Christian Slave* (1855).[89]

Comical treatments of slave life which served the cause of compromise were intermingled with Stowe's commentary on slavery's morally damaging effects. After opening with the strains of "Ole Kintuck in de Arternoon," *The Christian Slave* proceeded with blacks speaking in distorted and absurdly mispronounced dialect, acting shiftless, and telling bad jokes. Described as "rather a funny specimen in the Jim Crow line," Topsy never seemed able to get through her daily catechism without causing a good deal of laughter:

> *Ophelia:* Into what state did the fall bring all mankind?
> *Topsy:* Fall brought all mankind into a state of sin and misery. Please ma'am —?
> *Ophelia:* What, Topsy?
> *Topsy:* Dat ar state Kintuck? De Lor' knows dey has sin and misery 'nough dar![90]

In this manner, "sin and misery," humor and gaiety joined hands on the antebellum stage in a dramatic expression of white America's preference for union and for popular entertainment which made real-world tensions psychologically manageable. Sometimes this meant accepting obvious contradictions with a smile. When, for example, Ophelia asked Topsy to describe her household duties, the young slave replied: "Fetch water — and wash dishes — and rub knives — and wait on folks — and dance breakdowns." This perplexing juxtaposition of play and work — of cheerful and harsh plantation images — enabled audiences to recognize the wrongs of slavery while at the same time remaining undisturbed about their acquiescent racist attitudes.[91]

CHAPTER 3
Black Americans Fight Back

We wish to plead our own cause. Too long have
others spoken for us.
John Browne Russwurm, 1827

Uneasily coexisting with white-authored portrayals of southern plantation life was a world of black histories, novels, poetry, and drama. Although the nature of racial oppression in the United States limited much
of this pre-Civil War creative resistance to folk forms, Afro-Americans
nonetheless contributed their versions of slave life to American popular
culture. Black authors recorded different interpretations of slavery than
those accepted by white contemporaries. Indeed, their interpretations varied
so greatly from white norms that they might best be described as counter-
visions of the black condition under slavery.

Afro-American historians responded to cultural stereotypes of slaves in
texts which infused the black past with dignity and pride. Black poets countered pejorative portraits of Afro-American mental and physical disability
in verse that encouraged self-definition and self-esteem. Black novelists and
playwrights denied that slaves were helpless and dependent by highlight-
ing the bondsmen's noble souls, heroism, and the deceptions necessary to
survive in a racist society.

Collectively, these images reflect a distinctively Afro-American perspective forged by the creation and maintenance of institutionalized black enslavement. Resulting from no innate tendency of mind, but rather from
shared experiences with bondage and caste, folk culture, and separate institutions, this other view of American life was a cultural echo of a sociological reality. From the days of the "unthinking decision" to equate blacks
with slaves and slaves with blacks, people of African descent had been
considered too different to be included in white socioeconomic life. Refusing to accept the harsh implications of this widespread opinion of blacks
as outsiders, Afro-American writers adopted an important and prophetic
leadership role. While lashing out against false piety, misinformation, and
racism, these individuals also spoke of intraracial solidarity and of rejecting white standards. Even as they battled for the recognition of black rights
within American society, they attempted to speed the growth of intellectual and spiritual independence. Afro-American writers did not wait for

50

white approval, but instead proceeded to secure liberty for their people with the powers of self-definition and self-respect.

In their portrayals of slavery informed by personal experience, the early Afro-American historians, playwrights, novelists, and poets were no mere imitators of their white contemporaries. Black and white creative expression might have appeared similar in style, but in terms of content and spirit they often stood in quarrelsome contrast. This divergence itself suggests the psychological importance of the pre-Civil War struggle over slavery. Black writers refused to concede the battle to their powerful adversaries and fought back through the creation and promotion of literature which declared an alternative slave imagery.

Black Americans sought to assemble and preserve their historical tradition in the pre-Civil War era, despite laws which discouraged black literacy. Within an atmosphere inimical to self-esteem, black slaves uncovered and shared knowledge of their group history and culture. In covert classrooms in the field, cabin, and "hush-harbor," bondsmen learned to mitigate the influence of their masters' allegations of black inferiority.[1]

Slaves who were very young when they were separated from their parents often found it difficult even to determine their own birth date, but a well-placed question from an inquiring mind often yielded a surprising quantity of useful information. A Maryland slave, future abolitionist Frederick Douglass, took this approach to uncovering his heritage: as a youngster, Douglass inquired into the origin and nature of slavery. Since his questions were put to children only a little older and better informed than himself, the youth did not solve his problems easily. As he wrote in 1848: "The very first mental effort that I now remember on my part, was an attempt to solve the mystery, Why am I a slave?" He was told that God had made all things, that blacks were created to be servants of white masters, and that God was good and knew what was best for all of His creatures. Since these explanations conflicted with his own idea of goodness, Douglass continued his search for historical cause. By questioning older members of the slave community, he discovered that several could relate in detail the experience of their enslavement in Africa. Armed with this new information, the seven-year-old concluded that it was "not *color*, but *crime*, not *God*, but *man*" who had shaped the origins of black bondage. This sense of black history, along with a "burning hatred of slavery," motivated and informed his work and that of his black colleagues in history, fiction, poetry, and drama.[2]

Members of the antebellum free black community explored black history by organizing literary and library societies. In a nation which allowed Afro-Americans little access to formal education, these community organizations provided much needed support and focus for black self-education efforts. Groups such as Philadelphia's Reading Room Society, Boston's Adelphic Union for the Promotion of Literature and Science, and the Philomathean and Phoenix Societies of New York City developed circulating libraries, conducted surveys, and sponsored lectures on historical, moral, and scientific topics.[3]

In addition to providing a forum for discussing Afro-America's history, black literary societies and "Committees of Colored Gentlemen" encouraged research and publication. Early works by Robert Benjamin Lewis, James W. C. Pennington, Christopher Rush, James McCune Smith, William Cooper Nell, Martin Delany, and James Theodore Holly differed markedly from the writings of their white contemporaries. The volumes penned by these individuals told of the leadership roles held by blacks in antiquity, recounted the exploits of black soldiers in wartime, and outlined the rise and progress of Afro-American institutions such as the black church.[4]

To a large extent, such histories were written with a purpose other than to chronicle past events. Believing that black Americans would continue to suffer from the lack of a history, Afro-American authors wrote to correct the historical record. As antebellum emigrationist Holly described it, he and his colleagues wanted to "inflame the latent embers of self-respect, that the cruelty and injustice of our oppressors, have nearly extinguished in our bosoms, during the midnight chill of centuries, that we have clanked the galling chains of slavery." Author William Cooper Nell felt that "the names which others neglect should only be the more sacredly our care."[5]

In order to rewrite the history of their people, black writers contradicted several assumptions about slavery which were commonly accepted in pre-Civil War society. To counter the idea that slavery existed because Africans were natural slaves, former bondsman James W. C. Pennington traced the history of Spanish colonization in the Americas. By showing that Europeans enslaved Native Americans before they imported captive African labor gangs, he was able to claim that the concept of bondage was well established before blacks arrived. Surely then, he asserted, "slavery on this continent did not originate in the condition of the Africans." Euro-American avarice and not Afro-American biology, initiated and perpetuated the exploitation of red and black peoples.[6]

Black authors also spoke out against the assumption that the African homeland was uncivilized. In his *Treatise on the Intellectual Character, and Civil and Political Condition of the Colored People of the United States* (1837), Boston minister Hosea Easton noted the contributions which the West had made to the arts and sciences, but questioned "whether they are anywhere near its standard, as they once existed in Africa." Said to have been founded in 2188 B.C. by a son of Ham, he presented the kingdom of Egypt as the showpiece of African achievement. Its people noble, generous, and possessed of "true greatness," Egypt was credited with having done more to "cultivate such improvements as comports to the happiness of mankind, than all the descendants of Japhet[h] put together." According to Easton, Africa's contributions to world culture would be far more evident had not Europeans destroyed "every vestige of history" which fell into their hands during their raids of the continent.[7]

Easton and writers such as black physician-editor Martin R. Delany were not content to praise the achievements of ancient Africa; they also launched bitter attacks on the Euro-American character. After summarizing the history of Europe from 49 A.D. to 1667, Easton characterized this historical record as a "motley mixture of barbarism and civilization, of fraud and philanthropy, of patriotism and avarice, of religion and bloodshed." Moreover, the whites' checkered career in Europe had scarcely been improved by the Atlantic crossing. To Easton's mind, almost all Europeans — and especially Americans — retained in principle, if not in manner, "all the characteristics of their barbarous and avaricious ancestors." These writers offered their audiences spirited reading and recorded none of the paternalism that pervaded white historians' references to black civilization. Their work began with a distinctly different purpose — to represent black civilization as a historical treasure, not a racial deficit.[8]

Early black historians emphasized self-definition as vital to self-respect. Delany's *Condition, Elevation, Emigration, and Destiny of the Colored People of the United States* (1852) was particularly outspoken on this subject. Perhaps more aware of the shortcomings of romantic racialism than many, Delany reminded his readers that antislavery friends had "promised a great deal more than they have ever been able half to fulfill." Even in reform circles blacks continued to be considered less than equal by white antislavery leaders. Whites presumed to "*think* for, dictate to, and *know* better what suited colored people, than they knew for themselves." As a result of this usurpation, even well-intentioned white-authored histories of the Afro-American people failed to properly or fairly present black perspectives. Since Delany argued that "moral and mental" servitude fostered physical bondage, he championed the practical philosophy that "every people should be the originators of their own designs, the projector of their own schemes, and creators of the events that lead to their destiny." To this end his histories would be "a mere introduction to what will henceforth emanate from the pen of colored men and women."[9]

Further divorcing themselves from the unspoken assumptions and self-serving biases of white historians, Afro-American writers focused upon two areas which were underdeveloped by whites — slave achievement and the interconnection between prejudice and bondage. Black histories spoke often of individuals who had led distinguished lives while slaves and of those ex-slaves who exercised sound judgment and vigorous intellect. There is one such account of a slave with "the talents of correct and rapid calculation." According to this story, a black Virginian named Thomas Fuller once was asked how many seconds there were in seventy years, seven months, and seven days. He provided the correct answer in a minute and a half. Another example praises in detail the "unremitting industry and economy" of the Cuffe family. Specifically, father John Cuffe's thrifty industry made it possible for him to become a prosperous freeman who owned his own land.[10]

According to black writers, there would be many more such case studies of Afro-American advancement were it not for the pervasive influence of American racism. More than most of their white counterparts, black commentators on the American past were determined to state their views on the role which slavery had played in the development of the nation's unhealthy racial climate. Discussion of these matters was accorded an important place in their works. In a chapter entitled: "On the Nature of the Prejudice of the White Population of the United States, in its Malignant Exercise Towards the Colored People," Easton claimed that slavery incorporated "all, and every thing, that is bad on earth and in hell." It was this evil institution which was the true cause of prejudice. In like manner, Pennington examined "American prejudice against color" in a chapter of his *Text Book of the Origin and History, &c. &c. of the Colored People* (1841) — concluding that "slavery is the fountain of this bitter stream. The prejudice of which I have been speaking would not exist but for this corrupt fountain."[11]

Perhaps if these black writers failed to delve into the many intricacies of the slavery-racism continuum later probed by twentieth-century students of the "unthinking decision," they at least prepared their readers for the developments of the 1860s. Though the antebellum era ended in civil war and legally sanctioned racial slavery disappeared, social and legal sanctions thrived. During the postwar years black historians reminded their people — and all others who would listen — that historical studies could function as an encouragement to self-respect, self-definition, and intellectual freedom. If Martin Delany was at least partially correct in believing that mental servitude led to physical bondage, then their intellectual pursuits could someday help to secure a more complete freedom.

The sense of purpose seen in these histories can also be found in other forms of pre-Civil War black expression. The earliest black poets were able to publish only socially conservative poetry, but by 1830 black poets began to voice a strong protest ethic which was at once part of the growing antebellum reform spirit and at the same time more truly liberating than the poems of their white counterparts. Between 1830 and the Civil War Afro-American poets analyzed American ideological conflicts, critiqued current events, and provided readers with insights into surviving spiritually in a hostile land.

Initially, Afro-American poetry seemed to be more concerned with the issues of Christian piety and morality than with protesting the wrongs of slavery. Jupiter Hammon, the first black poet to have his verse published in America, has long been considered socially conservative. His poem, titled "The Kind Master and the Dutiful Servant" (1783), perfectly expresses the attitudes of an obedient and satisfied slave:

Master

My Servant, lovely is the Lord,
    And blest those servants be,
That truly love his holy word,
    And thus will follow me.

Servant

Dear Master, that's my whole delight,
    Thy pleasure for to do;
As for grace and truth's in sight,
    Thus far I'll surely go.[12]

In addition to advocating Christian piety in his poems, this Long Island slave also preached patient acquiescence to the slave system. In his *Address to the Negroes in the State of New-York* (1787) he tells his black audience that they should "think very little" of their "bondage in this life." By arguing that if the abolition of chattel slavery is a part of God's grand design "he will do it in his own time and way," Hammon seemed to be accommodating conservative white social values. In fact, he seemed to confirm proslavery assertions that Christianized bondsmen had "reason to bless God for ever" for bringing them to America.[13]

The seventy-year-old Hammon recognized that his life as a slave had been "so much better than most slaves have had," and that he "had more advantages and privileges . . . than many white people have enjoyed." For elderly servants such as himself, Hammon reasoned that "it may be more for our own comfort to remain as we are." Without their masters' help the aged bondsmen might be unable to take care of themselves in a free labor economy. While he did not wish for his own freedom, Hammon wrote that he "should be glad if others, especially the young Negroes, were to be free." Liberty was an important goal worth seeking, if one could get it honestly. He believed that this truth was not only self-evident — known "from our own feelings" — but that it had been reaffirmed by the rhetoric, goals, and conduct of the Revolution. Disappointed that the war had not more immediately improved life for blacks, Hammon nevertheless felt gains had been made by the antislavery effort. Moreover, he entreated free blacks to "lead quiet and peaceable lives in all Godliness and honesty" in order to discredit claims that manumission led to idleness, drunkenness, and thievery. For their own good and happiness, and for the sake of their "poor brethren, who are still in bondage," he cautioned free blacks against taking "to bad courses."[14]

Jupiter Hammon's blend of faith-based resignation and hope was attractive enough to certain of his contemporaries that the Pennsylvania Society for Promoting the Abolition of Slavery reprinted his *Address* in an edition of 500 copies.[15] This recognition tells us almost as much about the spirit of the Society as it does about the achievement of Hammon, but it pales in comparison to the attention given poet Phillis Wheatley. Torn from her own culture at an early age, largely isolated from mainstream black society, and educated in the neoclassical tradition, the Boston slave's use of primarily Greco-Roman and religious imagery diffused her occasional protests against bondage and thus obscured her expressions of race consciousness. Wheatley's first book of verse, *Poems on Various Subjects, Religious and Moral*, was published in 1773, shortly after she was manumitted.

One poem in this volume, entitled "To the Right Honourable William, Earl of Dartmouth," told of the poet's deep desire to see freedom rather than "wanton *Tyranny*" rule in her adopted North American homeland. Personal experience as a black slave — and not blind patriotism or ideological dogmatism — informed her view:

> I, young in life, by seeming cruel fate
> Was snatch'd from *Afric's* fancy'd happy seat:
> What pangs excruciating must molest,
> What sorrows labour in my parent's breast?
> Steel'd was that soul and by no misery mov'd
> That from a father seiz'd his babe belov'd:
> Such, such my case. And can I then but pray
> Others may never feel tyrannic sway?[16]

In another poem, "On being brought from Africa to America," she again expressed her awareness of black struggles in a white-dominated society. Though she joined Hammon in the belief that God had rescued her from paganism, she also criticized whites for their shallow understanding of spiritual equality:

Some view our sable race with scornful eye,
"Their colour is a diabolic die."
Remember, *Christians, Negroes,* black as *Cain,*
May be refin'd, and join th' angelic train.[17]

By placing "diabolic die" within quotations and capitalizing "Negroes,"
Wheatley suggested that while others might attach negative connotations
to blackness, she would not. Like Hammon, she was not simply a poet,
she was an "Afric" poet.[18]

Restrained by the dictates of the neoclassical, by the influences of
eighteenth-century social training, and by a dependence upon patrons, publishers, and other "beneficent intermediaries," the earliest black poets
presented guarded images both of themselves and of black slavery. Their
work was not, however, wholly devoid of racial consciousness and personal protestations for reform. Indeed, as organized reform efforts increased in scope and militancy, black poetry became more openly expressive
of a distinctly Afro-American point of view.[19] By 1830, Hammon's po-
litely worded concern for the freedom of young slaves assumed a bolder
form with a bolder author:

Slavery, oh, thou cruel stain,
Thou dost fill my heart with pain:
See my brother, there he stands
Chained by slavery's cruel bands.

Could we not feel a brother's woes,
Relieve the wants he undergoes,
Snatch him from slavery's cruel smart,
And to him freedom's joy impart?[20]

By 1830, Wheatley's occasionally expressed identification with blackness
found a more forceful and enthusiastic voice:

Black I am, oh! daughters fair!
But my beauty is most rare.
Black, indeed, appears my skin,
Beauteous, comely, all within.[21]

Like the poems of white reformers, Afro-American verse published between 1830 and the Civil War addressed the nation's longstanding hypocrisy on the issues of slavery and freedom. Both church and state were criticized for failing to live up to religious and constitutional professions of
principle. In a manner which must have seemed shockingly unpatriotic to

many, black poets asked: "Where—where is the nation so erring as we, /
Who claims the proud name of the 'HOME OF THE FREE'?" Boldly declaring
that black Americans were unhappy in being forced to dwell "upon the
shaking ground of tyranny," they made a mockery of much that was sacred in white majoritarian culture.[22] Black separatist James M. Whitfield
expressed this spirit when, with considerable sarcasm, he penned the lines:

> America, it is to thee,
> Thou boasted land of liberty,—
> It is to thee I raise my song,
> Thou land of blood, and crime, and wrong.[23]

In describing the American Constitution as "a sepulchre of whited lies"
and American religion as a seedbed of "heathenism," such writers shared
the conviction of white antislavery voices that the "clanking of chains, /
Make sounds of strange discord on Liberty's plains." Unlike these white
poets, however, some blacks were reluctant to believe that it was possible
to rescue now deeply corrupted national principles. Perhaps, they seemed
to suggest, the construction of a humanistic, Christian, egalitarian society
could only be carried out in another, less polluted context. For those writers who feared that the United States was incapable of erasing "the deep
blot of thy foul degradation," separation—either physical or psychological
—challenged integration as a motivating ethic.[24] By the late 1850s, continued oppression in America prompted black poet Frances Ellen Watkins
to insist:

> You may make my grave wherever you will,
> In a lowly vale or a lofty hill;
> You may make it among earth's humblest graves,
> But not in a land where men are slaves.[25]

Personal experience and racial unity bound many black poets more
tightly than ties of nationality could. When antebellum Afro-American
writers commented on current slavery-related events, they wrote with a
spirit and a sensitivity seldom matched by white reformers. Often having
had first-hand experience with both southern enslavement and northern
proscription, black authors felt a personal need to chasten, teach, uplift,
and reform and used their writing skills in fiction and poetry accordingly.
They condemned the 1850 Fugitive Slave Act as "a complete gewgaw, / Unworthy of the name of law" and warned that the Dred Scott decision of
1857 could very well ignite a confrontation which would "wrap the whole
South in wild conflagration." Moreover, they saw slave rebels such as the

Amistad's Joseph Cinque as a kinsman whose bold and noble example would "fire anew each freeman's heart." Certainly, wrote James Whitfield, Cinque's name would "stand on history's leaf, / Amid the mighty and the brave" because he had "scorned to live a cowering slave."[26]

On an even more personal level, the Afro-American poets shared their reactions to bondage with their readers and described slave survival techniques. While white writers concentrated on slaves' accommodation to oppressive conditions, black writers catalogued the ways in which people could triumph over bondage. Their poems advocated faith in the power of God, family, and the inner strength of black humanity.[27] According to North Carolina slave poet George Moses Horton, hope of a brighter future was essential to black survival:

> Must I dwell in Slavery's night,
> And all pleasure take its flight,
> Far beyond my feeble sight,
>   For ever?
>
> Worst of all, must hope grow dim,
> And withold her cheering beam?
> Rather let me sleep and dream
>   For ever!
>
> Something still my heart surveys,
> Groping through this dreary maze;
> Is it Hope?—then burn and blaze
>   For ever![28]

Other writers valued the family as a stabilizing force in a world of unpredictable events. Just as likely as white reformist verse to evoke sympathy, black depictions of slave auctions contained an added dimension which revealed the vital importance of family ties. For the young woman torn from loved ones in "The Slave Girl's Farewell," it was her mother who had been "the only hope my fond heart knew; / Or e'er shall know again." Similarly, Frances Ellen Watkins' "Fugitive's Wife" declared that "one thing cheered my lowly cot— / My husband was with me." These were images of the black family wherein love and support were joyously sustaining, a "fountain gushing ever new, / Amid life's desert wild."[29]

When separated from their kin, the bondsmen described by Afro-American poets had options other than suicide or submission. As described in Watkins' "Tennessee Hero" and Joseph C. Holly's "Fugitive," black slaves could choose to try an escape. By doing so, slaves risked their lives in order to reclaim the "heaven born right" of personal freedom. An escape did not betray those left behind, because even if unsuccessful, the attempt alone was spiritually liberating. With "a tameless light" flashing from his eyes, his heart beating "firm and true," a bold spirit would continue to resist enslavement. This slave could not be molded into any of the existing stereotypical black personalities.[30]

The liberating themes of strength, self-definition, and survival were also important to black novelists and playwrights in antebellum America. Pioneering Afro-American authors such as William Wells Brown, Frank J. Webb, Martin Delany, and Frederick Douglass often defined strength as bravery and rebelliousness, self-definition as purposeful pride, and survival as the ability to understand the oppressor without being understood by him. Whenever these qualities appeared in slave characters, they illustrated the dramatic difference between black and white visions of slave life in America.

Based upon an actual mutiny on board the slave ship *Creole* in 1841, Frederick Douglass' "The Heroic Slave" (1853) can be read as an abolitionist tool and as a record of pre-Civil War black thought regarding slave rebellions. The black reformer's hero was a "tall, symmetrical, round, and strong" slave named Madison Washington. Described by Douglass as "one to be sought as a friend, but to be dreaded as an enemy," Washington combined intelligence with bravery and had "the head to conceive, and the hand to execute." Radiating a "mesmeric power which is the invariable accompaniment of genius," he served as "general-in-chief" of the *Creole* rebels.[31]

Guided by personal experience, Douglass vividly described how Washington triumphed over self-doubt. From an initial feeling that his life was "worse than worthless," Washington came to realize that he could overcome his "*galling* consciousness of cowardice and indecision." He declared that he had wronged himself — that he was no coward: "*Liberty* I will have . . . or die in the attempt to gain it." Douglass goes on to say that as a result "at that moment he was free, at least in spirit."[32]

Having taken this first step, Douglass' hero experiences a series of epic adventures, each preparing him for the ultimate test. Finally, aboard the storm-swept *Creole*, Washington gained his victory by leading a successful surprise attack from the slave ship's hold. Though fellow rebels advised otherwise, Washington refused to execute their white captors and instead demanded that the slaves be granted their "rightful freedom." This noble restraint earned him the begrudging respect of the whites. As one sailor remembered: "I forgot his blackness in the dignity of his manner, and the eloquence of his speech. It seemed as if the souls of both the great dead (whose names he bore) had entered him."[33]

After courageously piloting the ship through a fierce squall, Madison Washington docked the brig at a Nassau wharf amidst the deafening cheers of sympathizers. Through personal courage and bold struggle, Douglass' hero had proven himself to be a man who "loved liberty as well as did Patrick Henry,— who deserved it as much as Thomas Jefferson,— and who fought for it with a valor as high, an arm as strong, and against odds as great, as he who led all the armies of the American colonies through the great war for freedom and independence." To Douglass, the black freedom-fighter was in no respect inferior to white Revolutionary War heroes. Washington's exploits compellingly contradicted literary portraits of fragile, child-like noble savages.[34]

"The Heroic Slave" was not the only example of early black writing which spoke of equality, nor was this elusive goal expressed solely in political terms. Afro-American playwrights and novelists carefully distinguished between equality and imitation.[35] Their white characters often exhibited abhorrent personal and behavioral defects. The slaveholders brutalized other human beings by feeding them roach-infested food, clothing them in tatters, and whipping them until "the flesh turn[ed] open in gashes streaming down with gore." Moreover, these cruelties did not stop with the slaves. Commonly, free blacks and helpless whites also were kidnapped and sold or cruelly flogged by bloodthirsty representatives of the plantation regime.[36]

According to Martin Delany, author of the serialized novel *Blake; or, The Huts of America* (1859), blacks would do well to rely upon their individual sense of values and self-worth.[37] His account of plantation life portrayed the master as "a silly, stupid old dolt, an inordinate blabber and wine bibber" and then went on to describe a slave family:

> Sampson was a black, tall, stoutly built, and manly, possessing much general intelligence, and a good-looking person. His wife a neat, intelligent, handsome little woman, the complexion of himself, was the mother of a most interesting family of five pretty children, three boys and two girls.[38]

Black novelists and playwrights often celebrated individual psychological victories over the oppressor. If such purposeful deception resulted in masters believing that their servants were childlike or ineptly comical, that was the masters' problem. Afro-American writers portrayed aberrant slave behavior as an important part of a well-planned survival game in which the slaves, of necessity, had to know more about the slaveholders than the slaveholders knew of them. Bondsmen in black-authored accounts interpreted their owners' every change in mood with astonishing precision, used celebrations to conceal illegal activities, and referred to masters as "da 'sarned ole scamp" or "dat ole cuss" whenever possible.[39] Even the death of the plantation patriarch could demand duplicity:

> At four o'clock at morn the family was called
>   Around the old man's dying bed;
> And oh! but I laughed to myself when I heard
>   That the old man's spirit had fled.
> Mr. Carlton cried, and so did I pretend;
>   Young mistress very nearly went mad;
> And the old parson's groans did the heavens fairly rend;
>   But I tell you I felt mighty glad.[40]

On occasion, planter-deprecating humor was enjoyed in a context that embarrassed the slaveholder and endangered the slave. In *Clotel* (1853), author William Wells Brown created a scene in which an infamously cruel planter named John Peck tried to convince a group of northern visitors that he was a kind slaveholder. To win the slaves' good will for the day, Peck treated each of them to a dram of whisky. In return, the hands were to drink to their master's health or offer a complimentary toast in the presence of the white guests. He offered the cup to Jack—the "cleverest and most witty" slave on the farm: "Now, Jack, give us something rich. . . . We have raised the finest crop of cotton that's been seen in these parts for many a day. Now give us a toast on cotton; come, Jack, give us something to laugh at." Taking the whisky in his right hand and putting his left to his head, the bondsman began to "scratch his wool" like the dull-witted slaves of minstrelsy. Then he toasted his master's agricultural achievements with a slyly worded critique of southern labor exploitation:

> The big bee flies high,
>   The little bee makes the honey;
> The black folks makes the cotton,
> And the white folks gets the money.[41]

Other accounts examined southern whites who, though they were not planters, shared slaveholding selfishness and greed. William Wells Brown created two of the most memorable such characters in his theatrical satire, *The Escape; or, A Leap for Freedom* (1858). A profit-mongering Maryland physician named Dr. Gaines had become concerned that his practice was poorly located:

> *Dr. Gaines:* I see by the New Orleans papers that the yellow fever is raging there to a fearful extent. Men of my profession are reaping a harvest in that section this year. I would that we could have a touch of the yellow fever here, for I think I could invent a medicine that would cure it. But the yellow fever is a luxury

that we medical men in this climate can't expect to enjoy; yet we may hope for the cholera.

Eminently supportive of her husband's career goals, his wife replied:

> *Mrs. Gaines:* Yes, I would be glad to see it more sickly here, so that your business might prosper. But we are always unfortunate. Every body here seems to be in good health, and I am afraid that they'll keep so. However, we must hope for the best. We must trust in the Lord. Providence may possibly send some disease amongst us for our benefit.[42]

Along with their portrayals of planters and physicians, black writers recorded a fresh perspective on a third group of professionals — ministers. In black-authored plays and novels, theology often reinforced slaveholders' prerogative and southern social practices. Christian ministers used their catechisms to teach subservience to planters' wishes, allowed slave auctions in church sanctuaries, and even traded in slaves to pay "travellin' expenses." Antebellum black literature characterized these spiritual leaders as hypocritical, shortsighted, and racist. In *The Escape* Reverend Pinchen unquestioningly assumed that the antebellum class system extended into more heavenly realms. After one of his visions, a house servant named Hannah asked if he had seen her "ole man Ben" in heaven. "No, Hannah," he replied tersely, "I didn't go amongst the niggers."[43]

Black authors condemned slaveholding theologians and encouraged slaves to abandon the white gospel because it was "false preaching" from "the stony hearts of . . . pretended Christians." Advocating black religion as a liberating alternative, these novels claimed that it would give bondsmen "a hope this side of the vale of tears" and "something on this earth as well as a promise of things in another world." Instead of serving their masters' interests, blacks could choose to live by their own interpretation of the gospel and take another step toward spiritual liberation. Though dealing with whites required continued duplicity, the choice for black believers was straightforward. According to Aunt Dafney and Ned in *Clotel*: "Dey all de time tellin' dat de lord made us for to work for dem, and I don't believe a word of it. . . . Uncle Simon can beat dat sermon all to pieces."[44]

Bold enough to contradict prevailing stereotypes of the slaves' spiritual, physical, and psychological state, black writers did not hesitate to address still another weighty contemporary problem: miscegenation. White and black writers agreed that light-skinned slaves faced great obstacles because of their mixed parentage, but the two groups of authors focused on opposing sources of these difficulties. Mulattos characterized by whites were condemned because of their black heritage; mulattos characterized by blacks were sometimes tragic figures, but they were more importantly people who struggled heroically against racial prejudice.[45]

The tragic octoroon most often was portrayed in fiction by white authors as a beautiful young woman who had been raised and educated as a white child in the home of her wealthy slaveholding father. Possessing only the slightest evidence of "Negro blood," she discovered her true status only upon the death of the planter. Then, sold through a crass, lower-class slave dealer who tried to rape her or sell her as a concubine, the fair-skinned and virtuous woman died of shame or committed suicide when she failed to regain her original status.[46] Readers were reminded that in the American South even a "bright, gay creature . . . worth her weight in sunshine" was doomed to slavery—and an early death—if marked with the "ineffaceable curse of Cain." As described by Zoe, the heroine of Dion Boucicault's Louisiana plantation drama, *The Octoroon* (1859), the prognosis for such a condition was bleak:

> Of the blood that feeds my heart, one drop in eight is black— bright red as the rest may be, that one drop poisons all the flood; those seven bright drops give me love like yours—hope like yours —ambition like yours—life hung with passions like dew-drops on the morning flowers; but the one black drop gives me despair, for I'm an unclean thing—forbidden by the laws—I'm an Octoroon![47]

Such treatments suggested that it was the "white blood" which gave these slaves their above-average intelligence, their attractive physique, and their inability to adapt to slavery.

As with authors who were ex-slaves, some black writers could bring personal experience to their treatments of miscegenation. William Wells Brown had such a family history. Not only was his slave mother said to be a daughter of Daniel Boone, but early in life he learned that his own father, a close relative of his master, was connected with one of Kentucky's oldest, wealthiest, and most aristocratic families. When he grew older, Brown was hired out as a superintendent of slave gangs headed for New Orleans. In his memoirs he tells of overhearing slave-trader James Walker offer a beautiful quadroon a choice—either she would return to his Missouri farm as his housekeeper/mistress or be sold as a field hand to "the worst plantation on the river." Reluctantly selecting the first, she and their four children were eventually sold as slaves so that Walker could marry a white woman. The quadroon's experience was of special concern to Brown because his own sister met with a similar fate.[48]

In *Clotel*, consequently, Brown portrays the forces of miscegenation as coercive and demoralizing to black self-esteem. His heroine had a face "of pure Anglo-Saxon; her long black wavy hair done up in the neatest manner; her form tall and graceful." She was a very intelligent sixteen-year-old slave who white men described as a "Real Albino, fit for a fancy girl for any one"; but Brown's virtuous heroine would not willingly become part of this system of "immorality and vice."[49]

Cast aside when her owner and politically ambitious common-law husband married a wealthy white woman, Clotel refused to be his mistress. She continued to refuse such attention from all of her subsequent owners. Finally, after a series of unsuccessful escapes, she jumped off a bridge and into the river in one last desperate leap for freedom.[50]

Brown portrayed Clotel's final exit from a compassionless world as an heroic act by a brave woman who fought tenaciously to maintain her own value system. Though his novel contained many elements of the noble savage stereotype, *Clotel* helped to push antebellum black literature beyond the limitations of the usual story line with its emphasis on the durability of the human spirit. All slaves — whether octoroon or dark-skinned — relied upon a personal wellspring of strength which gave them a unifying resiliency and sense of self:

> You may place the slave where you please; you may dry up to your utmost the fountains of his feelings, the springs of his thought; you may yoke him to your labour, as an ox which liveth only to work, and worketh only to live; you may put him under any process which, without destroying his value as a slave, will debase and crush him as a rational being; you may do this, and *the idea that he was born to be free will survive it all.* It is allied to his hope of immortality; it is the ethereal part of his nature, which oppression cannot reach.[51]

During the antebellum era, Afro-American writers also began to discuss the skin-color prejudices which existed within the black community. As a logical extension of their critique of white society, these authors reminded their readers that there were "traitors, even among colored people" who posed a real threat to racial unity. Mulattos ashamed of their black heritage, along with blacks who assumed too much from skin color, characteristically compromised unity and community integrity. Emulating slaveholding whites in mind and manner was not an exclusively mulatto caste fault: to be a "rale wite folk's nigga" was a matter of choice.[52]

Martin Delany examined one facet of this argument in *Blake* when he warned his mulatto readers away from taking advantage of American racism by "leaving their connections with the blacks and turning entirely over to the whites." In Richmond and Charleston "Negro-fearing master-fathers" had taught the mulatto community to harbor "the strongest prejudice and hatreds" against "pure-blooded Negroes." Shy among the blacks and fearful of the whites, these people were said to "go sneaking about with the countenance of a criminal, of one conscious of having done wrong to his fellows." They were "the least happy of all the classes" because they denied their own oppression and disregarded the strengths of their history.[53]

As they criticized complexional distinctions, black authors sought to promote racial unity by reminding readers that many "most excellent mulattos and quadroons" condemned such wrongheaded beliefs. These writers created mulatto characters who fought against intraracial division by helping to free enslaved relatives, sheltering and feeding runaways, and risking their lives posing as slaveholders in escape plans. Their stories sought to prove that being born a mulatto did not prevent an individual from faithfully adhering to the common interests and goals of the Afro-American people.[54]

Whether they were criticizing northerners or southerners, Anglo-or Afro-Americans, black writers promoted images of black pride, cooperation, self-definition, strength, and survival. Their purpose was clear: to undermine what Delany termed the "studied policy" of whites to "keep the blacks in subjection and their spirits below a sentiment of self-respect." In retrospect, the choice of weapons in this pre-Civil War crusade seem somehow rather undramatic — the history text, poem, short story, novel, and play. Nevertheless, the issues of intellectual, psychological, and physical freedom were compelling. Black authors approached these issues with a consensus that attested to their determination to resist American racism. The degree to which these issues necessarily dominated their literature underscores the invidious nature of the slave labor system. The Civil War would only be a beginning to the lengthy, arduous process of eradicating its influences.[55]

CHAPTER 4

From Slave to Citizen, 1861–1965

> You can be up to your boobies in white satin, with gardenias in your hair and no sugar cane for miles, but you can still be working on a plantation.
>
> Billie Holiday, 1956

In the century following the Civil War, a multitude of social changes made an impression upon American popular culture and its accepted images of blacks. Freed from slavery, some four million black Americans, their children, and their children's children engaged in a painfully slow quest for the inalienable rights guaranteed to them. As they made progress in literacy, social mobility, and political and economic influence, Afro-Americans found a growing number of people who were willing to accept their interpretations of the antebellum slave experience. Nevertheless, by the time of the Civil War's centennial, it became apparent that a good deal remained to be accomplished both by those who would complete the modern civil rights crusade and by those who would disown, discredit, and abolish pejorative racial stereotypes.

The evolution of views regarding the slaves' role in the war illustrates the basic trends in American popular culture during the postbellum years.[1] Within the 1861–1965 period, historians' shifting attitudes toward black history reflected not only attempts to revise traditional beliefs about slaves and masters, but also the social changes involved in the evolution of modern America. Well into the twentieth century, white historians continued to give stereotypical reasons to explain why slaves responded either reluctantly or eagerly to the arrival of Union troops.

According to University of Kansas historian William Watson Davis in *Civil War and Reconstruction in Florida* (1913), well-fed, well-housed, and well-treated bondsmen had little reason to upset the social discipline of plantation life. Blacks who worked in the Big House "loved 'their white people' and in return were loved with a sincerity proven by experience." To this group of servants the slaveholder "confided his women and little children" when he went away to fight. True to "their rearing in the family circles of the South's aristocracy," the house servants' dutiful devotion and "high-minded humanity" was said to have been underrated and often over-looked by the "meddlesome, conscience-stricken people of another section."[2]

Other writers expanded upon Davis' comments by including field hands in the ranks of the faithful. Walter L. Fleming's 1905 book, *Civil War and Reconstruction in Alabama*, credited the surprising tranquility of planta-tion life during the war to the slaves' desire to "acquit themselves faith-fully" of the whites' trust, to their intense fear and dislike of the northern invaders, and to the calming effect which religion had upon the black com-munity. According to Fleming, Afro-Americans were "constitutionally good-natured," remained as faithful to a harsh master as to one who "treated them as men and brothers," seemed virtually incapable of harboring mal-ice or hatred, and "lacked the capacity for organization" under their own leaders. No wonder that only "negroes of bad character or young boys deserted to the enemy or gave information to their armies."[3]

When they examined the motivations of slaves who refused to be con-trolled by the "logical sequence of mutual dependence, trust, and attach-ment," these writers assembled a compelling array of explanations that assumed the slaves weren't responsible for their own behavior.[4] For exam-ple, they argued that Union troops operating in the South urged the bonds-men into rebellion and encouraged them to loot and burn. Black troops in particular were blamed for giving their brothers and sisters "false im-pressions of the new and glorious condition that was before them." Other accounts described Union forces as veritable body-snatchers who "captured and carried off" unsuspecting bondsmen for eventual use as laborers in the Federal camps.[5]

Historians continued to see blacks as children, uniquely susceptible to coercion and manipulation by wily northerners. In various parts of the occupied South, the pageantry and color of military parades supposedly produced a "mental exhilaration" in slaves which was wholly incompatible with "the simple and monotonous life of the plantation."[6] Once introduced to such "fanciful ideas of what freedom meant," the misled and inexperi-enced freemen cast their lot with Lincoln's army.[7]

The historical writings of Afro-Americans such as W. E. B. DuBois, Jo-seph T. Wilson, and Charles Wesley critiqued this interpretation of the black Civil War experience.[8] Along with three 1938 revisionist studies by Bell Wiley, Herbert Aptheker, and Harvey Wish, the ideas defended by these scholars eventually worked an important historiographical transfor-mation.[9] Their cumulative effect began to discourage stereotype-filled in-terpretations, and after 1940 more historians spoke more often of a "great exodus" of slaves which "practically stripped most plantations of workers."[10] While the historiographical record continued to contain misinterpretations, by the mid-nineteen sixties new research appeared which demonstrated the humanity, self-direction, and practical intelligence of blacks during the Civil War. The slaves fled their plantation homes whenever possible. Immunized to danger, they quit slavery "by their own impulse" and thus began a migration to the northern lines that was "unparallelled in American annals for daring, sacrifice and heroism." Dissatisfied with their status, encouraged by the winds of war and of freedom, and determined to reunite their broken families, their history disproved the stereotypical image of black slaves. Even those who chose to remain on the plantations until after the war were credited with "shrewdness and prudence." Possessing a clear understanding of "the nature of the revolution going on around them," they bided their time with the knowledge that the "hour of freedom was drawing nearer by the minute."[11]

Life on the New Plantation

Historians writing during the years immediately following the Civil War found it difficult to eliminate its lingering influence from their work. Although many authors claimed impartiality, they could not keep their vow when discussing slavery-related topics. The issues and tensions of the times betrayed the objectivity of authors, whether sympathizing with or condemning the Union effort.[12] Those who had supported abolition spoke of "rebellion resisted and defeated" in their accounts of the war. Presenting their political viewpoints as historical fact, these individuals celebrated the triumph of the North over "the most oppressive, grinding, and detestable military despotism of which history furnishes a record."[13]

Authors in this school of thought offered detailed accounts of the rise and fall of what they called the Slave Power. From the first, they claimed, a greedy and ambitious class of Americans had been determined to secure and maintain control of the government. Initially sympathetic to the British aristocracy, this privileged caste became economically as well as politically influential after Eli Whitney's cotton gin stimulated and commercialized American agriculture. As profits soared, the slave labor system lost the patriarchal features which had made it tolerable, while southern landowners left unturned "no stone which would contribute to the fostering and to the extension of African Slavery."[14]

In choosing to disregard the enlightened philanthropy and the awakened conscience which abolished slavery in the North, members of a slaveholding oligarchy were thought to be planning the destruction of the Union and threatening the republican form of government. Southerners were aristocrats and monarchists who despised northern civilization for the freedoms it offered.[15] In its campaign to appropriate the natural rights of millions, the Slave Power had usurped almost total control of a political party which originally had looked to states' rights as a bulwark of individual rights. Employing this party doctrine for an entirely different and far less noble purpose, slaveholders thus had succeeded in gaining and maintaining control of the South for their own purposes.[16]

These historical accounts went on to claim that the Slave Power gradually came to control every branch of the national government. Comprising a political force more potent than any that had ever before appeared in American politics, the plantation oligarchy dominated James Buchanan's presidency. They greedily tried to extend their powers even further by advocating the territorial expansion of the slave system, by overturning the Missouri Compromise, by passing the Fugitive Slave Act, and by engineering the Dred Scott decision.[17]

Despite these successes the Slave Power had serious problems. According to Unionist historians, during the late 1850s slaveholders became aware of a widespread resistance to their continued supremacy. When the opposition succeeded in electing an antislavery President in 1860, the southern oligarchs refused to submit to Constitutional authority. Too long accustomed to power to surrender it without a battle, the Slave Power "raised the standard of revolution, and plunged the nation into a bloody contest for the preservation of its threatened life."[18]

This school of history maintained that the ensuing war was less a popular revolution than a conspiracy among slaveholding elites to crush all loyalty to the Union. Press and pulpit—as well as less discreet tools of the Confederate cause such as "the hangman's rope, the incendiary's torch, and the slave-hunter's blood-hound"—were used to coerce resisters. It was only through lies and intimidation that an apparent majority of the southern people committed themselves to the "desperate design of destroying the National Government." Pro-Union histories thus argued that the determined efforts of a few misguided and unprincipled men had threatened the power and welfare of a nation and dashed the hopes of freedom loving people around the world.[19]

To the pro-Union historians of the postbellum era the slave system bore responsibility for a vast array of sins. As black historian and Union Army veteran George Washington Williams phrased it, black bondage had "touched the brightest features of social life, and they faded under the contact of its poisonous breath." Few escaped slavery's polluting and demoralizing influence. It brutalized and degraded the mind of the master to the extent that normal human sensibilities were crowded out by base and consuming desires. Under the influence of slavery, whites became licentious, profligate, cruel, and selfish. Extravagant in their use of authority over the chattels, southerners encouraged violence and immorality: "cotton and cupidity led captive the reason of the South."[20]

Slavery not only had corrupted the South, it had bankrupted southerners financially as well. Blinded by tradition and pretension, planters could not see that their agricultural system was wasteful. Shunning modern farming techniques in favor of a vicious cycle of land acquisition, exhaustion, and expansion, they had impoverished rich soils within a few years. While the slave worked, the planter "lolled under the shade of his piazza, drinking, smoking, talking, sleeping," or else he squandered a year's profits on racing, gambling, or the luxuries of city life. As a result, unlike businessmen and capitalists in the North, the slaveholders were "notoriously slow in paying debts, and required a long credit." Northern merchants and manufacturers consequently thought of the region as inhospitable to business.[21]

Postbellum pro-Union writers also described the Old South as inhospitable to free white laborers. Immigrants to the United States shunned the slave section "like a pestilence," and poor southern whites lacked opportunities to improve their circumstances. Oppressed by the competition of the bond labor system and unable to climb higher on the social ladder because of slaveholders' opposition to public schooling, these illiterate whites could hope for no higher status than that of plantation overseer. Their pitiable lives proved that "slavery created a caste even among those of the ruling race."[22]

The accusation that slavery had threatened the national democratic heritage did not go unanswered. Refusing to accept the idea that southern social relationships were fraudulent and exploitative, writers sympathetic to southern society termed the concept of a Slave Power "the most preposterous phantom ever evoked, to spread needless alarm and to work incalculable and irretrievable mischief." According to these authors, it was the ranting of northern fanatics that disturbed the peace of the nation.[23]

In the postwar South, a bitter dispute over the morality of slavery and the motivation of slaveholders was waged by writers who felt that even a militarily defeated section had an obligation to preserve its history. Authors of Confederate military and social history dedicated themselves to vindicating southern society from the accusations of their northern foes. Smarting from charges that southerners were semi-barbarous people who had conspired to destroy the Union in order to perpetuate slavery, they hoped to correct the historical record with more accurate accounts of the region which produced the nation's first president.[24]

Though southern historians had ridiculed the concept of a Slave Power, they did not deny the role of fanaticism and conspiracy in events surrounding the Civil War. Unflattering descriptions of John Brown, William Lloyd Garrison, and Abraham Lincoln which appeared in the new southern chronicles confirmed the degree to which northerners had been misled. As a supporter of the lawless Underground Railroad, Brown was a head-

strong and reckless fanatic; Garrison was a sincere extremist, patently un-
qualified for leadership; and Lincoln was incapable of grasping generali-
ties and "liable to be led by sharper minds and more resolute wills."[25]

These fanatics and fools had inspired the North to participate in an immoral and imperialistic conspiracy. Jealous of the planters' "superior refine-
ments of scholarship and manners" and opposed to the maintenance of
a sectional political equilibrium, northerners had used the issue of slavery
to manipulate public opinion. They had deceived people into believing that
an irrepressible moral conflict was imminent in order to create a "conve-
nient ground of dispute" for enhancing their own power and influence.
To prosouthern historians, African servitude in America may have served
as an occasion for intersectional hostilities, but it was far from being their
cause. The bond labor system had been introduced into the South through
"international co-operative action, and . . . agreement among the States
of the Union." Northern politicos ignored this agreement and invented a
mythical Slave Power enemy. As a result, southerners witnessed "their States
insulted, their property destroyed, their lives menaced, the laws of the Union
reviled and the Constitution spurned."[26]

After describing the low morals and high ambition of northern politicians, postbellum pro-South writers constructed contrasting portraits of
southern leadership elites. Histories written during the 1860–1900 period
were informed by the personal opinion of these agricultural elites as revealed in biographies, autobiographies, and reminiscences penned by ex-
planters or their kin. While hesitant about the uncritical acceptance of
slavery evident in such sources, the era's historians generally viewed reminiscences as useful in counteracting the misrepresentations of abolition literature. The circulation of such accounts hopefully would "engender a more
just judgment of the white man who lived under the Old Regime in the
South." The old slaveholding class — and their social theories — became the
focus of those who were determined to create a New South chronicle of
the slave era. As far as a valid black view of the pre-Civil War years was
concerned, most white historians dismissed the possibility; since American slaves had no recorded history and no control over their destiny, their
story must "follow the tracks they have made in the history of another
people."[27]

As histories in reminiscence form, these volumes accorded slaveholders
a status and character remarkably similar to that of gentleman planters
in the earlier southern romance novel. Emphasizing distinctively southern
qualities, the new chronicles refurbished the image of the landed squire
and claimed that he had existed in fact as well as in fiction. The benevolent and polite planter offered a striking contrast to the sly and unscrupulous Yankee politician. Such accounts underscored a theme which reverberated throughout histories of this genre: that the southern-dominated

national government of the 1850s had "threatened nothing in the North, sought nothing from it, desired to disturb nothing in it."[28]

The slaveholding heroes of these reminiscences were remarkable individuals whose character, deportment, intellect, generosity, and bravery were all without question. Whether highly educated or barely literate, their rugged lives had prepared these planters for survival in the postwar South. As eulogized in Jeanette Walworth's *Southern Silhouettes* (1887), Colonel Benny Sims had commanded extraordinary respect before the war, and no less so after the Confederate defeat. The qualities which had given him "the dignity of a Roman senator" and had made him a responsible slaveholder now prompted his continued concern for confused and displaced freedmen.[29]

The New South chronicles recorded and lauded this patronizing attitude which regarded blacks as "fellow beings with like passions as ourselves, but as socially inferior to us, occupying the place of 'hewers of wood and drawers of water.'" Despite the obstacles created by postwar conditions, the southern gentry would continue "the work allotted them by God, civilizing and elevating an inferior race in the scale of intelligence and comfort." Never again, it was said, would African-Americans find a people "so kind and true to them as the Southerners have been."[30]

The antebellum description of the slave system as a mutually beneficial social arrangement remained basically unchanged by the Civil War years. Southern postbellum historians modified it only insofar as they emphasized the strength of the master-slave bond by describing it as a sacred trust. They provided evidence of whites' benevolence by recounting scenes of generosity, tolerance, and religious instruction. In one particularly stirring account, the wife of a wealthy merchant celebrated her twenty-seventh birthday by personally selecting 464 different presents which she parceled out to the slaves on two of the family plantations—a custom that was, no doubt, "one of the distinguishing features of the civilization."[31]

Southern whites were said to have shown their concern for the slaves in other than material ways, too. The plantation patriarchs of memoirs tolerated most of their servants' mistakes. In some cases, this meant that a slaveholder could expect to severely discipline an individual field hand "only once in a lifetime." According to his wife's biography of his life, Mississippi slaveholder and Confederate leader Jefferson Davis had a special phrase for this southern character trait: "toughing it out." One story of his patience told of how Davis won the sympathies of a mulatto woman he employed to cook his meals. Apparently a poor match for the job, one morning she neglected to prepare breakfast. Uncomplaining, the planter drank a cup of milk and went about the day's business. Later, at noontime, she again failed to prepare a meal, but again he did not complain. Finally, after the cook missed dinner that night Davis broke his silence.

With no trace of hurt, outrage, or even sarcasm in his voice, he "mildly" told her: "Do not trouble yourself; just give over trying to-night and catch up for breakfast." In the end, despite his empty stomach, Davis apparently had his reward. By practicing still another family maxim which held that "the less people are governed, the more submissive they will be to control," he won the slaves' esteem and loyalty. With a reciprocity typical in such accounts, all of the Davis slaves "loved him, and were willing to bear any little impertinence on his part cheerfully."[32]

The spiritual component of plantation paternalism rejected the idea that blacks could be slaves only and emphasized the planters' responsibility to provide them with religious instruction. Reminiscences such as Mary Ross Banks' *Bright Days in the Old Plantation Time* (1882) describe the success of Christian duty in improving the lives of both races. An elderly white woman recalls her childhood years with an industrious black woman known as Granny Sabra. Even though partially paralyzed, Granny worked diligently at her knitting in order to keep herself supplied with the small comforts of slave life. She received even greater reward, however, from devotion to her religion and to her teachers: "de Scripters nuver soun' ser sweet, an' Jesus nuver seems ser nigh, ez when Miss Mattie reads ter me, an' tells me 'bout Hiz preshus promises." Banks completes this picture of mutual trust and respect when she admits to having spent "some of the purest, happiest hours" learning "some of the best lessons of my life" at the knee of this same Granny Sabra. Antebellum planter paternalism thus bound both master and slave with ties of warmth and affection.[33]

To the postwar writers of these memoirs, the generosity, virtue, and compassion of the planter and his family typified antebellum southern civilization. The genteel planters of the slave era would be long remembered as symbols of a blessed and happy society which had "left its benignant influence behind it to sweeten and sustain its children." In one respect the accounts were unquestionably accurate. Postbellum admiration for a benevolent slaveholding class has influenced histories, novels, poetry, songs, and plays for over one hundred years.[34]

Refusing to concede the battleground of history to friends of the slaveholder, Union sympathizers championed their own heroes. In an already familiar way, they purported to be recording the only true accounts of events and people surrounding the Civil War. Their heroes were antislavery, pro-Union, and exceptionally virtuous. Wendell Phillips was "America's ablest orator,"—calm, highly principled, and determined; William Lloyd Garrison was an honest and distinguished reformer whose flawless character and moral convictions never wavered —"like a rock that stands stirless amid the conflicting agitation of the waves"; and mere mention of the name "Lincoln" evoked reverence.

These men represented an "unconquerable spirit of devotion, courage, and martyrdom" in the cause of freedom, but less well-known abolitionists earned honors, too.[35] Especially attractive to postwar writers were the men and women of the Underground Railroad. Although previous authors had recognized their importance to the antislavery crusade, it was the postwar generation that capitalized on the drama of Underground Railroad exploits. The self-sacrificing and principled conductors who would later become standard characters in American folklore first stood in determined opposition to the romanticized history of the southern planter.[36]

Authors of the underground's histories and reminiscences believed that its leaders' characters and motivations sharply differed from those of planters, overseers, and slave hunters. In northern accounts, an uncorruptible and unselfish group of men and women saw the nation's fugitive slave legislation as "diametrically opposed to the golden rule, and the example of Him." In acting upon this belief they sought to restore God-given rights to helpless, hunted fugitives and complete the mission to which Providence had called them. Though they violated federal law in helping escaped slaves, the conductors were described as heroically obedient to the higher laws of God. As Levi Coffin modestly explains in his account of Underground Railroad service: "What I had done I believed was simply a Christian duty and not for the purpose of being seen of men, or for notoriety, which I have never sought."[37]

Shunning notoriety did not always protect these antislavery heroes from the persecution, arrests, and other legal sanctions against helping fugitive slaves. Their memoirs described reformers who had been denounced as fanatics and disturbers of the public peace, then tarred and feathered, pelted with rotten eggs, imprisoned, and even murdered. In one 1890 biography, *Rev. Calvin Fairbank During Slavery Times: How He 'Fought the Good Fight' to Prepare 'The Way',* the author said he languished for seventeen years and four months in Kentucky prisons and received "thirty-five thousand, one hundred and five stripes" for illegally guiding some fifty slaves to the North. Other persecuted conductors found that their families were forced to share their suffering. Proslavery schoolmates taunted their children and in one instance the wife of a Pennsylvania martyr was said to have been so greatly affected by the plight of a young slave girl that her nerves never recovered. These accounts testified to a selflessness which proclaimed their faith in a "higher law, before which human statutes were impotent" and gave evidence of virtue against which the Confederacy could not hope to stand.[38]

Confident of their ability to withstand persecution and eventually defeat the wickedness of the greedy, the men and women of the Underground Railroad necessarily also had to be strong, self-reliant, and aggressive.[39]

But what of the fugitive slaves? How did they figure into this gripping drama of good and evil? For the most part, white conductors and their families occupied the center stage of these melodramatic histories and blacks were cast in secondary, supporting roles. Although several free black conductors were given credit for their active and valuable contributions to the operation of the clandestine transportation system, black fugitives often were characterized as possessing a "timid and fearful look, like that of hunted animals." Accounts which implied that few slaves would have escaped if left to their own devices described bondsmen who thought they could "just go down into the ground . . . and in some mysterious way be carried off" by the railroad. Slaves were said to have "skulked and stumbled along half the way to Lake Erie" before they accidentally found northern friends. Ignorant, half-clothed, and hungry, they were completely bewildered and "didn't know what to do, nor where to go." Luckily, Underground Railroad sympathizers then risked their own lives to shelter and feed these pitifully ill-prepared beings before sending them on to Canada. In this manner, postbellum antislavery writers recorded the story of the fugitive slave who reached free soil without "any forethought or management on his own part."[40]

Fortunately, not all postbellum histories and reminiscences linked freedom-seeking blacks with pre-Civil War stereotypes of bumbling, incompetent slaves. In some accounts, the virtue and daring of white conductors was matched by black fugitives. Robert C. Smedley's history of Underground Railroad operations in Chester County, Pennsylvania, told the dramatic stories of Black Pete, a strong, one-eyed fugitive who left his southern pursuers "more or less crippled from the rough handling he gave them"; of James Cummichael, a cunning and wise slave who rescued his wife from a well-guarded Louisiana-bound ship; and of the brave black mother who suffered a slaveholder's cat-o'-nine-tails rather than reveal the hiding place of her child. Eber M. Pettit and Levi Coffin wrote capsule biographies of individual slaves whose exploits gave credence to the view that "the fugitives as a class were among the ablest and [most] energetic of their race."[41]

While such accounts certainly contradicted traditional American images of enslaved blacks, it was William Still's *The Underground Rail Road* (1872) which focused most directly upon the fugitive slave as a hero. A black Philadelphia coal dealer and vigilance committee veteran, Still acknowledged the help of abolitionists, but he pointed out that "he who would be free, himself must strike the blow." Though he accepted the generalization that fugitive slaves were more intelligent than those who stayed on the plantation, Still remembered individual differences:

Anthony was of very powerful physical proportions, being six feet three inches in height, quite black, very intelligent, and of a temperament that would not submit to slavery.

Benjamin was twenty-seven years of age, small of stature, dark complexion, of a pleasant countenance, and quite smart.

Noah is only nineteen, quite dark, well-proportioned, and possessed of a fair average of common sense.

Perry is about twenty-seven years of age, decidedly colored, medium size and only of ordinary intellect.

[George]: Of course, mentally he was underdeveloped, nevertheless, possessed of enough mother-wit to make good his escape.[42]

In Still's account, the plantation runaways not only outwitted the southern planters, they played an important role in their own liberation: "such heroes in the days of Slavery, did much to make the infernal system insecure, and to keep alive the spirit of freedom in liberty-loving hearts the world over." With endurance, boldness, and stealth they resisted the physical and psychological chains of the Slave Power.[43]

The political divisions of the Civil War continued to be evident in historical accounts written in the twentieth century, but late nineteenth-century social and intellectual developments encouraged many historians toward a less antagonistic stance on slavery-related topics. In the two decades following President Rutherford B. Hayes' withdrawal of Federal troops from the South, historians began to ask if it was possible to discuss slavery and the Civil War "in the light of history and not as a matter of *politics*."[44] Soon thereafter a Princeton University professor named Woodrow Wilson offered an answer:

The general merits of the question of slavery in the United States, its establishment, its development, its social, political, and economic effects, it is now possible to discuss without passion. . . . doubtless for all of us the larger aspects of the matter are beyond reasonable question.[45]

Although this gradual post-Reconstruction substitution of consensus for conflict did not purposely seek to discredit the record of Afro-American involvement, the new historiographical trend in effect obscured black perspectives on the slave past.

Contributing to this development was the professionalization of historical study prompted by changes in American intellectual life and developments in modern scientific theory. During the last quarter of the nineteenth
century, research techniques introduced by scientists virtually compelled
historians to review the methodology of their own discipline. Specialization, objectivity, accuracy, and approach now required heavy reliance upon
primary source materials and thorough documentation. Historians replaced
personal opinion with an acquired and recognized scholarly expertise. This
generation of scholars did not work on an amateur or part-time basis —
they formed a community of teachers and researchers who were committed to history as a lifetime vocation. The new academics were employed
by departments of history, and they practiced their trade in colleges, research libraries, and professional associations. With a great respect for advanced training and specialization, scientific methodology, scholarly
monographs, and the study of contemporary political and legal institutions, they replaced the romance of earlier historical writing with a cautious and restrained dialogue. The measured and qualified judgments of
these professionals diffused conflict and promoted consensus.[46]

In American slavery studies, this consensus was manifested in what came
to be termed the Rhodes-Burgess Compromise. Although not necessarily
representative of late nineteenth-century professionals, both James Ford
Rhodes and John William Burgess were remarkably adept in distilling and
articulating the Spanish-American War era nationalism expressed by both
scientific and romantic writers.[47] Following their lead, fellow historians
took a more national approach to the traditionally sectional topics of slavery, the Civil War, and Reconstruction. These writers criticized the South
on one hand, and then criticized the North, blacks, and Reconstruction
on the other. Though slavery clearly was immoral in consensus history,
events in the post-Civil War South proved the necessity of white supremacy. In this way previous historical perspectives, whatever their bias, were
thought to be incorporated into a more balanced and thus more objective
view of the American past. Unfortunately, the compromise only modified
a vision of southern gentility already tainted with ethnocentrism and racial
prejudice.

Rhodes, a midwesterner and author of the influential multi-volume *History of the United States from the Compromise of 1850* (1893–1906), convinced his contemporaries that the differing proslavery and antislavery
perspectives were essentially compatible. Describing the slave labor system "as it may have appeared before the war to a fair-minded man," he
examined planters' abuse of the slaves. Some slaveholders, he concluded,
overworked blacks to the point of injuring them. Other masters callously
encouraged slave-breeding to increase the value of their estates. In regard

to legal and social sanctions for such abuse Rhodes recognized the slaves' lack of recourse: "The restraint of the law did not operate powerfully to prevent the killing of these unfortunates."[48]

The historian's understanding of the slave experience, however, did not extend beyond that necessary for reconciliation of certain political and professional viewpoints. If slaves were poorly fed and clothed it may have been the fault of forces beyond the planters' control. In fact, "It is more than probable," he wrote, "that the invention of the cotton-gin prevented the peaceful abolition of slavery." In any case, the worst abusers were not the southern white elite; instead it was the white overseer, "ignorant, frequently intemperate, always despotic and brutal," who dealt harshly with slaves. The degraded and unprincipled white supervisors in turn, according to Rhodes, found unusually cruel blacks to administer the harsh punishments. By absolving individual slaveholders, Rhodes made it possible to view the antebellum slave system as a national, impersonal institution for which no one could be blamed.[49]

The irony of the consensus approach, of course, is that it focused on white perspectives only. Revised descriptions of southern life tended to accept southern characterizations of white elites while reinforcing traditional attitudes toward blacks. Antebellum critics disputed the accuracy of Harriet Beecher Stowe's *Uncle Tom's Cabin* because its opening scene depicted a Kentucky gentleman entertaining a vulgar slave-dealer. Forty years later Rhodes agreed with Stowe's critics, asserting that the slaveholding gentility had most assuredly "looked upon slave dealers and auctioneers with contempt." Certainly, to Rhodes, slavery had been "a curse to the master" as well as "a wrong to the slave."[50]

A generation of historians, having identified slavery as a curse, proceeded to revitalize preexisting misrepresentations of Africans. Reconstructed during an era dominated by expansionist fervor and the twin concepts of racial evolution and Anglo-Saxon superiority, these pejorative stereotypes received a special stamp of approval from Rhodes. After a November, 1905, meeting with Theodore Roosevelt he noted: "The negroes, the President said, are 200,000 years behind [the whites]. (I suggested a million, an amendment which he accepted.)"[51] Accounts of blacks as slaves written during the late nineteenth and early twentieth centuries share this attitude. Eminently capable of distinguishing between the issues of freedom and equality, many of the era's historians reiterated variants of the pre-Civil War proslavery ideology even as they condemned "the peculiar institution."

Arguments forwarded by this generation begin with the assumption that the Afro-Americans' "alien and undeveloped" character had been a vital determinant of both slave behavior and southern social relationships. Unlike those nations of antiquity which had made slaves of debtors or enemy captives, the United States was said to have subjugated "an alien, uncouth-looking people, whom the Caucasian could hardly regard without mirth and contempt, even when moved to compassion for their wrongs." The untrained barbarians were so primitive that merely coming into contact with white culture would be to their advantage. While the scholars admitted that a slave had a hard life, they also found it difficult to imagine how the "aimless, good-natured, and improvident African could ever have been brought as a race to plow, to sow, to reap, to study, and at length to create thought, except for the tutelage of his slaveholding master." Indeed, some historical writers felt that the rigorous school of slavery had ended without fully preparing its students. Despite all their gains thus far, Afro-Americans had been released from bondage before they fully developed the skills, self-discipline and motivation of white workers. Certainly, equality was far in the distant future. Burdened with such assumptions, well-meaning historians could only hope and trust that "the same forces of evolution that have brought him to where he is now will bring him further."[52]

The social philosophy promoted in the historical and autobiographical writings of Booker T. Washington contributed importantly to societal acceptance of these notions. Undoubtedly aware that pointed criticism of antebellum plantation life might aggravate racial tensions in the New South, Afro-America's chief early twentieth-century spokesperson constructed an interpretation of slavery that would complement rather than detract from his overall program of interracial cooperation and economic advancement. To calm white fears of blacks, Washington described the Afro-American's acculturation in language designed to win both the good will of his "white neighbours" and the "opportunity for the peaceful development of those fundamental interests which are the same for both races."[53]

According to the well-known black educator, the majority of imported slaves had been "more submissive, more disposed to attach themselves and remain faithful to their masters, than any other race or class of people would have been under similar circumstances." Either because of prior training in Africa or because of their natural disposition, blacks neither pined away nor grew bitter in their chains. On the contrary, within a short time, slaves adjusted to the conditions of New World plantation life with a natural cheerfulness and affectionate sympathy for the white man. Washington reasoned that in the presence of such a compassionate and loving people, the only plausible cause for white anxiety must have been the slaveholders' recognition of the system's basic injustice and the realization that it was only human nature for an enslaved population to desire freedom.[54]

Washington did not accuse, or blame, or even identify any exclusive source of oppression, though he had been a slave himself. Like the professional historians of his day, the author of *Up From Slavery* (1901) and *The*

Story of the Negro (1909) depersonalized and nationalized slaveholders' responsibility. English and northern slave traders, southern landowners and slave-raiding West Africans all shared the responsibility for Afro-American bondage. In this context, the southern planter became "simply another unfortunate victim of the institution which the Nation unhappily had engrafted upon it at that time." Washington thus hoped to encourage acceptance of blacks by restating the abolitionist argument that slavery harmed both races. Approaching racism as a division generated by distrust, he tried to convince his readers that in the New South "the people of both races have discovered that their material and moral interests are so interlaced that if one race suffers the other must suffer too." He promoted a self-fulfilling prophesy in which white apprehensions disappeared as blacks progressed.[55]

Apparently Booker Washington did not fully calculate the degree to which his comments supported the status quo. His descriptions of institutional slavery were unflattering, but his desire to win the favor of southern whites muted the social impact of his writing. Unlike Martin Delany, Frederick Douglass, or William Still, he pointedly disavowed black bravado. Claiming that the black man had "gained just as little from the temporary power which he held during the Reconstruction time as he did from the successful and unsuccessful insurrections by which he sought to gain his freedom before the war," Washington dismissed slave rebel Nat Turner as "a dreamer . . . a fanatic" and divorced himself from the black politics of the postbellum period. When he championed increased respect for the black American on the basis of "his patience, his kindliness, and his lack of resentment toward those who do him wrong and injustice," he further entrenched common assumptions about racial differences. In an era of worldwide Euro-American expansionism such an argument only solidified stereotypes of aggressively dynamic Anglo-Saxons and passive, dependent, and emotionally incomplete Afro-Americans.[56]

The conciliatory view of slavery offered by Washington contributed to the historiographical reconciliation of the Rhodes school by further confusing the issues surrounding sectional compromise with those of interracial harmony. His inability to transform the slave stereotypes of his white contemporaries had telling consequences both for black Americans and for future historians. He missed an opportunity to issue a bold, revisionist statement on slave life and personality, and so missed a chance to deaden the influence of lingering associations between black and slave personalities. Without motivation to do otherwise, white historians continued to record black history within the limitations of traditional assumptions. When the time came to move beyond the late nineteenth-century compromise and consensus, historians would follow another, but disturbingly familiar, vision of the plantation South formulated by a former Georgia farm boy named Ulrich Bonnell Phillips.

Phillips' interpretation of black bondage became popular at a time when historians were reacting to perceived excesses of professional history. During the first three decades of the twentieth century, critics accused leading historians of promoting pedantic and uninteresting literature. Influenced by the social and political reforms of the Progressive era, a new generation of writers emphasized the social utility of history: they thought historical studies ought to be relevant to contemporary life. As they gained support for this approach their histories became at once more readable and more openly opinionated. In the case of slavery, the moderation and balance of consensus history was gradually replaced with interpretations dominated by the values and perspectives of the southern planter.[57]

Ulrich Phillips and his approach to southern history exactly fit the new trend. His sectional focus, economic emphasis, and fluid writing style offered his readers relief from his predecessors' nationalistic, fact-laden monographs on developing political and judicial institutions. Phillips' doctoral studies at Columbia University taught him the necessary skills for advanced research. His conclusions — documented by state, county, town, and plantation records — were powerfully influential and unquestionably biased. While believing that "to get into the records is to get away from the stereotypes," Phillips also projected his own values into the historical records. He did not see any conflict in the combination.[58]

Certain of the conclusions produced by Phillips' selection and ordering of the records had special ties to his personal experience.[59] Born into a Georgian family with a slaveholding heritage, Phillips remembered his childhood as idyllic. One story that appears in his work describes his attempt to harvest a cotton crop. After a short time in the fields his cramped hands and aching back forced Phillips to hire a black woman and her children to finish the job. On this occasion he found the work difficult, but he later claimed that the widespread image of the exhausted black laborer was preposterous. As he noted in 1918, "anyone who has had experience with negro labor may reasonably be skeptical when told that healthy, well fed negroes, whether slave or free, can by any routine insistence of the employer be driven beyond the point at which fatigue begins to be injurious."[60]

The Georgian's view of the South also carried the conviction that though postbellum whites had a responsibility to direct black progress, the freed slaves were not good students. Despite the transformation of the former bondsmen into sharecroppers, tenant farmers, and wage laborers, most blacks were said to be posing peculiar problems of economic and social adjustment as they continued to think and act in "distinctly negro-like ways." In Phillips' estimation, southern blacks of the early twentieth century maintained the same "easy-going, amiable, serio-comic obedience and the same personal attachments to white men, as well as the same sturdy light-heartedness and the same love of laughter and of rhythm, which distinguished their forbears." Certainly there were the exceptional, more civilized Afro-Americans, he offered, but they had become so by borrowing from Anglo-Saxon culture and not through any originality of their own. To say that a member of this small educated elite could serve as a more effective role model for the average black man than could the white southerner was "to argue that the reflected light of the moon is brighter and more effective than the direct rays of the sun." To Phillips, the Afro-American even though free remained an inferior, dependent caste within southern society.[61]

Instead of considering his southern heritage as a possible source of bias, Phillips argued that it uniquely qualified him for his work. He was convinced that the history of the United States had been "written by Boston and largely written wrong." Modern interpretations of the southern tradition still suffered from the prejudices of northern society, he maintained, and as a result the literature was inadequate and full of errors. Phillips predicted that the South would remain a baffling puzzle to all outsiders "until insiders give the clues for its solution," until its history was written by men who had inherited southern traditions.[62]

In his major works on black bondage, *American Negro Slavery* (1918) and *Life and Labor in the Old South* (1929), Phillips drew a portrait of the plantation South which significantly improved the historical image of "the peculiar institution." With colorful phrasing and careful ordering of evidence, the professor redeemed his homeland from the accusations of abolitionsts and politicians. More important, since his predecessors had nationalized moral responsibility for slavery, Phillips' revision of ante-bellum southern history helped to soothe the conscience of an entire nation.

In order to make the slaveholders' world more understandable to his urban contemporaries, Phillips made extensive use of allusion and analogy. Because these devices helped to present unfamiliar concepts in familiar ways, his work tempered the conflict between slavery and democratic ideals. The slave labor system seemed less ominous—the plantation became a school in speech and conduct, a homestead, a parish, and a variety show all at once. The labor force now was likened to "a conscript army" living in "weather-tight" barracks and on constant, but moderate fatigue duty. The white captain of this army commanded benevolently, aided by his lieutenant and sergeant (his overseer and foreman, respectively). The three worked together to instruct the slaves through both precept and example—an educational method familiar to those who had visited a "'social settlement' in a modern city slum."[63]

Having primed his audience with this updating of Old South terminology, Phillips proceeded to articulate perspectives on slavery-related topics which would continue to demand the attention of historians long after the decline of urban settlement houses. With one hand resting on the planter's account book and the other on the pulse of the racially segregated American social order, he penned some of slave historiography's most memorable statements:

> Negroes in America . . . were as completely broken from their tribal stems as if they had been brought from the planet Mars.[64]

> In the main the American Negroes ruled not even themselves. They were more or less contentedly slaves, with grievances from time to time but not ambition. With "hazy pasts and reckless futures," they lived in each moment as it flew, and left "Old Massa" to take such thought as the morrow might need.[65]

> The generality of planters . . . considered it hopeless to make their field hands into thorough workmen or full-fledged men, and contented themselves with very moderate achievement. Tiring of endless correction and unfruitful exhortation, they relied somewhat supinely upon authority with a tone of kindly patronage and a baffled acquiescence in slack service.[66]

> Plantation slavery had in strictly business aspects at least as many drawbacks as it had attractions. But in the large it was less a business than a life; it made fewer fortunes than it made men.[67]

> The scheme of life had imperfections which all but the blind could see. But its face was on the whole so gracious that modifications might easily be lamented, and projects of revolution regarded with a shudder.[68]

Impressed by the Georgian's prose, research, and background, his contemporaries lavished praise upon Phillips' work. As winner of the 1928 Little, Brown and Company award for the best unpublished manuscript on American history, *Life and Labor in the Old South* was especially honored. Reviewers raved about the book's contribution to historiography. His writing was considered brilliant, tactful, and realistic. He had provided Americans with the definitive history of plantation life in the Old South. Furthermore, Phillips had uncovered "the astonishing, interwoven homogeneity of southern society, in which all interests were bound up into a whole."[69]

His death in 1934 prompted predictions that his influence would be long-lived, and as late as 1961 the American Historical Association's *Guide to Historical Literature* still described Phillips as "one of the most learned students" of the antebellum southern region. His work, the guide said, provided "an excellent picture of the pre-Civil War South."[70] Perhaps more indicative of his impact, however, was the widespread incorporation of Phillips' views into succeeding generations of college textbooks and popular histories. Phillips' studies of the South were extensively noted, quoted, and paraphrased in textbooks published during the years between the two World Wars. As his interpretation of plantation society spread throughout the profession, students and general readers learned that slaves did not need or want to consider their future, that they were unconcerned with their own enslavement, that they enjoyed a lifetime annuity which became a financial burden to their owners, that they delighted in ecstatic religious exercises, picnics, and barbecues, and that they "were often happier than their masters."[71]

Ulrich Phillips' domination of slave historiography is a result of more than his research skill and writing ability. In an important sense, Phillips acquired and maintained professional influence because both he and the society in which he lived believed in variants of the same socioeconomic and racial ideologies. During an era of political, economic, and social progressivism, Phillips supported the ethic of "conservative progress." His plan for modernizing and developing the southern economy promoted a combination of past and present values that introduced, in effect, a new plantation system.[72]

From his position as a leading expert on southern history, Phillips rationalized white managerial control over a predominantly black labor force by recasting slave stereotypes. The new plantation would reestablish units of production large enough to justify increased investment in modern machinery, yet small enough to enable white managers to have close personal contact with — and control over — black laborers.[73]

This updating and reform of the inefficient tenant farming system would give blacks "a renewed association with the best of the Southern people (always the negroes' best friends) and enable them to use their imitative faculties and make further progress in acquiring the white man's civilization." Under a modern wage-labor plan, southern blacks could hope to advance their status; and at the very least they would be rescued from their post-emancipation "tendency . . . to lapse back toward barbarism." With the help of white managers and supervisors, this plan would bring "order out of existing chaos" in southern agriculture while serving as "the best means of offsetting the ignorance and laziness of the negro laborers."[74] Phillips and his generation of progressives did not see any conflict between the ideals of twentieth-century economic and political reform and prevailing racial attitudes. To many Americans, progressivism was for whites only. As one progressive journalist reasoned: "The Great Teacher never preached the flat equality of men, social or otherwise."[75]

To trace the scope and intensity of the opposition to Phillips' description of master-slave relationships is to map the gradual liberalization of white American social attitudes toward black people. Initially, criticism of the historian's work came from black reviewers of *American Negro Slavery* and *Life and Labor in the Old South.* If white colleagues occasionally lamented that Phillips' plantation-based approach neglected the manufacturing, mining, lumbering, and shipbuilding sectors, black critics charged him with far more serious historiographical crimes.[76] Their chief complaint was that he really had not addressed the subject of slaves under slavery, but instead had concentrated on American slaveholders, their land, and their crops. In the same way that an historian of the New England fisheries would "say very little about the species figuring in the industry, but more about the life of the people participating in it," Phillips' works were criticized for celebrating the "slaveholding superman" while treating antebellum blacks as subhuman. To Afro-American reviewers, Phillips' "inability to fathom the negro mind," his mistrust of "Negro sources," and his heavy reliance upon the records of large planters had so biased him that "without exception" he portrayed slavery from the masters' point of view. Collectively, his studies defended an institution which had been "at best a mistake and at worst a crime."[77]

During the 1930s and 1940s, white critics joined the attack on Phillips' view of the Old South. As they experienced the dislocations of economic depression and witnessed the excesses of Nazi ideology, American intellectuals became more sensitive to racial issues. Insofar as historians rejected long-assumed correlations between race, culture, and intellect, they began to question generalizations about blacks as slaves. A key target of these revisions was the claim that white benevolence had given slaves little reason to think about "the unknown attractions of freedom."[78]

At one point in the evolution of slave stereotypes it was generally conceded that fugitives were atypical slaves. "Unenlightened and submissive by nature," the average bondsman accepted punishment without resistance. Following the general outline of the planters' perspective, historians hypothesized that while an individual might rebel, such behavior was aberrant and classified as deluded, fanatic, or even childlike. Slave insurrectionary activity must have been rare because it would only have aggravated restrictions on blacks. Slaveholders so effectively controlled blacks that by 1860 "the negro was completely cowed."[79]

Chief among those who disputed such notions of slave docility was the pioneering Marxist historian Herbert Aptheker. In applying aspects of class struggle ideology to the plantation South, he revealed a side of collective slave behavior which previously had been recognized by Afro-American writers but overlooked by most whites. In *American Negro Slave Revolts* (1943) and in his many published essays and addresses on slave conspiracies, rebellions, and guerrilla warfare, Aptheker redefined the slave experience: "for ninety per cent of the years of its existence and throughout some ninety per cent of the area it blighted, American slavery was, as Karl Marx stated, 'a commercial system of exploitation.'" Uncowed by this tyranny, black slaves (aided not infrequently by poor whites) struggled to regain their elemental human rights. He claimed that as they did so, the bondsmen participated in at least two hundred and fifty reported conspiracies and revolts. Like Phillips, Aptheker believed in modern applications of historical achievement. Recognition of a black resistance effort not only would discredit the historiographical cliché of slave contentment; it also would provide both black and white Americans with the confidence and courage necessary to fight their common oppressors — the "industrial and financial overlords and the plantation oligarchs" who stood in the way of universal liberty, equality, and prosperity. Herbert Aptheker did not accept Phillips' proposal for a new southern plantation system. Instead, he championed a multiracial revolt of the people who would be exploited by it.[80]

Aptheker's claims for a revolutionary black tradition were greeted with a good deal of skepticism. His detractors accused him of being subjective and undiscriminating, accepting abolitionist descriptions of the Old South, and exaggerating the rebelliousness of the slave community. He claimed too much for the revolutionary tradition. Nevertheless, this Marxist scholar succeeded in writing previously unexplored possibilities into the historical record. His contribution eased the task of later authors who, though neither Afro-American nor Marxist, saw the inaccuracies of Phillips' work.[81]

By the end of the 1960s, major components of Phillips' interpretation had been discredited in historical literature. The modern Civil Rights Movement cultivated a recognition of erroneous, inaccurate, and dangerous preconceptions about blacks which permeated books like *American Negro Slavery* and *Life and Labor in the Old South.* Essays by Richard Hofstadter, Kenneth M. Stampp, and Ruben Kugler echoed earlier critiques by black reviewers — this time the audience was more accepting. Again Phillips was criticized for misreading, misrepresenting, or omitting important sources of information, assuming Afro-American inferiority, and most importantly, failing to view bondage from the standpoint of the slave.[82]

The result of reassessing Phillips' influential interpretation of plantation slavery was a rethinking and rewriting of American history textbooks. In the twenty years which followed the close of World War II, college texts increasingly reflected their authors' newfound awareness of racial prejudice and of the role which racism had played in American history. Although they declared it difficult to make objective judgments about contemporary racial relationships, white writers traced the origins of racism to the colonial era, blamed antislavery advocates for their lack of commitment to racial equality, and criticized postbellum historians for perpetuating a view of the Old South that was tainted by the concept of biological superiority.[83] As these ideas gained acceptance within the academic community, Phillips' influence seemed to diminish. The intellectual conceptualizations and research findings of John Hope Franklin's *From Slavery to Freedom* (1947) and Kenneth M. Stampp's *The Peculiar Institution* (1956) reoriented slave historiography. With the appearance of these studies, the profession witnessed the end of an era dominated by a single monolithic interpretation of the Old South.[84]

Educated at Fisk and Harvard during the depression years, Franklin was appointed to a professorship at Howard University in the same year that his influential Afro-American history text first appeared. The black historian believed Phillips to be an apologist for slaveholders; his book purposefully discredits Phillips' findings. John Hope Franklin assumed that slaves were intelligent and discontented. He described a slave community teeming with carpenters, masons, mechanics, and inventors. According to Franklin, the fact that blacks were permitted to acquire these skills proved neither white benevolence nor black tractability. In fact, bondsmen were "natural enemies" of the slaveholders. They sabotaged crops, broke tools, burned barns, and poisoned or stabbed their white oppressors. Long before the Underground Railroad became an effective antislavery device, blacks resisted slavery by leaving the plantations. Those who did not flee stayed behind to protest their abuse and mistreatment, long work hours, family separation, forced concubinage, and inadequate housing with a series of revolts and conspiracies. The resistance "began with the institution and did not end until slavery was abolished," and bondsmen accepted the accompanying bloodshed as an inevitable price of liberty. The tensions and panic that resulted were inherent in the slave labor system. Far from being a civilizing force, the system fostered mutual interracial misunderstanding, suspicion, and hatred.[85]

John Hope Franklin's attack on Old South stereotypes contributed to Kenneth Stampp's revisionist study of the southern plantation system. Modifying Ulrich Phillips' idea that the past could be a key to the present, the University of California, Berkeley professor believed that an historian's "knowledge of the present is clearly a key to his understanding of the past." Modern advancements in the social and natural sciences armed Stampp with arguments supporting the basic irrelevance of race: "the slaves were merely ordinary human beings . . . innately Negroes *are*, after all, only white men with black skins, nothing more, nothing less."[86]

The Peculiar Institution directly countered the teachings of *American Negro Slavery*. Contrary to Phillips' portrait of social harmony, Stampp found that fear was one of the planter's major tools for managing his human property. Slavery, above all, brought "maximum efficiency" to the organization and exploitation of labor. Instead of acculturating African peoples to white patterns of social behavior, instead of educating blacks to be responsible and moral citizens, institutional slavery merely trained them to be slaves.[87]

Stampp carefully researched original source materials before he concluded that there was little evidence of slaveholding "*chiefly* to gain status, or to help the South solve its 'race problem,' or from a patriarchal sense of duty to the Negroes." By examining plantation account books, diaries, journals, and correspondence, Stampp met Phillips on common historiographical ground; but even as he demolished the image of slavery as a benevolent and reciprocal arrangement, his choice of documentary sources reinforced a traditional emphasis on the white southern planter. His was an important but inconclusive step in fashioning a new beginning for American slavery studies. As subsequent research in black history revealed, "for proper balance and perspective slavery must be viewed through the eyes of the Negro as well as through the eyes of the white master." Though Stampp recognized this, he could not accomplish it within the boundaries of his own work. During the late 1960s and throughout the following decade, his successors' increased use of Afro-American testimony and source materials would bring the slave to the center of slave historiography.[88]

The Black Storyteller

Though slavery had been abolished, antebellum attitudes toward the Afro-American continued to influence postwar literature. Like their historian counterparts, white American novelists, short story writers, and poets practiced a literary paternalism that encouraged perpetuation of traditional slave characterizations. Indeed, the stereotypes persisted for over a century, prompting one scholar to lament in 1970: "We do not know how to portray the black man because there is no tradition of his adequate portrayal."[89]

It would have seemed unnecessarily pessimistic in the 1860s to predict such little progress for the years to come. The volatile atmosphere of the war years curtailed both production and distribution of proslavery fiction from the South. Northern writers provided their reading public with variants of the most popular scenes of the day—the Civil War, departing soldiers, personal sacrifice, and battlefield heroism. On occasion, Yankee patriotism and optimism thus encouraged literary images of Afro-American grit and promise.[90]

Northern novelists and poets were not timid in their advocacy of the Union cause, nor were they unenthusiastic when called upon to contribute their arts to the war effort. Their support of a total military victory took two forms. The first detailed southern tyranny, conspiracy, and betrayal; the second emphasized love of the Union and patriotic heroism. It is the latter form which most often produced unique portrayals of black characters.[91] In at least two novels of the Civil War era, *Peculiar: A Tale of the Great Transition* (1864) and *Cudjo's Cave* (1863), the authors transcended antebellum views of black intelligence, stamina, and racial equality. The slave heroes seen in these works differ significantly from those pictured in the literature of pre-Civil War romantic racialism.

The author of *Peculiar* was Epes Sargent, a Boston editor, abolitionist, and spiritualist. He told his northern reading public the story of a bold fugitive slave who fought for the Union in the 11th Louisiana African Regiment. Christened "Peculiar Institution" (and nicknamed "Peek") by a drunken plantation overseer, Sargent's slave-soldier was a man of dignity. Unlike the fictional black man "who always says 'massa,' and speaks a gibberish indicated to the eye by a cheap misspelling of words," his speech was refined—lacking any trace of "the African peculiarity." A listener who had not seen him "would have supposed it was an educated white gentleman who was speaking."[92]

Peculiar also was a man of action. Like his white counterparts in Civil War fiction, the fugitive slave inspired the men of his company. With almost superhuman courage he battled the Confederates in spirited hand-to-hand combat. Peek eventually "fell nobly, as he always desired to fall, in the cause of freedom and humanity," but his death did not mark the tragic end of yet another noble savage. In Sargent's story, Peek left a legacy to the postwar generation of freedmen represented by his seventeen-year-old son, Sterling. Reunited with his father on the battlefield, he had "fought by Peek's side and under his eye with heroic defiance of danger." Sterling's bravery and strength of character testified to a movement away from stereotypical treatments of Afro-Americans.[93]

Such a development seemed even more likely after the appearance of J. T. Trowbridge's novel about a pair of Tennessee fugitives named Pomp and Cudjo. Designed specifically to fuel Union loyalties and win support for an alliance with slave-soldiers, *Cudjo's Cave* detailed two contrasting images of slave personality.[94]

After escaping from his cruel white overseer, Cudjo, a native African, lived in a secluded mountain cave. A covert bartering network supplied him with ammunition and provisions in exchange for game and animal skins. As described by Trowbridge, Cudjo seemed apelike, unacculturated, and unskilled with the English language. He knew bits of spirituals, but he practiced the "fire-worshipping fanaticism" of his ancestors and looked "far more like a demon of the cave than a human being."[95]

Unlike this simple and barbaric cave-dweller, Trowbridge's second fugitive slave character was "magnificently proportioned, straight as a pillar, and black as ebony." Pomp possessed both enormous strength and a demeanor that inspired calmness and trust. He preferred the powers of reason to those of violence and would endanger his own life rather than violate his principles. The black plantation doctor had escaped his master's estate, but he returned to retrieve his medicine case from the bedside of the sleeping slaveholder: "Having got what I wanted, I came away, but I had changed knives with him, and left mine sticking in the bedstead over his head, so that he might know I had been there, and not accuse any one else of the theft." Pomp later joined forces with Cudjo to fight against the Confederacy.[96]

In this seemingly unlikely alliance, Pomp supplied the brains and Cudjo the brawn. Far different from most of the slave images created by white authors, Pomp had mastered advanced abolitionist theory. His dispassionate discourse upon the implications of the Civil War contained biblical references and key elements of eighteenth century European philosophy. Cudjo, on the other hand, tended to express his most complex emotions by "waving . . . flaring pine-knots over his head, and shouting." He entered the fray against the Confederates shrieking, "Kill! kill! kill!"[97]

In the novel's battlefield finale, the mortally wounded Cudjo died — but not before he had choked the life from his hated overseer. Pomp survived the battle and, we are told, his "intrepidity, intelligence, and wonderful celerity of movement," contributed to the Union victory. Thus, in *Cudjo's Cave*, the noble savage died and the values and promise of Afro-American individuality survived to face the challenges of the postbellum world.[98]

For a brief period of time it seemed that there was little opposition to positive portrayals of blacks.[99] When counter images began to appear after the war, they unilaterally endorsed romanticized visions of southern gentility and slave loyalty.[100] This refurbishing of Old South imagery was initiated by the immediate postwar writing of Virginia author and lawyer John Esten Cooke, and by the short fiction and poetry which appeared in a Charlotte, North Carolina, monthly magazine called *The Land We Love.*

Cooke served as a Confederate officer during the war and, according to legend, he buried his silver spurs on the surrender ground at Appomattox to avoid delivering them to the Yankees. After the war he launched a writing career with the specific goal of defending the conquered South. Eventually, he based seven books upon his Civil War experiences.[101] Cooke's account of the war glorified the Confederate army officer. His historical fiction described southern military men who were born leaders – individuals who could "remain whole days and nights in the saddle, never growing weary; would march all night, fight all day, and then ride a dozen miles and dance until sunrise." One glance at such a man told that he had "passed through some terrible ordeal, and had come out, steel."[102]

Unwilling to leave his readers with the impression that only officers could be noble, Cooke described the spirit and loyalty of soldiers whose appearance was less commanding. "Burly, black-bearded giants, with thunderous voices and boastings" could falter on the field of battle, while timid, smooth-faced boys would "fight to the last and die unmoved" in support of the southern cause. According to Cooke, even the most improbable figure was emboldened with a southern "nerve and courage which only numbers could overwhelm." It was this vital, life-giving spirit which he sought to rekindle in the immediate postwar years.[103]

Given an air of authenticity by personal anecdotes and references to actual events, Cooke's melodramatic historical romances must have afforded Confederate veterans some satisfying reading. The storylines in *Surry of Eagle's-Nest* (1866) and *Hilt to Hilt* (1869) presumed that the Confederate defense of southern institutions had been a superb adventure, an heroic fight against nearly impossible odds. As such, the war effort failed only in a limited sense. As one of Cooke's characters shouts to northern readers: "You will never conquer us! We will never yield!" Insofar as these sentiments supported the status quo in southern race relations, they bode ill for a postwar conversion to the gospel of Afro-American capability and promise.[104]

The first issue of *The Land We Love* signaled another offensive against Yankee encroachment. Begun in May, 1866, General Daniel H. Hill's compendium of poetry, fiction, military history, and personality sketches claimed to be the only magazine devoted to "zealously vindicating . . . the truth of Southern history." By April, 1867, the monthly had attracted some 12,000 subscribers. Its pages reflect the major outlines of postbellum attempts to cultivate a specifically southern literary tradition.[105]

The Land We Love spoke of the courage, pride, and perseverance of white southerners. Poems celebrated the resolve of wartime heroes and urged the sons and daughters of the Confederacy ever to remain loyal to the South.[106] Short stories recounted the horrors of the war years in tales of murderous and marauding Yankees who terrorized the civilian population. Near famine conditions had been commonplace and the incidence of insanity had increased dramatically. Nevertheless, through it all, the southern spirit survived to tell the story:[107]

> We wear flushed cheeks, and conquer rising tears, but we neither blush nor weep for shame; for true Southrons have lain in the fiery furnace, and bear the ring of good metal within their souls.[108]

Devoted to their cause, the contributors to *The Land We Love* emerged from the war in no mood to compromise their southern traditions.

When this particular group of writers focused upon the Civil War era slave population, they reaffirmed antebellum views; but more importantly, they reaffirmed an unwillingness to adopt any other perspective. The operative word in postbellum southern literature was "loyalty." Whether the story was set in the calm, prosperous days before the war or in the chaotic atmosphere that followed, blacks were portrayed as dependent upon and supremely loyal to their white folks. In one anonymous Reconstruction era poem titled "Mammy," an aged, fervently religious, and loving domestic servant prefers her master's family over "'white trash' whom she cannot tolerate." Mammy had nursed her master when he was a baby and she now enjoys a familiar, yet respectful relationship to the planter's family: "*All* to her is dear devotion whom the angels bend to bless, / All our thoughts of her are blended with a holy tenderness." Subtitled "A Home Picture of 1860," the poem seems to sigh for the days when planters could reward their loyal servants properly.[109]

Less fortunate, but no less dependent, was a free black characterized as a pitiful victim of wartime dislocation. Published in May, 1868, a poem titled "Poor Tom" described an ex-slaveholder's encounter with a wretched, shivering, and wasted black man returning from "Freedom, the pitiless" to die at his former master's feet. Muttering only one word, "Home!" he expired because "Freedom fell with a flail / On Tom, and made him DIE!" In the tradition of antebellum proslavery literature, this poem and others like it envisioned nothing but suffering for blacks who were denied the protections of white paternalistic supervision.[110]

By their unwillingness to capitulate in the postwar debate over the nature of slavery and the character of the Civil War, southern writers of the 1860s further threatened newborn possibilities for more positive portrayals of Afro-Americans. The climate of reconciliation which had affected historical perspectives also influenced late nineteenth-century literature. Eventually, national conditions became more favorable to the South's point of view.

During the 1870s, northern publishers and readers took a new interest in literature by southern authors. Editors at newly established magazines such as *Lippincott's* and *Scribner's* were receptive to southern material which muted antagonisms and colored the South with an innocent and picturesque localism. Thus, their poetry and prose tended to glorify the South, but not at the expense of new northern friends. Modified to lessen the incidence of Yankee villainy, postbellum southern writing became nationally influential. Before the end of the 1880s, the South was one of the most popular settings for American fiction. Novelists' characterizations of this once-outcast section were so generally favorable that one contemporary observer commented: "Not only is the epoch of the war the favorite field of American fiction to-day, but the Confederate soldier is the popular hero. Our literature has become not only Southern in type, but distinctly Confederate in sympathy."[111]

A nationwide enthusiasm for local color writing encouraged such portrayals and reinforced the postwar national consciousness. Picturesque landscapes, regional dialects, provincial manners, and local legends proved good material for promoting a North-South reconciliation because the colorful details celebrated and legitimized regional diversity.

The South suited the needs and purposes of local color writers admirably. In addition to providing a variety of picturesque backdrops for fictional tales, the section possessed a rich history and a suitably rustic cast of characters. Along with hearty North Carolina mountaineers, romantic Louisiana Creoles, and homespun Georgia Crackers, Afro-American slaves and ex-slaves were well represented in the works of the local color school. In some cases, free blacks were portrayed as simple-hearted, childlike peasants who enjoyed the affectionate indulgence of paternalistic whites. These images left the impression that the Civil War had settled all of the nation's racial problems and that black America would prosper with the help of southern whites. When antebellum slaves were depicted similarly, readers might even be led to question the necessity of the war. Whether they portrayed slaves or ex-slaves, local color descriptions of southern plantation life facilitated interregional reconciliation by retaining traditional attitudes toward blacks and modifying wartime characterizations by white northerners. Having weathered the military and political storms of the 1860s and 1870s, many whites in both North and South were content to read about loyal black servants who needed guidance from their social and intellectual superiors.[112]

Local color writers showed a keen interest in using what they perceived to be accurate southern Afro-American dialect. It was not unusual for a magazine article to be prefaced by a note explaining the black speech transcribed in oftentimes lengthy narrative passages. On occasion, as in the case of Sidney and Clifford Lanier's introduction to "Uncle Jim's Baptist Revival-Hymn" (1876), these instructions could be quite detailed:

> the phrase "peerten up" means substantially *to spur up*, and is an active form of the adjective "peert" (probably a corruption of *pert*), which is so common in the South, and which has much the sig-

nification of "smart" in New England, as e.g., a "peert" horse, in antithesis to a "sorry"—i.e., poor, mean, lazy one.[113]

Postbellum attempts to recreate Afro-American dialect eventually brought about a technical improvement in recording black speech patterns. Unfortunately, as was the case with the more haphazard dialect of earlier writers, nonstandard English was only one more weapon in an arsenal of joke material based on misconceptions. The grammatical innovations sometimes merely gave an unwarranted air of anthropological authenticity to popular stereotypes.[114]

Seemingly with new accuracy, authors portrayed slaves and ex-slaves discussing some variant of the loyalty theme. Readers were informed that Afro-Americans had been loyal to their white folks before and during the Civil War. Indeed, this long-term, friendly relationship between black and white southerners had survived this war just as it had survived the Revolutionary War because as children, master and slave had "bofe . . . nussed . . . at one breast." Thereafter, they may have had their petty differences and quarrels, but plantation stories generally characterized the two races as having a harmonious partnership during the postwar era. In this manner, the developing interregional accord blended with an image of interracial kinship in which the masters and the slaves were as close as "two fibe-cent pieces in one dime."[115]

One recurring formula for developing this theme described an ex-slave reminiscing about the Old South. Virginia-born author Thomas Nelson Page was particularly adept at crafting this type of memoir. Page's black characters were wholly devoted to the interests of the white gentry because their self-worth depended upon that of their owners. The ex-slaves thus yearned for the abundance of pre-Civil War times. Blessed with memories that recalled the past "jes' like 'twuz yistiddy," they remembered plantation communities that "jes' wallowed an' roll' in wealf." Some planters had so many cattle and hogs that they "mec' de hill-sides look like black." Flocks of sheep had been so large that they "'peared like clouds on a moon-shine night." "We wuz rich den," the ex-slaves recalled, "quarters on ev'y hill, an' niggers mo' 'n you could tell dee names." Page's post-Civil War image of the slave added a new element to the canon of southern writers—slaves had not only enjoyed their status in white society; they were sorry to have lost it. "Dem wuz good ole times. . . . Dey wuz, in fac'! . . . Dyar warn' no trouble nor nothin', . . . ain' nuver gwine forgit it!"[116]

Page was not alone in his desire to refurbish the image of the South or in his use of the slave memoir technique. Collectively, postwar southern authors developed a singularly compelling literary device which shaped the popular imagination. They disseminated and popularized a caricature of the elderly ex-bondsman who, blessed with a jolly disposition, a commodious lap, and a keenly developed ability to spin tales, veritably mesmerized young white children with stories from antebellum black folklife. While the storyteller could be young or old, male or female, by far the best known of these figures was a white-haired uncle named Remus.[117]

First appearing in the Atlanta *Constitution* during the latter part of the 1870s, Uncle Remus was created by white humorist Joel Chandler Harris. As a teenager in rural Georgia, Harris apprenticed at a literary paper called the *Countryman*. His work there exposed him to local folklore and the plantation sages who eventually became familiar as a composite portrait of post-Civil War black life. Originally used as a vehicle for commenting on contemporary Atlanta customs, it was as a rural story teller that Remus became a nationally recognized folk philosopher.[118]

Having witnessed the passing of most of his own generation, Uncle Remus was content to spend his remaining days as a privileged family servant to Miss Sally, the daughter of his former owner. He did no great amount of work, but neither was he idle. Considering himself a partner in the operation of the plantation, he tended his own watermelon and cotton patches, fed the stock, tanned leather, and manufactured shoes, horse collars, fish baskets, mops, and ax handles. He had "all the prejudices of caste and pride of family" characteristic of the antebellum master-slave relationship. Though Remus sometimes could be a trifle overbearing and quarrelsome, his relationship with Miss Sally was evidence of the fact that he had "nothing but pleasant memories of the discipline of slavery."[119]

Invariably accompanied by his mistress' young son, the elderly servant also instructed readers in antebellum Afro-American folk culture. As he half-soled a shoe or oiled a harness in the carriage-house, Uncle Remus might be asked: "Do geese stand on one leg all night, or do they sit down to sleep?" The kind storyteller then answered the child's question with a tale about "Why the Guinea-Fowls are Speckled," "Why Mr. Possum Loves Peace," or "Why the Negro is Black." Since, "like all the negroes," Remus was "very superstitious, and believed more or less in witches and witchcraft," these stories were not dryly anthropological, but instead drew heavily upon the imagination. With this vast reservoir of material at his disposal — and with the remarkable ability to imitate sounds as complex as the tuning of a fiddle or a terrapin talking under water — the ex-slave introduced his young charge to the world of "genuine folk-lore tales."[120]

Harris further authenticated his character by claiming "long familiarity with the manifold peculiarities of the negro mind," though he was not a trained folklorist. "To be frank," he admitted, "I did not know much about folk-lore, and I didn't think that anybody else did." He intended only to "preserve the stories dear to Southern children in the dialect of the cotton plantations." Despite his disclaimers of academic expertise, Harris convinced his postbellum audience that Uncle Remus represented the genuine flavor of the old plantation. According to Thomas Nelson Page: "No man who has ever written has known one-tenth part about the negro that Mr. Harris knows."[121]

In fact, Mr. Harris's portrayal of southern blacks is strikingly similar to those of his white predecessors. In "A Story of the War" (1880), Uncle Remus remembers how the Civil War upset plantation life to the unprecedented necessity of placing him in charge. With the master and white overseer gone, the loyal servant adeptly performed the role of a demanding but generous white planter:

> I had dem niggers up en in de fiel' long 'fo' day, en de way dey did wuk wuz a caution. Ef dey didn't earnt der vittles dat season den I ain't name Remus. But dey wuz tuk keer un. Dey had plenty er cloze en plenty er grub, en dey wuz de fattes' niggers in de settlement.[122]

It was a perfect example of the racial harmony and reciprocity idealized by proslavery advocates — and it was popular thirty years after Appomattox.

The old man's loyalties were further tested by the arrival of Union troops. In preparation for this intrusion Uncle Remus hid all the stock and the grain and fodder supply, sharpened his axe, marched into the mansion sitting-room, and took his stand behind Ole Miss and Miss Sally "w'iles de Yankees ransack de place."[123]

With the safety of the white women assured, the ever diligent Remus took his master's rifle from its rack and proceeded to check on the stock. On his way through the woods, he happened upon a Yankee who was about to shoot his beloved master. In an instant, he raised the rifle, shut his eyes, "en let de man have all she had." After the war, when asked why he had shot a Union soldier to protect a slaveholder, Uncle Remus defended his action: "it sorter made cole chills run up my back; but w'en I see dat man take aim, . . . I des disremembered all 'bout freedom en lammed aloose."[124]

Infused with the conciliatory spirit of the era, "A Story of the War" concluded with the ex-slave's description of how he and Miss Sally nursed the wounded Yankee back to health. Not long thereafter, the southern belle married the northern soldier and they produced a son — the child whom Harris once described as a "product of that practical reconstruction which has been going on to some extent since the war in spite of the politicians." In this allegorical tale of sectional reconciliation Uncle Remus could narrate "from the standpoint of a Southerner, and with the air of one who expected his hearers to thoroughly sympathize with him." For the white readers of the late nineteenth century, Joel Chandler Harris had created an impression of interregional and interracial good will: "whatever is truly Southern is likewise truly American." Though readers who had been saddened by the tragic story of Harriet Beecher Stowe's Uncle Tom might have disagreed before the war, they now could put aside past differences as they enjoyed the heart-warming tales spun by Uncle Remus — a surviving kinsman cut from remarkably familiar cloth.[125]

Since the days of Uncle Remus' greatest popularity, the nature of Joel Chandler Harris' overall contribution to American letters has been subjected to a fair amount of analysis. Critics have labeled him "a leading proponent of the plantation myth" and have charged him with distorting "hate-imbued" black folk materials through the use of pastoral settings.[126] In commenting upon Uncle Remus they have pointed out that the storyteller's comical struggles with the complexities of a modernizing America made the ex-slave seem ridiculously dense. As a result, already existing stereotypes of black incapacity were reinforced whenever Remus attempted to fathom the workings of the telephone, the phonograph, or the trolley car.[127]

Certainly Harris did help to perpetuate misconceptions about black people well into the twentieth century. While claiming the ability to "think in the negro dialect," he could not speak without the prejudices of his times. His literary creations mirrored his sociological assumptions and were compatible with his journalistic observations. Although white local color writers like Harris may have thought carefully about setting, costume, and dialect, theirs still differed from their black contemporaries' treatments of racial pride, cooperation, self-definition, strength, and survival.[128]

Upon first view, the slave images created by postwar black writers seem to belie any claims to uniqueness. Afro-American poets produced some of the most conciliatory and demeaning dialect verse of the times. When Daniel Webster Davis, James David Corrothers, or James Edwin Campbell spoke of black America's long-term addiction to hogmeat, steaming buckwheat cakes, possum, and sweet potatoes, they seemed to be affirming popular portrayals of the Old South. According to such writers, the region still was a place where black contentment was commonplace and only "de banjo an' de fiddle" ever "gits er dahky soon to shoutin'."[129]

Nevertheless, other black poets persisted in their demands for equality. The Ohio-born orator-poet James Madison Bell spoke of "a deathless kinship — a relation, / A brotherhood that knows no bounds, / Pervading earth in every station / Where e're the human form is found." When these poets wrote of a reconciliation between black and white, North and South into "one broad land, all free and blest," they were hoping for the eventual creation of a more egalitarian nation — one which would be "a real

Republic—free! uncurs'd!" There, "without respect to birth or hue," the black American could stand "sublime in his creation, / Begirt with freedom as his due."[130] This hope survived despite the deluge of late nineteenth-century dialect verse and it remained kindled in the works of poet Paul Laurence Dunbar and author Charles Waddell Chesnutt.

Like others of his generation, Dunbar faced a vexing personal dilemma —he had to decide whether to work within the confines of white literary convention or to break with popular expectations and risk alienating a large segment of his reading public. On many occasions, Dunbar seemed exceedingly eager to win and to hold his white audience. Colorful, faithful retainers are legion in Dunbar's poetry and prose. They found great personal satisfaction in laboring for white people, sang their praises and were suitably devastated whenever tragedy befell them.[131]

Neither did Dunbar risk disapproval over the issues of sectional and interracial reconciliation. In "Mammy Peggy's Pride" (1900), Bartley Northcope, the new northern owner of a Virginia plantation, considered the burdens of the defeated white southerners. With a reassuring compassion, he explained:

> These Southerners cannot understand that we sympathize with their misfortunes. But we do. They forget how our sympathies have been trained. We were first taught to sympathize with the slave, and now that he is free, and needs less, perhaps, of our sympathy, this, by a transition, as easy as it is natural, is transferred to his master.[132]

Lest readers think that the ex-slaves were less charitable than Yankee planters, Dunbar wrote "Nelse Hatton's Vengeance" (1898)—a tale which described how one black man conquered his bitterness toward his former enslavement. Discovering that his master had become a destitute beggar, Nelse gave him a suit and some money along with reassurances that nothing much had changed: "You're goin' back to Kintucky, an' you're goin' back a gentleman. I kin he'p you, an' I will. You're welcome to the last I have." Certainly, scenes such as these suggest that Dunbar was willing to make, as one observer noted, "a few concessions to convention and sentiment."[133]

The popularity of his dialect writing obscured the fact that Dunbar used standard English in his novels, in more than half of his poems, and in most of his short stories. Perhaps even less well understood by his readers were his personal dissatisfactions with the dialect convention. He chose this arena originally because he was as skilled as his contemporaries and so hoped to gain a hearing, but Dunbar soon discovered that his readers did not want him to write anything but dialect. On occasion, his poetry spoke disparagingly of the acclaim which greeted each new "jingle in a broken tongue." With a veiled rage he described the practical necessities which forced black writers to "wear the mask that grins and lies" even while "in ouah innards we is p'intly mad ez sin." Thus, with a keen sense of disappointment he lamented: "I've kept on doing the same things, and doing them no better. I have never gotten to the things I really wanted to do."[134]

Whether or not his writings were personally satisfying, the poet's inner militancy and race pride refused to be completely suppressed by the dialect mask.[135] Even though his elderly black characters stereotypically longed for the Old South of antebellum days, there was an important difference between his portrayal of their reminiscences and those current in white-authored stories. Ex-slaves in the latter tended to identify with their masters. By Dunbar's account, the postbellum blacks often spoke of their ties to the slave community.

In one example of this nostalgia, titled "The Deserted Plantation," a black narrator explains his loyalty to former days. Everyone else had left the plantation, but he had stayed behind to "watch de deah ol' place an' tend it / Ez I used to in de happy days gone by." It wasn't slavery which had so enriched his life; it wasn't his white masters, either. It was instead "all dat loved me an' dat I loved."

> Whah's ol' Uncle Mordecai an' Uncle Aaron?
> Whah's Aunt Doshy, Sam, an' Kit, an all de res'?
> Whah's ol' Tom de da'ky fiddlah, how's he farin'?
> Whah's de gals dat used to sing an' dance de bes'?[136]

In Dunbar's world of dialect and local color, when black characters remembered the pre-Civil War past, they remembered their families and friends. This was their reconciliation.

Like Dunbar, Charles W. Chesnutt chafed at the literary restrictions and popular stereotypes of turn-of-the-century America. He judged Thomas Nelson Page guilty of "disguising the harshness of slavery under the mask of sentiment" and he identified the distinguishing characteristic of prevailing images of slaves to be a "dog-like fidelity to their old master, for whom they have been willing to sacrifice almost life itself." Such characters undoubtedly existed, but as he noted in a June, 1890, letter to novelist George Washington Cable: "I can't write about those people, or rather I won't write about them." Instead, he created Uncle Julius, a black counter-image to Joel Chandler Harris's more famous plantation storyteller.[137]

In Chesnutt's first novel, *The Conjure Woman* (1899), this venerable, white-haired Afro-American narrator recounted a series of folk tales to a white couple who had gone South after the war to start a vineyard. Although he spoke in dialect and constantly craved "'possum," "watermill-yums," and "scuppernon' wine," Uncle Julius McAdoo was less stereotypical than first appearances would indicate. Presented in a familiar format, Uncle Julius' stories spoke of a far more antagonistic master-slave relationship than the one described by white local color writers. Chesnutt had appropriated a literary form popularized by Joel Chandler Harris and then adapted it to confront white readers with a more controversial interpretation of slavery.[138]

Commenting upon his stories, Chesnutt once said that "in every instance Julius had an axe to grind." Unlike Harris, Chesnutt did not choose to place his slave-era tales in an innocuous setting. Instead, the stories told by his shrewd coachman represented generations of black conflict with white overlords. He described in bone-chilling detail a slaveholder who "nebber 'peared ter hab no feelin' fer nobody" and an overseer who "behin' his back dey useter call . . . Ole Nick, en de name suited 'im ter a T." Insensitive and greedy white men would even stoop to separate mother from child, noting with corrupt rationalization: "niggers is made ter wuk, en dey ain' got no time fer no sich foolis'ness ez babies."[139]

According to Uncle Julius, however, blacks were far from helpless in defending themselves against the brutalities of plantation life. As sly as the storyteller, the slaves fought back by appropriating white-owned goods, by waging psychological warfare, and by continually testing the limits of slaveholders' authority.[140] Chesnutt's counter-offensive revealed dimensions of human personality missing from black characters created by white writers.

In one particular story, titled "The Conjurer's Revenge," Uncle Julius described the activities of a slave whom he had known in his younger days. Primus loved to dance, drink, and run around, and he was patently unwilling to have his courting and partying limited in any way. Despite the fact that his nighttime absences from the plantation brought him into serious confrontation with a local black conjurer, it never seemed to alter his relationship with white people. Primus continued his evening excursions between the slave quarters and the free black settlement unimpeded by white authority. The fun-loving bondsmen created and maintained this niche of freedom because he also had a deadly serious side to his personality. According to Uncle Julius, whenever Primus felt he was being treated unfairly, he became so stubborn and sulky that "de w'ite folks couldn' ha'dly do nuffin wid 'im." More than this, he could be positively "dange'ous w'en he got in dem stubborn spells." The slaveholders decided that he was one slave "dey'd ruther not fool wid," and the reader is left the impression that Primus himself might be the conjurer's revenge.[141]

As early twentieth-century readers became bored with the dialect vogue and local color writing passed from public favor, black authors were able to pick up where Chesnutt left off in developing a tradition for a distinctly Afro-American view of the slave experience. They condemned historical and literary treatments which had "at all times, held the Negro up to contemptuous gaze, and pictured him as a fawning fool!" Echoing Dunbar, they ever more openly raged at the conventional necessity of speaking from behind the minstrel mask. Although they acknowledged the constraints which influenced earlier writers, they were determined to avoid the demeaning use of dialect "even as a *tour de force.*" In fact, in 1927 Countee Cullen advised against using it at all: "In a day when artificiality is so vigorously condemned, the Negro poet would be foolish indeed to turn to dialect." Instead, the Afro-American literary community of the 1920s and 1930s concentrated on celebrating the "New Negro."[142]

The turn of the century sparked the black protest effort and soon the Niagara Movement, the National Association for the Advancement of Colored People, the National Urban League, and the Universal Negro Improvement Association were all at work representing the interests of their members. A generation which, as Alain Locke described it, seemed "suddenly to have slipped from under the tyranny of social intimidation" became actively engaged in "shaking off the psychology of imitation and implied inferiority." The New Negro writers of the Harlem Renaissance era sought to express this spiritual emancipation both by anticipating a glorious future and by celebrating key Afro-American contributions to the national past. To their mind, the past was indeed a living prologue to that future.[143]

When New Negroes scanned the future, they spoke of providing for, promoting, and protecting their own group destiny, but they also described the black American as a collaborator and participant in American civilization. Infused with the ethos of cultural pluralism, these writers spread the word that blacks had demonstrated their talents and energies in the past and that they would continue to do so in the future. Harlem Renaissance writers meant to preserve the indisputable truth that Afro-Americans had, as James Weldon Johnson phrased it, "bought a rightful sonship here, / And we have more than paid the price."[144]

Afro-American writers of the 1920s and 1930s witnessed the passing of the antebellum generation and recorded the life stories of these "gnarled sentinels of time and tide." They hoped the slaves' histories would provide inspiration and encouragement for their own and future generations. These stories taught twentieth-century blacks to persevere, to struggle, and the men and women of the slave era were portrayed with admiration for their ability to endure great hardships.[145]

In his poem, "The Negro Mother" (1931), Langston Hughes created a black American materfamilias of epic stature. The narrator begins the poem with a description of the "long dark way / That I had to climb, that I had to know / In order that the race might live and grow." Overcoming three hundred years of suffering and deprivation, she explains how she persevered. Armed with a song, a prayer, and a heavenly dream, this black mother encouraged readers to continue her fight for equality:

> All you dark children in the world out there,
> Remember my sweat, my pain, my despair.
> Remember my years, heavy with sorrow —
> And make of those years a torch for tomorrow.
> Make of my past a road to the light
> Out of the darkness, the ignorance, the night.[146]

For writers like Hughes, the nation's experience with slavery left a legacy capable of providing contemporary black Americans with strong role models for the future — no Uncle Toms or Aunt Minnies need apply.[147]

Black authors of the pre-World War II era promoted role models as a necessary defense against the demeaning stereotypes which continued to flourish within American society. Many black Americans remained mired in poverty, without land, homes, or stable incomes. With starvation ever at their door they were exploited, dispirited, and in urgent need of the inspiration of their people's history. Hughes and his compatriots could remind readers of the continuing ties which bound southern blacks to the perverse whims and stringent demands of King Cotton.[148]

For those Afro-Americans who had escaped poverty, there was a nagging fear that they had also relinquished their heritage, and ultimately their self-esteem. In "Children's Children" (1932), Sterling Brown chided a modern generation of affluent blacks who, with "paled faces, coppered lips, / And sleek hair cajoled to Caucasian straightness," restlessly and reluctantly acknowledged their ancestors. Preferring popular music — "saccharine melodies of loving and its fevers" — to the melancholy songs of the slaves, they seemed disrespectful of those responsible for their prosperity. Moreover, they appeared to be jettisoning key elements of their Afro-American folk culture in a frenzied scramble to obtain status and acceptance within the white world. In Brown's words: "They have forgotten / What had to be endured — ".[149]

Black writers tried to renew both the hope of the poor and the memories of the prosperous by recalling the nature and purpose of the struggle against slavery; but they were equally interested in reminding readers that black America's confrontation with poverty and injustice was far from over. According to Mingo, the free black insurrectionist of Arna Bontemps' 1936 novel, *Black Thunder:* "You ain't free for true till all yo' kin peoples is free with you. You ain't sure 'nough free till you gets treated like any other mens."[150]

As they spoke of perseverance and unity, these characterizations of the slave era delineated the historical roots of contemporary racial oppression. Afro-Americans wrote about slavery with the bitterness of a people still greatly afflicted by white America's attitude toward racial inequality. A modern era of disfranchisement, discrimination, and segregation required a new awareness of an old adversary.

In the hope that their brothers and sisters would deal cautiously with white America, black authors recounted the horrors of the Atlantic slave trade and detailed the institutionalized denial of human rights which afflicted New World plantation laborers.[151] They denigrated slaveholders — calling them "white scum" — and described slaves who nurtured a deep enmity toward whites for the physical and emotional cruelties of the slave labor system. When a fictional bondsman responded to the sum of slavery's abuses by cursing, "God gone smite ye! Gone smite ye like your pappy and mammy afore ye and your grandpappy now! God gone smite ye," he was issuing a warning which reflected the depth and staying power of black anger.[152]

Relatively few white authors responded to black America by challenging the assumptions and teachings of the plantation tradition. Mainstream popular culture continued to promote many of the traditional interpretations of nineteenth-century black culture.[153] Having learned little from Afro-American views of the antebellum world, white writers were thought to have "little to say, but say it over and over."[154] No fictional work of its day more clearly illustrates this point than Margaret Mitchell's *Gone With the Wind* (1936).

As a daughter of Atlanta, Mitchell inherited a set of general impressions about the Civil War South which later influenced her writing. Her claims to accuracy almost exactly duplicate those of antebellum and postbellum authors. Vowing that she had written "nothing that was not true, nothing that I could not prove," Mitchell collected research material for her novel in antebellum and Civil War era newspapers, history books, reminiscences, and "the Lord knows how many unpublished letters and diaries." With the additional aid of a seventeen page glossary of Afro-American dialect, she hoped that her characters would not be seen as "lavender-and-lace-moonlight-on-the-magnolias people."[155]

Whatever her intention, Margaret Mitchell did construct a fantastically popular novel from her experience and research. Over one million copies of *Gone With the Wind* were sold within six months of publication. As a Book-of-the-Month Club selection and recipient of the 1937 Pulitzer Prize for fiction, the novel brought its author so much notoriety that two secretaries were required to help her cope with the ensuing deluge of correspondence. Attracted by this outpouring of interest in the book, David O. Selznick purchased the motion picture rights for $50,000. By the time his film reached the nation's theaters, there was no doubt that American popular culture had canonized Mitchell's story of the Civil War. In 1939, fans sealed the book into a time capsule at the New York World's Fair, not to be disturbed until the year 6939.[156]

According to Margaret Mitchell, life in antebellum rural Georgia was a little crude when judged by the standards of Augusta, Savannah, or Charleston, but it did have its advantages. In this "pleasant land of white houses, peaceful plowed fields and sluggish yellow rivers," parents could raise their children in an atmosphere that would promote "vigor and alertness." Neither slack nor soft, these frontier settlers may have lacked the social graces of planters in more thickly populated regions, but they were no less skilled in the things that mattered. They liked "raising good cotton, riding well, shooting straight, dancing lightly, squiring the ladies with elegance and carrying one's liquor like a gentleman."[157]

The planters of north Georgia also considered themselves good slaveholders. At great expense they tried to unite and preserve the black nuclear family. Risking her own health, a good planter's wife persisted in "hoppin' up at night time nursin' niggers an' po' w'ite trash dat could ten' to deyseff." Equally unselfish in the practice of her religion, the mistress of the Big House shared her faith with the houseservants and thanked God daily for "the health and happiness of her home, her family and her negroes." These selfless deeds were greatly appreciated by the slaves, some of whom expressed their gratitude with vows of voluntary servility: "I'm gwine do my bes' fo' you and show you I ain't forgettin'."[158]

Although they may have been devoted, the slaves in *Gone With the Wind* were usually quite inept in the actual performance of their duties. Without careful and constant white supervision, their blundering inefficiency became all too apparent. Furniture went undusted, meals were served late, and dirty linen accumulated in the laundress' hamper. If one was gentle with the slaves, said heroine Scarlett O'Hara, they would merely "sit in the kitchen all day, talking endlessly." Yet, since it would have been unfair to harshly discipline such dull-witted dependents, the response to the slave's shortcomings usually consisted of empty threats and bluster. "I swear," went the typical lament, "darkies are more trouble. Sometimes I think the Abolitionists have got the right idea."[159]

According to black critic George S. Schuyler, Margaret Mitchell's conceptualization of the antebellum South was grossly inaccurate. He labeled her "a feminist, a modern, a Confederate in slacks, but a Confederate nevertheless." In Schuyler's opinion, *Gone With the Wind* may have been awarded a Pulitzer Prize by white America, but the book more correctly ought to be recognized as an obstacle to equal rights. For those black Americans who had learned a different version of antebellum southern history, Mitchell's novel was "just another Rebel propaganda tract."[160] Mitchell, in response to criticisms of her book, announced that she did not intend to allow "trouble-making Professional Negroes" to alter her feelings toward "the race with whom my relations have always been those of affection and mutual respect."[161]

Though popular culture continued its romance with the Old South, disenchanted white authors eventually began to cultivate a less traditional relationship with southern history. Like historians of the 1930s and 40s who acknowledged and utilized the perspectives of their Afro-American colleagues, proponents of twentieth-century literary realism echoed the sentiments and restated certain themes developed by slavery's black critics. Writers who had rejected dialect verse and local color fiction were concerned that their works accurately depicted southern life. Motivated by the harsh realities of their own era's social and economic problems, they sought solutions in new perspectives on the Old South.[162]

Their search revealed the financial underpinnings of the antebellum labor system. More willing than their predecessors to explore the proposition that slaveholders had owned people as property, this school of writers stripped the cloak of benevolent paternalism from the master/slave relationship. Slaveholders were characterized as unwilling to economize during hard times, and capable of sacrificing the black family in the interest of their own financial security. Unlike the planters in *Gone With the Wind* who reunited kinsmen at great personal expense, these hard-hearted barons thought only of protecting their investment: "I don't know whether niggers is going up or down," said one slaveholder in a 1931 plantation novel, "so I'm selling and waiting for conditions to settle."[163]

In addition to describing their ungentlemanly adherence to some of the less savory principles of the market economy, these accounts portrayed slaveholders who were almost as poor as their slaves, only slightly more educated than their slaves, and just as prone to boasting and poor judgment as any stock minstrel character. Like Thomas Sutpen in William Faulkner's *Absalom, Absalom!* (1936), the pioneering planter could arrive at the sight of a future estate "with a horse and two pistols and a name which nobody ever heard before . . . seeking someplace to hide himself." After stealing a section of land from the Indians, he and his slaves might proceed to "drag . . . house and gardens out of virgin swamp" and to plant the acreage with borrowed seed cotton. Though his effort may have won a certain type of frontier social status and respectability, he still wore coarse clothing and "always smelled of his own dogs."[164]

Planters such as these rarely lived in lordly splendor. The interior of a log home might contain a small library, but in general the cabin bore little resemblance to the Tara of *Gone With the Wind*.[165] Even the titles on the bookshelves raised doubts about the planter's relationship to the landed gentry of tradition:

> a Coke upon Littleton, a Josephus, a Koran, a volume of Mississippi Reports dated 1848, a Jeremy Taylor, a Napoleon's Maxims, a thousand and ninety-eight page treatise on astrology, a History of Werewolf Men in England, Ireland and Scotland . . . a complete Walter Scott, a complete Fenimore Cooper, a paper-bound Dumas. . . .[166]

Lacking the customary trappings of the southern romance, such characterizations more critically scrutinized the personal weaknesses of slaveholders. In the process, it became apparent that some would suffer economic ruin. Those who were too fond of strong drink, gambling, or land speculation found that their depleted savings were insufficient to cover customary expenses during hard times. Even if they could temporarily bolster their egos with "a flourish of manners before the ladies" or by boasting about their lineage, such planters could not ignore their poverty. Forced to supplement their income through part-time jobs, and reduced to a slave's diet of corn pone and sweet potatoes, the unlucky slaveholder suspected that "sometimes, since we have grown so dirt-poor, even our darkies laugh at our grand talk."[167]

During times like these, claims of white supremacy rang hollow with the slaveholders' ignorance, indulgence, and impoverishment. White characters in white-authored stories about the antebellum era were now being portrayed as both greatly dependent upon and fearful of their black slaves. In part, white characters began to fear blacks once they realized the falsehoods of white supremacy; but black characters in these novels often cultivated fear and distrust as necessary for their own protection.[168] In this way, twentieth-century America was introduced to the idea that if blacks could be just as capable as whites, they could be just as threatening:

> Their bowing and scraping; and underneath it all, their watching ways — their great brown eyes forever following you around. All just standing there, and watching you always, and more than ever when your back was turned — standing, watching, saying nothing.[169]

Forced to be on continual guard against these deceptively docile bondsmen, planters might be heard to muse disgustedly, "How close we come
to the niggers without knowing anything about them."[170]

Sometimes the planter did confront the rage of a bondsman who had
grown "bone-tired waitin' on white folks." The slave's response may have
taken the form of a threat: "Doan you cuss at me, Boss," he might say,
"Ah's wise man dis mawnin' an' Ah ain' gwina stan' no cussin'—leastways
not frum yawl"; or it may have been stated as fact: "Marster, if you hadn't
got me, I'd a got you."[171] The most chilling characterization of quiet revenge, however, was named Uncle Jimbilly, the Uncle Remus—or, more
correctly, the Uncle Julius—of the twentieth century.

Created by the Texas-born short story writer Katherine Anne Porter,
Uncle Jimbilly was an intimidating and somewhat mysterious figure. Hobbled by the rheumatic afflictions of old age, the elderly handyman spent
much of his time telling ghost stories to white children and carving minia-
ture wooden tombstones for their dead pets. As he talked in a low, broken,
abstracted murmur, he "dwelt much on the horrors of slave times."[172]

Uncle Jimbilly told his young listeners that the slaves of the rice swamps
had perished "by de thousands and tens upon thousands." He described
the rice planters' sadistic punishments in horrifying detail:

> Dey used to stake 'em out all day and all night, and all day and
> all night and all day wid dey hans and feet tied so dey couldn't
> scretch and let de muskeeters eat 'em alive. De muskeeters 'ud bite
> 'em tell dey was all swole up like a balloon all over, and you could
> heah 'em howlin and prayin all ovah the swamp.[173]

If they didn't die in the swamps, according to Uncle Jimbilly, planters would
resort to whipping them with "gret big leather strops inch thick long as
yo' ahm, wid round holes bored in 'em so's evey time dey hit 'em de hide
and de meat done come off dey bones in little round chunks."[174]

The grim accounts provoked, in Porter's words, "tinglings of embarrass-
ment" among Uncle Jimbilly's listeners. Despite the gap between the young
white audience and the Afro-American slave experience, the storyteller's
macabre tales of torment and inhumanity left an impression upon their
young minds. Nothing could have been more impersonal and distant than
Jimbilly's manner of talking about slavery, but his listeners nevertheless
"wriggled a little and felt guilty."[175]

These latest modifications of popular plantation stereotypes portrayed
slavery in a manner long familiar to Afro-American writers and their reading public. Such depictions of antebellum brutality and resistance now
would be introduced to a wider and increasingly diverse audience. It seemed

that white writers were becoming more accepting of black perspectives and more critical of stereotypical treatments. Nonetheless, the changes were not unequivocal improvements. The gulf between treatments of slaves in white- as opposed to black-authored literature continued, even while authors searched for a common understanding. Perhaps, as civil rights leader Martin Luther King, Jr., proposed, the search itself signalled a beginning that was "a long and satisfactory distance from nothing." Or perhaps, a common vision would always be an elusive and impossible goal as long as the society of which it was a part remained divided and fearful.[176]

Technicolor Dixie

The social changes represented by the transition from Uncle Remus to Uncle Julius to Uncle Jimbilly also were mirrored in the music and drama of the post-Civil War century. By the mid-1960s, Afro-American songwriters and playwrights could point with pride to the growing influence of the black perspective on slavery. As with literature and history, their opportunities to gain a hearing were growing as Americans moved away from antebellum attitudes. In the context of American popular song, this long and difficult journey began with the singing of "Dixie."

Originally written as a concluding "walk-around" for Bryant's Minstrels in 1859, "Dixie's Land" in its many variations demonstrates minstrelsy's capacity for compromise even during wartime. Initially performed by burnt cork minstrels on Broadway, it gained widespread popularity after being incorporated as a drill song in a New Orleans production of the play *Pocahontas*. From there it was spread throughout the South by Confederate soldiers and pirated sheet music sales. The lyrics in most versions celebrated "de land ob cotton" where "de whites grow fat, an' de niggers fatter."[177]

The song's composer, Daniel Decatur Emmett, struck a harmonious chord for whites with his description of northern blacks who longed to "lib and die in Dixie." It was played at the inauguration of Jefferson Davis in February 1861 and accompanied countless Confederate soldiers into battle. Southern military versions sent foot soldiers off to be "strong as lions, swift as eagles" to "rout the band, / That comes to conquer Dixie."[178] Yankee variations reclaimed Dixie for the Union and encouraged southerners to believe in the inevitability of a Union victory:

> Away down South in the land of traitors,
> Rattlesnakes and alligators,
> Right away, come away, right away, come away.
> Where cotton's king and men are chattels,

> Union boys will win the battles,
> Right away, come away, right away, come away.[179]

However modified, it was the original version of "Dixie," with its description of ex-slaves longing for the "buck-wheat cakes an 'Ingen' batter" of the plantation South, which survived the war. Both during and after the conflict, this sprightly minstrel song expressed the sentiments of those white northerners who could not accept ex-slaves as co-workers in the building of a prosperous postbellum economy. The message of "Dixie" was that blacks were an unequal, unwelcome element in Yankee society. Representing both northern and southern attitudes toward Afro-Americans' destiny, the song popularized and promoted ideological and political compromise on issues of race. As such, it supported the status quo in American race relations.[180]

Other Civil War songs forwarded the disturbing idea that whites were being denied their rightful place in society and their God-given liberties because of the war. Some spoke bitterly of free white people being oppressed by conflicts surrounding the slavery question. To the northern anti-draft advocate, wartime conscription meant that the drafted, "like felons," were "chained / To negroes called 'their betters.'" To the determined Confederate, Abraham Lincoln and his generals had only one goal in mind — to "fetter the free man" under the pretext of liberating the slave.[181] To the peace advocate, the issue was equally clear-cut — freedom for southern blacks was not worth the sacrifice of life, liberty, or luxury. As one soldier lamented in an 1863 song:

> It's monsus fine for the Bobolition line,
>   With mouths ful o' pumpkin pie,
> To preach in meetin' agin' retreatin' —
>   Why don't they come theirselves and try?
> . . . .
> War is mighty fine to them that's drinking wine
>   At the big hotels in York;
> But as for *lousy* me, that's lost his liberty,
>   *Peace* is the right sort o' talk.[182]

Wartime songs recorded white society's attachment to principles and freedoms which they reluctantly shared with members of a long-established slave caste.

During the years of civil conflict, Americans anxiously contemplated the possibility that if they "to the Union prove[d] true," they would be encouraging the notion that "the nigger is as good a man as you." One way in which leaders of the free black community of the 1860s hoped to popularize this idea was through Afro-American enrollment in the Union Army ranks.[183] Although these supporters of black regiments endorsed the troops' capabilities, songwriters were less approving. In A. C. D. Sandie's "Ole Uncle Abrum's Comin'", for example, newly liberated slaves appeared more interested in creature comforts than in the Union army. As their masters fled from the Yankee invaders, leaders of the slave community urged their brothers and sisters to "git into de parlor / As fast as yer can, / And set upon de sofy / Wid yer feet on de divan." Allowing white northerners to fight the battle for them, the slaves in such songs were perfectly willing to "fight de South . . . / All by de 'word ob mouth'.[184]

There were songs, nonetheless, that celebrated Afro-American military might:

> McClellan went to Richmond with two hundred thousand brave;
> He said, "Keep back the niggers" and the Union he would save.
> Little Mac he had his way, still the Union is in tears,
> *NOW* they call for the help of the colored volunteers.
> . . . .
> So rally, boys, rally, let us never mind the past;
> We had a hard road to travel, but our day is coming fast;
> For God is for the right, and we have no need to fear,
> The Union must be saved by the colored volunteer.[185]

The songwriter's praise accurately estimated their relative contribution to the Union cause; but the more than 200,000 black troops could not convince white northerners that Afro-Americans were their equals. As an 1864 song called "Sambo's Right to Be Kilt" put it, a white man wouldn't "at all object, / If Sambo's body should stop a ball / That's comin' for me direct," but an extension of blacks' rights into other areas held little attraction for white Americans.[186]

Burnt cork minstrelsy enthusiastically supported these inequalities in its portrayals of both free and enslaved blacks. Both during and after the war, abusive comedy skits, song lyrics, and stereotypical caricatures continued to evoke howls of laughter from minstrel show audiences. Cowardly in wartime, inept in freedom, the Afro-American minstrel character was a walking argument for a postbellum extension of racial subordination. Slave recruits who did not understand even the most elementary military maneuvers fled the battlefield "when dey smell de bullets."[187] If they weren't bumbling and cowardly soldiers, blacks were characterized as confused about white America's work-ethic. In a skit entitled "Lost His Situation," an ex-slave had no sense of responsibility and refused to be told what to do. His employer, he said, made unfair demands:

He wanted me to be at work by nine o'clock in de mornin' an' he 'jected ef I took more dan two hours fo' my dinner. He didn't want me to smoke cigarettes durin' business hours, an he wanted me to stop readin' de mornin' paper ef a customer kim in. He didn't want me to frow peanut shucks nor water mellun rinds on de flo' an' he 'fused to raise my wages. Finally he said he didn't want me no mo' no how, so I got disgusted an' quit.[188]

Certainly such a fellow stood in desperate need of the legendary paternalistic supervision of southern whites. He needed considerable direction in order to function at even the lowest levels of skill and responsibility.

The minstrel portrayal of black political expectations during the era of Reconstruction took similar directions. In one skit of the 1870s, a black character named Josiar described the benefits of "de swivel rights bill" then under consideration by Congress. According to Josiar, the proposed legislation would permit blacks to ride free on the railroads, smoke in the ladies' car, and put their feet "on de percussions of de seats wheneber we dam please." The new law would allow black travelers to stay at the best hotels, to eat at the head of the main dining room table, and then afterward to "lay around in de parlor, and spit on de carpets." Even the Afro-Americans' afterlife was to be affected by the bill. Under federal law, the deceased would be placed in "italic coffins wid looking glasses on de top," and would be buried "on top of de white folks" in order to be the first to respond to Gabriel's call on resurrection day. He made, in effect, a cogent case for continuing white supervision of black America.[189]

Despite the promises of freedom, ex-slaves in minstrel shows more often longed for the plantation kitchen than the hotel dining room; in other words, they longed for life as a slave. In one postwar skit, an ex-slave reminisced about the days when he would "sit under de shade ob de tree and listen to de little birds sing and read my little bible; take off my hat to de white folks as dey passed by, and dey used to gib me silber." Preoccupied with visions of a good master and good rum, the blackfaced minstrel greatly preferred an old-time possum hunt and barbecue to a fancy meal in a northern hotel. Freedom had separated these characters from the ways of life they enjoyed most. If they couldn't live in the South anymore, at least an elderly ex-slave could hope to be buried there: "I wants ter see de ol' home 'fore I die. . . . Let me go back chillun to dat sunny southern lan'."[190]

Burnt cork minstrel shows offered the public variations on old themes, but black minstrel troupes were often equally unable to ignore prevailing stereotypes. Building upon a small antebellum base, these traveling companies began to appear more frequently after the Civil War. Since northern audiences were both curious about the newly emancipated slaves and eager for entertainment, they flocked to see Brooker and Clayton's Georgia Minstrels, Smallwood's Great Contraband Minstrels and Brass Band, the Georgia Slave Troupe Minstrels, and other such assemblages. The black minstrels billed themselves as representatives of the Negro race and tried to capitalize on this by convincing audiences that competing burnt cork companies were, at best, inferior imitations.[191]

Recent scholarship maintains that in certain instances Afro-American minstrel companies did portray antebellum black life differently than white companies. Black minstrels' nostalgic postwar longing for family and friends often surpassed their desire to reunite with their white masters. Black minstrels were more likely than whites to criticize slavery and celebrate their freedom. They were also more likely to perform authentic Afro-American religious music. In contrast, one burnt-cork burlesque named "Come To De Gospel Show!" described heaven as a place where there would be "lots to eat in de land above . . . / All kinds of pie that a nigger can love."[192]

As comparative newcomers to the minstrel stage, the black companies were at a disadvantage. Black showmen found that audiences demanded the conventions of slave characterizations developed by white companies. Furthermore, whites owned or managed many of the most successful postwar troupes.[193] As a result, the overall thrust of Afro-American minstrelsy was anything but revolutionary. Indeed, the substitution of black actors for white actors in burnt cork may have served only to solidify time-honored stereotypes. If these genuine Negroes behaved in much the same manner as their white imitators, who could question the fundamental accuracy of the minstrelsy interpretation of slave life and culture? In this context, rather than being an inaccurate, demeaning form of public ridicule, the whites' mimicry was one of the higher forms of show business flattery.

Prominent among those black artists whose songs were popular but conventional were James Bland, Sam Lucas, James Putnam, and Gussie L. Davis. Tunes like "Carry Me Back to Old Virginny," "Dis Darkey's Growing Old," "When Gabriel Blows His Trumpet, I'll Be Dar," and "I Long to See Old Massa's Face Again" reinforced images of slave loyalty and docility. A black minstrel company of the 1870s that performed such songs profited from convincing, melancholy visions of black people pining for their Mississippi homes where "previous to the war . . . the darkies liv'd so happy gay and free."[194]

Minstrels were not the only black performers in the public eye in late nineteenth-century America. "Banjo Comiques" such as Billy Kersands and Ike Simond also tried to make a living by pleasing white audiences. Even though talented in song and dance, their primary contribution to reeducating white America would be to reserve a place on stage for future generations of Afro-American performers. They could offer little in the way of contradictory testimony regarding the character of black people or the nature of slavery.[195]

The education that black performers did offer made thorough use of familiar formulas. In a promotional interview which appeared in the *New York Clipper* in 1882, a black member of the white-owned and managed Callender's Consolidated Colored Minstrels described an upcoming performance:

> dar am to be de genuine plantation darky on de stage. . . . de scene on de lebbee and all de old plantation frolics and de cotton-field sports will be pictured so natural dat de audience will tink dey is down in Louisiana wid cotton bales, alligators, canebrakes and cypress swamps all 'round dem. . . . We will hab de ole time fiddles, and de ole-time rosin, and de ole-time yaller gals, and de ole-time cotton pickins, and de ole-time coon hunts, and de ole-time breakdowns.[196]

The minstrel promoted himself as an expert on southern life. He assured the reporter that he was "a rale brack Efiopian" and that he had "de papers to proove it." He also described his family's journey from the African homeland—where warring tribes "nebber took no prisoners, kase dey eat dem up as fast det kotch dem"—to what he termed "modern cibbilization." As a Louisiana slave, he had been taught how to pick cotton, plant tobacco, and "mash de big green worm on de 'backer plant." Through this process of acculturation, he claimed to have been on his way to becoming a "'spectable colored citizen" of Louisiana. Unfortunately, the Civil War interrupted his labors and destroyed his fine prospects. All was not lost, however, because he luckily found employment "up Norf" in the glamorous and soul-satisfying field of postbellum black minstrelsy.[197]

According to this black character, all varieties of late nineteenth-century Americans could benefit from attending a minstrel performance. Former southern planters—especially those who had been impoverished by the war—were certain to be so moved by the minstrels' recreation of the good old days that they would sit in their seats and cry. Captivated by "dese trufes ob de plantation," northern whites would murmur, "I wish de Almighty had painted me brack as dese brack fellers up dere dat am making all dis music." The promotion also promised to appeal to blacks who had been waiting for years to "get into a rale genuine show, what ain't got no sawdust, nor cheers, nor non of dem white tomfolleries." The cast was composed solely of "rale brack darkies whose granddadies use to lib in Africa among de tigers and elephants." Callender's minstrel spectacular would take them back to the days of their youth. Through the magical mechanism of the stage, the black theatergoer could "be hisself once more and forget dat he eber had any trouble."[198]

So it was that the "forgetting of troubles" continued to be one of minstrelsy's key social functions. Both black and white minstrels adeptly ignored the implications of their characterizations as the country moved toward reconciliation. Instead of challenging prevailing conventions, black minstrelsy reinforced them. The era which black historian Rayford Logan has termed the nadir of Afro-American political life may also have been the zenith of white sociocultural influence upon black artistry.[199]

The drama of this postbellum period also reflected the nation's willingness to compromise on the issue of equality for ex-slaves. During the Civil War, most plays were either pro-South or pro-Union.[200] During the late nineteenth-century era of reconciliation, wartime hostilities were transformed into bilateral testimonials for national unity. Slave characters had an important role to play in these developments — a role remarkably similar to the one which they had played in the wartime southern theater.

As with the literature of the time, the identifying quality for slave characters was loyalty to their white masters. In an 1862 Confederate play titled *The Guerrillas*, a brave servant named Jerry saved his master from the gallows and was rewarded with his freedom. He responded by breaking into tears, moaning and begging: "If you'se tired of old Jerry, jis take him out in de field and shoot him, but don't send him away from you; don't set him free." Here was the prototype for later depictions of slave devotion.[201]

Using the utmost restraint, dramatists of the postwar era avoided sectional bias. Instead, they offered their audiences melodramatic Civil War plays depicting the divided sympathies, mutual valor, and eventual reconciliation of Union and Confederate forces. A recurring formula for developing this theme began with a romance between a northern soldier and a southern belle. Their courtship invariably became a metaphor for the Civil War —"a lover's quarrel"— until the war's end prompted them to "*wed* for good" and join in a union which "*nothing can separate*." The love-smitten Colonel Harvey Brant of William Gillette's *Held by the Enemy* (1886) drew his southern sweetheart into his arms and told her "love has no North or South. . . . Listen, darling — this frightful struggle will be over — *soon — soon!* — Everything will be forgiven and forgotten — everything but the glorious bravery on both sides!" Even less subtle in promoting the reconciliation theme, Bronson Howard's *Shenandoah* (1888), unites *five* pairs of lovers separated by their political sympathies during the war.[202]

As portrayed in the theater, black slaves did not share in the reconciliation because they never waivered in their devotion to southern life or to the cause of the Confederacy. Their loyalties remained undivided before, during, and after the war. Theatrical backdrops for these depictions of Afro-American faithfulness added to the overall effect. When, for example, the curtains parted on opening night at David Belasco's *The Heart of Maryland* (1895), the audience was treated to a marvelously romantic picture of the old plantation:

> *Scene:* Old Colonial homestead with veranda facing road. . . .
> Vines droop over lower corner. . . . A brook runs from R.,
> nearly to C. and disappears among meadows at back. Water
> lilies grow in it and the bank is covered with grasses. An old
> moss-covered, low-pitched rustic bridge crosses stream, over-
> hanging boughs bend over bridge. . . . Effect of lowland lights
> comes from valley at back and sunlight bathes all in a tender
> glow. . . . A soft melody is played at rise of curtain.[203]

For white audiences, whether northern or southern, easygoing and good-natured slave characters contributed an air of quiet cooperation and comic relief to postbellum portraits of the planter's world. Belasco's Uncle Dan'l, for example, was overindulged by his owners and had little use for work. He preferred to eat watermelon and nap in the shade. Even when the Civil War threatened his master's estate, he continued to be preoccupied with visions of ripe melons and unscrupulous melon thieves. Instead of praying for freedom, Uncle Dan'l could only lament, "More sojers am comin'. Lord help the million patch and strengthen them chickens' wings."[204]

Other slaves were characterized as being more concerned for their own-ers' well-being than their own. During the war they continued to be de-voted to the white folks whom they had raised from infancy.[205] As the young southern heroine despaired in *Barbara Frietchie, The Frederick Girl* (1899), her black mammy comforted her with assurances of a Confeder-ate victory:

> *Barbara Frietchie:* Oh, Mammy Lu! Is the fighting over?
> *Mammy Lu:* Yaas, missy, or you wouldn't have cotched dis ole
> niggah woman out! We ain't heard no shots in our house fo'
> dis long time.
> *Barbara Frietchie:* And *we've lost!* [despairingly]
> *Mammy Lu:* Lor' save us, no, honey! Frederick's a Rebel town
> again, bress de Lord![206]

In a play titled *Belle Lamar: An Episode of the Civil War* (1874), a slave character named Uncle Dan is confronted by the contradictions of his Rebel loyalties. Captured while serving as a guide for Confederate troops, he answered a Union soldier's question about freedom with philosophic resignation: "Dunno 'zackly — wot all dat is Curnel," he replied, "an' I guess Uncle Dan is too old to larn."[207]

Other slaves were portrayed as willing to sacrifice their lives for their masters. In Gillette's *Held by the Enemy*, an elderly black slave named Rufus loyally hobbled into Union Army headquarters and offered himself as a substitute for his captured master. He reasoned that since "de law aren't no respecter o' pussons," it was only proper to have "'rangements made so's dat Ah kin be shot unstead o' him." When this request was refused, Rufus tried to bribe the soldier with his life's savings. Rebuffed once again, the elderly slave concluded that not even a Yankee would think the exchange of his life for that of Master Gordon "a fa'r bargin."[208] Such portrayals became the norm in late nineteenth-century theater. Their prevalence and uniformity illustrate the importance of a white American consensus in the reunification of North and South. The spread of proslavery attitudes into northern postwar popular culture reassured whites across the nation that though they may have disagreed intensely about the slave labor system, they were in complete agreement about Anglo-Saxon superiority. The ultimate success of their hidden agenda depended upon sustaining the belief that blacks would accept, indeed wanted, second-class status and continued white supervision. So, on the postbellum American stage, when white characters asked black characters for help, the ex-slaves eagerly answered "Yes. . . . , we's all ready to go whar ebber yo'-alls want us ter go."[209] This was the white hope at the end of the century. This was the heritage of the national experience with slavery and racism.

By 1900 a new form of theater began to amuse urban America. During the first fifteen years of the twentieth century vaudeville circuits thrived as they introduced their audiences to the fascinating world of mind readers, magicians, animal acts, and cornball comedians. Although the developing motion picture industry eventually replaced traveling companies such as Leavitt's Gigantic Vaudeville Stars and Sargent's Great Vaudeville Company, vaudevillian theater was, in its heyday, an immensely popular form of mass entertainment.[210]

Owing a great deal to minstrel comedy, vaudeville gradually absorbed certain of minstrelsy's methods and values as well as a large portion of its national audience. For a time, the two forms of theater differed only in name. Much broader in focus than in earlier years, a minstrel show could now include "The Siamese Twins! The Hindoo Ballet Dancers! The Trick Elephants! The Chinese Giants! The Headless Man!" Sharing the stage with vaudeville's jugglers, bird imitators, puppeteers, and acrobats was a diverse assortment of ethnic impersonators and comedians. Crude burlesques of Irish, Dutch, Jewish, and Afro-American physiognomy, dress, speech, and social customs found favor with audiences who had been weaned on the slapstick minstrel tradition. The new theater was innovative only insofar as it brought new life to old stereotypes.[211]

Although they did not always use black dialect, white entertainers in the early twentieth century continued to use blackface makeup. Some, such as comedian James Francis Dooley, claimed that "blacking up is like putting on a mask"—it hid the performer's nervousness. Other burnt cork comics admitted that blackface was simply a prop to gain audience acceptance. Comedians were sure to be funny if they wore a pair of big shoes, a set of old, ill-fitting clothing, and a few dabs of black makeup. According to one veteran performer, "working in white face demanded a personality which many of the guys didn't have, but when blackened up with a big white mouth they looked funny and got over easier."[212]

Because it pandered to public taste and opinion, vaudeville had little reason to alter stereotypes upon which many of its stock routines were based. Instead, vaudeville writers manipulated existing images of blacks and popularized them within more modern contexts. Thus, as Afro-Americans migrated to the North in increasingly large numbers, Al Jolson blacked up and sang the praises of southern life: "Is it true what they say about Dixie?" he asked. "Does the sun really shine all the time? Do the sweet magnolias blossom at everybody's door? Do the folks keep eating 'possom till they can't eat no more? . . . That's where I belong!"[213]

White performers like Jolson may have hoped to encourage interracial agreement and good will; but their portrayals of blacks lost even minimal contact with reality as long as vaudeville remained loyal to shopworn imagery. Content to entertain their audiences with formulaic and stereotypical characterizations that dated back over a century, vaudeville performers left their patrons ill-prepared for life in a modern, more competitive, multiracial world.[214]

Black performers were trapped within the conservative conventions of theater. Bert Williams and George Walker are two particularly good examples. Billed for a time as "Two Real Coons" in order to distinguish themselves from white comedians in makeup, they dressed as twentieth-century versions of Jim Crow and Dandy Jim. Concealing a strong and healthy body with shabby clothes and slouching posture, Williams played the stereotypical loser—the lazy, dull-witted, uneducated Negro who somehow made everything go wrong. If he "never got nothin' from Nobody" it was because of his own indolence and stupidity.[215]

Dressed in faddish, impractical street clothes, a silk cravat, and gaudy two-toned shoes, singing comedian George Walker played the accompanying role of the Broadway swell. He teamed up with Williams for *In Dahomey* (1902), and he later played Bon Bon Buddy to his partner's Skunkton

Bowser in *Bandanna Land* (1907). His signature song in the latter production blatantly reiterates the theme that blacks would accept second-class status:

> I'm Bon Bon Buddy the Chocolate Drop,
> The Chocolate Drop that's me.
> I've gained no Fame,
> But I'm not ashamed,
> I'm satisfied with my Nick Name,
> I'm Bon Bon Buddy the Chocolate Drop,
> The Chocolate Drop that's me.[216]

Both actors were restricted by the values of their white audience, and their performances reinforced those same values.[217]

Bert Williams complained that playing a stereotyped character was one of the few ways blacks could "get before the public and prove what ability we might possess." With big time show business dominated by white tastes and finances, Afro-American performers sometimes had little choice in what could be considered major career decisions. As Williams told an interviewer during his years with the Ziegfeld Follies, "If I were free to do as I like, I would give both sides of the shiftless darkey, the pathos as well as the fun." Unfortunately, the role of the ignorant, inept black character had become, in George Walker's words, "a race institution."[218]

In the meantime, black America had been nurturing an alternative to the confines of white theater. Using the turn-of-the-century Afro-American musical review as a foundation, the infrastructure of black theater began to rise even before the engaging refrain of "Bon Bon Buddy" faded from memory. Beginning in the early 1890s, productions such as *The Creole Show* (1891), *The Octoroons* (1895), and *Oriental America* (1896) modified the minstrel/vaudeville ethic in several ways. Although similar to previous forms of entertainment, these variety shows made new use of black talent. Afro-American chorus lines and singers began to replace Tambo and Bones. Black stage managers and producers wrote scripts that had structure and thematic continuity. Instead of automatically ending performances with the traditional cakewalk, black singers and actors now entertained their audiences with selections from Faust, Rigoletto, and Carmen.[219] As Will Marion Cook, the musical director and composer of one such musical recalled, these developments were viewed as important milestones in the history and theater of black Americans:

> Negroes were at last on Broadway, and there to stay. Gone was the uff-dah of the minstrel! Gone the Massa Linkum stuff! We

were artists and we were going a long, long way. We had the world on a string tied to a runnin' red-geared wagon on a downhill pull.[220]

Cook's enthusiasm definitely was contagious. Afro-American dramatists of the Harlem Renaissance era celebrated human potential. Their goal was to create a national network of black playwrights, actors, musicians, and dancers who could develop and perform their craft in a supportive atmosphere. They abandoned the effort to please white audiences with demeaning slapstick antics and instead directed their attention to the Afro-American folk tradition and to contemporary issues of black life.[221] Some of the productions took a second look at prevailing images of blacks as slaves.

By 1913, W. E. B. DuBois had adapted his historian's perspective to the needs of black theatergoers. Presented to New York City audiences during the National Emancipation Exposition of that year, DuBois' "The People of Peoples and Their Gifts to Men" was typical of the black history pageants that were to follow. Each of its six acts celebrated a significant contribution which "the eldest and strongest of the races of mankind" had made to world civilization. The pageant transported the audience from Iron Age Africa, to the splendid palaces of the Nile, and to the court of Mansa Musa, Muhammadan king of medieval Mali. Moving to the modern era, the "gifts" of Humiliation, Struggle, and Freedom were then presented. In these tributes to black people of more recent times, the Afro-American fight against institutional slavery took on epic proportions. By the end of the pageant, the forces of Greed, Vice, Luxury, and Cruelty had been defeated. In their place stood symbolic figures of "the Laborer, the Artisan, the Servant of Men, the Merchant, the Inventor, the Musician, the Actor, the Teacher." The enslaved had risen from the "valley of the shadow of death" and had proven that blacks could "bear even the Hell of Christian slavery and live."[222]

Later dramatists added a veritable cavalcade of black heroes and heroines to DuBois' list of historical images. They wrote inspiring portrayals of Phillis Wheatley, Harriet Tubman, Sojourner Truth, and Fannie Jackson Coppin, among others. The biographical accounts celebrated both the past and the future by defining the struggle for freedom as a life-long commitment which could not fail: "Once started, you gotta go on or die – thar ain't gonna be no turnin' back."[223]

The life of abolitionist hero Frederick Douglass proved to be an especially popular subject for plays which focused on the themes of education, perseverance, and racial solidarity. In Georgia Douglas Johnson's *Frederick Douglass* (1935), he was portrayed as a young slave with an unquenchable thirst for knowledge. He scavenged scraps of newspaper from the streets

of Baltimore, dried and pressed the damp, wrinkled sheets, and then cajoled white playmates into helping him learn to read. When asked whether
he had feared for his safety, he replied coolly, "[Whites] caught me an'
nearly killed me many a time. They took all my papers away, but pshaw!
I whirled right around an' found some more an' learned harder than I
ever had."[224]

Dorothy Guinn's *Out of the Dark* (1924) also emphasized the importance of education, but the struggle to gain it, and its application, were
shown to be equally crucial to the cause of human freedom. There were
those born enslaved whose "genius overcame all the shackles laid upon
them by human hands." Douglass had used his hard-won skills so that
modern-day black Americans could use theirs. In turn, according to Guinn,
they should do the same for future generations by learning from his
example:

> If you feel, O men and women, that there are great obstacles to-
> day, think of Frederick Douglass, born a slave in Maryland — he
> who suffered all the worst hardships of that institution, yet who
> after his escape to the North became an ardent fighter for the
> freedom of his people. [225]

Urging their audiences to be "courageous in the midst of dire adversity,"
black dramatists reiterated these history-based themes long after the Harlem Renaissance generation had retired from the stage. In their determination to portray "what it means to be colored in America," black playwrights
of the 1920s and 1930s rejected vaudeville's degrading format. Instead,
they wrote within the tradition of black theater which began with William Wells Brown and Martin Delany. Their conscious attempt to present
material "sincerely and truthfully without recourse to objectionable caricatures and stereotypes" demonstrates their commitment to the self esteem
of the black individual.[226]

Given an open society, adequate financing, and freedom from coercion,
it is conceivable that these determined writers could have significantly
changed white America's perceptions of blacks as slaves. This was not to
be. Transfixed by their culture's past, white playwrights proved to be remarkably resistant to rapid change. If the plantation slave was appearing
less frequently, his formulaic blunders were "still incorporated in the [stage]
negro of the present time." The adaptation of the slave persona to more
modern settings seldom disrupted the continuity of prevailing images. The
inept plantation hand and the self-sacrificing Mammy may have moved
to the city, but they were just as inept and just as self-sacrificing in their
new urban environment. Overall, white theatrical characterizations of Afro-

Americans remained much as they were before the Civil War. By the end of the 1930s, as one critic concluded, "for all of its growing liberal attitude" Broadway remained "entranced with the stereotypes of the exotic primitive, the comic stooge and the tragic mulatto."[227]

As the flickering images of the first kinetoscope travelogues and documentaries metamorphosed into longer and more complex films, woolly-headed, thick-lipped white actors and actresses in blackface roles appeared before the cameras much as they had on the vaudeville stage. By the time of World War I, feature-length films of five reels or more were being distributed through some 17,000 American theaters. The black characters silently continued to fit the pattern of racial inferiority cut centuries before.[228]

During and immediately following the semi-centennial celebration of the end of the Civil War, white filmmakers produced a bevy of nostalgic movies set in the slave era. If the black characters in these films took any action at all, it was almost always to reject Yankee promises of freedom. They loyally embraced slavery as the proper organizing principle of their lives. In *For Massa's Sake* (1911), a devoted chattel was so attached to his master that he volunteered to be sold in order to pay the white man's gambling debts. Luckily, the slaveholder discovered a gold mine and the servant was spared a heart-breaking separation.[229]

In similar fashion, the two-part drama *His Trust* and *His Trust Fulfilled* (1911) focused on an elderly servant who saved his master's family from their burning home and sheltered them in his tiny cabin throughout the war. Willingly, he sacrificed his own meager savings so that young Missy could be properly educated. At the conclusion of the second film, Old George, played by a white actor in blackface, saw that his master's daughter was safely wed to a prosperous English cousin and then turned to his own affairs. As a reward for his long and faithful service, the aged bondsman received the bridegroom's grateful handshake and his master's saber. Back at his cabin, the loyal servant fondled the treasured sword, happy in the realization that he had not betrayed his owner's trust.[230]

White audiences not only accepted such characterizations, they complained about small variations. In response to a film about the Civil War called *The Soldiers Ring* (1911), one viewer in particular felt that a black house servant had shown an intolerably "stiff unwillingness in placing chairs for the Confederate generals." Violations of a racial etiquette dominated by pre-Civil War values were forbidden by the laws of popular taste.[231]

The intensity and direction of whites' attitudes on this issue can be measured by the controversy surrounding David Wark Griffith's *The Birth of a Nation.* In this 1915 melodrama of the Civil War and Reconstruction, Griffith gave new life to proslavery arguments. According to this Kentucky-born son of a former Confederate colonel, free blacks threatened society. They had to be monitored constantly by patriotic organizations like the Ku Klux Klan. In the film, even good slaves could regress into savages. Happy and contented with their lot before the war—dancing, singing, and clowning in the quarters—black people became brutes when denied the advantages of bondage. They made a mockery of southern social customs, political practices, and time-honored moral codes, and thus were capable of destroying treasured American institutions.[232]

D. W. Griffith described his twelve reel, three hour celebration of white supremacy as accurate and impartial. He claimed that the film was based on "an overwhelming compilation of authentic evidence and testimony" and that his version of southern history required "no apology, no defense, no 'explanations.'"[233] Some viewers disagreed.

Although a Los Angeles audience survey suggested that only 23 of some 2,500 viewers objected to the film, less charitable views soon surfaced in other parts of the country. During an early screening at New York City's Liberty Theatre, both blacks and whites demonstrated against the film, claiming that Griffith's production libeled "10,000,000 loyal American Negroes." In Boston protest marchers, stink bombs, rotten eggs, interracial fist fights, and police billy clubs disrupted its premiere. On the national level, the NAACP sent letters to governors of all the states urging them to use their powers to prevent the showing of *The Birth of a Nation*. Concerned that the film would undermine national morale, the *Crisis* cited the tragic case of Edward Manson as an example of the movie's influence. Manson, a black fifteen-year-old high school student, was killed in cold blood by a white man who had just come from a showing of Griffith's interpretation of southern history.[234]

Griffith professed shock at Afro-American protests and attempts at censorship. "I am not now and never have been 'anti-Negro' or 'anti' any other race," he responded. "My attitude towards the Negroes has always been one of affection and brotherly feeling." According to the white filmmaker, to say otherwise would be "like saying I am against children, as they were our children, whom we loved and cared for all our lives." Needless to say, Afro-Americans remained unconvinced and Griffith faced organized black protest against *The Birth of a Nation* for the remainder of his days in show business.[235]

The controversy which enveloped *The Birth of a Nation* encouraged black talent within the motion picture industry to advance their own interpretations. As readers of the *Crisis* were told in December, 1915, even a racist movie could serve a useful purpose if it "jolts the Negro into a campaign of counter publicity." The article urged black Americans to begin a campaign to reeducate whites. "The Negro has a history of which he need not be ashamed," trumpeted the *Crisis*, "but he will wait a long, long time for white men to write this history in all fairness for the consumption of the great white public."[236]

Afro-American writers and producers took advantage of this opportunity in an effort to build a community of filmmakers outside the world of Hollywood convention. They hoped to combat traditional stereotypes by casting Afro-American actors and actresses as detectives, gangsters, cowhands, romantic lovers, and other figures common to the silver screen. By the late 1920s there were at least a dozen small, independent black production companies making full-length features and newsreels for use in inner city cinemas, on black vaudeville circuits, and at once-a-week matinees in "white" theaters. Most of these films were set in the North, within a twentieth-century urban context.[237]

Like their counterparts in the black theater movement, these early filmmakers lacked the capital, equipment, and experience to compete with a well-established film industry that rebuffed their achievements. As silent films gave way to sound, the black production companies' weak financial position left them in a poor position to draw viewers. White attempts to control the inner city market, a lack of bookings in white-owned theaters, and cutthroat competition all contributed to the struggles of the Afro-American film industry. Moreover, as the National Urban League's Elmer Anderson Carter lamented, traditional racial attitudes had proven to be "a tremendous obstacle in the way of those whose creative instincts lead them to see the beauty and pathos in Negro life." By the end of the Depression years, black films for black audiences were being made almost exclusively by whites.[238]

In retrospect, the creation of a black motion picture industry during the 1930s seems hopelessly idealistic. Hollywood casting policies restricted black actors and actresses to a limited number of roles — some forty percent of which were maids and butlers. When not playing domestic servants, black performers were offered roles as dull-witted comics or pagan tribesmen. When a strong black role did surface, the publicity promoted it on the basis of racist stereotyping, rather than on the skill of the actor or grace of the screenplay. The advertisements for Paul Robeson's dynamic portrayal of *The Emperor Jones* (1933) promised that "your heart will beat with the tom-toms at this tragedy of a roaring buck from Harlem, who swapped a pullman porter's cap for a tyrant's crown." Promotional campaigns of this nature placed even the most powerful black performances under the veil of white definition and control.[239]

Throughout the Depression there was little noticeable change in portrayals of blacks as slaves. House servants remained especially obedient and well mannered. In *Jezebel*, a 1938 Warner Brothers film, Uncle Cato was a model of the fully domesticated slave of the Old South. He both knew and accepted his place in American society. On one occasion, a white friend he had known for years offered Uncle Cato a mint julep. Humbly noting that it "ain't hardly proper" for master and slave to share a social drink, Cato left the room so that he could sip his drink in the pantry.[240]

A 1935 Shirley Temple film, *The Littlest Rebel*, featured an equally trustworthy black servant named Uncle Billy (played by Bill "Bojangles" Robinson). His greatest joy was to dance for little Virgie Cary and her friends. The action takes place in the Civil War South, and when little Virgie asks Uncle Billy to explain what the fighting is all about, he stumbles around for an answer and then says: "there's a white man up North who wants to free the slaves." Clearly excluding himself from the group of people who might want to be free, he soon joins his young mistress in a series of impromptu tap dancing fund raisers. The cause is a noble one—to finance a trip north so that Virgie can visit her imprisoned father and plead for his release from a Yankee prison camp. Eventually, the black guardian and his sprightly white ward earn their fare to Washington and convince President Lincoln to pardon the Confederate officer. Thus the loyal servant helps save his master from being shot as a southern spy.[241]

In the 1936 film, *So Red the Rose*, a group of rebellious servants almost revolted in response to the promises of freedom. A deceptive slave named Cato (Clarence Muse) forecast that the arrival of northern troops would herald the beginning of a grand new era of wealth and leisure. "No more plowing," he promised his followers. "No more breaking new ground . . . no more planting . . . no more chopping cotton! Just sittin' in the sun!" The hands drove off horses, scrambled about the chicken coops, lunged for pigs, and shouted boisterously, "I got mine! I got mine!" Concerned that the noise might disturb her critically ill father, plantation mistress Valette Bedford (Margaret Sullavan) took matters into her own hands. She immediately quelled the rebellion by treating one of the ringleaders to a slap across the face and by reminding the bondsmen how well they had been treated in the past. Recalled to their humble duty of upholding the foundations of southern civilization, they abandoned their revelry and resumed their duties. As might be expected, the southern press thought that *So Red the Rose* was, in the words of the Baton Rouge *Morning Advocate*, "probably the best motion picture on the Old South ever to reach the screen."[242]

Such praise paled in comparison to the accolades which greeted the most honored Civil War film of the decade, *Gone With the Wind* (1939). The big screen adaptation of Margaret Mitchell's best-seller was an elaborate and expensive undertaking. Costing nearly $4 million to produce, the almost four-hour drama included 59 actors and actresses, 2,400 extras, 1,100 horses, and 375 pigs, mules, cows, oxen, sheep, and dogs. Filmed largely in the San Fernando Valley and on the grounds of a private estate in Pasadena, boxcar loads of imported dirt and brick dust were used to simulate the reddish soil of Georgia. In order to whet the appetite of the ticket-buying public, highly publicized searches were made to cast the major roles. Producer David O. Selznick even screen tested the Roosevelts' cook, Elizabeth McDuffie, for the role of Scarlett O'Hara's Mammy. The competition for these on-screen parts was so spirited that Margaret Mitchell, at home in Atlanta, was forced to complain about the "people [who] turn up with their colored cooks and butlers and demand that I send them to Hollywood to portray 'Mammy' and 'Uncle Peter.'" After more than two years in production, the film premiered in Atlanta with elaborate hoopla. Within twelve months it had garnered ten Academy Awards and had been seen by some 25 million Americans. By 1943 it had grossed four times as much as its closest competitor, Walt Disney's *Snow White and the Seven Dwarfs*. Reissued seven times since 1939, the epic wartime love story maintained its freshness through conversion to wide-screen, 70 mm projection, the addition of stereophonic sound, and the restoration of its fading Technicolor hues. When first shown on television in 1976, it broke all viewing records for an individual program. In sum, *Gone With the Wind* became an entertainment industry institution.[243]

The movie portrayed blacks in conventional, stereotypical ways, but it did avoid the vicious racism of *The Birth of a Nation*. In part, this was due to a series of prerelease protests launched by the NAACP, the National Urban League, and the National Negro Congress, among others. Their objections eventually led the filmmakers to excise lines such as "Ah nare milked no cow, Miz Scarlett, ah's a house nigguh" and to limit the use of potentially inflammatory scenes involving black attacks upon white women. Despite these changes, the movie received a cool reception from the Afro-American press and was picketed in several cities.[244]

Critics specifically objected to the way in which the film depicted black slaves. As noted by the *Pittsburgh Courier*, many of the bondsmen were portrayed as little more than "happy house servants and unthinking, hapless clods." The scatter-brained Prissy (Butterfly McQueen) was so afraid of Yankees, cannon fire, and "daid folkses," that she became positively immobilized during times of crisis. Aunt "Pittypat" Hamilton's elderly coachman, Uncle Peter (Eddie Anderson), cheerfully performed the duties of his station — carrying white women over mud puddles and defending their honor against Yankee insults. The hulking Big Sam (Everett Brown) proudly served the Confederate cause by digging "de ditches fo' de w'ite gempmums ter hide in w'en de Yankees comes." Pork, played by Oscar Polk, adopted the Rebel cause and beamed at the prospect of receiving a gold watch engraved with the phrase "Well done, good and faithful servant." Even Mammy (Hattie McDaniel), the most dignified and compelling slave character in the film, lacked dimension. Authoritative in her motherly care of Scarlett, she seemed more concerned that her mistress' milk-white shoulders might be "gittin' freckled" than with the welfare of the black community. Black Americans cheered Hattie McDaniel's Best Supporting Actress award in 1940, but they did not necessarily approve of the role she played. To many, *Gone With the Wind* wasted more black talent than it used. It was, as one contemporary observer noted, merely "the LATEST picture in the Hollywood campaign of presenting pictures of the past to conform to the PREJUDICES of the present."[245]

Fortunately, during the 1940s and 1950s it became increasingly clear that the crudest and most vicious stereotypes of blacks were too dated to have relevance in the postwar world. Nevertheless, characterizations of Afro-Americans in post-World War II films continued to be controlled by whites. Hollywood found it exceedingly difficult to break with tradition. As a result, black actors and actresses were cast in a wider variety of roles and historical settings, but black producers found the industry unreceptive. Tough-minded films like *Intruder in the Dust* (1949) and *Home of the Brave* (1949) could be shown alongside modern versions of the idyllic South of slaveholding days. Millions of the nation's children learned about black folklore from the docile Uncle Remus in Walt Disney's often-reissued *Song of the South* (1946). On the eve of the Black Power revolution of the 1960s, it was still necessary to ask, as did Afro-American lyricist Andy Razaf some 25 years earlier: "Are Hollywood producers mindful of their harmful acts, / Or are they just plain ignorant and do not know the facts?"[246]

The motion picture industry apparently had transformed stereotypes of slaves into less obvious versions. The film adaptation of Robert Penn Warren's 1955 novel, *Band of Angels*, for example, starred Sidney Poitier as a vengeful, sometimes militant fugitive slave. Poitier's Rau-Ru was angered both by cruel slaveholders and by light-skinned blacks who would deny their Afro-American ancestry. He wanted to celebrate the beginning of the Civil War by delivering his slave-trading master (Clark Gable) to the Union Army hangman. It was a forgiving heart that beat beneath Rau-Ru's stern exterior, however. When reminded of how the white man had spared him from certain death at the hands of black African slave raiders and of how a kind master had raised, educated, and made him his confidant, Rau-Ru changed his mind and helped the Confederate escape.

At best, *Band of Angels* conveyed the notion that some slaveholders were fair-minded masters like Gable and some were corrupt, immoral, and cruel. By extension then, some black slaves were capable of exercising leadership and good judgment, like Poitier, and others were hot-tempered and unruly.

The combined effect of the opposing images was at worst contradiction, and at best balance. In either case, the opening scene of *Band of Angels* provided a context from which the audience could judge all that followed. As they glanced up from taking their first few nibbles of popcorn, moviegoers witnessed a frantic chase in which slavecatchers and hounds were in hot pursuit of a pair of fugitives headed for Ohio. The bondsmen were caught and returned to their master's Kentucky plantation. There they were met by Massa Starr, the very image of benevolent white power. Confronting the slaves in front of his mansion's colonnade, the white-suited Starr listened patiently as the terrified slaves blamed each other for the escape. Although he pronounced them guilty of breaking the law, Starr tempered his judgment with the reminder that since the offenders were new to his plantation they could not have known he would treat them fairly. Nevertheless, their wrongdoing had to be recognized for what it was — a threat to the established order of southern life. The planter then sentenced the two fugitives to a shift at weeding the plantation cemetery. While in one sense his punishment seemed a gentle one, in another sense it minimized the issue of personal freedom. Once again, this time in film, the combination of images and events suggested that *if* planters were benevolent, then blacks would accept slavery.[247]

In 1959, while viewing what he later termed a "ridiculous version of slavery entitled *Band of Angels*," black novelist John Oliver Killens suddenly burst into laughter. Surely, he thought, such scenes must have been "put into the film for comic relief." Unfortunately, almost one hundred years of public debate had made little impact on the popular culture of America. As the modern Civil Rights Movement gathered momentum, the motion picture industry continued to carry on the traditions of Dixie.[248]

By 1965, Killens had assembled a bitter list of complaints against the filmmaking community. He accused Hollywood of being the most "anti-Negro influence" in twentieth-century America. Moreover, claiming that "the brainwashers have never in history become the unbrainwashers," he asserted that slaveholders would never willingly create free societies. To Killens' mind, white Americans never gave up their role as masters. Instead, they had tried to keep Afro-Americans in "economic, social, sentimental, psychological" slavery by teaching that blacks were innately inferior beings. Hollywood "more than any other institution" created and promoted this image.[249]

Ironically, whites had become slaves to their own brainwashing, according to Killens, since it was clear that Afro-Americans could not accept anything less than total equality. In fact, blacks had a mission to be "the basic folk to free this country." Like the antebellum bondsmen, modern-day black Americans eagerly awaited "the day, the hour, the moment" of freedom.

They refused to wait patiently while whites procrastinated over their fate and over the future course of the nation. After experiencing the long, hot, and violent summers of the late 1960s, many Americans — both black and white — would come to the conclusion that the conflict between American ideals and realities made further procrastination unthinkable.[250]

CHAPTER 5

The Debate Continues, 1965–1980

> You all better get them grins off'n your faces. You think old master's dead, but he just liable not to be.
>
> Loften Mitchell's Mrs. Black in
> *Tell Pharaoh* (1967)

The marriage of the American intellectual community to popular culture was consummated in the late 1960s with an unprecedented level of student activism on college campuses. The social and political values popularized during this era were as much a part of the public education process as classroom lectures. Marches, rallies, and student strikes — they all focused attention on national priorities as a generation of college students demanded public debate. One hundred years after the Civil War, conflict now seemed to be an acknowledged component of American society. The liberal arts college provided both the structure and opportunity for participating in this social revolution and so became an essential ingredient in the movement toward realigning American realities with long-misplaced ideals. The heady aura of the late 1960s left the unmistakable impression that young, vibrant, anti-establishment intellectuals could represent, and in turn influence, popular culture.[1]

At a time when social change was an accepted offspring of higher education, a rapid (and sometimes unwelcome) spread of Black Studies courses became a key component of the unprecedented public response to the King assassination, the urban riots in Watts, Newark, and Detroit, and American involvement in Vietnam. Designed specifically to meet the demand for a new sense of racial justice, such courses sought to expose the historical patterns of American exploitation, violence, and racism.[2] At the same time, Afro-American students began to immerse themselves in a "new blackness." During the last half of the 1960s, a vital segment of black America became totally disillusioned with the goals of integration, abandoned time-honored middle class values, and instead adopted Black Power as a vehicle for spiritual liberation. Northern universities recruiting black students found that they demanded curriculum changes to make studies more relevant to current needs. Even on all-black campuses activists charged that traditional departments had made only token efforts to revise their programs. Since existing academic units seemed either unwilling or unable to respond in a satisfactory manner to insistent demands for a black-oriented curriculum, there seemed no alternative but to create separate Afro-American Studies departments and programs.[3]

Like Martin Delany, William Still, W.E.B. DuBois and other contributors to the record of Afro-American history and culture, Black Studies advocates tried to correct historical misconceptions, to boost black pride, and to further the cause of black solidarity. Unlike their predecessors, the activists, writers, and scholars of the Vietnam War era could champion their views from within the highly visible and purportedly influential American university system. White America could not ignore them any longer. The following commentary outlines the extent to which these upheavals and revelations have influenced popular accounts of blacks as slaves.[4]

Black History Revised

During the late 1960s, black history advocates were given their first real opportunity to prove the validity and worth of their specialty in the country's major institutions of higher education. Nonetheless, it was not a new specialty. The determined efforts of earlier black scholars had already mapped the weaknesses of traditional white-authored texts and monographs, just as they had established the usefulness and purpose of exploring the black past. Contemporary debates over the role of black history in higher education continued to center around issues which were identified initially by previous generations of black historians. Not even the modern emphasis upon Pan-African and interdisciplinary approaches was a wholly new construction.[5]

Following the Civil War, students of black history established historical societies in order to research and preserve their past. Philadelphia's American Negro Historical Society (ANHS) was typical of such groups in that it sought to "collect relics, literature and historical facts relative to the Negro race, illustrating their progress and development" in the United States. Active from the 1890s to the early 1920s, the ANHS sponsored free public lectures, some of which it published in pamphlet form. Papers on various historical topics were read and discussed at monthly meetings. The membership included ministers, journalists, artists, postal clerks, lawyers, a produce dealer, and at least one wood carver. Along with groups such as the Bethel Literary and Historical Association of Washington, D.C., the Negro Society for Historical Research, and the American Negro Academy, the ANHS encouraged lay interest in black history and paved the way for the formation of the Association for the Study of Negro Life and History (ASNLH) in 1915.[6]

Through the devotion and determination of Carter G. Woodson, the second black American to receive a doctorate in history from Harvard University, the ASNLH inaugurated an ambitious program to insure that blacks would "escape the awful fate of becoming a negligible factor in the thought of the world." After most philanthropic funding sources refused to help him, Woodson contracted a $400 debt in order to publish the first issue of the *Journal of Negro History* in 1916.[7] Thereafter, the quarterly served as the major scholarly publication concerned with the black experience. Early volumes contained reprinted documents, brief biographies, studies of developing Afro-American institutions, and commentary upon historically important white friends — and enemies — of reform.

Carter Woodson's involvement in the publication and popularization of black historical studies did not stop with directing Association activities and editing its quarterly. Carefully choosing his words, Woodson once noted that while white publishers "may not be prejudiced," it was obvious that they were "not interested in the Negro."[8] To surmount the distribution problems plaguing black authors, Woodson organized a private corporation called Associated Publishers to spread the black history gospel in book form. A significant number of pioneering monographs on black historical topics were written under the auspices of the Association. Woodson also used ASNLH funds to collect and preserve important manuscript materials, to promote the annual celebration of Negro History Week, and to initiate the publication of the *Negro History Bulletin* in 1937.[9]

For his many accomplishments Carter Woodson earned the title "Father of Black History," but many black scholars during the 1920s and 1930s recognized, respected, and worked to preserve the collective heritage of Afro-Americans. In the years which encompassed the Harlem-centered "New Negro Movement" national awareness and concern grew. According to Afro-American historian Benjamin Brawley, "as never before the Negro began to realize that the ultimate burden of his salvation rested upon himself, and he learned to respect and to depend upon himself accordingly."[10]

Though black Americans attached great importance to their history, the nation's all-white colleges and universities not only ignored black history, they generally overlooked the needs of black students or denied them entrance altogether. The number of Afro-Americans attending college expanded during the 1920s, but most earned their degrees from "historically Negro colleges." At the end of the decade only one black graduate in five would receive his/her baccalaureate degree from a northern school.[11]

There are a number of social and economic reasons for this disparity between black and white educational opportunities. The most telling reason, however, came from a white administrator responding to W. E. B. DuBois' request for information. In a study designed to supplement the findings of *The College-Bred Negro* (1900), DuBois mailed letters to various institutions asking for the names and addresses of their Afro-American graduates, an evaluation of their achievements, and a general estimation of student and administration attitudes toward black students. In his reply, one administrator summarized the situation bluntly: "We have never had any Negro or any person with Negro blood graduate from [this college] in its history. I have not found a student in the state that would tolerate a Negro in the college. And it is even worse since the Johnson-Jeffries fight."[12]

Accepting relatively few black students and employing even fewer Afro-American professors, white colleges saw no need to offer courses in black history.[13] In a 1919 survey of "Negro life and history" as taught in the nation's schools, Carter Woodson concluded that while a handful of northern universities offered courses dealing with various aspects of the "race problem," such classes actually may have fueled racist assumptions. Instead of attempting to "arrive at some understanding as to how the Negro may be improved," investigations into "Modern Race Problems" often "degenerated into a discussion of the race as a menace and the justification of preventative measures inaugurated by the whites."[14]

While northern colleges seemed to assume that knowing more about blacks would do little to solve contemporary social problems, southern schools were even less willing to make changes. As Woodson reported, the colleges of the South proceeded "on the basis that they know too much about the Negro already." Consequently, the curriculum of white southern schools offered even fewer courses on black life and history than did their northern counterparts.[15]

As an alternative to the white-dominated educational process, black colleges could have provided the facilities and support missing elsewhere. Unfortunately, during the early decades of the century, black higher education operated under constraints which inhibited both the ability and the will of educators to campaign for Black Studies. Already severe financial restraints were further taxed by allocations to remedial programs for graduates of substandard secondary schools. Remaining funds more often developed traditional courses than Black Studies curricula because those were the courses which defined the word "educated." Furthermore, white benefactors could not conceive of a liberal arts curriculum for these schools which differed significantly from that offered by northern colleges. In an 1895 address to a group of Atlanta University students, United States Commissioner of Education William T. Harris echoed the feelings of many white educators when he noted: "As our civilization is largely derived from the

Greeks and Romans and as Negroes of America are to share it with the Anglo-Saxons, it is very important that the bright minds among them would get acquainted with it, as other have done, through the study of Latin and Greek." Thus, from their founding, black liberal arts colleges offered a classical education with an emphasis on Greek, Latin, Mathematics, and English literature.[16]

By the 1920s there were some seventy-nine black colleges in the United States. Fisk was recognized as the leading liberal arts school, Tuskegee and Hampton were the most prominent industrial institutes, and Howard the only black multiversity. Prompted by rising confidence and consciousness, Afro-American students began to protest the structure of their education. They rejected white paternalistic leadership and launched disruptive class boycotts to protest strict dress and disciplinary codes, compulsory chapel and ROTC attendance, the prohibition of fraternities and sororities, and the stereotypical use of spirituals at white-attended fund-raising and social events.[17]

Though they moved black colleges toward curriculum changes, the student protests of the 1920s did not trigger a Black Studies revolution. The campus movements were far more concerned about deemphasizing vocational training than they were with black history and culture, and the students feared that their schools undermined integrationist goals. They hoped to join the mainstream of American life fully prepared by the type of quality liberal arts education offered at northern schools. On those campuses where the protests failed to achieve lasting results, students faced the very real possibility that their education would continue to be directed by social and educational conservatives. In the opinion of one keen observer, Langston Hughes, to set foot on such campuses was akin to "going back to mid-Victorian England, or Massachusetts in the days of the witch-burning Puritans." With course content controlled by "old and mossbacked presidents, orthodox ministers or missionary principals," these schools produced graduates who were "spineless Uncle Toms, uninformed, and full of mental and moral evasions."[18]

Some black educators nonetheless saw a way to prepare students for life in white America without diminishing their self-esteem. To Howard University's Kelly Miller, for example, an ideal black curriculum would "embrace those subjects which lead (1) to discipline, (2) to culture, and (3) to a knowledge of the facts and factors of racial life." For educators of Miller's persuasion, the mandate of the Negro college was a broad one. Black schools had to "garner, treasure and nourish group tradition," stimulate black scholarship, and supply "the cultural guidance of the race."[19]

Gradually, as black faculty were trained and hired in increasing numbers, black colleges began to do a better job of acquainting students with their heritage. Carter G. Woodson offered a course on "The Negro in American History" to juniors and seniors at Howard in 1919. During the 1921–22 academic year, Fisk introduced a sociology course entitled "Problems of Negro Life" as well as a class in "Negro Music and Composition." Following a ten week student protest in 1925, black history and literature were added to the Fisk curriculum. By 1931, Tuskegee Institute offered eight courses and West Virginia State College five courses primarily concerned with the black experience. Three years later, a survey of fifty-eight black colleges and universities revealed the existence of over one-hundred courses on black history, literature, and race relations topics.[20]

Despite these gains, black students continued to feel that their educational opportunities suffered from racist assumptions. In a 1930s survey conducted by Fisk University one young professional man reflected upon his educational experiences and complained:

> The curriculum in white schools is planned to meet the needs of the *average white student*. Most Negro schools are mere mimics of the large white schools, woefully failing to take into consideration the economic, social and traditional background of the race. . . . Instead, in the Negro schools too often the professor (a product of some big white school) is content to read off to his classes some notes that he took at Harvard or Yale. As long as such practices are followed Negro youth will continue to be miseducated.[21]

Hobbled by uncertain financial support, staffing problems, and tradition-bound accrediting agencies or state boards of education, black schools tended toward the imitative rather than the innovative in terms of curriculum emphasis.[22]

Seeking to transcend the limitations of their undergraduate education, Afro-Americans attending graduate school acquired credentials which would enable them to accelerate the pace of change. Initially small in number, blacks doing post-graduate work made a determined effort to examine key aspects of black life in their thesis research. Of the sixty-seven who received doctorates in the social sciences to 1943, forty-nine wrote their dissertations on Afro-American topics.[23] They published their work diligently, both in book and article form. As one white scholar noted in 1942: "The Negroes are energetically rewriting the history of the race." Building steadily upon the groundwork of their predecessors, these scholars provided both foundation and inspiration for the Black Studies movement of the late 1960s.[24]

The changes in curriculum and research emphases promoted by black scholars did not go unnoticed by their white colleagues. With renewed interest, white historians took yet another look at the history of black slaves in America. Stanley M. Elkins' *Slavery: A Problem in American Institutional and Intellectual Life* (1959) contributed to an ever more complex understanding of black bondage by expanding upon Kenneth Stampp's teaching that one of the slaveholders' major goals in managing human property was "to make them stand in fear."[25]

Elkins, a historian at Smith College, began his research by questioning certain assumptions held by white liberal scholars of the post-Ulrich Phillips era. Elkins argued that if slavery was as physically and psychologically harsh as the record showed, then it was unlikely slaves could have thought and acted like "free, white Anglo-Saxon Americans." The concept of inherited racial inferiority was "consigned to oblivion," but Elkins felt compelled to identify the specific mechanism which had created the childlike, dependent slave personality described by Phillips. Seeking to study this perplexing question from a new vantage point, he turned from history to psychology in search of answers.[26]

Drawing an analogy between black slavery and the World War II Nazi concentration camp, Elkins suggested that Americans had created a system of oppression so destructive that it left its victims childlike and dependent. Much like Ulrich Phillips' "Sambo," the exasperating but lovable plantation slave typically was "docile but irresponsible, loyal but lazy, humble but chronically given to lying and stealing." Sambo proved that "granted sufficient power you could do terrible things to personality."[27]

Critics of his book charged that Elkins had overdrawn his analogy to concentration camps, and that he consequently underestimated the role of the black community in slave life. The historian answered these criticisms with a countercharge that his detractors expressed "a very American unwillingness to believe that even slavery could really touch the 'inner man'." Revised and reissued in 1968, *Slavery* asserted that "few ethnic groups seem to have been so thoroughly and effectively detached from their prior cultural connections as was the case in the Negro's transit from Africa to North America."[28]

Elkins' interpretation of the role and contribution of the African heritage to American culture did not mesh well with the research agenda of black historians. He had violated three key premises of contemporary Black Studies scholarship: 1) that there is a specifically African contribution to the United States' cultural mix, 2) that a slave folk culture, distinct from Euro-American culture, could and did serve as an effective form of physical and psychological resistance, and 3) that a close study of evidence from slaves themselves was the mandatory starting point for an acceptable treatment of slavery. Therefore, it is understandable why a black historian, Yale

University's John W. Blassingame, decided it was time to provide his colleagues with a history that utilized these assumptions.[29]

As one reviewer pointed out, Stanley Elkins stalked the pages of Blassingame's *The Slave Community* (1972) like a ghost.[30] He took a determined stand on the issues raised in Elkins' work and promoted the view that the Afro-American slave was a multidimensional human being:

> . . . [he] used his wits to escape from work and punishment, preserved his manhood in the quarters, feigned humility, identified with masters and worked industriously only when he was treated humanely, simulated deference, was hostilely submissive and occasionally obstinate, ungovernable, and rebellious.[31]

Some slaves may have seemed docile and childish, admitted Blassingame, but blacks in bondage were adept at masking their true feelings while in the presence of whites. Through a process of feigning ignorance and humility, most managed to avoid internalizing the roles demanded of them by antebellum racial etiquette. In sum, the same range of personality types existed in the quarters as in the Big House. (Elkins responded to Blassingame's assertions by commenting: "If slavery in practice made no more difference than that, perhaps the entire subject of slavery is less important than we thought.")[32]

With Blassingame's approach, the master-slave relationship by itself did not define black behavior. A poor analogue to the death-dealing German concentration camp, the Old South plantation controlled slaves only on a limited basis because they spent a good deal of time free from close scrutiny by whites. Blacks found a variety of role models within their own extended families, and so they were more successful than concentration camp prisoners in escaping the full psychological impact of their oppression. Thus the slaves' struggle for survival could have been difficult without necessarily destroying their African/Afro-American culture. In fact, the black community provided its members with a wide variety of cultural traditions with which they could transcend the most repressive aspects of their captivity.[33]

The Slave Community's findings were based upon slaves' own accounts of their antebellum experiences. Inferring that earlier historians deliberately ignored these sources because "blacks emerge from them as men who survived an inhuman institution," Blassingame claimed that there was no better way to understand the slaves than through their personal records. Instead of rejecting potentially important source materials as too subjective, historians ought to place the black autobiographies alongside the planters' records. Blassingame urged his colleagues to let each account of the slave era stand or fall on its own merits; but first historians must abandon old habits and "consider the testimony of those witnesses our less enlightened predecessors damned to perdition."[34]

Though *The Slave Community* has been criticized for being "too brief and impressionistic" to do justice to its subject, there is no doubt that Blassingame had succeeded in his effort "to bring the slave onto the historical stage to speak for himself." With a new respect for the cautious, scholarly use of the black autobiographies, southern black folk culture, and slave reminiscences, historians sought to meet the challenges posed by Blassingame's work.[35]

Bolstered by the increased availability of slave testimony, Albert Raboteau's *Slave Religion* (1978) and Thomas Webber's *Deep Like the Rivers* (1978) described both the religious and the secular educational mechanisms that blacks utilized to "form and control a world of their own values and definitions."[36] Lawrence Levine's *Black Culture and Black Consciousness* (1977) and Dena Epstein's *Sinful Tunes and Spirituals* (1977) deepened the profession's understanding of Afro-American folk culture and helped to legitimize the use of oral history as a research tool.[37] In his massive *Roll, Jordan, Roll* (1974) Eugene Genovese painted an intriguing portrait of "the world the slaves made," but did not neglect their relationship with the planters.[38] William Van Deburg's *The Slave Drivers* (1979) was the first book to deal wholly with a slave elite while Herbert Gutman's long-awaited study of *The Black Family in Slavery and Freedom* (1976) fleshed out Blassingame's commentary on the family life of the slave quarters community.[39] Even more broadly based texts such as Leslie Howard Owens' *This Species of Property* (1976) and Nathan Huggins' *Black Odyssey* (1977) assumed that Afro-American slaves were "more resilient, less malleable, and less able to live without some sense of cultural cohesion, individual autonomy, and self-worth" than many earlier scholars had maintained.[40]

As the revolution in slavery studies progressed, historians began to apply statistical and econometric techniques to their analyses of the slave system. The most controversial product of this approach was *Time on the Cross: The Economics of American Negro Slavery*. Stanley Elkins grounded his assertions about the slave personality in psychological theory while John Blassingame utilized antebellum black-authored narratives. In 1974, Robert William Fogel and Stanley L. Engerman forwarded a conceptualization of the slave experience based upon quantifiable data.[41] Their stated goal was straightforward: to "correct the perversion of the history of blacks"—to strike down, for all time, the belief that black Americans were "without culture, without achievement, and without development for their first two hundred and fifty years on American soil."[42]

Following an initial series of favorable reviews, *Time on the Cross* was subjected to a withering attack from both black and white critics who branded the book socially unacceptable and methodologically weak. At least one reviewer likened its authors to "perversely self-righteous snake-root salesmen." Charges that the two volume quantitative study was at once vicious, false, and contrived eventually surfaced in disagreements over certain of the historians' key conclusions, the manner in which they arrived at those conclusions, and the way in which the findings were presented to the profession and to the reading public.[43]

As part of a broader effort to reconstruct the history of American economic development on a quantitative basis, *Time on the Cross* claimed to have corrected traditional characterizations of the slave economy. The authors argued that the material conditions of slave life compared favorably with the standard of living attained by contemporary free industrial workers; that the extent of the slaves' exploitation by their owners was much lower than had been presumed by historians such as Stampp and Elkins; and that planters had been remarkably successful in their attempts to mold the slaves into diligent workers by convincing them to adopt the Protestant work ethic and Victorian attitudes toward family life.[44]

For some reviewers, these conclusions were far too similar to those made by Ulrich Phillips to be acceptable. To those who likened Fogel and Engerman to proslavery ideologues it mattered little what methodology had been used to formulate and support such wrongheaded findings. *Time on the Cross* was a portrait of slavery viewed through "the wrong end of the telescope" and written from the vantage point of the masters. As such, it represented a type of achievement-oriented history which tolerated the exploitation of black Horatio Algers by white business entrepreneurs.[45]

For other reviewers, *Time on the Cross* had inadequately and inappropriately adapted a quantitative methodology to the study of the black past. Faulty procedures, imprecision, unrealistic assumptions, persistent bias, and carelessness plagued the authors' conclusions, according to some critics. Said to have been overly zealous and shortsighted, Fogel and Engerman stood accused of failing to meet the essential preconditions for using quantifiable materials in a creative and scientific manner.[46]

The publicity which accompanied the publication of *Time on the Cross* added to the controversy. Unlike most academic books, this study was vigorously promoted. While the mass market audience watched Fogel and Engerman debate black sociologist Kenneth Clark on the "Today" show, history professors found their campus mailboxes bulging with advance review copies and advertisements for the book.[47] These promotional efforts fueled charges that the authors were attempting to intimidate historians not expert in quantitative techniques. As a result of this professional backlash, many historians were encouraged in the belief that *Time on the Cross* portrayed slavery as a far too collegial institution. As one critic noted, before Fogel's and Engerman's benign plantation images, the word "oppression" soon faded away and "the angry slogans of the 1960s on historic black grievances seem strangely beside the point."[48]

Questions surrounding the relationship between black suffering and resiliency proved to be obstacles which no single methodology could overcome. In the case of Fogel and Engerman, many of their conclusions sympathized with efforts to reject images of battered, dispirited, and helpless slaves. *Time on the Cross* seemed nonetheless to heighten contemporary fears that white historians remained eager to deny black America's claims to hardship reparations. For all the controversy, however, slavery studies during the 1970s reached an unprecedented level of consensus regarding the value of interdisciplinary work, black source materials, and the contributions of slaves to southern history, and more generally, to American history. The slave experience came to be viewed as a triumph of the human spirit over adversity.[49] Since both black and white academics could be numbered among those who had reached this same general conclusion, there was hope that the lingering influence of antebellum stereotypes might at last disappear.

High Expectations and Low Art

In literature, the issues of black history surfaced in critics' reactions to William Styron's *The Confessions of Nat Turner* (1967). While white reviewers generally praised the best-selling novel for its accuracy and insight, most black reviewers saw it as yet another example of white America's determination to misrepresent the Afro-American past.[50] The most severe critics labeled *Nat Turner* "an anathema," a "witches' brew of Freudian psychology," a "throwback to the racist writing of the 1930's and 1940's." In an era when civil rights and Black Power advocates campaigned to increase public awareness of racism, the book was seen as an attempt to "escape the judgment of history embodied in Nat Turner and his spiritual sons of the twentieth century."[51]

Styron's version of southern history portrayed Nat Turner as a man victimized by the "madness of nigger existence." The duplicities of slavery demanded that he live "as if straddling two worlds of the mind and spirit." Part of his life was spent "playing always the good nigger a little touched in the head with religion." At other times he fell under the spell of the troubling visions which foreshadowed his insurrection of 1831. Turner was "nearly torn apart by frights and apprehensions," and when the time came to spill white blood, Nat could be seen stealing off "to retch dry spasms in the bushes."[52]

Styron's slave insurrectionist was greatly attracted to a pale belle with auburn hair named Miss Emmeline Turner. The twenty-five year old daughter of his owner was, in Nat's estimation, the most beautiful of all the white ladies who "seemed to float like bubbles in an immaculate effulgence of purity and perfection." He secretly watched and worshipped her, waiting "with a kind of raw hunger" for a moment when she might pause to look up at the sky and "let her fair and slender fingers pass lightly over her damp brow." Unable to control his passions completely, Styron describes Turner stealing away into the woods to masturbate against a tree trunk. According to the Afro-American critics, this aspect of Styron's characterization shifted the novel's focus away from the historical act of insurrection. Instead, the author elevated the southern white woman to a position of central importance in determining black behavior. Such a scenario clearly perpetuated hackneyed racist beliefs and insulted the black community.[53]

Through the imagination of this Pulitzer Prize winning white author, twentieth-century readers also learned that the antebellum slaves were a cowardly and degraded "shit-eating people." Turner described his fellow bondsmen with phrases like "God's mindless outcasts," "Snivelin' black toadeatin' white man's bootlickin' scum," "spiritless and spineless wretches," and "animals" who "deserved to be sold." In case readers might think that Nat Turner had somehow managed to escape such influences, they are assured that he too had been mentally "hamstrung from the moment of [his] first baby-squall on a bare clay floor." Slavery was so effectively oppressive that Styron's hero could be sent into "demented ecstasy" just by imagining himself to be "white as clabber cheese, white, stark white, white as a marble Episcopalian."[54]

Nat Turner lacked sensitivity to the racial climate of the 1960s, but more than this it lacked an awareness of an entire tradition of fictional portrayals just like it. Styron hoped to convince his audience that he had created a unique perspective. The fact that relatively little was known about the 1831 slave conspiracy made it "a wonderful ground for exploration imaginatively." As he explained in a prepublication interview, "the beauty for me of Nat as a subject is the fact that I can use whatever responsible imagination I have trying to create my own myth."[55] In truth, he only updated the longstanding opinion that bold, disruptive slaves were aberrations on the normally peaceful plantation scene. Styron rejected the idea that blacks could have sustained an organized effort to undermine a slave system "unique in its psychological oppressiveness — the worst the world has ever known." The vast majority had been "reduced to the status of children, illiterate, tranquillized, totally defenseless, ciphers and ants."[56]

A second novel about this black folk hero appeared that same year. Daniel Panger's *Ol' Prophet Nat* (1967) generated only a modest amount of attention, though its treatment of Nat Turner was more unique — and far less demeaning — than Styron's portrayal. Panger chose to describe Nat Turner as a man whose internal conflicts represented his struggle to understand and maintain personal values. Though he sometimes despaired, Panger's Turner never abandoned his trust in God. Treating adversity as a test of worthiness, the slave rebel likened himself to ancient Christian martyrs who suffered for their deeply-held beliefs. Like them, he might occasionally question the reason for his continued existence. He might even question the existence of a Supreme Being; but in the end he would leave such doubts and fears behind him and fight the slaves' oppressors with "the Lord on our side."[57]

Unlike Styron's characterization, Panger's Nat Turner was not held spellbound by the daughters of slaveholders. They, too, were responsible for the cruelties he had witnessed and experienced. He swore an oath of vengeance against the planters and "their soft white women," but proclaimed a vow of eternal love to his young black bride.[58] Certainly, few could match her radiant beauty:

> Her rich dark lips were parted, the tips of her flashing teeth catching specks of sunlight. The black curl of her hair looked as soft as that of a frisky lamb. Her broad fine nose seemed to melt into her sunny smile. She was all brown and velvety like a young colt after it rubs against its mother.[59]

In *Ol' Prophet Nat*, Panger characterizes Turner as willing to recognize the destructive psychological consequences of slavery without blaming or ridiculing the slaves. Some may have become like dogs who were whipped too often —"dogs that lick their master's hand, the same hand that held the whip, when that hand gives the beast a piece of meat." He did not condemn blacks for this, however, because it was the master, not the slave, who planted and nurtured the "evil seeds" of self-hate. Turner offered fellow slaves an alternative; he promised to "protect them against any harm, to tell them over and over that everything would be all right, finally to see them settled safely, their liberty secure." They joined his revolt as a statement of their humanity, and though some betrayed him, Turner refused to criticize his comrades. Instead, he maintained that it was "a hard thing to change from a slave to a free man in one night." After all, it took the children of Israel forty years of wandering before they lost "the ways of the slave."[60]

Daniel Panger's *Ol' Prophet Nat* definitely was an improvement over the stereotypical treatment of blacks in white-authored historical fiction, but it did not satisfy the uncompromising and militant demands of Black Power advocates for a wholesale revolution in portrayals of the Afro-American experience. Believing that the descendants of the antebellum slaves continued to be exiled within America and subjected to cruel modern slave codes enforced by "remnants of slave-drivers dressed in cop uniforms," embittered Afro-American writers experienced a sense of *deja vu* during the Black Power era. "Sometimes i get the feeling that i have been here before," wrote Brooklyn poet Mae Jackson, "plantations are still the same / (jails they are now called)." Fearing that the past would repeat itself endlessly, such writers asked themselves whether they actually would have to "shoot the white man dead to free the nigger in his head." As another black poet put it, with the proper mind-set the solution became quite simple: "Tick, tock, toe / Three whiteys in a row / Bang, Bang, Bang."[61]

If Afro-American writers could see little difference between the slave existence and their own, they did visualize a radically different postrevolution world. The Afro-American people would create a new millennial kingdom dedicated to black pride, unity, and freedom. It would contain newly-renamed landmarks such as Huey Newton street, Muhammed Ali square, the city of Marcus Garvey, and the state of Malcolm X. Under the auspices of the millennial kingdom a new approach to education would "rip those dead white people" off the schoolhouse walls, replacing them with a "Black Hall of Fame." Before long there would be "black angels in all the books and a black Christchild in Mary's arms." There would even be black Easter bunnies, black fairies, black santas, black nursery rhymes, and black ice cream. Indeed, a black God would set the world right again by placing control in "the hands of human beings."[62]

In order to erase the influence of white-authored accounts of black life, Afro-American authors sought to "deniggerize" slave portraiture by inspiring their characters with a sense of Black Power. As a result, the antebellum slave communities described in these works reverberated with an infectious spirit of political protest. Distrustful of most whites, the bondsmen reminded one another that there was "no sicha' thing as a good and kindly massa." Like their descendants who lived in modern-day Watts, Newark, or Bedford-Stuyvesant, they often challenged white authority figures. In Afro-American characterizations, slaves were described as so loyal to the black community that even the most dull-witted white man could recognize that "all these black bastards is in cahoots." Brooding, militant, "pure black ain't-been-messed-with, and . . . damn proud of it," they represented the Black Power movement in literature. The authors warned their readers that blacks had been second-class American citizens for far too long. White America could not destroy them when they were enslaved, and blacks would continue to consider a true and final liberation the only possible alternative to racial conflict.[63]

The link between the Afro-American historical experience and contemporary black literature is particularly strong because of the deadly slow pace of change in American race relations. Novelists such as Ernest J. Gaines and Margaret Walker, for example, could bring a unique perspective to their writings on the antebellum era by recalling personal encounters with both white racism and the oral traditions of plantation storytellers.

Gaines, whose *The Autobiography of Miss Jane Pittman* (1971) provided a compelling portrait of black American strength and endurance, could remember working in the fields near New Roads, Louisiana, for the paltry sum of fifty cents per day. It was there that he acquired his understanding of the Negro as America's "peasantry." In later life, after he had moved to California and launched a successful writing career, Gaines told a journalist that his early days were "not too much different from the way things could have been when my ancestors were in slavery." Basing his understanding of black history upon his own youthful experiences as well as upon the oral histories of several generations of southern blacks, Gaines concluded that white writers, coming from outside this tradition, simply didn't "put my people into books the way that I knew them."[64]

In like manner, Margaret Walker anchored her fiction with personal history. Enthralled by the "harrowing tales" of Georgia slave life told by her maternal grandmother, young Walker promised the elderly woman that someday she would write a book about the family's antebellum experiences. After years of sporadic historical and genealogical research, Walker published *Jubilee* in 1966. Like her grandmother, the Jackson State College English professor hoped to "set the record straight where Black people are concerned." As she noted in an interview transcribed during the early 1970s, "I know what the struggle of black people has been. I'm black, and I have been through some terrible stuff."[65]

After Gaines and Walker had prepared the way, a free lance writer named Alex Haley further established black oral history as a reference tool for modern historical fiction. Though he would be accused of creating a romanticized vision of the Afro-American quest for identity, Haley popularized both black history and an image of slaves struggling with social injustice. Possessed by a consuming passion to learn all that he could about a man whom his grandmother called "The African," Haley began a lengthy, detective-like search for the story of his enslaved African ancestor, Kunta Kinte.

Armed with the surviving remnants of Kinte's story and a few unfamiliar African words, Haley supplemented his knowledge of the family's history through research in archival sources and conferences with specialists in African linguistics and oral history. Eventually, during a crucial meeting with an elderly griot in a small West African village, he uncovered his family's tie to the ancestral lineage of the Kinte clan of Juffure, The Gambia. From this base of genealogical information, Haley wrote *Roots* (1976), a best-selling novel that tried to give readers the "feeling of what slavery had been." Billed as "the saga of a people," the book became a chronicle of inspiration and vicarious wish fulfillment for black Americans less able to spare the time, effort, and money needed for extensive genealogical research. According to Haley, although slavery had stolen from blacks "all insight into what they had been," now, because of *Roots*, "many could adopt his family patriarch as their family patriarch. During the mid-1970s, Haley's Kunta Kinte became the black American's "symbolic . . . ancestor out of Africa."[66]

Haley's novel reaffirmed the proud and militant spirit of blackness which defined the Black Power movement. As described in one literary commentary, Haley's ancestors were "winners to a man." By contrast, whites often were perceived by *Roots'* black characters as inhuman, or subhuman, bogeymen. Echoing Gaines and Walker, Alex Haley claimed that only "a real black man, a man who knows what it is to be black" could have written *Roots*. Pressing the point of historical truth even further, he held that to the best of his knowledge, "every statement in *Roots* is accurate in terms of authenticity."[67]

A predominantly white group of critics challenged the black author's claims to accuracy with charges that "on page after page there are factual errors as well as distortions." In addition to uncovering flaws in his description of southern crop patterns, slave prices, and plantation size, critics berated Haley for creating a "romance of African history." *Roots* created the illusion of "a lost Eden" to which, in the fifteenth century, "Satan came in the guise of a white man." Most critical to this debate were the accusations leveled by British reporter Mark Ottaway. In a copyrighted article written for the *Sunday Times*, Ottaway suggested that Haley had been misled by the elderly Gambian griot—"a man of notorious unreliability who knew in advance what Haley wanted to hear." According to Ottaway, who had researched the Kunta Kinte story in Gambia, Haley had come up short in his attempt to link his African and Afro-American ancestors. Although appealing simultaneously to "the black American quest for identity and to white American guilt," the factual basis of the *Roots* story was said to be "more tenuous than anyone had thought."[68]

Beset by Ottaway's charges as well as by a series of plagiarism suits, Haley lamented the fact that Afro-Americans could not yet reconstruct and popularize a worthy account of their ancestral heritage "without someone taking a cheap shot to torpedo it." In the estimation of Haley and

his supporters, black Americans of the 1970s needed "a place called Eden
. . . a Pilgrim's Rock" upon which to build their future in the United States.
Unfortunately, critics who continued to "demean anything Black people
have to say about the slavery experience" frustrated their efforts to reclaim
black history and prolonged the black/white impasse on slave imagery.
As Haley noted in a 1977 interview with his nemesis, Mark Ottaway, "You
have your interpretation of history. I have mine."[69]

Not all black novelists have shared Haley's perspectives in equal measure. For example, the early popular fiction of Georgia-born Afro-American
novelist Frank Yerby contains descriptions of slaves who dearly loved their
owners, bragged about their own selling prices, preferred white lovers to
black, betrayed attempts at insurrection, and admitted that they "weren't
ready" to govern themselves in the postbellum world. Although his earliest works were said to offer "noteworthy departures" from the stereotypes
seen in conventional white-authored historical fiction, it wasn't until he
created the Dahomean slave hero of *A Darkness at Ingraham's Crest* (1979)
that Yerby addressed the more militant demands of the times.[70]

On the surface, Frank Yerby seemed somewhat ill-suited to the task of
upholding the Black Power perspective in American literature. His career
as the "prince of pulpsters" began with the publication of the best-selling
The Foxes of Harrow in 1946 and grew with the subsequent publication
of more than twenty other escapist novels set in various historical periods.
Over 25 million copies of these books have been sold, making Yerby by
some estimates the wealthiest black writer in history.[71]

Thinking of himself as an entertainer rather than a preacher or a teacher,
Yerby appeared to be unmoved by critics who argued that, lacking a "social function," black fiction was at its best trivial, and at its worst dangerous to the goals of Afro-American liberation. "Look," he told an interviewer
in 1975, "if your only theme is 'Oh, God, I'm Black and look how badly
they treat me,' people get tired of that. . . . I have an audience of utter,
nasty bigots. Great art demands great audiences, that's very clear. You give
me a great audience and I'll produce the great art." Claiming to be proud
of his race, but refusing to "flaunt it," Yerby criticized the Black Power movement for its use of Afro-American literature as "apologetics." He believed
that Black Studies departments were created by black students who "found
the ordinary going in a university too difficult and wanted something they
could get through more easily."[72]

Given his position on these issues, it is not surprising to find that Yerby's early novels possessed relatively little of what he termed "the tendency
to defend." As a result, many of his African and Afro-American characters
were anything but heroic role models. In the introduction to *The Dahomean* (1971), he stated his position clearly by saying that he refused to

make the black characters "either more or less than what they were." On the other hand, Yerby's plantation fiction contained very few good slave-holders. Instead, these whites were only a generation removed from the avaricious adventurers, criminals, and misfits who had first settled and exploited the South. It was a region "about which more lies have been solemnly told and believed than any other comparable section of earth." The planters' uneducated and foul-mouthed abuse of the English language was matched by living quarters only "one cut above a dogtrot cabin." He told readers of *The Dahomean* that he wrote such characterizations "to correct, so far as it is possible, the Anglo-Saxon reader's historical perspective."[73]

Although Yerby's early work did contain examples of rebellious bondsmen, in general he portrayed broken slaves.[74] Controlled by uncouth and sometimes brutal slaveholders they had been reduced from proud, industrious, warlike peoples of West Africa to "the state of tortured, neurotic, self-hating caricatures of humanity." Indeed, his definitions of "slaves" and of "men" often appeared to be mutually exclusive. At times, Yerby's conviction that complacent antebellum blacks made "such good slaves" appeared out of step with trends in black-authored slave portraiture. Nevertheless, with the publication of *A Darkness at Ingraham's Crest* Yerby initiated a reconciliation with the muse of Black Power.[75]

The chief character of *Ingraham's Crest* was Hwesu/Wesley Parks, an enslaved governor of the Dahomean province of Alladah. According to Yerby, this fearless, strong, and tall leader "was not a nigger and a thing," but rather "an African and—a man." Yerby's slave hero had lost none of his proud bearing in the Atlantic crossing. As one white character said, he never did "*anything* niggerish." He just stood there, "smiling a little or not a-tall, enwrapped in a dignity so visible it's like a Roman Senator's toga." Whites viewed him as a threat because he considered their race to be composed of inferior, "foolish children." Recognizing his fierce pride and unquenchable self-confidence, the slaveholders saw in Parks the weakness of their claims to superiority.[76]

With the help of *Tau Vudun,* or ancestor gods, Yerby's slave hero worked the sorcerer's art on white people. Gifted with an ability to see into the future, Parks could also "project thoughts, ideas, dreams—from miles away—into other people's heads." His most amazing power, though, turned his white adversaries into puppets. Through mind control, he could strike enemies dumb or freeze them in their tracks. He could stop a slaveholder's whip and if he tried hard enough, he even could make it rain. Like a black, caped, comic book crusader, the clever slave performed these "Voodoo tricks," as the whites called them, and then simply took "a quick sidewise dancing step—and merged with the night." Since he was confident that his hypnotic powers were more than a match for his weak opponents, the exiled African ruler frowned on killing and preferred to shame and humiliate his oppressors. If, in Yerby's novel, revolutionary militancy did not exactly spring from the masses of oppressed slaves, the masses were at least favored by having within their midst the most incredible representative of Black Power ever to appear in American historical fiction.[77]

Whatever the shortcomings of Frank Yerby's early characterizations of black slaves, they seem relatively inoffensive when compared to those of the Falconhurst series. The basic concern of these novels was to detail the patterns of sadistic sex, nymphomania, incest, and general promiscuity that prevailed on a fictional slave-breeding plantation. Written by white novelists — Kyle Onstott, Lance Horner, and Harry Whittington — the series began in 1957 with the publication of Onstott's *Mandingo* and continues through *Scandal of Falconhurst* (1980). More than this, the Falconhurst books have set the standard for dozens of other sex and slavery novels.[78]

None of the three contributors to the series could be considered knowledgeable about the black experience. Onstott, who was 70 years old when *Mandingo* was published, had spent most of his adult life in California judging dog shows and writing books on dog breeding. Claiming that he had always been "horrified and strangely drawn to slavery," he spent five years writing the first of the series that was to sell over 16 million copies by the mid-1970s.[79] According to his son, Onstott considered his work unworthy of a second glance:

> My father's method of writing was to put a Ouiji board on his lap and then he'd get a box of big white paper and a box of soft pencils. He didn't bother with things like paragraphs, chapters or page numbers. While he'd write, he'd just drop the pages on the floor. Then I'd come home, gather the pages and put in paragraphs, number the pages, and try to edit. He hated to go back over what he had written. He'd say to me: "You don't expect me to return to my vomit, do you?"[80]

The second and third contributors to the series may have worked more systematically, but they were just as estranged from the Afro-American folk tradition. Lance Horner, in his spare time, churned out fourteen long novels in approximately fifteen years.[81] After both Onstott and Horner died, the Falconhurst series was continued by Harry Whittington. Writing under various pseudonyms, this short story writer and novelist has authored the last two Falconhurst books as well as a number of novelettes for *Male, Stag,* and *Adam* magazines. His non-Falconhurst works include *Sailors Weekend* (1952), *Backwoods Hussy* (1952), *Wild Oats* (1953), and *Desire in the Dust* (1955).[82]

The Falconhurst novels reveled in white sexual exploitation of black slaves. White men had the power to honor a black woman simply by bedding her. Though she could never be too young for this, she was always ready and passionately willing. White women, in turn, rejected sex with white men in favor of the well-endowed virility of young black males. The slaves took pride in their qualities as breeding stock and dreamt constantly and restlessly of their next opportunity to demonstrate their skills. Black women and black men slept together without love and willingly switched partners on orders from their owners.[83]

Even when compared to the incredibly degenerate white residents, most of the African-Americans at Falconhurst appeared savage and subhuman. Slaves enjoyed viewing and even participating in disciplinary whippings and castrations because the sight of suffering satisfied the "sadistic impulses in their African background." They "ate like hogs," "coupled like goats," and sang "primitive" obscene folk songs while they worked.[84]

At Falconhurst, blacks and whites came together only through their degradation. After comparing these images with those proud, noble, even superhuman slave heroes created by contemporary black novelists, one can only wonder how contemporary Euro-Americans view their Afro-American neighbors. There is no doubt, however, that blacks and whites have critically different visions of the realities of slave life. This persistent gap is modern evidence of sociocultural distinctions made long before twentieth-century writers traded claims of historical accuracy, literary license, and racial superiority.

The Hollywood Whitewash

The popular culture arenas of stage, screen, and television had never been particularly responsive to charges of racism, but the threatening pronouncements of the Black Power era did have some impact. Afro-American playwrights, producers, directors, actors and actresses of this era renewed their vow to drive "'Uncle Tom' and all that he connotes" from the nation's theaters. That this effort ultimately fell short of achieving its stated goal is testimony to the fundamental conservatism of American mass entertainment.[85]

The antipathy which advocates of the "new blackness" felt toward white America is the theme of Herbert Stokes' *The Uncle Toms* (1968). In this community theater production, two groups of Afro-American youths become involved in a street corner confrontation over the meaning of black brotherhood. The first group, children of janitors and laundresses employed by whites, dislike their own skin color and ridicule members of the second group for refusing to love or to respect white people. Recognizing that these young men need an education in "blackness," the more militant group tries to convince them that "we are all black brothers and we must stick together." The first group eventually abandons their belief that "the white man is the only person that can teach or tell us anything." "We have been very stupid," they confess, "our eyes have been closed for a long time." Henceforth, they would consider themselves to be black in both mind and body. Vowing to drive the pale-skinned oppressors "off our planet," both groups then shake hands and proclaim undying loyalty to the Black Power brotherhood.[86]

Slaves portrayed in the Afro-American Revolutionary Theater of the late 1960s were equally determined to seek out and redeem any Uncle Tom in their midst. They succeeded most of the time with a scenario that removes any doubt about the need for militancy. Over a century after the Civil War, Black Power advocates decided it was time to form a united front from which to accuse and attack white America. They wrote for a "theatre of Victims," viewing the past through the victims' eyes and encouraging the suffering masses of today to recognize their collective strength. Moreover, according to playwright LeRoi Jones (Imamu Amiri Baraka), the Afro-American Revolutionary Theater could "help in the slaughter of these dim-witted fat bellied white guys who somehow believe that the rest of the world is here for them to slobber on." The slave characters created by such writers served as footsoldiers in this twentieth-century crusade to radicalize black America and liberate its people both from the integrationist ethic and from white sociocultural domination.[87]

In the drama of the Black Revolutionary Theater, acquiescent slaves were a corrupt form of humanity created and nurtured by whites. Some were handpicked in the West African slave markets. These "beaten men" already had been defeated by black warlords who would "kill anyone who tries to take from them what is theirs." Others became docile because of the pressing brutality of white owners who kept them mired in mental and physical filth, misery, and degradation. These individuals lived in a hat-in-hand existence, betraying slave revolts and chirping to their masters that the slave life made them "happy as a brand new monkey ass." The descendants of these slaves were said to be the elitist, pinstripe-suited, non-violent preachers of the Civil Rights Movement. According to the militant playwrights of the Black Power era, such individuals either would convert or be killed as the long-awaited revolution swept through black America.[88]

Some of the slave characters created by these dramatists had thrown off their mental shackles and converted to militancy even before the chant of "Rise, Rise, Rise/Cut these ties,/Black Man Rise" echoed through the quarters. Others, like the docile Billy in Clifford Mason's *Gabriel* (1968), had to be shamed or physically shaken into joining the cause. Militant slave leaders believed that to have a black skin and not regard slavery as "the sin of the world" was itself a greater sin. As Mason's Gabriel says, "When I think of how the white man has made me hate myself and believe that he's everything that's good and wise and noble, then I know what being a slave really means." This realization was the essential first step toward physical rebellion against the white man's authority.[89]

The rebellions described in these Revolutionary Theater productions were highly charged, bloody confrontations that joined the overt, militant actions of *the people* to the covert strategies of a slave leadership elite. The formerly complacent masses revealed their true spirit by burning plantations, celebrating their master's death as if it were a joyous holiday, and banding together in Union Army blue to destroy the Confederacy. With this new level of commitment it no longer would be enough to die a hero: "Die proud," fumed Gabriel, "And what good is that to anybody? The idea is to win, not to die proud."[90]

Black playwrights of the late 1960s portrayed slave heroes who roamed through time and space, caring deeply about and relating on a personal level to the "nightmarish pain" of the Afro-American people. Members of a self-proclaimed "fantastic race," they struggled for their own freedom and for the freedom of "house slaves and field hands and thousands of others." They fought for "all of Africa that never struck for itself" and they fought so that slave youngsters could grow up to be proud adults. As militant blacks were "getting smashed and bashed but fighting back," they taught by example that the future of the nation could be shaped by the actions of its people.[91]

Although it would "take all the people together to make any real change" in the American system of racial exploitation, the prospects were so glorious that no one would be able to resist joining the revolution. A victory of black over white would turn the entire world topsy-turvy—blacks would judge their former oppressors in the nation's highest courts and afterwards enjoy refreshments served by "little white boys whose fathers will be hanging from the nearest trees." In such a world all things would be new. After destroying the white devil "like a slaughtered hog," a proud, vibrant black civilization would flourish.[92]

In the insurrectionist's dream, the only acceptable goal was total revolution. Less militant tactics or less sweeping goals undermined and compromised the whole effort. To the dramatists of Black Power, black acquiescence and white domination were either temporary or terminal conditions. Thus, on the straight and narrow road to liberation, slave heroes issued the ultimate threat: "I'll kill you. I'll kill you all. Oh, it's the only way. It's all that's left. It's got to happen someday."[93]

The movies and television programs which appeared during the heyday of Black Power drama obviously continued to stereotype blacks, seemingly unaware of the revolution taking place in black theater. The militant spirit of Black Power found its way into movies and television, to be sure, but primarily in characterizations that tacitly endorsed traditional stereotypes.

One exception to Hollywood's continued conservatism, *The Scalphunters* (1968), focused on Joseph Winfield Lee, a fugitive slave played by veteran actor Ossie Davis. In this Black Power era film, the central character rejected the ambiguities of traditional slave portrayals. There was no question about the ideology guiding Joseph Lee. The Louisiana fugitive challenged white authority with a slyness and sass that radiated the modern spirit of "blackness." The level-headed Lee manipulated whites whenever he could, and if this didn't work he shed his usual reserve for a fist fight — all the while demanding that he be called *Mister* Lee.[94]

Because he had worked for well-educated white southerners, Joseph Lee could read and write. He knew the Latin names of most desert plants and was familiar with the major characters of ancient history. Beyond the question of literacy, Lee believed that whites lacked the grit and tenacity which enabled black people to survive slavery. In one of many arguments with his chief antagonist, trapper Joe Bass (Burt Lancaster), he revealed his true estimation of white manhood by declaring, "You know how long you'd last as a colored man — about one minute!" Bass eventually seems to agree with him. After the pair survive a series of frontier adventures, the white trapper develops a begrudging respect for the fugitive's survival skills: "Throw you in the pig pen and you come out Vice President of the hogs."[95]

Ossie Davis was soon cast again as a slave — this time flogged to death in the movie version of John Oliver Killens' *Slaves* (1969). Although filmed on location at two northern Louisiana plantations, this small budget melodrama was peppered with incongruous references to contemporary racial consciousness. Director Herbert Biberman constructed an Old South in which slaveholders spouted black history, adorned their mansions with African art — and drove the slaves to revolt through inhumane treatment.[96]

In *Slaves*, plantation workers put their thoughts on the evils of slavery and the nature of black discontent into music. The score for the film described the hands "singin' 'bout the Jubilo" because "when your baby's born a slave the cradle is her grave and all she'll ever know is the white man reap what the black man sow." Nevertheless, even though whites treated their human property like animals, the slaves recognized their own self-worth. As the title song declared, "I'm a man, ain't no boy. I'm a man. I'm a man. I'm a man. I ain't no slave either. Lord, I'm a man!" Dionne Warwick, who played a mulatto mistress in the film, considered *Slaves* to be a pioneering statement of affirmation for the Afro-American perspective.[97]

Most of the next decade's message films, if they dealt with the subject of slavery at all, tended either to be comedic satire (*Skin Game,* 1971), western gunfighting adventure (*The Legend of Nigger Charley,* 1972, and *The Soul of Nigger Charley,* 1973), or sexual titillation (*Mandingo,* 1975, and *Drum,* 1976).[98] For a 1970s view of the antebellum South, connoisseurs of plantation films had to turn on the television. During this era, the largest and most influential entertainment medium in the country confronted the Afro-American past reluctantly. When this conservative force met head-on with the social demands of the era, sparks flew as critics debated the accuracy of competing plantation images.

Like many of their motion picture counterparts, black television entertainers of the 1950s and early 1960s found that they were most likely to be cast as domestics, comics, or as musical guests on variety shows hosted by Arthur Godfrey, Ed Sullivan, or Milton Berle. In 1962, a survey of black appearances on prime-time television spanning a two-week period revealed that no blacks appeared in 309 of 398 half-hour units of programming. Of the remaining units that did contain blacks as cast members, about one-third featured Afro-Americans as singers, dancers, or musicians. They appeared next most often in documentary and hard news shows. Despite pioneering but shortlived variety series hosted by singers Nat "King" Cole (1957) and Sammy Davis, Jr. (1966), the on-screen impact of Afro-American entertainers remained mimimal throughout most of the sixties.[99]

As in other areas of American society, the racial turmoil of the late 1960s encouraged network directors to rethink their casting policies. Citing the medium for its failure to "portray the Negro as a matter of routine and in the context of the total society," the National Advisory Commission on Civil Disorders criticized television executives for contributing to the division of the nation into "two societies, one black, one white—separate and unequal." The networks responded with castings that included Greg Morris on "Mission: Impossible," Bill Cosby on "I Spy," Gail Fisher on "Mannix," and Clarence Williams III on "Mod Squad."[100]

Among others affected, veteran actress Ruby Dee recognized that these changes did not necessarily represent a lasting commitment to black representation on television. "We are the most commodity-conscious nation in the world," she remarked in 1968. "The Black man is the commodity this year. If Black people sell, they'll be back. If they don't, they won't." Thus, with white awareness of black society at an all-time high, Afro-American roles increased dramatically during the late 1960s. The continued "sale" of these characters depended heavily upon whites' viewing tastes, the growth of black consumers' buying power, and ultimately, upon programming decisions of network executives. As one such executive at ABC noted in 1979, "We must be able to get an audience to a show and then be able to keep it there. It's all commerce."[101]

Successful commercial television depended on the expertise and savvy of marketing executives, and the popularity of any individual program owed a great deal to the skill and perception of its writers, producers, casting directors, and technicians. These behind-the-scenes figures often were as important as the on-screen cast in determining whether a new series or a special won an audience. During the 1965–1980 period these key managerial positions were monopolized by whites who had, at best, tenuous connections with the real-world black experience. Those who lived and worked in the West Coast film colony faced additional problems of geographic and social class insularity.[102]

Afro-American advocacy groups such as the National Black Media Coalition have been consistent in their critiques of the entertainment programming produced in this environment. Citing as evidence the industry's long-term emphasis upon formulaic situation comedies as opposed to any realistic black-oriented dramatic series, they complain that the basic problem has been access. As noted by stage and film actor Brock Peters, "Until blacks can fully participate in those productions we will not get the quality scripts that realistically portray our lifestyle and culture and contributions to this society." Even when the necessity of black participation seems most obvious, television's conservative influence has left black critics dissatisfied.[103]

Historical dramatizations such as "The Autobiography of Miss Jane Pittman" (1974), "Roots" (1977), and "A Woman Called Moses" (1978) brought acclaim to their black cast members and stirred new interest both in Afro-American history and in the works of historical fiction upon which they were based. However, "A Woman Called Moses," NBC's four hour dramatization of Harriet Tubman's life, was said to have suffered from an intrusive white presence. Critics likened Orson Welles' scene-setting narration to that of a television announcer "auditioning to play the Almighty." His portentous introductions made Cicely Tyson's Tubman appear "otherworldly and unreal — presumably to excuse the kind of woman she was."[104]

In similar fashion, the television version of *Jane Pittman* "whitewashed and thereby diminished" the impact of Ernest J. Gaines's story. Unlike the original, Tracy Keenan Wynn's screenplay included a white narrator who had "absolutely . . . no business being there." This uninvited intrusion into black history was thought to be "tantamount to rape." His presence served as a telling reminder that "the white oppressor still has an overseer mentality." The television industry had, in effect, refused to let a black artist tell the story. Since the norms of the mass media were distinguished only by their "racism and artistic mediocrity," this decision seemed particularly unsettling.[105]

The assertion that television interpretations of slave culture were filtered through a "white lens" surfaced again during the airing of television's biggest Old South blockbuster, "Roots." Filmed on location in Georgia and California prior to (but not released until after) the publication of Alex Haley's family history, this version of *Roots* was an immediate hit. The first episode of the twelve hour mini-series was the sixth most popular show in television history. The final episode on January 30, 1977, attracted almost ninety million viewers, surpassing *Gone With the Wind* and eleven Super Bowl telecasts as the highest rated show of all time. By the end of "Roots Week," ABC announced that a record 130 million Americans, representing eighty-five percent of all TV-equipped homes, had watched at least part of the series.[106]

The television adaptation of Haley's book cost $6 million and generated many times more than that in commercial spin-offs. The tremendous success of both the book and the mini-series inspired entrepreneurs to offer "Mandinka Maiden" T-shirts and plaques, mail-order "Root Tracing Kits" complete with imitation parchment genealogical charts, and newly-recorded "Roots music." This last product line celebrated sentiments such as "Africa's our homeland, our man is fit to test. / Though life is hard, the warrior's life is best"; and " . . . 'stead of bein' a nigga in Carolina, rather be a free man in Hell."[107]

Once unleashed, the "Roots" phenomenon spread rapidly into still other areas of American sociocultural life. Over a half million high schools were provided with supplementary materials on the series by the National Education Association. Over two hundred colleges were said to be giving academic credit to those who watched the show. A public opinion poll conducted after the series aired revealed that Alex Haley, a stocky, fifty-six-year-old writer, had become the third most admired black man in America among Afro-American youth — surpassed only by boxer Muhammad Ali and Motown singer Stevie Wonder. Confronted with this wide-ranging assault on the hearts, minds, and wallets of the nation, commentators on popular culture began to ask an important question — Why *this* show?[108]

Explanations for the cross-cultural popularity of "Roots" ranged from the suggestion that it celebrated patriotic values to the hypothesis that television had finally discovered its multi-ethnic audience. Perhaps there was a subconscious need for a highly mobile, technologically oriented people to find "rootedness in their pasts and security in their families." It could have been that the Vietnam and Watergate debacles were causing Americans to reach out, like Kunta Kinte, for a more stable, more worthy national identity. Overall, the greatest attractiveness of the mini-series may have been, as suggested by historian Benjamin Quarles, "the threat of violence, the appeal of sex, all building up to a wonderful climax — all the things that make for good television."[109]

Quarles' theory raised more complex questions. How faithful was this television program to black history? How had it changed from Haley's original? To one group of "Roots" critics, the answers were obvious. The show had become popular among whites because of the alterations and distortions made to please them. In the view of black psychiatrist Dr. Frances Welsing, those who read Haley's book and those who saw the televised version "were given two entirely different images." The book unambiguously celebrated black culture, but, according to Welsing, "there was something missing in the black images presented on television."[110]

The critics charged that compromises resulted from a partial substitution of white for black perspectives on the African/Afro-American past. Complaints about everything from the opening statement—that the Haley family history had begun in "primitive Africa"—to the length and polish of Kizzy's (played by Leslie Uggams) nails began in the belief that the series was "contrived, commercialized and romanticized." Striving to create entertainment "that informed, that got a big audience and made a lot of money," executive producer David L. Wolper admitted that he "wasn't even trying to appeal to blacks." He knew that his potential audience was ninety percent nonblack so he tried to "reach the maximum white audience" by casting, with Haley's approval, well-known white actors and actresses in roles that barely existed in the original version of Kunta Kinte's story.[111]

Performers like Robert Reed, who was best known as a good father on the comedy series, "The Brady Bunch," or Ralph Waite of "The Waltons," or Ed Asner of "The Mary Tyler Moore Show" and "Lou Grant" were difficult to perceive as slave-traders and slaveholders because of their family-oriented images. Others, like football great O. J. Simpson and "Mission: Impossible" beauty Lynda Day George, seem to have been employed principally for their commercial appeal. In this respect, *Roots* was, as the critics contended, flagrantly dissected and reassembled.[112]

Nevertheless, enough of the book's "blackness" survived the passage through Hollywood's gauntlet of white screenwriters, directors, and casting heads to anger a significant number of critics.[113] This predominantly white group of prime-time reviewers blasted the series for magnifying "the extraordinarily lopsided nature of Haley's story." Critical of black characters who constantly wore "their machismo on their sleeves" and offended that antebellum whites were portrayed as "cruel, inhuman, immoral, pretentiously mannered, inured to human suffering, calloused in their emotions, obsessed with property and propriety and order," these commentators barely suppressed their anger over reports that the show had spawned minor racial disturbances in several cities.[114]

To the National Urban League's Vernon Jordan, the historical drama was "the single most spectacular educational experience in race relations in

America"; but in the eyes of William Loeb, outspoken publisher of the *Union Leader,* it was "a pinko plot to make white Americans feel so much guilt and shame that they would accept the Soviet takeover of Africa." Alex Haley defended the telefilm with stories of blacks who wrote him to say, "thank you for giving us our history" and of whites who praised the show, saying, "I didn't know; I never knew." William Styron called it "dishonest tripe"; Nancy Reagan felt that the series was "inflammatory"; and David Duke, Grand Wizard of the Ku Klux Klan, proposed filming an eight-part Reconstruction documentary that would counteract a "vicious malignment of the white population in America." If nothing else, this national debate over the ABC telecast discouraged illusions about the imminent disappearance of longstanding divisions within American society.[115]

The broadcast of a made-for-TV movie called "Beulah Land" (1980) confirmed black critics' doubts about the industry's sensitivity to racial issues. This three part NBC mini-series was based on a novel by the same name that originally had been billed as "*Gone With the Wind,* with sex!"[116] Written by a white Georgia novelist, Lonnie Coleman, and first published in 1973, the adaptation of Coleman's book for television was controversial almost from the beginning. By the time the first segment aired on October 7, 1980, the television movie had become the center of a recall campaign designed to prevent its appearance. Opponents described it as "an imbalanced, stereotypical and pathologically erotic view of life in and beyond the slave quarters that only the most prurient tastes could savor."[117]

According to members of the NAACP-supported Coalition Against the Airing of Beulah Land, the six hour mini-series would offend and misinform the viewing public. No black historians or consultants advised the project. Members of the Coalition claimed that "there is no black point of view in this movie," that the producers failed to understand the concerns of Afro-Americans, and that the series as a whole was filmed and packaged in a way that was "intensely offensive and degrading to black people." Although initially characterizing his critics as "misguided zealots who are shooting from the hip and spouting off at the mouth," executive producer David Gerber reedited those portions of the film deemed most likely to perpetuate the image of slaves as ignorant and dependent. The network also brought in, as a last minute advisor, Yale historian John Blassingame. Said Blassingame, who refused to recommend the film to the National Education Association: "I think as entertainment it works, but if I had to choose a film to show on slavery, this would not be the one."[118]

Filmed in Natchez, but supposedly depicting Georgia plantation life between 1827 and 1874, "Beulah Land" focused on the lives, loves, marital problems, and infidelities of white planter families. In this context, black slaves often appeared only in the background, scurrying about the cabin row or hustling across the barnyard as if late to a midday luncheon. When scenes did include the black servants, they contained many of the elements of proslavery stereotypes. For example, the belief that bondsmen had little respect for one another was reinforced by a kitchen maid who referred to a fellow servant as a "shiftless good-for-nothin' flap jaw." In another scene, the southern blacks' legendary rejection of free society (and its supposed benefits) was depicted when a character named Floyd returned to Beulah Land after an unhappy stay in Canada and Alaska. Offered the job of foreman, the former bondsman betrayed his eagerness to gain status and authority by proclaiming, "I like the ring of that!"

According to antebellum southern norms, good whites taught young slave children everything they needed to know to function successfully as adults. At the Beulah Land school, black youths were taught to read and recite "I will wash my hands before dinner." Bad whites, on the other hand, were coarse, lower class individuals who found great pleasure in saying things like "this blacksnake is thirsty boy, so stay out of its way." The worst whites in the movie, however, were the Yankee troops of the Civil War era. Surly and vicious, these villains killed in cold blood, raped slave women, beat up children, and desecrated graves in their search for "the spoils of war."[119]

As suggested by the film's critics, "Beulah Land" seemed like a step back in time as far as popular stereotypes were concerned. It was not simply that the series failed as "revolutionary television." Clearly, none of the major networks would accept responsibility for fomenting a Black Power revolution.[120] More precisely, the problem with "Beulah Land" was that it so easily, so glibly, reverted to racist formulas in order to portray the antebellum slave system. On this Georgia plantation born of Old South images and new Hollywood priorities, the past became, in effect, the present. In Beulah Land, Uncle Tom and his kin appeared alive and well. Attacked, shamed, maligned, and occasionally forced into hiding, Tom entered the decade of the 1980s in the driver's seat of the white folks' carriage. The most influential institutions of American popular culture had made their own "unthinking decision" to endorse traditional stereotypes. That Afro-Americans consistently and bitterly contested such a view of history can only affirm the essential validity of their position on the irrepressibility of the Afro-American spirit.

CHAPTER 6
Conclusion

> One does not worship, display, or teach culture; one acknowledges it as a whole way of life grounded in history, and one necessarily lives a culture.
>
> Houston A. Baker, Jr., 1971

By the end of the 1970s America had evolved from a country that endorsed slavery to a nation that consigns it to history. Nevertheless black and white interpretations of the slave experience have, to a remarkable degree, remained distinctly different. As Afro-Americans become more influential in white society so, too, will their perspectives on history. The incomplete recognition now granted to the black view of slavery represents the larger inequalities within American society and the incomplete acceptance of black people by white Americans.

Noticeable strides in narrowing the gap were made in the ivory tower world of higher education during the late 1960s. Black Power ideology and black students' presence on the nation's campuses argued forcefully for the academy's long overdue recognition that, as one history text review panel noted:

> Negroes were not just another immigrant group: no other group could be so readily identified by its color, no other group was so systematically enslaved, and no other group has been subjected to as persistent and virulent discrimination.[1]

This new awareness and appreciation for Afro-American history was endorsed by teacher education directors, curriculum committees, and textbook writers.[2] By the mid-1970s history texts and slavery books appeared which depicted the antebellum slave community in a manner that would have pleased the early advocates and practitioners of black history studies.[3]

Even as the textbook writers acknowledged "the large amount of slave unrest that from time to time shook the whole fabric of the planter's kingdom," institutional forces swung the pendulum back toward more traditional notions of black America.[4] Intellectual conservatism and cultural inertia kept the popular culture from recognizing the power and authenticity of the slave experience. As the case of Frank Yerby and his slave hero

Hwesu/Wesley Parks suggests, it is possible that Black Studies eventually will be seen as having been more important in radicalizing blacks than in reeducating whites.

As the economy weakened, university budgets tightened, and Black Studies enrollments leveled off during the late 1970s, the prospect of witnessing the spread of the Black Power/Black Studies perspective to the larger culture dimmed.[5] Mass market forms of socialization and education in slave imagery proved to be remarkably resistant to change. Not even Alex Haley's well promoted, massively popular multimedia blockbuster could clear the pulp novel racks and television screens of time-honored pejorative caricatures of blacks as slaves. Perhaps black identity, as portrayed in the mass culture, was, after all, doomed to be merely a sickly reflection of continuing white psychological needs. Perhaps, too, the only lasting contribution of the 1960s protests would be their legacy of unanswered questions and unaddressed issues.

At the close of the decade, black and white America, as viewed through the lens of slave images, remained divided, troubled, and confused. Despite statistical evidence pointing to the growth of an upwardly mobile black middle class, it seemed clear that such progress had to be measured against past hardships rather than future possibilities. Afro-Americans still lived with the history of their exploitation and with the knowledge that both white civility and black economic gains tend to deteriorate rather rapidly in a depressed economy. This was a gloomy forecast for the early years of the 1980s.[6]

Amidst such gloom, I have attempted to maintain the optimistic belief that, eventually, the nation and its popular culture will achieve liberation. Nevertheless, one afternoon on a break from my research, a strange, unnerving sensation overtook my sense of optimism. As I walked to the drinking fountain, a notation in the margin of a graduate school, minority student recruitment poster caught my eye. Haphazardly, perhaps hurriedly, scrawled in felt pen was the hate-filled and chilling message: "Go back to Liberia! Who needs niggers?" At the very same moment that the impact of these words hit me, I thought I heard — indistinctly and just for an instant — the dull metallic clank of chains being dragged across wooden planking.

NOTES
SELECTED BIBLIOGRAPHY
INDEX

NOTES

INTRODUCTION

1 At various times in the nation's history, the line between juvenile and adult publications has been a difficult one to fix. In addition, defining "American" can be problematic when United States citizens become expatriates or when foreign nationals arrive in this country, establish residence, and then return to their former homeland a few years later. The author has considered these contextual and definitional problems on a case by case basis and has attempted to focus the study upon materials produced by and for adult Americans.

2 Plato, *The Republic* (ca. 370 B.C.), trans. Benjamin Jowett (New York: Books, Inc., 1943), pp. 334–52.

3 For further commentary on the relationship between art and life in American society and culture, see Herbert J. Gans, *Popular Culture and High Culture: An Analysis and Evaluation of Taste* (New York: Basic Books, Inc., 1974); Milton C. Albrecht, "The Relationship of Literature and Society," *American Journal of Sociology* 59 (March 1954): 425–36; Terence Martin, "Social Institutions in the Early American Novel," *American Quarterly* 9 (Spring 1957): 72–84; Carl N. Degler, "Why Historians Change Their Minds," *Pacific Historical Review* 45 (May 1976): 167–84; Andrew Tudor, *Image and Influence: Studies in the Sociology of Film* (New York: St. Martin's Press, 1975).

CHAPTER 1. *From African to Slave, 1619–1830*

1 For an historiographical survey of this literature, see Raymond Starr, "Historians and the Origins of British North American Slavery," *Historian* 36 (November 1973):1–18. See also Peter Wood, "'I Did the Best I Could for My Day': The Study of Early Black History during the Second Reconstruction, 1960 to 1976," *William and Mary Quarterly* 35 (April 1978): 185–225.

2 For Jordan's most influential writing on this subject, see "The Influence of the West Indies on the Origins of New England Slavery," *William and Mary Quarterly* 18 (April 1961):243–50; "Modern Tensions and the Origins of American Slavery," *Journal of Southern History* 28 (February 1962):18–30; *White Over Black: American Attitudes Toward the Negro, 1550–1812* (Chapel Hill: University of North Carolina Press, 1968). For studies of early English attitudes toward African peoples, see also Katherine George, "The Civilized West Looks at Primitive Africa, 1400–1800: A Study in Ethnocentrism," *Isis* 49 (March 1958):62–72; Charles H. Lyons, *To Wash an Aethiop White: British Ideas About Black African Educability, 1530–1960* (New York: Columbia University Teachers College Press, 1975); Anthony J. Barker, *The African Link: British Attitudes to the Negro in the Era of the Atlantic Slave Trade, 1550–1807* (London:

Frank Cass, 1978); and Philip D. Curtin, *The Image of Africa: British Ideas and Action, 1780–1850* (Madison: University of Wisconsin Press, 1964).

3 John Smith, *The Generall Historie of Virginia, New England & The Summer Isles Together with The True Travels, Adventures and Observations, and A Sea Grammar,* 2 vols. (Glasgow: James MacLehose and Sons, 1907 [London: Michael Sparkes, 1624]), 1:247; Salma Hale, *History of the United States, From Their First Settlement as Colonies to the Close of the War With Great Britain, In 1815* (London: John Miller, 1826), p. 24. See also Robert Beverly, *The History and Present State of Virginia,* ed. Louis B. Wright (Chapel Hill: University of North Carolina Press, 1947 [London: R. Parker, 1705]), p. 48; William Stith, *The History of the First Discovery and Settlement of Virginia* (New York: Johnson Reprint Corporation, 1969 [Williamsburg: William Parks, 1747]), p. 182; John McCulloch, *A Concise History of the United States, from the Discovery of America, till 1813* (Philadelphia: W. McCulloch, 1813), p. 25. For an interesting perspective on Smith's source of information and the use made of it by later writers, see Wesley Frank Craven, "Twenty Negroes to Jamestown in 1619?" *Virginia Quarterly Review* 47 (Summer 1971):416–20.

4 Stith, *Settlement of Virginia,* p. 182; William Douglass, *A Summary, Historical and Political, of the First Planting, Progressive Improvements and Present State of the British Settlements in North-America,* 2 vols. (Boston: R. Baldwin, 1755), 2:360.

5 Peter Gay, *A Loss of Mastery: Puritan Historians in Colonial America* (New York: Vintage Books, 1968 [Berkeley: University of California Press, 1966]), pp. 21, 24; Kenneth B. Murdock, *Literature & Theology in Colonial New England* (New York: Harper Torchbooks, 1963 [Cambridge: Harvard University Press, 1949]), pp. 80, 88, 93; Kenneth B. Murdock, "Clio in the Wilderness: History and Biography in Puritan New England," *Church History* 24 (September 1955):229–30. For representative histories of the Indian wars, see William Hubbard, *The History of the Indian Wars in New England* (London: Thomas Parkhurst, 1677) and John Mason, *A Brief History of the Pequot War* (Boston: S. Kneeland & T. Green, 1736).

6 Samuel Eliot Morison, *The Intellectual Life of Colonial New England* (Ithaca: Great Seal Books, 1960 [New York: New York University Press, 1956]), pp. 42–43; and Herbert B. Adams, *The Study of History in American Colleges and Universities* (Washington, D.C.: Government Printing Office, 1887), pp. 17, 20.

7 The first college courses in American history were probably those offered at William and Mary in 1821 and at the College of Charleston in 1828. Separate departments of history were first established at the University of North Carolina (1853) and the University of Michigan (1855). George H. Callcott, *History in the United States, 1800–1860: Its Practice and Purpose* (Baltimore: The Johns Hopkins Press, 1970), pp. 60–61.

8 Hellmut Lehmann-Haupt, Lawrence C. Wroth, and Rollo G. Silver, *The Book in America: A History of the Making and Selling of Books in the United States* (New York: R. R. Bowker, 1952), pp. 32–33; John Tebbel, *A History of Book*

Publishing in the United States, vol. 1, *The Creation of an Industry, 1630–1865* (New York: R. R. Bowker, 1972), pp. 147–48. For a study of how adherence to a particular theory might have discouraged interest in the writing of history, see Stow Persons, "The Cyclical Theory of History in Eighteenth Century America," *American Quarterly* 6 (Summer 1954): 147–63.

9 Edmund Randolph, *History of Virginia*, ed. Arthur H. Shaffer (Charlottesville: University Press of Virginia, 1970), p. 269; Hale, *History of the United States*, p. 31.

10 John Burk, *The History of Virginia, from Its First Settlement to the Present Day*, 4 vols. (Petersburg, Va.: Dickson & Pescud, 1804), 1:212; Thomas Hutchinson, *The History of the Colony and Province of Massachusetts-Bay*, ed. Laurence Shaw Mayo, 3 vols. (Cambridge: Harvard University Press, 1936 [Boston: Thomas & John Fleet, 1764]), 1:374; McCulloch, *Concise History*, p. 244.

11 McCulloch, *Concise History*, pp. 232, 244.

12 Benedict S. Seidman, "Historical Writing in the United States, 1775–1830" (M.A. thesis, University of Wisconsin, 1941), pp. 6–8; David Ramsay, *The History of South-Carolina, From Its First Settlement in 1670, to the Year 1808*, 2 vols. (Charleston: David Longworth, 1809), 1:22. See also Hale, *History of the United States*, pp. 463–64.

13 Seidman, "Historical Writing," p. 126; Frederick Butler, *A Complete History of the United States of America*, 3 vols. (Hartford, 1821), 1:vi. For an examination of history as education for eighteenth-century statesmen, see Edward McNall Burns, "The Philosophy of History of the Founding Fathers," *Historian* 16 (Spring 1954): 142–68.

14 Burk, *History of Virginia*, p. 211; Hugh McCall, *The History of Georgia*, 2 vols. (Atlanta: A.B. Caldwell, 1909 [Savannah: Seymour & Williams, 1811]), 1:3–4; David Ramsay, *History of the United States, from their First Settlement As English Colonies, in 1607, To The Year 1808*, 3 vols. (Philadelphia: M. Carey and Son, 1818), 1:53, 248–50. See also Randolph, *History of Virginia*, p. 96.

15 For an early, impassioned proslavery history which claimed that Georgia's prohibition of slave labor had made the colony an object of pity and ridicule, see Patrick Tailfer, Hugh Anderson, and David Douglas, *A True and Historical Narrative of the Colony of Georgia in America* (Charles-Town: P. Timothy, 1741). For a rebuttal to their position, see Benjamin Martyn, *An Account Showing the Progress of the Colony of Georgia in America from its first Establishment* (Annapolis: Jonas Green, 1742).

16 James D. Hart, *The Popular Book: A History of America's Literary Taste* (New York: Oxford University Press, 1950), pp. 50, 53–54; Lillie Deming Loshe, *The Early American Novel* (New York: Columbia University Press, 1907), pp. 1–2, 27; Timothy Dwight, *Travels in New-England and New-York*, 4 vols. (London: W. Baynes and Son, 1823), 1:477. For Dwight's personal, poetic vision of God's just vengeance upon West Indian slaveholders, see his *Greenfield Hill: A Poem in Seven Parts* (New York: Childs and Swaine, 1794), pp. 37–41.

17 Aphra Behn, *Oroonoko: or, the Royal Slave* (New York: W. W. Norton &

Company, 1973 [London: Will. Canning, 1688]), pp. 68–75. For an evaluation of the book as a work which represents a distinct genre in the evolution of the English novel, see Edwin D. Johnson, "Aphra Behn's 'Oroonoko,'" *Journal of Negro History* 10 (July 1925):334–42. For other British models of tragic Africans, see Thomas George Street, *Aura; or The Slave* (London: J. Stevenson, 1788) and Anna Maria Mackenzie, *Slavery: or The Times* (London: G.G.J. and J. Robinsons and J. Dennis, 1792).

18 For Defoe's picture of servants and slaves in late seventeenth-century Virginia and Maryland, see *Col. Jacque* (London: Oxford University Press, 1965) [London: J. Brotherton, 1722]), pp. 117–73. For a description of the more unsavory aspects of West Indian slavery in the 1760s, see Edward Bancroft's epistolary novel, *The History of Charles Wentworth, Esq.*, 3 vols. (New York: Garland Publishing, Inc., 1975 [London: T. Becket, 1770]), 2:175–98.

19 Thomas Branagan, *Avenia, or a Tragical Poem, on the Oppression of the Human Species; and Infringement on the Rights of Man* (Philadelphia: J. Cline, 1810 [Philadelphia: Silas Engles and Samuel Wood, 1805]), p. 19. A discussion of the author's literary career may be found in Lewis Leary, "Thomas Branagan: Republican Rhetoric and Romanticism in America," *Pennsylvania Magazine of History and Biography* 77 (July 1953):332–52.

20 Thomas Branagan, *The Penitential Tyrant* (Philadelphia, 1805), p. 60.

21 Africus, "The Tears of a Slave," *Freedom's Journal* 1 (14 March 1828):202.

22 "Intrepidity of a Negro Woman," *Massachusetts Magazine* 3 (December 1791): 728. For evaluations of black characters in early short fiction, see Jack B. Moore, "Images of the Negro in Early American Short Fiction," *Mississippi Quarterly* 22 (Winter 1968/69):47–57; Mukhtar Ali Isani, "Far from 'Gambia's Golden Shore': The Black in Late Eighteenth-Century American Imaginative Literature," *William and Mary Quarterly* 36 (July 1979):353–72.

23 *The American in Algiers, or the Patriot of Seventy-Six in Captivity* (New York: J. Buel, 1797), pp. 28, 32. See also "A Negro's Lamentation," *Monthly Magazine and American Review* 3 (November 1800):398.

24 "The Negro," *Weekly Magazine* 1 (3 February 1798):11–12.

25 Branagan, *Penitential Tyrant*, p. 77. For other fictional accounts of slave suicide and death, see "The Desperate Negroe," *Massachusetts Magazine* 5 (October 1793):583–84; L. B., "Niko—A Fragment," *New-York Weekly Magazine* 1 (27 January 1796):239; "Extraordinary Friendship of Two Negroes," *Philadelphia Minerva* 3 (16 December 1797):3.

26 *A Poetical Epistle to the Enslaved Africans. . . .* (Philadelphia: Joseph Crukshank, 1790), p. 11.

27 "The Negro Boy," *Providence Gazette and Country Journal* 29 (18 August 1792):4; "The Negro Boy. Sold for a Metal Watch by an African Prince," *Philadelphia Minerva* 3 (28 October 1797):4. See also Joel Barlow, *The Columbiad* (Washington, D.C.: Joseph Milligan, 1825), pp. 272–81.

28 Mary Hamlin Writing Book, 1812, David Campbell Papers, Duke University, Durham, North Carolina, cited in Duncan J. MacLeod, *Slavery, Race and the American Revolution* (London: Cambridge University Press, 1974), p. 144.

North-South differences were noted briefly in William Hill Brown's early epistolary novel, *The Power of Sympathy* (Columbus: Ohio State University Press, 1969 [Boston: Isaiah Thomas and Company, 1789]), pp. 53–54, where he describes white southerners as "haughtier," more "tenacious of honour," and possessed of a more "aristocratick temper" than the "open, generous and communicative" citizens of nonslaveholding states.

29 For an early satirical debate on slavery, see Hugh Henry Brackenridge, *Modern Chivalry* (New York: American Book Company, 1937 [Philadelphia: John McCulloch, 1792]), pp. 134–40.

30 Hart, *Popular Book*, p. 80.

31 There were between sixty and eighty novels written in the United States prior to 1820. A number of these were less than 50 pages in length. *The Spy* was Cooper's first work after his amateurish *Precaution* (1820). During his career, he created more than fifty black characters — seven of them were full portraits. Terence Martin, "Social Institutions in the Early American Novel," *American Quarterly* 9 (Spring 1957):72; Charles Hampton Nilon, "Some Aspects of the Treatment of Negro Characters by Five Representative American Novelists: Cooper, Melville, Tourgee, Glasgow, Faulkner" (Ph.D. diss., University of Wisconsin, 1952), p. 1.

32 James Fenimore Cooper, *The Spy; a Tale of the Neutral Ground* (New York: Dodd, Mead & Company, 1946 [New York: Wiley & Halsted, 1821]), pp. 10, 28, 35, 43, 67, 76, 201.

33 Nilon, "Treatment of Negro Characters," pp. 11–13; Cooper, *Spy*, pp. 28, 272, 277.

34 Cooper, *Spy*, pp. 61, 100, 104, 201–3.

35 Therman B. O'Daniel, "Cooper's Treatment of the Negro," *Phylon* 8 (June 1947):168; Cooper, *Spy*, pp. 10, 24, 26, 98–99. For a brief fictional treatment of an elderly black servant who told ghost stories and who was described as "one of these old weatherbeaten wiseacres of negroes," see Washington Irving, *Salmagundi: or, The Whim-Whams and Opinions of Launcelot Langstaff, Esq. and Others* (London: T. Davison, 1824 [New York: David Longworth, 1807]), pp. 278–81.

36 For commentary on Tucker's contribution to the plantation tradition in literature, see Robert Colin McLean, *George Tucker: Moral Philosopher and Man of Letters* (Chapel Hill: University of North Carolina Press, 1961), pp. 188–92; Richard Beale Davis, "The 'Virginia Novel' Before *Swallow Barn*," *Virginia Magazine of History and Biography* 71 (July 1963):285–89, 292; William F. Mugleston, "Southern Literature as History: Slavery in the Antebellum Novel," *History Teacher* 8 (November 1974):20–22; William R. Taylor, *Cavalier and Yankee: The Old South and American National Character* (New York: Harper Torchbooks, 1969 [New York: George Braziller, Inc., 1961]), pp. 149, 302–3.

37 George Tucker, *The Valley of Shenandoah; or, Memoirs of the Graysons*, 2 vols. (New York: Charles Wiley, 1824), 2:44–45; Mugleston, "Southern Literature as History," p. 21.

38 Tucker, *Valley*, 2:206–10.

39 Ibid., 1:61–62.

40 Ibid., 2:211–13.

41 Ibid., 1:63; James Fenimore Cooper, *The American Democrat, or Hints on the Social and Civic Relations of the United States of America* (New York: Alfred A. Knopf, 1931 [Cooperstown: H. & E. Phinney, 1838]), p. 165. For the development of Cooper's and Tucker's views on issues of slavery and race, see also Robert E. Spiller, "Fenimore Cooper's Defense of Slave-Owning America," *American Historical Review* 35 (April 1930): 575–82; Max L. Griffin, "Cooper's Attitude Toward the South," *Studies in Philology* 48 (January 1951):67–76; James Fenimore Cooper, *Notions of the Americans: Picked Up by a Travelling Bachelor*, 2 vols. (Philadelphia: Carey, Lea & Carey, 1828), 2:259–77; McLean, *George Tucker*, pp. 175–202; Tipton R. Snavely, *George Tucker as Political Economist* (Charlottesville: University Press of Virginia, 1964), pp. 134–53.

42 Nilon, "Treatment of Negro Characters," p. 3.

43 Richard Moody, *America Takes the Stage: Romanticism in American Drama and Theatre, 1750–1900* (Bloomington: Indiana University Press, 1955), p. 188; and Hugh F. Rankin, *The Theater in Colonial America* (Chapel Hill: University of North Carolina Press, 1965), p. 2.

44 The play was performed on the American stage in New York City as early as 1783 and later appeared in Philadelphia (1792), Charleston (1795), and Boston (1796). Thomas Southerne, *Oroonoko* in *The Modern British Drama*, ed. Walter Scott, 5 vols. (London: William Miller, 1811 [London: H. Playford, B. Tooke, and S. Buckley, 1696]) 1:493; John Daniel Collins, "American Drama in Antislavery Agitation, 1792–1861" (Ph.D. diss., State University of Iowa, 1963), p. 21.

45 Isaac Bickerstaffe, *The Padlock* (London: Sadler and Co., n.d. [London: W. Griffin, 1768]), p. 16.

46 Ibid., p. 19. For other British plays with comic black figures, see George Colman, *The Africans; Or, War, Love, And Duty* (London: John Cumberland, 1808) and *Inkle and Yarico* (London: G.G.J. & J. Robinson, 1787).

47 John Murdock, *The Politicians; or, A State of Things* (Philadelphia, 1798), p. 19.

48 Ibid., p. 20.

49 Ibid., p. 30. For modern literary commentary on *The Politicians*, see Alfonso Sherman, "The Diversity of Treatment of the Negro Character in American Drama Prior to 1860" (Ph.D. diss., Indiana University, 1964), pp. 47–50; and Stanley Glenn, "The Development of the Negro Character in American Comedy Before the Civil War," *Southern Speech Journal* 26 (Winter 1960): 138–39.

50 Richard Walser, "Negro Dialect in Eighteenth-Century American Drama," *American Speech* 30 (December 1955):269, 271.

51 Robert Munford, *The Candidates; or the Humours of a Virginia Election*, ed. Jay B. Hubbell and Douglass Adair (Williamsburg: Institute of Early American History and Culture, 1948 [Petersburg: William Prentis, 1798]), p. 19.

52 A. B. Lindsley, *Love and Friendship; or, Yankee Notions* (New York: D. Longworth, 1809), p. 13.

53 For other early examples of attempts at black dialect, see the speaking parts of Caesar in Charles Powell Clinch, *The Spy, A Tale of the Neutral Ground* in *Metamora & Other Plays*, ed. Eugene R. Page (Princeton: Princeton University Press, 1941), pp. 57–105; Debauchee in *Occurrences of the Times* (Boston: Benjamin Russell, 1789); Cuffy in Samuel Low, *The Politician Out-Witted* (New York: W. Ross, 1789).

54 John Leacock, *The Fall of British Tyranny; or, American Liberty Triumphant* in *Representative Plays by American Dramatists*, ed. Montrose J. Moses, 3 vols. (New York: E. P. Dutton & Company, 1918–1925 [Philadelphia: Styner and Cist, 1776]), 1:331–33.

55 Ibid., pp. 328–29.

56 Samuel Woodworth, *The Forest Rose; or, American Farmers* (Boston: William V. Spencer, 1855 [New York: Hopkins and Morris, 1825]). p. 12. For a similar scene, see Mary Clarke, *The Benevolent Lawyers; or, Villainy Detected* (Philadelphia, 1823), p. 56.

57 David Ewen, *The Story of America's Musical Theater* (Philadelphia: Chilton Book Company, 1968), p. 1; S. Foster Damon, "The Negro in Early American Songsters," *Papers of the Bibliographical Society of America* 28 (1934):133; Arthur Hobson Quinn, *A History of the American Drama: From the Beginning to the Civil War* (New York: Appleton-Century-Crofts, Inc., 1951), p. 332.

58 John Murdock, *The Beau Metamorphized; or The Generous Maid* (Philadelphia: Joseph C. Charles, 1800), p. iv.

59 John Murdock, *The Triumphs of Love; or Happy Reconciliation* (Philadelphia: R. Folwell, 1795), pp. 19, 51.

60 Ibid., pp. 51–53. For more early song and dance, see the antics of a house servant named Cesar in Lazarus Beach, *Jonathan Postfree; or, the Honest Yankee* (New York: David Longworth, 1807), p. 28.

61 Murdock, *Triumphs of Love*, pp. 53, 67–68.

62 Ibid., pp. 68–69.

63 Loften Mitchell, *Black Drama: The Story of the American Negro in the Theatre* (New York: Hawthorn Books, Inc., 1967), p. 18; Alan W. C. Green, "'Jim Crow,' 'Zip Coon': The Northern Origins of Negro Minstrelsy," *Massachusetts Review* 11 (Spring 1970):395; Murdock, *Triumphs of Love*, p. 42.

CHAPTER 2. *The Debate Begins, 1830–1861*

1 Of the 145, there were 34 clergymen, 32 lawyers and statesmen, 18 publishers, 17 physicians and scientists, 9 teachers, 9 gentlemen, 7 journalists, 7 archivists and librarians, 5 businessmen, 4 artists and engravers, 2 planters, and 1 historian. George H. Callcott, *History in the United States, 1800–1860: Its Practice and Purpose* (Baltimore: The Johns Hopkins Press, 1970), pp. 61, 68–71. For a listing of the texts available to antebellum students, see William F. Russell, "Historical Text-books Published before 1861," *History Teachers' Magazine* 6 (April 1915): 122–25. For background on John McCulloch's early his-

tories, see Alice Winifred Spieseke, *The First Textbooks in American History and their Compiler John M'Culloch* (New York: Bureau of Publications, Teachers College, Columbia University, 1938).

2 Callcott, *History in the United States*, p. 59; Frederick M. Binder, *The Age of the Common School, 1830–1865* (New York: John Wiley & Sons, 1974), p. 141; Clement Eaton, *Freedom of Thought in the Old South* (Durham: Duke University Press, 1940), p. 197; Jeptha Root Simms to Lyman Copeland Draper, 12 December 1849, reprinted in William B. Hesseltine and Larry Gara, "History Publishing in 1849," *Historian* 16 (Spring 1954):141.

3 Harvey Wish, *The American Historian: A Social-Intellectual History of the Writing of the American Past* (New York: Oxford University Press, 1960), pp. 72, 75; Russel B. Nye, *George Bancroft: Brahmin Rebel* (New York: Alfred A. Knopf, 1944), pp. 187–88; George Bancroft, *History of the United States, from the Discovery of the American Continent*, 10 vols. (Boston: Little, Brown, and Company, 1834–1875), 1:vi;.3:398. Volumes one through eight appeared prior to the Civil War. Volume nine was published in 1866 and volume ten in 1875.

4 Wish, *American Historian*, p. 78; John Spencer Bassett, *The Middle Group of American Historians* (New York: The Macmillan Company, 1917), p. 204; Bancroft, *History*, 3:397.

5 David Levin, *History as Romantic Art: Bancroft, Prescott, Motley, and Parkman* (New York: Harcourt, Brace & World, Inc., 1963 [Stanford: Stanford University Press, 1959]), pp. 79–81; Wish, *American Historian*, p. 86.

6 Bancroft, *History*, 1:159, 177–78; 3:410–13. He also criticized the Dutch, claiming: "That New York is not a slave-state like Carolina, is due to climate, and not to the superior humanity of its founders." Bancroft, *History*, 2:303.

7 Bancroft, *History*, 2:193.

8 Bancroft, *History*, 1:159–61.

9 Bancroft, *History*, 3:403–4, 406.

10 Ibid., pp. 406, 408.

11 Robert H. Canary, *George Bancroft* (New York: Twayne Publishers, Inc., 1974), p. 40; Nye, *George Bancroft*, pp. 82, 135, 146, 147, 211, 222; Bassett, *Middle Group*, p. 194; Lorraine A. Williams, "Northern Intellectual Reaction to the Policy of Emancipation," *Journal of Negro History* 46 (July 1961):179–80; Leonard I. Sweet, *Black Images of America, 1784–1870* (New York: W. W. Norton & Company, Inc., 1976), p. 17.

12 Bancroft, *History*, 1:159, 165; 3:402–3; 8:225, 321. David Brion Davis has noted that in dealing with the relationship between slavery and America's destiny Bancroft "resorted to a curious mixture of assumptions which reflected inconsistencies prevalent in American thought from late colonial times to the twentieth century." See David Brion Davis, *The Problem of Slavery in Western Culture* (Ithaca: Cornell University Press, 1966), p. 21.

13 Boston *Evening Telegraph*, 29 November 1854, reprinted in Martha M. Pingel, *An American Utilitarian: Richard Hildreth as a Philosopher* (New York: Columbia University Press, 1948), pp. 199–200.

14 George Bourne, *Picture of Slavery in the United States of America* (Middletown, Conn.: Edwin Hunt, 1834), pp. 25, 155, 156. For a sampling of histories which approach Bourne's blend of reform and history, see William E. Channing, *Slavery* (Boston: James Munroe and Company, 1835); William Goodell, *Slavery and Anti-Slavery: A History of the Great Struggle in Both Hemispheres* (New York, 1853).

15 Thomas R. R. Cobb, *An Inquiry into the Law of Negro Slavery in the United States of America* (Philadelphia: T. & J. W. Johnson & Co., 1858), pp. 36, 40; George S. Sawyer, *Southern Institutes; or An Inquiry into the Origin and Early Prevalence of Slavery and the Slave-Trade* (Philadelphia: J. B. Lippincott & Co., 1858), p. 222.

16 Cobb, *Inquiry,* p. 49; John Fletcher, *Studies On Slavery, In Easy Lessons* (Natchez: Jackson Warner, 1852), p. 174; Thomas R. R. Cobb, *An Historical Sketch of Slavery, from the Earliest Periods* (Philadelphia: T. & J. W. Johnson & Co., 1858), pp. cli–clii, clviii–clx, ccxii–ccxxi, ccxxxiv, ccxliv, cclxvi, cclxviii.

17 Josiah Priest, *Slavery as it relates to the Negro, or African Race* (Albany: C. VanBenthuysen and Co., 1843), p. 264; J. K. Paulding, *Slavery in the United States* (New York: Harper & Brothers, 1835), p. 9; George Tucker, *The History of the United States, from Their Colonization to the End of the Twenty-Sixth Congress, in 1841,* 4 vols. (Philadelphia: J. B. Lippincott & Co., 1856–1858), 3:263, 4:426–27, 432–33.

18 Tucker, *History,* 3:263, 4:431–32; Priest, *Slavery,* p. 224.

19 Tucker, *History,* 1:98, Bancroft, *History,* 3:17.

20 William Lloyd Garrison, "To Louis Kossuth," in *The Liberty Bell* (Boston: National Anti-Slavery Bazaar, 1853), p. 298.

21 William Allen Butler, "At Richmond," *National Anti-Slavery Standard* 20 (8 October 1859):4.

22 M. Roland Markham, *Alcar, The Captive Creole; A Story of the South, in Verse* (Homer, N. Y.: Jos. R. Dixon, 1857), p. 83.

23 Ibid., p. 71. See also "The Auction Sale," *National Anti-Slavery Standard* 19 (19 March 1859):4.

24 "The Slave Mother," *National Anti-Slavery Standard* 20 (4 June 1859):4.

25 See, for example, "To the Christian Mother," *National Anti-Slavery Standard* 19 (11 September 1858):4; "The Slave Mother," *Liberator* 3 (30 November 1833):192.

26 Daniel Ricketson, "Ho! Help!" in *The Liberty Bell* (Boston: National Anti-Slavery Bazaar, 1858), p. 208. See also John Greenleaf Whittier, "Expostulation," in *The Complete Poetical Works of Whittier* (Boston: Houghton Mifflin Company, 1894 [1834]), p. 268; James Russell Lowell, "On the Capture of Fugitive Slaves Near Washington," in *The Complete Poetical Works of James Russell Lowell* (Boston: Houghton Mifflin Company, 1917 [1845]), pp. 82–83; and William Denton, "Appeal to America," in *Poems for Reformers* (Dayton, Ohio: William and Elizabeth M. F. Denton, 1856), p. 52.

27 John Greenleaf Whittier, "The Christian Slave," in *Poetical Works of Whittier,* [1843], p. 289.

28 Lorenzo Dow Turner, *Anti-Slavery Sentiment in American Literature Prior to 1865* (Washington, D. C.: Association for the Study of Negro Life and History, 1929), pp. 72, 78; John Herbert Nelson, *The Negro Character in American Literature* (College Park, Maryland: McGrath Publishing Company, 1968 [Lawrence, Kansas: University of Kansas, Department of Journalism Press, 1926]), pp. 74–75.

29 H. G. Nicholas, "Uncle Tom's Cabin, 1852–1952," *American Heritage* 4 (Winter 1953):22; J. C. Furnas, *Goodbye to Uncle Tom* (New York: William Sloane Associates, 1956), pp. 59–60; James D. Hart, *The Popular Book: A History of America's Literary Taste* (New York: Oxford University Press, 1950), pp. 110–12. For a more detailed literary history of *Uncle Tom's Cabin*, see E. Bruce Kirkham, *The Building of Uncle Tom's Cabin* (Knoxville: University of Tennessee Press, 1977).

30 Harriet Beecher Stowe, *A Key to Uncle Tom's Cabin. Presenting the Original Facts and Documents Upon Which the Story is Founded, Together with Corroborative Statements Verifying the Truth of the Work* (Boston: John P. Jewett and Company, 1853), p. 1; Harriet Beecher Stowe, *Uncle Tom's Cabin* (New York: Washington Square Press, Inc., 1966 [Boston: John P. Jewett and Company, 1852]), p. 452. Charles Nichols, "The Origins of Uncle Tom's Cabin," *Phylon* 19 (Fall 1958):329; Furnas, *Goodbye to Uncle Tom*, pp. 23–27; Stowe, *Key*, p. 1.

31 Stowe, *Key*, pp. v, 233; Stowe, *Uncle Tom's Cabin*, p. 35.

32 Stowe, *Uncle Tom's Cabin*, p. 15; John William Ward, "*Uncle Tom's Cabin*, As a Matter of Historical Fact," *Columbia University Forum* 9 (Winter 1966): 42. For conflicting modern commentary on the human dimensions of Stowe's characters, see Randall M. Miller, "Mrs. Stowe's Negro: George Harris' Negritude in *Uncle Tom's Cabin*," *Colby Library Quarterly* 10 (December 1974): 521–26; Benjamin F. Hudson, "Another View of 'Uncle Tom,'" *Phylon* 24 (Spring 1963):79–87; Ernest Cassara, "The Rehabilitation of Uncle Tom: Significant Themes in Mrs. Stowe's Antislavery Novel," *CLA Journal* 17 (December 1973):230–40; Thomas P. Riggio, "*Uncle Tom* Reconstructed: A Neglected Chapter in the History of a Book," *American Quarterly* 28 (Spring 1976):56–70; Alfred R. Ferguson, "The Abolition of Blacks in Abolitionist Fiction, 1830–1860," *Journal of Black Studies* 5 (December 1974):137–41, 155; David W. Levy, "Racial Stereotypes in Antislavery Fiction," *Phylon* 31 (Fall 1970):265–79; Jaclyn C. Palmer, "Images of Slavery: Black and White Writers," *Negro History Bulletin* 41 (September-October 1978):888–89; Herbert Hill, "'Uncle Tom': An Enduring American Myth," *Crisis* 72 (May 1965):289–95, 325; James Baldwin, "Everybody's Protest Novel," *Partisan Review* 16 (June 1949):578–85; Furnas, *Goodbye to Uncle Tom*, pp. 48–54.

33 Stowe, *Uncle Tom's Cabin*, pp. 353–54.

34 Ibid., pp. 354, 361, 366.

35 Stowe, *Uncle Tom's Cabin*, p. 354. For poetic visions of hopelessly crushed, maddened, or dehumanized slaves, see William Cullen Bryant, "The African Chief," in *The Poetical Works of William Cullen Bryant*, ed. Parke Godwin,

2 vols. (New York: D. Appleton and Company, 1883 [1825]), 1:141–43; Elizabeth Margaret Chandler, "Summer Morning," in *The Poetical Works of Elizabeth Margaret Chandler* (Philadelphia: Lemuel Howell, 1836), p. 75; Louisa J. Hall, "Birth in the Slave's Hut," in *The Liberty Bell* (Boston: National Anti-Slavery Bazaar, 1849), pp. 42–44; William Lloyd Garrison, "To Kossuth," in *The Liberty Bell* (Boston: National Anti-Slavery Bazaar, 1852), pp. 260–61; Henry Wadsworth Longfellow, "The Slave in the Dismal Swamp," in *The Complete Poetical Works of Longfellow* (Boston: Houghton Mifflin Company, 1922 [1842]), pp. 21–22.

36 Stowe, *Uncle Tom's Cabin*, pp. xix, 2, 30, 97, 183–84, 294, 404.

37 George M. Fredrickson, *The Black Image in the White Mind: The Debate on Afro-American Character and Destiny, 1817–1914* (New York: Harper Torchbooks, 1972 [New York: Harper & Row, 1971]), pp. 97–129. For additional modern commentary on racism in the antislavery movement, see Robert L. Allen, *Reluctant Reformers: Racism and Social Reform Movements in the United States,* (Washington, D. C.: Howard University Press, 1974), pp. 11–48; Leon F. Litwack, "The Emancipation of the Negro Abolitionist," in *The Antislavery Vanguard: New Essays on the Abolitionists,* ed. Martin Duberman (Princeton: Princeton University Press, 1965), pp. 137–55; William H. Pease and Jane H. Pease, "Antislavery Ambivalence: Immediatism, Expediency, Race," *American Quarterly* 17 (Winter 1965):682–95; James M. McPherson, *The Struggle for Equality: Abolitionists and the Negro in the Civil War and Reconstruction* (Princeton: Princeton University Press, 1964), pp. 134–53.

38 Jeannette Reid Tandy, "Pro-Slavery Propaganda in American Fiction of the Fifties," *South Atlantic Quarterly* 21 (January 1922):41; Nelson, *Negro Character,* p. 87; E. J. Stearns, *Notes on Uncle Tom's Cabin: Being a Logical Answer to its Allegations and Inferences Against Slavery as an Institution* (Philadelphia: Lippincott, Grambo & Co., 1853), pp. 145, 155, 156; A. Woodward, *A Review of Uncle Tom's Cabin; or An Essay on Slavery* (Cincinnati: Applegate & Co., 1853), pp. 35, 36, 40–41; Mary H. Eastman, *Aunt Phillis's Cabin; or, Southern Life as it Is* (Philadelphia: Lippincott, Grambo & Co., 1852), p. 266. For a summary of the contemporary literary reviews of *Uncle Tom's Cabin,* see Severn Duvall, "*Uncle Tom's Cabin:* The Sinister Side of the Patriarchy," *New England Quarterly* 36 (March 1963):13–21. For a contemporary critique of the reviewers, see F. C. Adams, *Uncle Tom at Home: A Review of the Reviewers and Repudiators of Uncle Tom's Cabin By Mrs. Stowe* (Philadelphia: Willis P. Hazard, 1853). For a case study of the reaction to Stowe's novel in one southern city, see Joseph P. Roppolo, "Harriet Beecher Stowe and New Orleans: A Study in Hate," *New England Quarterly* 30 (September 1957): 346–62.

39 W. J. Grayson, *The Hireling and the Slave* (Charleston: John Russell, 1855 [Charleston: John Russell, 1854]), p. 44. In line three Grayson was referring to British traveler Frances Trollope, whose *Domestic Manners of the Americans* (London: Whittaker, Treacher & Co., 1832) forwarded a generally unfavorable portrait of slavery.

40 Charles Jacobs Peterson [J. Thornton Randolph], *The Cabin and Parlor; or, Slaves and Masters* (Philadelphia: T. B. Peterson, 1852), pp. 3, 6. Authors' published claims to historical accuracy were, on occasion, contradicted by private statements. In 1856, southern anti-Stowe editor and novelist William Gilmore Simms wrote to a friend: "My novels aim at something more than the story. I am really . . . revising history." William Gilmore Simms to John Reuben Thompson, 7 February 1856, in *The Letters of William Gilmore Simms*, ed. Mary C. Simms Oliphant, Alfred Taylor Odell, and T. C. Duncan Eaves, 5 vols. (Columbia, S. C.: University of South Carolina Press, 1952–1956), 3: 421. See also Drew Gilpin Faust, *A Sacred Circle: The Dilemma of the Intellectual in the Old South, 1840–1860* (Baltimore: The Johns Hopkins University Press, 1977), pp. 74–75; S. P. C. Duvall, "W. G. Simms's Review of Mrs. Stowe," *American Literature* 30 (March 1958):107–17; Joseph V. Ridgely, "*Woodcraft:* Simms's First Answer to *Uncle Tom's Cabin*," *American Literature* 31 (January 1960):421–33.

41 Caroline E. Rush, *The North and South, or Slavery and Its Contrasts* (Philadelphia: Crissy & Markley, 1852), pp. 128–30, 136; Grayson, *Hireling and the Slave*, p. ix; Peterson, *Cabin and Parlor*, p. 91; Eastman, *Aunt Phillis's Cabin*, pp. 73–74; Caroline Lee Hentz, *The Planter's Northern Bride* (Chapel Hill: University of North Carolina Press, 1970 [Philadelphia: Parry & McMillan, 1854]), p. 32. See also Sarah Josepha Hale, *Northwood; or Life North and South: Showing the True Character of Both* (New York: H. Long & Brother, 1852). For commentary on the origins of this argument, see Milton Cantor, "The Image of the Negro in Colonial Literature," *New England Quarterly* 36 (December 1963):468. For discussion of this sentiment as it was expressed in the larger society, see Wilfred Carsel, "The Slaveholder's Indictment of Northern Wage Slavery," *Journal of Southern History* 6 (November 1940):504–20; Marcus Cunliffe, *Chattel Slavery and Wage Slavery: The Anglo-American Context, 1830–1860* (Athens: University of Georgia Press, 1979). For literature critical of British "wage slavery," see M. Estes, *Tit For Tat* (New York: Garret & Company, 1856), pp. i–ii, 226–29; Lucien B. Chase, *English Serfdom and American Slavery: or, Ourselves — as Others See Us* (New York: Negro Universities Press, 1968 [New York: H. Lang & Brother, 1854]), pp. 86–87, 207–11; Grayson, *Hireling and the Slave*, pp. 21–24.

42 Eastman, *Aunt Phillis's Cabin*, pp. 70–71. For antislavery depictions of North-South differences, see Harriet Beecher Stowe, *Dred; A Tale of the Great Dismal Swamp*, 2 vols. (Boston: Phillips, Sampson and Company, 1856), 1:129–30, 267–68; John H. Hoopes, "Tell Me Not of the Sunny South," *National Era* 9 (5 April 1855):1. For a study of southern authors' views of slavery in southern cities, see Alan Dowty, "Urban Slavery in Pro-Southern Fiction of the 1850's," *Journal of Southern History* 32 (February 1966):25–41.

43 Grayson, *Hireling and the Slave*, p. 27.

44 Ibid., p. viii.

45 Nehemiah Adams, *The Sable Cloud: A Southern Tale, with Northern Comments* (Westport: Negro Universities Press, 1970 [Boston: Ticknor and Fields,

1861]), pp. 59–61. See also Robert Criswell, *'Uncle Tom's Cabin' Contrasted with Buckingham Hall* (New York: D. Fanshaw, 1852), pp. 38–39, 57, 149–50.

46 Peterson, *Cabin and Parlor*, pp. 39, 47. See also William Gilmore Simms, "The Hunter of Calawassee; A Legend of South Carolina," in *Poems Descriptive, Dramatic, Legendary and Contemplative*, 2 vols. (New York: Redfield, 1853), 1:290. For a vivid description of "abolitionist hypocrisy," see the characterization of Thomas Brainard in Hentz, *Planter's Northern Bride*, pp. 448–60, 501, 514, 526.

47 Rollin G. Osterweis, *Romanticism and Nationalism in the Old South* (New Haven: Yale University Press, 1949), 215. For additional commentary on Scott's influence and popularity in the South, see Hart, *Popular Book*, pp. 76–77; Jay B. Hubbell, *The South in American Literature, 1607–1900* (Durham: Duke University Press, 1954), pp. 188–93; and William R. Taylor, *Cavalier and Yankee: The Old South and American National Character* (New York: Harper Torchbooks, 1969 [New York: George Braziller, Inc., 1961]), pp. 177–88.

48 Taylor, *Cavalier and Yankee*, p. 310. See also Addison Gayle, Jr., "Cultural Hegemony: The Southern White Writer and American Letters," in *Amistad 1*, ed. John A. Williams and Charles F. Harris (New York: Vintage Books, 1970), pp. 7–9. Kennedy's *Swallow Barn, or A Sojourn in the Old Dominion*, 2 vols. (Philadelphia: Carey & Lea, 1832) is particularly interesting not only because of the southern scenes and characters which it helped to popularize, but also because it had "a somewhat critical revisal" in 1851. The latter edition was less satirical and even more sentimental than the original. It was designed to serve as "an antidote to this abolition mischief." See J. P. Kennedy, *Swallow Barn, or A Sojourn in the Old Dominion* (New York: George P. Putnam, 1851), pp. 7–11; John Pendleton Kennedy to William Gilmore Simms, 8 March 1851, quoted in Jean Fagan Yellin, *The Intricate Knot: Black Figures in American Literature, 1776–1863* (New York: New York University Press, 1972), p. 59. Both versions were well received by southern reviewers and seen as "a series of most agreeable and faithful sketches of Virginia life, drawn by the hand of a master." *Southern Literary Messenger* 17 (December 1851):764. For a summary of the reviews, see Charles H. Bohner, *John Pendleton Kennedy: Gentleman from Baltimore* (Baltimore: The John Hopkins Press, 1961), pp. 73, 87–88. For further modern commentary, see Paul C. Wermuth, "Swallow Barn: A Virginia Idyll," *Virginia Cavalcade* 9 (Summer 1959):30–34; Alan Henry Rose, "The Image of the Negro in the Pre-Civil-War Novels of John Pendleton Kennedy and William Gilmore Simms," *Journal of American Studies* 4 (1970): 217–26.

49 Caroline Lee Hentz, *Robert Graham* (Philadelphia: T. B. Peterson, 1855), pp. 107–9; Kennedy, *Swallow Barn*, [1832], 1:19–20, 28, 32, 190; 2:223–24; Peterson, *Cabin and Parlor*, p. 11.

50 Kennedy, *Swallow Barn* [1832], 2:55, 225, 243; Kennedy, *Swallow Barn*, [1851], p. 453; W. L. G. Smith, *Life at the South: or 'Uncle Tom's Cabin' as it is* (Buffalo: Geo. H. Derby and Co., 1852), p. 518.

51 Channing, *Slavery*, p. 65.

52 Carl Wittke, *Tambo and Bones: A History of the American Minstrel Stage* (Durham: Duke University Press, 1930), p. 41; Alan W. C. Green, "'Jim Crow,' 'Zip Coon': The Northern Origins of Negro Minstrelsy," *Massachusetts Review* 11 (Spring 1970):387–88, 391, 395; Robert C. Toll, *Blacking Up: The Minstrel Show in Nineteenth-Century America* (New York: Oxford University Press, 1974), pp. 33–34, 65, 270–72; Alexander Saxton, "Blackface Minstrelsy and Jacksonian Ideology," *American Quarterly* 27 (March 1975):4. For commentary on minstrel acts in circuses, see Harry R. Edwall, "The Golden Era of Minstrelsy in Memphis: A Reconstruction," *West Tennessee Historical Society Papers* 9 (1955):43. See also Philip Graham, *Showboats: The History of an American Institution* (Austin: University of Texas Press, 1951), pp. 23–24.

53 Gary D. Engle, ed., *This Grotesque Essence: Plays from the American Minstrel Stage* (Baton Rouge: Louisiana State University Press, 1978), pp. xxi–xxiii; Toll, *Blacking Up*, pp. 52–57. Antebellum theater audiences were composed of both black and white viewers. In the North, Afro-Americans usually shared the gallery with whites. When not excluded altogether, blacks attending southern shows were the exclusive occupants of the highest tier of seats. In the South, theatergoing slaves had to produce a pass from their owners in order to gain admission. Free blacks seeking privacy or prestige could obtain box seats within the gallery. David Grimsted, *Melodrama Unveiled: American Theater and Culture, 1800–1850* (Chicago: University of Chicago Press, 1968), p. 53; James H. Dormon, Jr., *Theater in the Ante Bellum South, 1815–1861* (Chapel Hill: University of North Carolina Press, 1967), pp. 233–36.

54 Hans Nathan, *Dan Emmett and the Rise of Early Negro Minstrelsy* (Norman: University of Oklahoma Press, 1962), pp. 50–51; Wittke, *Tambo and Bones*, pp. 8–9; Richard Moody, *America Takes the Stage: Romanticism in American Drama and Theatre, 1750–1900* (Bloomington: Indiana University Press, 1955), p. 42.

55 George C. D. Odell, *Annals of the New York Stage*, 15 vols. (New York: Columbia University Press, 1927–1949), 4:372.

56 Robert C. Toll, "Behind the Blackface: Minstrel Men and Minstrel Myths," *American Heritage* 29 (April-May, 1978):95; Toll, *Blacking Up*, pp. 40–51, 60; Moody, *America Takes the Stage*, pp. 33, 55; Saxton, "Blackface Minstrelsy," pp. 7, 14; Wittke, *Tambo and Bones*, p. 166, 175; Richard Orton, "Black Folk Entertainments and the Evolution of American Minstrelsy," *Negro History Bulletin* 41 (September-October 1978):885, 887; Frank Costellow Davidson, "The Rise, Development, Decline and Influence of the American Minstrel Show" (Ph.D. diss., New York University, 1952), pp. 107–8. For contemporary commentary on minstrel authenticity, see Frances Anne Kemble, *Journal of a Residence on a Georgian Plantation in 1838–1839* (New York: New American Library, 1975 [New York: Harper and Brothers, 1863]), p. 131; Henry George Spaulding, "Under the Palmetto," *Continental Monthly* 4 (August 1863):200; J. J. Turx, "Negro Minstrelsy—Ancient and Modern," *Putnam's Monthly* 5 (January 1855):75, 79.

57 Dailey Paskman and Sigmund Spaeth, *"Gentlemen, Be Seated!" A Parade of the Old-Time Minstrels* (Garden City, N.Y.: Doubleday, Doran & Company, 1928), p. 29.

58 Francis Pendleton Gaines, *The Southern Plantation: A Study in the Development and the Accuracy of a Tradition* (New York: Columbia University Press, 1924), p. 128; Saxton, "Blackface Minstrelsy," p. 4. For a sampling of pre-minstrel era songs which commented on slave-related issues, see William Reeve, "The Desponding Negro" in *The American Musical Miscellany* (Northampton, Mass.: Daniel Wright and Company, 1798), pp. 166-68; R. C. Dallas, "Bonja Song" in *Series of Old American Songs Reproduced in Facsimile From Original or Early Editions in the Harris Collection of American Poetry and Plays, Brown University,* ed. S. Foster Damon (Providence: Brown University Library, 1936 [ca. 1820]), pp. 34-35.

59 Robert P. Nevin, "Stephen C. Foster and Negro Minstrelsy," *Atlantic Monthly* 20 (November 1867):608-16; Wittke, *Tambo and Bones,* pp. 174-76.

60 Wittke, *Tambo and Bones,* p. 176; Theodore W. Johnson, "Black Images in American Popular Song, 1840-1910" (Ph.D. diss., Northwestern University, 1975), p. 50.

61 "I'm Sailin' On De Old Canal," in Elias Howe [Gumbo Chaff], *The Ethiopian Glee Book* (Boston: Elias Howe, 1848), p. 40.

62 "In De Wild Rackoon Track," in Howe, *Ethiopian Glee Book,* pp. 24-25.

63 Cool White, "Lubly Fan Will You Cum Out To Night?" in Damon, *Old American Songs,* [1844], p. 164; S. S. Steele, "Kate of Caroline," quoted in Johnson, "Black Images," [1847], p. 13; George Willig, Jr., "Clare De Kitchen," in Damon, *Old American Songs,* [1832], p. 62; "De Yaller Corn," in Howe, *Ethiopian Glee Book,* p. 12; "The Gal from the South," quoted in Wittke, *Tambo and Bones,* [ca. 1840s], p. 186.

64 E. Deaves, "Ginger's Tale of Lub," in *Christy's Panorama Songster* (New York: William H. Murphy, 1860), pp. 106-7; Dan Myers and Silas S. Steele, "Dandy Jim O'Caroline," in Howe, *Ethiopian Glee Book,* p. 7.

65 "Black Sam," in *Panorama Songster,* p. 133. For an interesting, theatrical portrayal of black arrogance, see Cato in J. E. Heath, *Whigs and Democrats; or, Love of No Politics* (Richmond: T. W. White, 1839).

66 Myers and Steele, "Dandy Jim" in Howe, *Ethiopian Glee Book,* p. 7.

67 "Black Sam," in *Panorama Songster,* p. 134.

68 "Over the Mountain," in Howe, *Ethiopian Glee Book,* p. 31. See also "Ole Joe Golden," in Howe, *Ethiopian Glee Book,* p. 36.

69 "Gaily de Niggers Dance," quoted in Cecil Lloyd Patterson, "A Different Drum: The Image of the Negro in the Nineteenth Century Popular Song Books" (Ph.D. diss., University of Pennsylvania, 1961 [ca. 1847]), p. 147; "De Ole Roast Possum," quoted in Patterson, "Different Drum," [ca. 1847] p. 148; Dan Emmett, "Elam Moore," reprinted in Nathan, *Dan Emmett,* [1854], p. 346; Stephen Collins Foster, "My Old Kentucky Home, Good-Night!" in *Stephen Foster Song Book,* ed. Richard Jackson (New York: Dover Publications, Inc., 1974 [1853]), pp. 68-69; "The Hut Where We Lived," quoted in Patterson, "Different

Drum," [ca. 1847], p. 146; "Sing, Sing! Darkies Sing," in Howe, *Ethiopian Glee Book*, pp. 16–17; Christy Minstrels, "We'll Have a Little Dance To Night Boys," quoted in Johnson, "Black Images," [1848], p. 22.

70 "Come, Niggas Arouse," quoted in Patterson," Different Drum," [ca. 1847], p. 149.

71 Dan Emmett, "Jonny Roach," reprinted in Nathan, *Dan Emmett*, [1859], p. 358. See also James Porter, Sr., and James W. Porter, "De Loved Ones at Home" (Philadelphia: Lee & Walker, 1852); Christy Minstrels, "I Long For My Old Home in Kentuck" (Philadelphia: J. E. Gould, 1852); Frank Spencer and Hattie Livingston, "The Young Folks at Home" (New York: Gould & Berry, 1852), J. H. Collins and Frank Sulzner, "The Slave's Return" (New York: William Hall & Son, 1851); Charles Soran and John H. Hewitt, "Pompey's Trip to New York" (Baltimore: Henry McCaffrey, 1853).

72 Dan Emmett, "I'm Going Home to Dixie," reprinted in Nathan, *Dan Emmett*, [1858], pp. 351–53; Stephen Collins Foster, "Old Folks at Home," in Jackson, *Foster Song Book*, [1851], pp. 101–3; Dan Emmett, "Loozyanna Low Grounds," reprinted in Nathan, *Dan Emmett*, [1859], p. 379. For images of slaves with unrealistic views of life outside the plantation world, see "Ching A Ring Chaw," in Damon, *Old American Songs*, [1833], pp. 65–66; L. Maria Child, "The Stars and Stripes," in *The Liberty Bell* (Boston: National Anti-Slavery Bazaar, 1858), pp. 132–33.

73 Eileen Southern, *The Music of Black Americans: A History* (New York: W. W. Norton & Company, 1971), pp. 126–28; George W. Clark, *The Harp of Freedom* (New York: Miller, Orton & Mulligan, 1856), p. iv. See also Vicki L. Eaklor, "Music in the American Antislavery Movement, 1830–1860" (M.A. thesis, Washington University, 1979).

74 John Greenleaf Whittier and George W. Clark, "Gone, Sold and Gone," in *The Liberty Minstrel*, ed. George W. Clark (New York, 1846), pp. 5–6.

75 William Lloyd Garrison, "Anti-Slavery Hymn #14," in *A Selection of Anti-Slavery Hymns, for the Use of the Friends of Emancipation*, ed. William Lloyd Garrison (Boston: Garrison & Knapp, 1834), p. 18; E. D. H., "Brothers Be Brave For the Pining Slave," in Clark, *Liberty Minstrel*, p. 28.

76 "I Am Monarch of Nought I Survey," in Clark, *Liberty Minstrel*, pp. 18–19.

77 Johnson, "Black Images," p. 37; Gaines, *Southern Plantation*, p. 130.

78 Paskman and Spaeth, *"Gentlemen, Be Seated!"* pp. 119–21.

79 "The Bee-Gum," reprinted in Nathan, *Dan Emmett*, [1833], p. 163; Charles White, "The Dinner Horn," in *Panorama Songster*, pp. 119–20; Angilo C. Lafferty, "There's Nothing Like It!" quoted in Johnson, "Black Images," [1856], p. 56.

80 Stephen Collins Foster, "Way Down In Ca-I-Ro," in Jackson, *Foster Song Book*, [1850], p. 151.

81 One exception to this trend was Robert Montgomery Bird's blank verse tragedy, *The Gladiator* (1831). This tacitly abolitionist drama was not performed south of St. Louis after 1847 because it offended proslavery advocates. See John Daniel Collins, "American Drama in Antislavery Agitation, 1792–1861" (Ph.D. diss., State University of Iowa, 1963), p. 115; Clement E. Foust,

The Life and Dramatic Works of Robert Montgomery Bird (New York: Knickerbocker Press, 1919), p. 51; Dormon, *Theater in the Ante Bellum South,* p. 277.

82 George Lionel Stevens, *The Patriot; or, Union and Freedom* (Boston: Marsh, Capen & Lyon, 1834), p. 20; Henry Clay Preuss, *Fashions and Follies of Washington Life* (Washington, D. C., 1857), p. 16; William Tappan Thompson, *Major Jones' Courtship; or, Adventures of a Christmas Eve* (Savannah: E. J. Purse, 1850), p. 56; Mrs. Sidney F. Bateman, *Self,* in *Representative Plays by American Dramatists,* ed. Montrose J. Moses, 3 vols. (New York: E. P. Dutton & Company, 1918–1925 [New York: S. French, 1856]), 2:715–16, 745–47, 763–64; Clifton W. Tayleure, *Horseshoe Robinson; or, The Battle of King's Mountain,* in Moses, *Representative Plays,* [New York: Samuel French, 1856], 2: 777, 784–85, 810–11; Moody, *America Takes the Stage,* p. 68.

83 John Brougham, *Dred; or, the Dismal Swamp* (New York: Samuel French, 1856), p. 4.

84 Ibid., pp. 5–7, 21.

85 Loften Mitchell, *Black Drama: The Story of the American Negro in the Theatre* (New York: Hawthorn Books, Inc., 1967), pp. 32–33; *Lynchburg Daily Virginian,* 10 January 1854; Dormon, *Theater in the Ante Bellum South,* pp. 278–80; Charles S. Watson, *Antebellum Charleston Dramatists* (University, Alabama: University of Alabama Press, 1976), p. 145; Frank Rahill, "America's Number One Hit," *Theatre Arts* 36 (October 1952):21; Richard Moody, "Uncle Tom, the Theater and Mrs. Stowe," *American Heritage* 6 (October 1955):33–34. For accounts of the national acceptance of Uncle Tom-based burlesques, see Toll, *Blacking Up,* pp. 90–96; Joseph P. Roppolo, "Uncle Tom in New Orleans: Three Lost Plays," *New England Quarterly* 27 (June 1954): 213–26.

86 G. C. Howard, "Oh! I'se So Wicked," reprinted in Harlowe R. Hoyt, *Town Hall Tonight* (Englewood Cliffs, N. J.: Prentice-Hall, Inc., 1955 [1854]), p. 63; George L. Aiken, *Uncle Tom's Cabin,* in Moses, *Representative Plays,* [New York: S. French, ca. 1852], 2:642.

87 Dan Rice, "Wait for the Wagon," quoted in Roppolo, "Three Lost Plays," p. 222.

88 Toll, *Blacking Up,* p. 94.

89 Moody, "Uncle Tom," p. 32; Furnas, *Goodbye to Uncle Tom,* pp. 260–61; Turner, *Anti-Slavery Sentiment,* p. 75.

90 Harriet Beecher Stowe, *The Christian Slave* (Boston: Phillips, Sampson & Company, 1855), pp. 1, 14, 34–35, 37, 41–42. For an account of two lost plays which, in their own way, promoted the theme of "No North, no South, but Justice and Fraternity," see the description of *Distant Relations; or, A Southerner in New York* (1859) and *The Old Plantation; or, The Real Uncle Tom* (1860) in Arthur Hobson Quinn, *A History of the American Drama: From the Beginning to the Civil War* (New York: Appleton-Century Crofts, Inc., 1951 [New York: Harper & Brothers, 1923]), p. 291.

91 Aiken, *Uncle Tom's Cabin,* p. 634.

CHAPTER 3. *Black Americans Fight Back*

1 For a more complete study of the slaves' educational efforts, see Thomas L. Webber, *Deep Like the Rivers: Education in the Slave Quarter Community, 1831–1865* (New York: W. W. Norton & Company, Inc., 1978).

2 Frederick Douglass to Thomas Auld, 3 September 1848, in *Anti-Slavery Bugle*, 29 September 1848; Frederick Douglass, *My Bondage and My Freedom* (New York: Dover Publications, Inc. 1969 [New York: Miller, Orton & Mulligan, 1855]), pp. 89–91; Frederick Douglass, *Life and Times of Frederick Douglass* (New York: Crowell-Collier Publishing Company, 1962 [Boston: DeWolfe, Fiske & Co., 1892]), p. 50. For the effect which written accounts of America's racial past had on Douglass, see his *Narrative of the Life of Frederick Douglass, An American Slave* (New York: New American Library, 1968 [Boston: Anti-Slavery Office, 1845]), pp. 54–55.

3 Dorothy B. Porter, "The Organized Educational Activities of Negro Literary Societies, 1828–1846," *Journal of Negro Education* 5 (October 1936):559–70.

4 See Robert Benjamin Lewis, *Light and Truth; Collected from the Bible and Ancient and Modern History, Containing the Universal History of the Colored and the Indian Race, from the Creation of the World to the Present Time* (Boston: B. F. Roberts, 1844); James W. C. Pennington, *A Text Book of the Origin and History, &c. &c. of the Colored People* (Hartford, Conn.: L. Skinner, 1841); Christopher Rush, *A Short Account of the Rise and Progress of the African Methodist Episcopal Church in America* (New York, 1843); James McCune Smith, *A Lecture on the Haytien Revolutions, with a Sketch of the Character of Toussaint L'Ouverture* (New York: D. Fanshaw, 1841); William Cooper Nell, *The Colored Patriots of the American Revolution* (Boston: Robert F. Wallcut, 1855); Martin Robison Delany, *The Condition, Elevation, Emigration and Destiny of the Colored People of the United States Politically Considered* (Philadelphia, 1852); James Theodore Holly, *A Vindication of the Capacity of the Negro Race for Self-Government, and Civilized Progress . . .* (New Haven: Afric-American Printing Co., 1857). For an evaluation of the works of these authors, see Helen Boardman, "The Rise of the Negro Historian," *Negro History Bulletin* 8 (April 1945):148–50; Earl E. Thorpe, *Black Historians: A Critique* (New York: William Morrow and Company, Inc., 1971), pp. 33–38.

5 Pennington, *Text Book*, p. 5; Holly, *Vindication*, reprinted in *Black Separatism and the Caribbean, 1860*, ed. Howard H. Bell (Ann Arbor: University of Michigan Press, 1970), p. 23; Nell, *Colored Patriots*, p. 379.

6 Pennington, *Text Book*, pp. 39–42.

7 Hosea Easton, *A Treatise on the Intellectual Character, and Civil and Political Condition of the Colored People of the U. States; and the Prejudice Exercised Towards Them: with a Sermon on the Duty of the Church to Them* (Boston: Isaac Knapp, 1837), pp. 12, 18. Easton's interpretation of Genesis 9–10 assumed that Noah's son Ham was the projenitor of the dark-skinned Egyptians and that Ham's brother Japheth was the forefather of the Indo-European Greeks.

8 Ibid., p. 19. For Delany's contrasting views of the "hardy and enduring" Africans and various "unprincipled" Englishmen, see Delany, *Condition*, pp. 53–56, 58.

9 Delany, *Condition*, pp. 7–8, 10, 25–29, 209. For additional criticism of the "pseudo-humanitarians," see Holly, *Vindication*, pp. 21–22.

10 Pennington, *Text Book*, pp. 48, 50; Nell, *Colored Patriots*, pp. 73–75, 270. For one of the Cuffe's early attempts at writing history, see Paul Cuffe, *A Brief Account of the Settlement and Present Situation of the Colony of Sierra Leone, in Africa* (New York: Samuel Wood, 1812).

11 Easton, *Treatise*, p. 38; Pennington, *Text Book*, pp. 89–90. See also Delany, *Condition*, pp. 26–29.

12 Jupiter Hammon, "The Kind Master and the Dutiful Servant," in *America's First Negro Poet: The Complete Works of Jupiter Hammon of Long Island*, ed. Stanley Austin Ransom, Jr. (Port Washington: Kennikat Press, 1970 [1783]), p. 59.

13 Jupiter Hammon, *An Address to the Negroes in the State of New-York* (New York: Carroll and Patterson, 1787) reprinted in Ransom, *Complete Works*, p. 117.

14 Ibid., pp. 107, 112–13, 117–18.

15 Oscar Wegelin, "Biographical Sketch of Jupiter Hammon," in Ransom, *Complete Works*, p. 33.

16 Phillis Wheatley, "To the Right Honourable William, Earl of Dartmouth, His Majesty's Principal Secretary of State for North-America, &c," in *Poems on Various Subjects, Religious and Moral* (Philadelphia: Joseph Crukshank, 1786 [London: A. Bell, 1773]), pp. 39–40. For further commentary by Wheatley on freedom and Africa, see Charles W. Akers, "'Our Modern Egyptians': Phillis Wheatley and the Whig Campaign Against Slavery in Revolutionary Boston," *Journal of Negro History* 60 (July 1975): 406–7; William H. Robinson, *Phillis Wheatley in the Black American Beginnings* (Detroit: Broadside Press, 1975), pp. 59–60.

17 Wheatley, *Poems*, p. 13.

18 Ibid., pp. 12, 50; Eugene B. Redmond, *Drumvoices: The Mission of Afro-American Poetry* (Garden City: Anchor Press/Doubleday, 1976), p. 56.

19 For further commentary on these constraints, see Arthur P. Davis, "Personal Elements in the Poetry of Phillis Wheatley," *Phylon* 14 (June 1953): 192–93, 198; M. A. Richmond, *Bid the Vassal Soar: Interpretive Essays on the Life and Poetry of Phillis Wheatley and George Moses Horton* (Washington, D.C.: Howard University Press, 1974), p. 54; Robinson, *Phillis Wheatley*, pp. 42, 45.

20 George R. Allen, "On Slavery," reprinted in *Early Negro Writing, 1760–1837*, ed. Dorothy Porter (Boston: Beacon Press, 1971 [1828]), p. 574.

21 "The Black Beauty," *Freedom's Journal* 1 (8 June 1827): 52.

22 Charles L. Reason, "Freedom," reprinted in *An Anthology of Verse by American Negroes*, eds. Newman Ivey White, Walter Clinton Jackson, James Hardy Dillard (Durham, N.C.: Trinity College Press, 1924 [1847]), p. 48. Ada, "My Country," *Liberator* 4 (4 January 1834): 4.

23 James M. Whitfield, "America," reprinted in *Early Black American Poets,* ed. William H. Robinson, Jr. (Dubuque: Wm. C. Brown Company, 1969 [1853]), p. 40.

24 Joseph C. Holly, "Injustice — not Law," in *Freedom's Offering, A Collection of Poems* (Rochester: Charles H. McDonnell, 1853), p. 27; Frances Ellen Watkins, "Bible Defense of Slavery," in *Poems on Miscellaneous Subjects* (Philadelphia: Merrihew & Thompson, 1857), p. 9; Watkins, "Eliza Harris," in *Poems,* p. 11; Holly, "The Patriot's Lament," in *Freedom's Offering,* p. 18.

25 Frances Ellen Watkins, "Bury Me in a Free Land," *National Anti-Slavery Standard* 19 (4 December 1858):1.

26 Joan R. Sherman, *Invisible Poets: Afro-Americans of the Nineteenth Century* (Urbana: University of Illinois Press, 1974), p. xxi; Elymas Payson Rogers, "On the Fugitive Slave Law," in Robinson, *Early Black American Poets,* [1855], p. 62; Frederick Douglass, speech in New York City, 11 May 1857, in *The Life and Writings of Frederick Douglass,* vol. 2: *Pre-Civil War Decade 1850–1860,* ed. Philip S. Foner (New York: International Publishers, 1950), p. 414; Whitfield, "To Cinque," in Robinson, *Early Black American Poets,* [1853], p. 49. For white-authored antebellum verse which displayed an heroic element in the slave character, see especially M. Roland Markham, *Alcar, the Captive Creole; A Story of the South, in Verse* (Homer, New York: Jos. R. Dixon, 1857), pp. 11–12; Sophia L. Little, "The Autograph of Sims," in *The Liberty Bell* (Boston: National Anti-Slavery Bazaar, 1852), pp. 69–70. For a modern account of Joseph Cinque's 1839 slave mutiny, see Mary Cable, *Black Odyssey: The Case of the Slave Ship Amistad* (New York: Viking Press, 1971).

27 See Ada, "The Slave," *Liberator* 7 (11 March 1837):44; A. Gibbs Campbell, "The Prayer of the Bondmen," *National Anti-Slavery Standard* 19 (9 April 1859):4.

28 George Moses Horton, "The Slave's Complaint," in *Poems by a Slave* (Philadelphia: Lewis Gunn, 1837), pp. 9–10. See also George Moses Horton, "On Hearing of the Intention of a Gentleman to Purchase the Poet's Freedom," in *Poems,* pp. 21–22.

29 Ada, "The Slave Girl's Farewell," *Liberator* 5 (27 June 1835): 104; Watkins, "The Fugitive's Wife," in *Poems,* p. 27; Watkins, "The Slave Mother," in *Poems,* p. 7.

30 Watkins, "Tennessee Hero," in *Poems,* pp. 33–34; Holly, "The Fugitive," in *Freedom's Offering,* pp. 19–20.

31 Frederick Douglass, "The Heroic Slave," *Frederick Douglass' Paper* (4–25 March 1853), reprinted in *Violence in the Black Imagination,* ed. Ronald T. Takaki (New York: Capricorn Books, 1972), pp. 40, 64. For a twentieth-century historian's account of the mutiny, see Howard Jones, "The Peculiar Institution and National Honor: The Case of the Creole Slave Revolt," *Civil War History* 21 (March 1975): 28–50.

32 Douglass, "Heroic Slave," pp. 39–40, 75. For an account of Douglass' personal struggle with slavery's psychological bonds, see Douglass, *My Bondage,* pp. 159–61, 166–69, 219–21, 246–47.

33 Douglass, "Heroic Slave," p. 75.

34 Ibid., pp. 37–38, 76–77. To compare Madison Washington with two of the boldest slave heroes created by white writers, see Richard Hildreth, *The Slave; or, Memoirs of Archy Moore*, 2 vols. (Boston: John H. Eastburn, 1836) and the depiction of Carlos in "The Fugitives," in *Star of Emancipation* (Boston: Massachusetts Female Emancipation Society, 1841).

35 Frank J. Webb, *The Garies and Their Friends* (London: G. Routledge & Co., 1857), p. 4. William Wells Brown, *The Escape; or, A Leap for Freedom* (New York: Prologue Press, 1969 [Boston: P. F. Wallcut, 1858]), pp. 13, 32.

36 Martin R. Delany, *Blake; or, The Huts of America* (Boston: Beacon Press, 1970 [*The Weekly Anglo-African*, 26 November 1861–24 May 1862]), pp. 51, 67, 76, 82; William Wells Brown, *Clotel; or, The President's Daughter: A Narrative of Slave Life in the United States* (New York: Collier Books, 1970 [London: Partridge & Oakey, 1853]), pp. 110–11; Douglass, "Heroic Slave," p. 53.

37 Delany, *Blake*, p. 33.

38 Ibid., pp. 83–84. For an interpretation of Delany's ideology as a forerunner of modern militancy, see John Zeugner, "A Note on Martin Delany's *Blake*, and Black Militancy," *Phylon* 32 (Spring 1971): 98–105.

39 Delaney, *Blake*, pp. 11, 37; Brown, *Escape*, p. 8.

40 Brown, *Clotel*, p. 119.

41 Ibid., pp. 107–8.

42 Brown, *Escape*, p. 5. See also Brown, *Clotel*, p. 80; Delany, *Blake*, p. 64.

43 Brown, *Escape*, pp. 15, 19, 23; Brown, *Clotel*, pp. 69–74; Delany, *Blake*, p. 26.

44 Delany, *Blake*, pp. 16, 18, 20, 41, 69; Brown, *Clotel*, pp. 73, 75. Martin Delany attacked *Uncle Tom's Cabin* both because of its stand on colonization and because he felt that Mrs. Stowe "knows nothing about us." For commentary on this matter and on the view that Delany's protagonist, Henry Holland, represented the antithesis of Tom, see Roger W. Hite, "'Stand Still and See the Salvation': The Rhetorical Design of Martin Delany's *Blake*," *Journal of Black Studies* 5 (December 1974):192–202; Jean Fagan Yellin, *The Intricate Knot: Black Figures in American Literature, 1776–1863* (New York: New York University Press, 1972), p. 197; Addison Gayle, Jr., *The Way of the New World: The Black Novel in America* (Garden City, N.Y.: Anchor Press/Doubleday, 1975), p. 21.

45 For examples of the tragic mulatto archetype, see John Townsend Trowbridge, *Neighbor Jackwood* (Boston: Phillips, Sampson and Company, 1857); Joseph Holt Ingraham, *The Quadroone; or, St. Michael's Day* (London: Richard Bentley, 1840); Henry Wadsworth Longfellow, "The Quadroon Girl," in *Poems on Slavery* (Cambridge: J. Owen, 1842); Mayne Reid, *The Quadroon; or, A Lover's Adventures in Louisiana* (New York: R. M. DeWitt, 1856); H. L. Hosmer, *Adela, the Octoroon* (Columbus: Follett, Foster & Co., 1860).

46 For further literary analysis of this tragic figure, see Jules Zanger, "The 'Tragic Octoroon' in Pre-Civil War Fiction," *American Quarterly* 18 (Spring 1966): 63–70 and Judith R. Berzon, *Neither White Nor Black: The Mulatto Charac-*

ter in American Fiction (New York: New York University Press, 1978), pp. 99–116.

47 Dion Boucicault, *The Octoroon; or, Life in Louisiana* (Upper Saddle River, N.J.: Literature House/Gregg Press, 1970 [New York: S. French, 1859]), pp. 4–5, 16–17. Upon its New York premiere in December, 1859, some critics panned this play as sensationalist and incendiary, but according to Joseph Jefferson, an antebellum actor who played *The Octoroon's* Salem Scudder, the drama was noncommittal. The dialogue and characters "made one feel for the South, but the action proclaimed against slavery, and called loudly for its abolition." In January, 1860, Christy's Minstrels staged a burlesque of the play starring "Zoeasy, the Moctoroon . . . unhappy descendant of a Gorilla." Sidney Kaplan, "The Octoroon: Early History of the Drama of Miscegenation," *Journal of Negro Education* 20 (Fall 1951): 547–57; Robert Hogan, *Dion Boucicault* (New York: Twayne Publishers, Inc., 1969), pp. 40, 73–74, 117; Joseph Jefferson, *The Autobiography of Joseph Jefferson* (New York: The Century Co., 1890), p. 214.

48 William Wells Brown, *The Narrative of William W. Brown, A Fugitive Slave* (Reading, Mass.: Addison-Wesley Publishing Company, 1969 [Boston: Anti-Slavery Office, 1848]), pp. 1, 18, 28; William Wells Brown, *The Black Man, His Antecedents, His Genius, and His Achievements* (New York: Thomas Hamilton, 1863), p. 11; Brown, *Clotel*, p. 1.

49 Brown, *Black Man*, pp. 18–19; Brown, *Clotel*, pp. 39–40, 42–43.

50 Brown, *Clotel*, pp. 82, 133, 177.

51 Ibid., pp. 119–20. For a recent fictional treatment of certain of the themes developed in *Clotel*, see Barbara Chase-Riboud, *Sally Hemings* (New York: Viking Press, 1979).

52 Brown, *Narrative*, p. 42; Delany, *Blake*, p. 28.

53 Delany, *Blake*, pp. 110, 116.

54 Ibid., pp. 111, 117–18, 137–38, 247; Brown, *Clotel*, p. 181–88; Webb, *Garies*, pp. 8–9, 13. For other views on mulatto characters in the fiction of Brown, Webb, and Delany, see Toni Trent, "Stratification Among Blacks by Black Authors," *Negro History Bulletin* 34 (December 1971): 179–81; Arthur P. Davis, *"The Garies and Their Friends:* A Neglected Pioneer Novel," *CLA Journal* 13 (September 1969): 27–34; James H. DeVries, "The Tradition of the Sentimental Novel in *The Garies and Their Friends,*" *CLA Journal* 17 (December 1973): 241–49; Robert E. Fleming, "Black, White, and Mulatto in Martin R. Delany's *Blake,*" *Negro History Bulletin* 36 (February 1973): 37–39.

55 Delany, *Blake*, p. 109.

CHAPTER 4. *From Slave to Citizen, 1861–1965*

1 For a bibliographical survey of this literature, see Clarence L. Mohr, "Southern Blacks in the Civil War: A Century of Historiography," *Journal of Negro History* 59 (April 1974):177–95.

2 William Watson Davis, *The Civil War and Reconstruction in Florida* (Gainesville: University of Florida Press, 1964 [New York: Columbia University Press, 1913]), pp. 218–19.

3 Walter L. Fleming, *Civil War and Reconstruction in Alabama* (New York: Columbia University Press, 1905), pp. 209–12. See also Charles C. Jones, Jr., "Negro Slaves During the Civil War," *Magazine of American History* 16 (August 1886):168–69; James Ford Rhodes, *History of the United States from the Compromise of 1850,* 7 vols. (New York: The Macmillan Company, 1893–1906), 5:460–61; James Kendall Hosmer, *The Appeal to Arms, 1861–1863* (New York: Harper & Brothers Publishers, 1907), pp. 203–4.

4 Jones, "Negro Slaves," p. 169.

5 Fleming, *Civil War and Reconstruction,* pp. 210–12, 269–70; James Kendall Hosmer, *Outcome of the Civil War, 1863–1865* (New York: Harper & Brothers Publishers, 1907), p. 209.

6 Davis, *Florida,* pp. 237–38. See also E. Merton Coulter, *The Civil War and Readjustment in Kentucky* (Chapel Hill: University of North Carolina Press, 1926), pp. 203–4.

7 James Ford Rhodes, *History of the Civil War, 1861–1865* (New York: The Macmillan Company, 1917), p. 381. See also Rhodes, *History of the United States,* 5:463–64; James Schouler, *History of the United States of America, Under the Constitution,* 7 vols. (New York: Dodd, Mead & Company, 1894–1913), 6:217.

8 W. E. Burghardt DuBois, *Black Reconstruction in America* (Cleveland: World Publishing Company, 1968 [New York: Harcourt, Brace and Company, 1935]), pp. 55–83; Joseph T. Wilson, *The Black Phalanx* (Hartford: American Publishing Company, 1890), p. 100; Charles H. Wesley, "The Employment of Negroes as Soldiers in the Confederate Army," *Journal of Negro History* 4 (July 1919):240–41. See also William Wells Brown, *The Negro in the American Rebellion* (Boston: Lee & Shepard, 1867) and George W. Williams, *A History of the Negro Troops in the War of the Rebellion, 1861–1865* (New York: Harper & Brothers, 1888).

9 See Bell Irvin Wiley, *Southern Negroes, 1861–1865* (New Haven; Yale University Press, 1938). See also Bell Irvin Wiley, "Southern Reaction to Federal Invasion," *Journal of Southern History* 16 (November 1950):499, "A Time of Greatness," *Journal of Southern History* 22 (February 1956):32, and *Embattled Confederates: An Illustrated History of Southerners at War* (New York: Harper & Row Publishers, 1964), pp. 231–44; Herbert Aptheker, *The Negro in the Civil War* (New York: International Publishers, 1938), *American Negro Slave Revolts* (New York: Columbia University Press, 1943), pp. 94–95, 359–67, and "Notes on Slave Conspiracies in Confederate Mississippi," *Journal of Negro History* 29 (January 1944): 75–79; Harvey Wish, "Slave Disloyalty Under the Confederacy," *Journal of Negro History* 23 (October 1938):435–50.

10 Charles P. Roland, *Louisiana Sugar Plantations During the American Civil War* (Leiden, The Netherlands: E. J. Brill, 1957), p. 101.

11 Benjamin Quarles, *The Negro in the Civil War* (Boston: Little, Brown and Company, 1953), pp. 53–54, 56, 63–64, 262; Allan Nevins, *War Becomes Revo-*

lution (New York: Charles Scribner's Sons, 1960), p. 296. See also Charles L. Wagandt, "The Army Versus Maryland Slavery, 1862–1864," *Civil War History* 10 (June 1964):141; Tinsley Lee Spraggins, "Mobilization of Negro Labor for the Department of Virginia and North Carolina, 1861–1865," *North Carolina Historical Review* 24 (April 1947):176; B. H. Nelson, "Some Aspects of Negro Life in North Carolina During the Civil War," *North Carolina Historical Review* 25 (April 1948):156. Joel Williamson, *After Slavery: The Negro in South Carolina During Reconstruction, 1861–1877* (Chapel Hill: University of North Carolina Press, 1965), p. 7.

For the further development of these views during the 1970s, see Leon F. Litwack, "Free at Last," in *Anonymous Americans: Explorations in Nineteenth-Century Social History*, ed. Tamara K. Hareven (Englewood Cliffs: Prentice-Hall, Inc., 1971), pp. 131–71; Peter Kolchin, *First Freedom: The Responses of Alabama's Blacks to Emancipation and Reconstruction* (Westport: Greenwood Press, 1972); Edmund L. Drago, "How Sherman's March Through Georgia Affected the Slaves," *Georgia Historical Quarterly* 57 (Fall 1973):361–75; Paul D. Escott, "The Context of Freedom: Georgia's Slaves During the Civil War," *Georgia Historical Quarterly* 58 (Spring 1974): 79–104; William F. Messner, "Black Violence and White Response: Louisiana, 1862," *Journal of Southern History* 41 (February 1975):19–38; C. Peter Ripley, *Slaves and Freedmen in Civil War Louisiana* (Baton Rouge: Louisiana State University Press, 1976); Bobby L. Lovett, "The Negro's Civil War in Tennessee, 1861–1865," *Journal of Negro History* 41 (January 1976):36–49; James L. Roark, *Masters Without Slaves: Southern Planters in the Civil War and Reconstruction* (New York: W. W. Norton & Company, 1977); William L. Van Deburg, "Elite Slave Behavior During the Civil War: Black Drivers and Foremen in Historiographical Perspective," *Southern Studies* 16 (Fall 1977):253–69; Leon F. Litwack, *Been in the Storm So Long: The Aftermath of Slavery* (New York: Alfred A. Knopf, 1979).

12 See Woodrow Wilson, *Division and Reunion, 1829–1889* (New York: Longmans, Green, and Co., 1902 [1898]), p. x; George W. Williams, *History of the Negro Race in America from 1619 to 1880*, 2 vols. (New York: G. P. Putnam's Sons, 1883), 1: x; John Clark Ridpath, *A Popular History of the United States of America, from the Aboriginal Times to the Present Day* (Cincinnati: Jones Brothers & Company, 1881), p. iv; James Schouler, *History of the United States of America, Under the Constitution*, 7 vols. (New York: Dodd, Mead & Company, 1894–1913), 4: iv; 6: vi.

13 Horace Greely, *The American Conflict: A History of the Great Rebellion in the United States of America, 1860–'65*, 2 vols. (Hartford: O. D. Case & Company, 1864–1866), 2: 7; John Minor Botts, *The Great Rebellion: Its Secret History, Rise, Progress, and Disastrous Failure* (New York: Harper & Brothers, 1866), p. v. See also Jesse T. Peck, *The History of the Great Republic, Considered from a Christian Stand-Point* (New York: W. C. Palmer, Jr., 1871), pp. viii, 83; Thomas P. Kettell, *History of the Great Rebellion* (Hartford: L. Stebbins, 1866), p. iv.

14 John A. Logan, *The Great Conspiracy: Its Origin and History* (New York: A. R. Hart & Co., 1886), pp. 462–63; Peck, *Great Republic,* pp. 45, 563; Alexander Johnston, *The United States: Its History and Constitution* (New York: Charles Scribner's Sons, 1889), p. 137.

15 James G. Blaine, *Twenty Years of Congress: From Lincoln to Garfield,* 2 vols. (Norwich, Conn.: Henry Bill Publishing Company, 1884–1886), 1: 177; Greeley, *American Conflict,* p. 7; Logan, *Great Conspiracy,* pp. 463, 466, 468; Johnston, *United States,* p. 138.

16 Henry Wilson, *History of the Rise and Fall of the Slave Power in America,* 3 vols. (Boston: James R. Osgood and Company, 1872–1877), 1: 2; Johnston, *United States,* p. 138; E. Benjamin Andrews, *History of the United States,* 2 vols. (New York: Charles Scribner's Sons, 1894), 2: 77.

17 Andrews, *History,* p. 59; William T. Alexander, *History of the Colored Race in America* (New Orleans: Palmetto Publishing Co., 1887), p. 156; John G. Nicolay, *The Outbreak of Rebellion* (New York: Charles Scribner's Sons, 1881), p. 2; Botts, *Great Rebellion,* p. 67; Blaine, *Twenty Years,* p. 256; Wilson, *Rise and Fall,* 2: 323, 533.

18 Blaine, *Twenty Years,* p. 257; Wilson, *Rise and Fall,* 1: vi–vii; Kettell, *Great Rebellion,* p. 31; William Cullen Bryant and Sydney Howard Gay, *A Popular History of the United States,* 4 vols. (New York: Charles Scribner's Sons, 1876–1881), 4: 435–36; Botts, *Great Rebellion,* pp. 220–21.

19 Benson J. Lossing, *A Centennial Edition of the History of the United States* (Hartford: Thomas Belknap, 1876), p. 545; Blaine, *Twenty Years,* p. 217. See also Nicolay, *Outbreak of Rebellion,* p. 2; Wilson, *Rise and Fall,* 1: v; John Robert Irelan, *The Republic; or A History of the United States of America in the Administrations, from the Monarchic Colonial Days to the Present Times,* 18 vols. (Chicago: Fairbanks and Palmer Publishing Co., 1886–1888), 16: 477, Kettell, *Great Rebellion,* p. 36.

20 Williams, *History of the Negro Race,* 1: 115, 294, 296, 323; 2: 36. See also William Wells Brown, *The Rising Son; or, the Antecedents and Advancement of the Colored Race* (Boston: A. G. Brown & Co., 1874), p. 291; Wilson, *Rise and Fall,* 2: 61.

21 Schouler, *History,* 2: 268–69; Andrews, *History,* p. 5; Alexander, *History,* pp. 143–44.

22 Schouler, *History,* 2: 269; Andrews, *History,* pp. 4–5; Alexander, *History,* pp. 144–45.

23 George Lunt, *The Origin of the Late War: Traced from the Beginning of the Constitution to the Revolt of the Southern States* (New York: D. Appleton and Company, 1867), p. 159.

24 See J. L. M. Curry, "Legal Justification of the South in Secession," in *Confederate Military History,* ed. Clement A. Evans, 13 vols. (Atlanta: Confederate Publishing Company, 1899), 1: 3–4; Thomas Nelson Page, "The Old South," in *The Old South: Essays Social and Political* (New York: Charles Scribner's Sons, 1892), p. 51; Thomas Nelson Page, "The Want of a History of the Southern People," in Page, *Old South,* pp. 253–55, 257, 266–69.

25 Clement A. Evans, "The Civil History of the Confederate States," in Evans, *Confederate Military History*, 1: 263–64, 277, 434–35; Lunt, *Late War*, p. 327. See also Edward A. Pollard, *The Lost Cause: A New Southern History of the War of the Confederates* (New York: E. B. Treat & Co., 1866), p. 80.

26 Jefferson Davis, *The Rise and Fall of the Confederate Government*, 2 vols. (New York: D. Appleton and Company, 1881), 1: vi–vii, 34, 78–80; Pollard, *Lost Cause*, pp. 48–49; Evans, "Civil History," pp. 257, 264–65, 320; Joseph Hodgson, *The Cradle of the Confederacy; or, the Times of Troup, Quitman and Yancey* (Mobile: The Register Publishing Office, 1876), pp. 221, 227.

27 John Spencer Bassett, *Slavery and Servitude in the Colony of North Carolina* (Baltimore: The Johns Hopkins Press, 1896), p. 11; Victoria V. Clayton, *White and Black Under the Old Regime* (Milwaukee: Young Churchman Co., 1899), p. 195. Even historians who were somewhat more modern in their approach to the selection of source material acknowledged the usefulness of white reminiscences. Although grounded in legislative and court records, Jeffrey Brackett's contribution to the Johns Hopkins University Studies in Historical and Political Science carried the following notation: "We have not attempted to describe 'the old plantation' of the South, for the task has been well done by some who knew it. For an interesting account of life on a large and well ordered plantation, see, for instance, 'Memorials of a Southern Planter,' by Susan Dabney Smedes." Jeffrey R. Brackett, *The Negro in Maryland: A Study of the Institution of Slavery* (Baltimore: N. Murray, 1889), p. 263.

28 Pollard, *Lost Cause*, p. 81.

29 Jeanette H. Walworth, *Southern Silhouettes* (New York: Henry Holt and Company, 1887), pp. 1–3, 12–13. See also Belle Kearney, *A Slaveholder's Daughter* (New York: Negro Universities Press, 1969 [New York: Abbey Press, 1900]), p. 5; H. S. Fulkerson, *Random Recollections of Early Days in Mississippi* (Vicksburg: Vicksburg Printing and Publishing Company, 1885), p. 15; Susan Dabney Smedes, *Memorials of a Southern Planter* (Baltimore: Cushings & Bailey, 1888), pp. 3–4.

30 Clayton, *White and Black*, p. 124; Letitia M. Burwell [Page Thacker], *Plantation Reminiscences* (Owensboro, Ky., 1878), p. 69.

31 Mary Ross Banks, *Bright Days in the Old Plantation Time* (Boston: Lee and Shepard, Publishers, 1882), pp. 147–51, 167–68; Thomas Nelson Page, "Social Life in Old Virginia Before the War," in Page, *Old South*, p. 171. For stories of other noble slaveholders, see George W. Paschal, *Ninety-Four Years: Agnes Paschal* (Washington, D.C., 1871), p. 60; Smedes, *Memorials*, pp. 47–48, 108–9. For accounts describing the postbellum influence of the "sacred bond" which developed between master and slave, see Frances B. Leigh, *Ten Years on a Georgia Plantation Since the War* (New York: Negro Universities Press, 1969 [London: R. Bently & Sons, 1883]), pp. 236–37; M. V. Moore, "Recollections of a Former Slaveholder," *New England Magazine* 4 (July 1891):665–71; John Hallum, *The Diary of an Old Lawyer; or, Scenes Behind the Curtain* (Nashville: Southwestern Publishing House, 1895), pp. 213–16; Clayton, *White and Black*, pp. 57–58, 125, 130–31; Varina Jefferson Davis, *Jefferson Davis, Ex-*

President of the Confederate States of America: A Memoir by His Wife, 2 vols. (New York: Belford Company, Publishers, 1890), 1: 173–74.

32 Smedes, *Memorials,* p. 190; Davis, *Jefferson Davis,* pp. 174, 177–78.

33 Banks, *Bright Days,* pp. 3, 19–20. See also R. Q. Mallard, *Plantation Life Before Emancipation* (Richmond: Whittet & Shepperson, 1892), p. 235.

34 Page, "Social Life," p. 185. See also Dabney Herndon Maury, *Recollections of a Virginian in the Mexican, Indian, and Civil Wars.* (New York: Charles Scribner's Sons, 1894), p. 12.

35 Nicolay, *Outbreak of Rebellion,* p. 47; Brown, *Rising Son,* pp. 394–96; Wilson, *Rise and Fall,* 1: 321.

36 Larry Gara, *The Liberty Line: The Legend of the Underground Railroad* (Lexington: University of Kentucky Press, 1961), pp. 2, 143, 163–64. See especially the antebellum musical celebration of the "railway under-ground" in William Wells Brown's *The Escape; or, A Leap for Freedom* (New York: Prologue Press, 1969 [Boston: P. F. Wallcut, 1858]), pp. 47–48.

37 Norman B. Wood, *The White Side of a Black Subject: A Vindication of the Afro-American Race* (Chicago: American Publishing House, 1897), pp. 168–69, 174; William Still, *The Underground Rail Road* (Philadelphia: Porter & Coates, 1872), p. 649; R. C. Smedley, *History of the Underground Railroad in Chester and the Neighboring Counties of Pennsylvania* (Lancaster: Office of the Journal, 1883), p. 55; Eber M. Pettit, *Sketches in the History of the Underground Railroad* (Fredonia, New York: W. McKinstry & Son, 1879), p. 35; Levi Coffin, *Reminiscences of Levi Coffin* (Cincinnati: The Robert Clarke Company, 1898 [Cincinnati: Western Tract Society, 1876]), p. i.

38 Smedley, *Underground Railroad,* pp. 34, 100, 105; John Hutchins, "The Underground Railroad," *Magazine of Western History,* 5 (March 1887):676; Pettit, *Sketches,* pp. xi, xiv; Calvin Fairbank, *Rev. Calvin Fairbank During Slavery Times: How He 'Fought the Good Fight' to Prepare 'The Way'* (Chicago: R. R. McCabe & Co., 1890), pp. 10–12.

39 For accounts of such individuals, see Laura S. Haviland, *A Woman's Life-Work: Labors and Experiences of Laura S. Haviland* (Chicago: C. V. Waite & Company, 1887 [Grand Rapids: S. B. Shaw, 1881]), p. 65; Fairbank, *Calvin Fairbank,* p. 27; G. W. E. Hill, "Underground Railroad Adventures," *Midland Monthly* 3 (February 1895):175.

40 James H. Fairchild, *The Underground Railroad* (Cleveland: Western Reserve Historical Society, 1895), p. 94; Marion Gleason McDougall, *Fugitive Slaves* (Boston: Ginn & Company, 1891), pp. 60–61; Pettit, *Sketches,* pp. 39, 90; Smedley, *Underground Railroad,* p. 92; Wilbur H. Siebert, *The Underground Railroad from Slavery to Freedom* (New York: The Macmillan Company, 1898), p. 87. For stories of free black agents see Smedley, *Underground Railroad,* pp. 45–47, 97.

41 Smedley, *Underground Railroad,* pp. 73–74, 159–61; Pettit, *Sketches,* pp. 27–33, 97–99, 113–15, 125–29, 157–64; Coffin, *Reminiscences,* pp. 139–43, 160–69; Hutchins, "Underground Railroad," p. 674.

42 Still, *Underground Rail Road,* pp. 2, 51, 63, 79, 97, 105, 145, 202.

43 Ibid., p. 202. For additional commentary on Still, see Gara, *Liberty Line*, pp. 175–78.

44 J. B. Henneman, "Historical Studies in the South Since the War," *Sewanee Review* 1 (May 1893):337.

45 Wilson, *Division and Reunion*, p. 123. See also Samuel Wylie Crawford, *The Genesis of the Civil War: The Story of Sumter, 1860–1861* (New York: C. L. Webster & Company, 1887), p. viii; Brackett, *Negro in Maryland*, p. 1.

46 For further commentary on the rise of scientific history and the professionalization of the discipline, see W. Stull Holt, "The Idea of Scientific History in America," *Journal of the History of Ideas* 1 (June 1940):352–62; Edward N. Saveth, "A Science of American History," *Diogenes* 26 (Summer 1959):107–22; Deborah L. Haines, "Scientific History as a Teaching Method: The Formative Years," *Journal of American History* 63 (March 1977):892–912; Bert James Loewenberg, *American History in American Thought: Christopher Columbus to Henry Adams* (New York: Simon and Schuster, 1972), pp. 344–45, 380–81; John Higham, *History: The Development of Historical Studies in the United States* (Englewood Cliffs, N.J.: Prentice-Hall, Inc., 1965), pp. 3–25, 92–103, 158–70.

47 A transitional figure in American historiography, Rhodes was one of the last great amateur historians. Leaving a successful Cleveland coal and iron business, he moved to Cambridge and then to Boston during the early 1890s in order to study and to write history. In 1898, he was elected President of the American Historical Association. His major work was the *History of the United States from the Compromise of 1850*, 7 vols. (New York: The Macmillan Company, 1893–1906). Burgess was the son of a slaveholding Tennessee Unionist who left the South at age 18 to study at Amherst College and at the universities of Berlin, Leipzig, and Göttingen. Upon his return, he was instrumental in the organization of graduate studies in political science and history at Columbia University. The revisionist views which he contributed to the Rhodes-Burgess Compromise are found in *The Civil War and the Constitution, 1859–1865*, 2 vols. (New York: C. Scribner's Sons, 1901) and *Reconstruction and the Constitution, 1866–1876* (New York: C. Scribner's Sons, 1902). His personal views on historiographical reconciliation can be found in capsule form in *The Middle Period, 1817–1858* (New York: Charles Scribner's Sons, 1897), pp. vii–xii.

48 Rhodes, *History*, 1: 303, 305–10.

49 Ibid., pp. 26, 306–8, 344. For further commentary on Rhodes' conciliatory stance, see Thomas J. Pressly, *Americans Interpret Their Civil War* (Princeton: Princeton University Press, 1954), pp. 135–49.

50 Rhodes, *History*, 1: 303, 324.

51 Memorandum of meeting with Theodore Roosevelt, 16 November 1905, quoted in M. A. DeWolfe Howe, *James Ford Rhodes: American Historian* (New York: D. Appleton and Company, 1929), p. 120. For further commentary on Rhodes' racial stereotyping—and on his belief that in part the "Negro problem" was a result of blacks raping white women—see John David Smith, "The Forma-

tive Period of American Slave Historiography, 1890–1920" (Ph.D. diss., University of Kentucky, 1977), pp. 36–37; Robert Cruden, "James Ford Rhodes and the Negro: A Study in the Problem of Objectivity," *Ohio History* 71 (July 1962):129–37. For a discussion of racism and Teutonism in the American historical profession of the late nineteenth and early twentieth centuries, see I. A. Newby, *Jim Crow's Defense: Anti-Negro Thought in America, 1900–1930* (Baton Rouge: Louisiana State University Press, 1965), pp. 52–82.

52 John Spencer Bassett, *A Short History of the United States* (New York: The Macmillan Company, 1913), p. 351; W. P. Harrison, *The Gospel Among the Slaves* (Nashville: Publishing House of the M. E. Church, South, 1893), p. 99; Schouler, *History*, 1: 4; Bassett, *Slavery and Servitude*, p. 12; Philip Alexander Bruce, *Economic History of Virginia in the Seventeenth Century*, 2 vols. (New York: Macmillan and Co., 1896), 2: 73, 108; Irelan, *Republic*, 16: 453; Hamilton W. Mabie and Marshal H. Bright, *The Memorial Story of America* (Philadelphia: John C. Winston & Co., 1892), pp. 291–92; Woodrow Wilson, *A History of the American People*, 5 vols. (New York: Harper & Brothers, 1902–1903), 4: 194–95.

53 Smith, "Formative Period," pp. 184, 192; Booker T. Washington, *The Story of the Negro: The Rise of the Race from Slavery*, 2 vols. (New York: Doubleday, Page & Company, 1909), 1: 184–85.

54 Washington, *Story of the Negro*, 1: 158, 179–80.

55 Ibid., pp. 144–46, 188; Booker T. Washington, *Up From Slavery* (New York: Bantam Books, 1963 [New York: A. L. Burt Company, 1901]), pp. 2, 11–12. For the role played by white journalist Max Bennett Thrasher in the writing of *Up From Slavery*, see Louis R. Harlan, *Booker T. Washington: The Making of a Black Leader, 1856–1901* (New York: Oxford University Press, 1972), pp. 246–47. For the role played by white journalist/sociologist Robert Ezra Park in the writing of *The Story of the Negro*, see *The Booker T. Washington Papers*, ed. Louis R. Harlan and Raymond W. Smock, 8 vols. (Urbana: University of Illinois Press, 1972–1979), 8: 203.

56 Washington, *Story of the Negro*, 1: 12, 182, 185; Washington, *Up From Slavery*, pp. 10–11.

57 For further commentary on these historiographical trends, see Higham, *History*, pp. 104–16, 171–211; Richard Hofstadter, *The Progressive Historians: Turner, Beard, Parrington* (New York: Alfred A. Knopf, 1968); Charles Crowe, "The Emergence of Progressive History," *Journal of the History of Ideas* 27 (January–March 1966):109–24. For an example of slavery studies which avoided interpretation in favor of reciting southern slave codes, legislative acts, and court proceedings, see Edward McCrady, *Slavery in the Province of South Carolina, 1670–1770* (Washington, D.C.: American Historical Association, 1896).

58 Ulrich B. Phillips, *Life and Labor in the Old South* (Boston: Little, Brown and Company, 1963 [Boston: Little, Brown and Company, 1929]), p. viii. See also Ulrich B. Phillips, *Georgia and State Rights* (Washington, D.C.: American Historical Association, 1902), pp. 5–6; "The Master Touch is Urged on Youth,"

New York Times (29 March 1931), sec. 3, p. 7. During his years as a student at the University of Georgia, at the University of Chicago, and at Columbia University, Phillips studied with John H. T. McPherson, Frederick Jackson Turner, William Archibald Dunning, John W. Burgess, and James Harvey Robinson. For commentary on Phillips' college career and on the influence of these professors, see Wendell Holmes Stephenson, *The South Lives in History: Southern Historians and Their Legacy* (Baton Rouge: Louisiana State University Press, 1955), pp. 59–60, 62–65, 87–89; Wendell H. Stephenson, "Ulrich B. Phillips: The University of Georgia and the Georgia Historical Society," *Georgia Historical Quarterly* 41 (June 1957):103–25; Ulrich B. Phillips, "The Traits and Contributions of Frederick Jackson Turner," *Agricultural History* 19 (January 1945):21.

59 At birth, the future historian was named Ulysses Bonnell Phillips in honor of the doctor who had attended the delivery. When he was twelve years old, Phillips became convinced that his given name had "damnyankee" connotations. With his parents' approval, "Ulrich" was selected to replace "Ulysses" so that his original initials could be preserved. Wood Gray, "Ulrich Bonnell Phillips," in *The Marcus W. Jernegan Essays in American Historiography*, ed. William T. Hutchinson (New York: Russell and Russell, 1958 [Chicago: University of Chicago Press, 1937]), pp. 355–56.

60 Phillips, *Life and Labor*, pp. 123–24; Ulrich Bonnell Phillips, *American Negro Slavery: A Survey of the Supply, Employment and Control of Negro Labor as Determined by the Plantation Regime* (Baton Rouge: Louisiana State University Press, 1969 [New York: D. Appleton and Company, 1918]), pp. 383–84, 386. For an account of other instances in which Phillips drew upon personal experience "to throw light upon the past," see Fred Landon, "Ulrich Bonnell Phillips: Historian of the South," *Journal of Southern History* 5 (August 1939): 367–68.

61 Phillips, *Life and Labor*, p. 338; Phillips, *American Negro Slavery*, preface, p. 2; Ulrich B. Phillips, "Black-Belt Labor, Slave and Free," in *Lectures and Addresses on the Negro in the South* (Charlottesville: Michie Company, 1915), p. 29; Ulrich B. Phillips, "The Plantation as a Civilizing Factor," *Sewanee Review* 12 (July 1904):265.

62 Smith, "Formative Period," pp. 248–49; Stephenson, *South Lives in History*, pp. 58, 79–80; Phillips to George J. Baldwin, 2 May 1903, Phillips Papers, Southern Historical Collection, University of North Carolina, Chapel Hill; Phillips to William W. Ball, 28 November 1923, W. W. Ball Papers, Duke University Library, Durham, North Carolina.

63 Phillips, *Life and Labor*, pp. 196–99, 201–3, 363.

64 Ibid., p. 160.

65 Ibid., p. 196.

66 Ibid., p. 200.

67 Phillips, *American Negro Slavery*, p. 401.

68 Phillips, *Life and Labor*, p. 366.

69 Allen Tate, review of *Life and Labor in the Old South*, in *New Republic*, 59

(10 July 1929): 211–12. See also C. P. Patterson, review of *American Negro Slavery*, in *Political Science Quarterly* 33 (September 1918):456; Tipton R. Snavely, review of *American Negro Slavery*, in *American Economic Review* 10 (June 1920):336; J. G. deRoulhac Hamilton, "Interpreting the Old South," *Virginia Quarterly Review* 5 (October 1929):631; Henry Steele Commager, review of *Life and Labor in the Old South*, in New York Herald Tribune *Books* 5 (19 May 1929):4; William K. Boyd, review of *Life and Labor in the Old South*, in *American Historical Review* 35 (October 1929):133; review of *Life and Labor in the Old South*, in *Sewanee Review* 38 (January 1930):124; Richard H. Shyrock, review of *Life and Labor in the Old South*, in *South Atlantic Quarterly* 29 (January 1930):96.

70 Fred Landon, "A Bibliography of the Writings of Professor Ulrich Bonnell Phillips," *Agricultural History* 8 (October 1934):198; American Historical Association, *Guide to Historical Literature* (New York: The Macmillan Company, 1961), pp. 725–26.

71 Edward Channing, *A History of the United States*, 6 vols. (New York: The Macmillan Company, 1905–1925), 5: 125; R. S. Cotterill, *The Old South: The Geographic, Economic, Social, Political, and Cultural Expansion, Institutions, and Nationalism of the Ante-bellum South* (Glendale, Calif.: Arthur H. Clark Company, 1939), p. 269; William B. Hesseltine, *A History of the South, 1607–1936* (New York: Prentice-Hall, Inc., 1936), p. 328; W. E. Woodward, *A New American History* (New York: Farrar & Rinehart, Inc., 1936), pp. 114, 412; John D. Hicks, *The Federal Union: A History of the United States to 1865*, 2 vols. (Boston: Houghton Mifflin Company, 1937), 1: 495–96. For an estimation of Phillips' influence upon studies of slavery in individual states, see Bennett H. Wall, "African Slavery," in *Writing Southern History: Essays in Historiography in Honor of Fletcher M. Green*, ed. Arthur S. Link and Rembert W. Patrick (Baton Rouge: Louisiana State University Press, 1965), pp. 185–86. For Phillips' influence upon elementary and secondary school history texts, see James McPherson, "The 'Saga' of Slavery: Setting the Textbooks Straight," *Changing Education* 1 (Winter 1967):26–33, 48.

72 Ulrich B. Phillips, "Conservatism and Progress in the Cotton Belt," *South Atlantic Quarterly* 3 (January 1904):2, 7–8; Ulrich B. Phillips, "The Economics of the Plantation," *South Atlantic Quarterly* 2 (July 1903):231, 233, 235.

73 Phillips was not alone in his advocacy of the new plantation. For one of the most extensive plantation plans of the day, see Enoch M. Banks, *The Economics of Land Tenure in Georgia* (New York: Columbia University Press, 1905). In the 1960s, various aspects of Phillips' system were still being discussed as progressive agricultural reforms. See Stephen J. Brannen, "Structural Change of the Individual Farm," in *The Structure of Southern Farms of the Future*, ed. Charles R. Pugh (Raleigh: Agricultural Policy Institute, North Carolina State University, 1969), pp. 25–38.

74 Phillips, "Plantation as a Civilizing Factor," pp. 258, 263–64; Phillips, "Economics of the Plantation," pp. 232, 235–36; Phillips, "Conservatism and Progress," p. 8. For commentary on other aspects of Phillips' ideology, see John

Herbert Roper, "A Case of Forgotten Identity: Ulrich B. Phillips as a Young Progressive," *Georgia Historical Quarterly* 60 (Summer 1976):165–75; Daniel Joseph Singal, "Ulrich B. Phillips: The Old South as the New," *Journal of American History* 63 (March 1977):871–91; William L. Van Deburg, "Ulrich B. Phillips: Progress and the Conservative Historian," *Georgia Historical Quarterly* 55 (Fall 1971):406–16.

75 Phillips, "Conservatism and Progress," pp. 2, 9; Ray Stannard Baker, *Following the Color Line: American Negro Citizenship in the Progressive Era* (New York: Harper Torchbooks, 1964 [New York: Doubleday, Page & Company, 1908]), pp. 302–7. For studies of the racial attitudes of the progressive reformers, see David W. Southern, *The Malignant Heritage: Yankee Progressives and the Negro Question, 1901–1914* (Chicago: Loyola University Press, 1968); Jack Temple Kirby, *Darkness at the Dawning: Race and Reform in the Progressive South* (Philadelphia: J. B. Lippincott Company, 1972); Robert L. Allen, *Reluctant Reformers: Racism and Social Reform Movements in the United States* (Washington, D.C.: Howard University Press, 1974), pp. 81–119.

76 See especially Charles W. Ramsdell, review of *Life and Labor in the Old South,* in *Mississippi Valley Historical Review* 17 (June 1930):162; Avery Craven, review of *Life and Labor in the Old South,* in *Political Science Quarterly* 45 (March 1930):135. In 1939 Carter G. Woodson, editor of the *Journal of Negro History,* wrote: "I must say that I have never heard one of them [Afro-American historians] speak of Phillips' work in a complimentary fashion. The impression I have is that they consider him the fearless pro-slavery champion of the South and its institutions." Carter G. Woodson to Philip Charles Newman, 12 December 1939, reprinted in Philip Charles Newman, "Ulrich Bonnell Phillips —The South's Foremost Historian," *Georgia Historical Quarterly* 25 (September 1941):258.

77 W. E. Burghardt DuBois, review of *American Negro Slavery,* in *American Political Science Review* 12 (November 1918):722–26; William M. Brewer, review of *Life and Labor in the Old South,* in *Journal of Negro History* 14 (October 1929):534–36; C. G. Woodson, review of *American Negro Slavery,* in *Mississippi Valley Historical Review* 5 (March 1919):480–82; [C. G. Woodson], review of *American Negro Slavery,* in *Journal of Negro History* 4 (January 1919):102–3. For a pointed black editorial which claimed that Phillips' comments upon modern southern agriculture demonstrated an astute "adroitness in bolstering up bad cases," see W. E. B. DuBois, "The Experts," *Crisis* 5 (March 1913):239–40.

78 For further background on this changing intellectual/racial climate, see Thomas F. Gossett, *Race: The History of an Idea in America* (New York: Schocken Books, 1965 [Dallas: Southern Methodist University Press, 1963]), pp. 409–59. For an early study that was critical of Phillips' views on slave breeding and trading, see Frederic Bancroft, *Slave-Trading in the Old South* (Baltimore: J. H. Furst Company, 1931), pp. 24, 27, 68, 208, 234–35, 283, 398.

79 Bassett, *Short History,* pp. 430, 470; James Wilford Garner and Henry Cabot Lodge, *The History of the United States,* 4 vols. (Philadelphia: John D. Morris

and Company, 1905), 3: 989; William Sidney Drewry, *The Southampton Insurrection* (Murfreesboro, N.C.: Johnson Publishing Company, 1968 [Washington, D.C.: The Neale Company, 1900]), pp. 18, 28–29, 35–36, 60, 116. For similar commentary from the late nineteenth-century, see Stephen B. Weeks, "The Slave Insurrection in Virginia, 1831," *Magazine of American History* 25 (June 1891):448–49; B. A. Hinsdale, "Some Features of the Old South," *Magazine of Western History* 5 (November 1886):5. For a black counterproposal, see Williams, *History of the Negro Race*, 2: 82–92.

80 Herbert Aptheker, *Essays in the History of the American Negro* (New York: International Publishers, 1964 [New York: International Publishers, 1945]), pp. 3–11, 69–70. See also Herbert Aptheker, *To Be Free: Studies in American Negro History* (New York: International Publishers, 1948), pp. 9–10, 30; Herbert Aptheker, *American Negro Slave Revolts* (New York: International Publishers, 1963 [New York: Columbia University Press, 1943]), pp. 162–63. To compare Aptheker's approach with that of a text which its author claimed was "the first extended Marxian history of America," see V. F. Calverton, *The Awakening of America*, 2 vols. (New York: The John Day Company, 1939), 1: vii–viii, 76, 271–82.

81 J. G. deRoulhac Hamilton, review of *American Negro Slave Revolts*, in *American Historical Review* 49 (April 1944):504–6; Theodore M. Whitfield, review of *American Negro Slave Revolts*, in *Journal of Southern History* 10 (February 1944):103–5; Bucklin Moon, review of *To Be Free*, in *Nation* 167 (31 July 1948):134–36. Chase C. Mooney, "The Literature of Slavery: A Re-Evaluation," *Indiana Magazine of History* 47 (September 1951):255.

82 Richard Hofstadter, "U. B. Phillips and the Plantation Legend," *Journal of Negro History* 29 (April 1944):109–24; Kenneth M. Stampp, "The Historian and Southern Negro Slavery," *American Historical Review* 57 (April 1952):613–24; Ruben F. Kugler, "U. B. Phillips' Use of Sources," *Journal of Negro History* 47 (July 1962):153–68.

83 Henry Bamford Parkes, *The American Experience: An Interpretation of the History and Civilization of the American People* (New York: Alfred A. Knopf, 1947), pp. 54, 213–15; Henry Bamford Parkes, *The United States of America: A History* (New York: Alfred A. Knopf, 1953), p. 206; Merle Curti, Richard H. Shryock, Thomas C. Cochran, and Fred Harvey Harrington, *An American History*, 2 vols. (New York: Harper & Brothers, 1950), 1: 325; Thomas A. Bailey, *The American Pageant* (Boston: D. C. Heath and Company, 1956), pp. 358, 366.

84 To trace the progress of revisions in the texts of two well-known white American historians, compare the treatment given "the cotton kingdom" in the following volumes: S. E. Morison, *The Oxford History of the United States, 1783–1917*, 2 vols. (London: Oxford University Press, 1927), 2: 1–24; Samuel Eliot Morison and Henry Steele Commager, *The Growth of the American Republic* (New York: Oxford University Press, 1930), pp. 411–26.; Samuel Eliot Morison and Henry Steele Commager, *The Growth of the American Republic*, 2 vols. (New York: Oxford University Press, 1950), 1: 533–50; Samuel Eliot

Morison and Henry Steele Commager, *The Growth of the American Republic,* 2 vols. (New York: Oxford University Press, 1962), 1: 521–39; Samuel Eliot Morison, *The Oxford History of the American People* (New York: Oxford University Press, 1965), pp. 500–515.

85 John Hope Franklin, *From Slavery to Freedom: A History of American Negroes* (New York: Alfred A. Knopf, 1947), pp. 177–78, 184–212, 602.

86 Kenneth M. Stampp, *The Peculiar Institution: Slavery in the Ante-Bellum South* (New York: Alfred A. Knopf, 1956), pp. vii, 8–11. For the story of one professional organization's battle with nonegalitarian social attitudes during the 1950s, see Ray Allen Billington, "From Association to Organization: The OAH in the Bad Old Days," *Journal of American History* 65 (June 1978): 75–84.

87 Stampp, *Peculiar Institution,* pp. 11–12, 34, 44, 73, 86, 141–91, 381–82.

88 Ibid., p. 387; Stampp, "Historian," p. 618. For additional commentary on Stampp's position in slave historiography, see David Brion Davis, "Slavery and the Post-World War II Historians," in *Slavery, Colonialism, and Racism,* ed. Sidney W. Mintz (New York: W. W. Norton & Company, 1974), pp. 1–16; Stanley M. Elkins, *Slavery: A Problem in American Institutional and Intellectual Life* (Chicago: University of Chicago Press, 1959), p. 20–23.

89 Perry Lentz, "Our Missing Epic: A Study in Novels About the American Civil War" (Ph.D. diss., Vanderbilt University, 1970), p. 608.

90 Jan Cohn, "The Negro Character in Northern Magazine Fiction of the 1860's," *New England Quarterly* 43 (December 1970):573. For detailed studies of this literary genre, see Richard Schuster, "American Civil War Novels to 1880" (Ph.D. diss., Columbia University, 1961); Ralph C. Most, "Civil War Fiction: 1890–1920" (Ph.D. diss., University of Pennsylvania, 1951); William Joseph Kimball, "The Civil War in American Novels: 1920–1939" (Ph.D. diss., Pennsylvania State University, 1957); and Lentz, "Missing Epic." See also Robert A. Lively, *Fiction Fights the Civil War: An Unfinished Chapter in the Literary History of the American People* (Chapel Hill: University of North Carolina Press, 1957); Lawrence S. Thompson, "The Civil War in Fiction," *Civil War History* 2 (March 1956):83–95; Louis D. Rubin, Jr., "The Image of an Army: The Civil War in Southern Fiction," in *Southern Writers: Appraisals in Our Time,* ed. R. C. Simonini, Jr. (Charlottesville: University Press of Virginia, 1964), pp. 50–70.

91 See James Roberts Gilmore [Edmund Kirke], *Among the Pines: or, South in Secession-Time* (New York: J. R. Gilmore, 1862), pp. 38–39, 91; John Pierpont, "Forward!" in *Lyrics of Loyalty,* ed. Frank Moore (New York: George P. Putnam, 1864), pp. 9–10; Henry Morford, *The Days of Shoddy* (Philadelphia: T. B. Peterson & Brothers, 1863), pp. 108–9. William Cullen Bryant, "Our Country's Call," in Moore, *Lyrics,* pp. 1–3; George Vandenhoff, "The Patriot Girl to Her Lover," in Moore, *Lyrics,* pp. 248–49.

92 Epes Sargent, *Peculiar: A Tale of the Great Transition* (New York: Carleton, 1864), p. 21.

93 Ibid., pp. 490, 494.

94 John Townsend Trowbridge, *My Own Story* (Boston: Houghton, Mifflin and Company, 1903), pp. 260, 262.

95 John Townsend Trowbridge, *Cudjo's Cave* (London: Ward, Lock, and Tyler, n.d. [Boston: Lothrop, Lee & Shepard Co., 1863]), pp. 55, 57, 63–64, 121, 128.

96 Ibid., pp. 55–57, 61, 63.

97 Ibid., pp. 67–68, 106–7, 197.

98 Ibid., pp. 200–201, 219. For an early postbellum story which detailed the possibilities of Afro-American advancement under white tutelage, see L. Maria Child, *A Romance of the Republic* (Boston: Ticknor and Fields, 1867).

99 Richard B. Harwell, "Gone with Miss Ravenel's Courage; or Bugles Blow So Red: A Note on the Civil War Novel," *New England Quarterly* 35 (June 1962): 256. Key wartime sustainers of the southern patriotic tradition were Augusta J. Evans, *Macaria; or, Altars of Sacrifice* (New York: G. W. Dillingham, 1896 [Richmond: West & Johnson, 1864]) and Paul Hamilton Hayne, "On the Chivalry of the Present Time," in *Poems of Paul Hamilton Hayne* (Boston: D. Lothrop and Company, 1882 [ca. 1861]), pp. 84–85. For contrasting poetic images of secessionist chilvalry, compare S. Henry Dickson, "South Carolina," in *War Poetry of the South*, ed. William Gilmore Simms (New York: Richardson & Company, 1866 [1860]), pp. 18–19 with "South Carolina—1865," in *Poetry, Lyrical, Narrative, and Satirical of the Civil War*, ed. Richard Grant White (New York: American News Company, 1866 [1865]), pp. 282–83.

100 For an early postbellum northern novel that adjudged the civilization of the planters to have been an anachronism incompatible with "the railroad, electric-telegraph, printing-press, inductive philosophy, and practical Christianity," see John William DeForest, *Miss Ravenel's Conversion from Secession to Loyalty* (New York: Harper & Brothers, 1867).

101 John O. Beaty, *John Esten Cooke, Virginian* (New York: Columbia University Press, 1922), pp. 85, 87, 108.

102 John Esten Cooke, *Hilt to Hilt; or Days and Nights on the Banks of the Shenandoah* (New York: G. W. Carleton, 1869), pp. 21, 110; John Esten Cooke, *Surry of Eagle's-Nest or the Memoirs of a Staff-Officer Serving in Virginia* (New York: G. W. Dillingham, 1889 [1866]), pp. 82–83.

103 Cooke, *Hilt to Hilt*, pp. 109–110; Cooke, *Surry*, p. 392.

104 John Sherwood Weber, "The American War Novel Dealing With the Revolutionary and Civil Wars" (Ph.D. diss., University of Wisconsin, 1947), pp. 85–86; Beaty, *John Esten Cooke*, p. 95; Cooke, *Surry*, p. 178.

105 Advertisement in *The Land We Love* 5 (October 1868):549. The Charlotte monthly was absorbed by *New Eclectic* in 1869. Frank Luther Mott, *A History of American Magazines*, 5 vols. (Cambridge: Harvard University Press, 1938–1968), 3: 46.

106 H. R. Jackson, "Stonewall Jackson," *The Land We Love* 5 (August 1868):291; Fanny Downing, "Dixie," *The Land We Love* 1 (October 1866):381; Buehring H. Jones, "My Southern Home," *The Land We Love* 4 (January 1868):229.

107 "In an Old Drawer," *The Land We Love* 6 (December 1868):156, 161; "The Texas Soldier," *The Land We Love* 2 (March 1867):346–47, 349; M. J. H., "Rose

Cottage," *The Land We Love* 6 (February 1869):284, 292; "Road-Side Stories," *The Land We Love* 1 (August 1866):258–61; "Only Son of His Mother," *The Land We Love* 5 (June 1868):158; L. Cary Wilden, "The Soldier Son," *The Land We Love* 5 (July 1868):230.

108 "John Smith, Esq.," *The Land We Love* 5 (July 1868):253.

109 "Mammy (A Home Picture of 1860)," *The Land We Love* 6 (March 1869): 389–90.

110 "Poor Tom," *The Land We Love* 5 (May 1868):23–24.

111 Jay B. Hubbell, *The South in American Literature, 1607–1900* (Durham: Duke University Press 1954), pp. 701, 740; Lawrence J. Friedman, *The White Savage: Racial Fantasies in the Postbellum South* (Englewood Cliffs: Prentice-Hall, Inc., 1970), pp. 60–61; Albion W. Tourgée, "The South as a Field for Fiction," *Forum* 6 (December 1888):405.

112 For a detailed study of southern local color fiction, see Merrill Maguire Skaggs, *The Folk of Southern Fiction* (Athens: University of Georgia Press, 1972). For further commentary on the sociopolitical influence of the local color movement, see Louis D. Rubin, Jr., "Southern Local Color and the Black Man," *Southern Review* 6 (October 1970):1011–30; Paul H. Buck, *The Road to Reunion, 1865–1900* (Boston: Little, Brown and Company, 1937), pp. 196–235; George R. Lamplugh, "The Image of the Negro in Popular Magazine Fiction, 1875–1900," *Journal of Negro History* 57 (April 1972):177–89; Rayford W. Logan, *The Betrayal of the Negro: From Rutherford B. Hayes to Woodrow Wilson* (New York: Collier Books, 1965), pp. 242–75. For a comparative study of Native Americans and black Americans as they appeared in periodicals of this era, see Charles R. Wilson, "Racial Reservations: Indians and Blacks in American Magazines, 1865–1900," *Journal of Popular Culture* 10 (Summer 1976):70–79.

113 Sidney and Clifford Lanier, "Uncle Jim's Baptist Revival-Hymn," *Scribner's Monthly* 12 (May 1876):142. See also H. S. Edwards, "How Sal Came Through," *Century* 39 (February 1890):582; Thomas Nelson Page, *In Ole Virginia: or, Marse Chan and Other Stories* (New York: Charles Scribner's Sons, 1887), p. viii.

114 For studies of the creation and use of black dialect such as "blim blammin'," "ding-busted" and "dad-fetchedes," by one of the most famous humorists of the era, see James Nathan Tidwell, "Mark Twain's Representation of Negro Speech," *American Speech* 17 (October 1942):174–76 and Lee A. Pederson, "Negro Speech in *The Adventures of Huckleberry Finn*," *Mark Twain Journal* 13 (Winter 1965):1–4.

115 Thomas Nelson Page, "Unc' Edinburg's Drowndin': A Plantation Echo," in Page, *Ole Virginia*, p. 41; A. C. Gordon and Thomas Nelson Page, *Befo' De War: Echoes in Negro Dialect* (New York: Charles Scribner's Sons, 1888), p. 118. For particularly interesting examples of loyalty and its rewards, see Maurice Thompson, "A Dusky Genius," *Century* 39 (April 1890):906–15; H. S. Edwards, "De Valley An' De Shadder," *Century* 35 (January 1888):468–77; Maurice Thompson, "Ben and Judas," *Century* 38 (October 1889):893–902. For an ear-

lier version of the theme, see Mrs. E. P. Campbell, "Uncle Gabriel's Account of His Campaigns," *Atlantic Monthly* 24 (August 1869):207–15.

116 Thomas Nelson Page, "Meh Lady: A Story of the War," in Page, *Ole Virginia*, p. 80; Thomas Nelson Page, "Marse Chan: A Tale of Old Virginia," in Page, *Ole Virginia*, pp. 4, 10; T. N. Page, "Uncle Gabe's White Folks," *Scribner's Monthly* 13 (April 1877):882; Page, "Unc' Edinburg's Drowndin'," pp. 40, 67–69.

117 For houseboy and Mammy storytellers, see Mary Hose, "Bushy and Jack," *Harper's New Monthly Magazine* 34 (April 1867):660–63; Sherwood Bonner, *Suwanee River Tales* (Freeport, N.Y.: Books for Libraries Press, 1972 [Boston: Roberts Brothers, 1884]), pp. 6–21.

118 Joel Chandler Harris, "An Accidental Author," *Lippincott's Magazine* 37 (April 1886):419; Julia Collier Harris, *The Life and Letters of Joel Chandler Harris* (London: Constable & Co., 1919). p. 34. For a fictionalized autobiographical account of Harris' education in folklore while at *The Countryman*, see Joel Chandler Harris, *On the Plantation: A Story of a Georgia Boy's Adventures During the War* (New York: D. Appleton and Company, 1892). An examination of Remus as elder statesman of the Atlanta Afro-American community is contained in Thomas H. English, "The Other Uncle Remus," *Georgia Review* 21 (Summer 1967):210–17.

119 Joel Chandler Harris, *Daddy Jake the Runaway and Short Stories Told After Dark* (New York: The Century Co., 1898 [1889]), pp. 152–53; Joel Chandler Harris, *Uncle Remus, His Songs and His Sayings* (New York: McKinlay, Stone & Mackenzie, 1908 [New York: D. Appleton and Company, 1880]), p. xvii.

120 Harris, *Uncle Remus*, pp. 3–4, 11–15, 69, 163–65; Joel Chandler Harris, *Nights with Uncle Remus: Myths and Legends of the Old Plantation* (New York: McKinlay, Stone & Mackenzie, 1911 [Boston: James R. Osgood and Company, 1883]), pp. 4, 48–49, 193–98; Harris, *Daddy Jake*, p. 139; Joel Chandler Harris to G. Laurence Gomme, 9 June 1883, in Harris, *Life and Letters*, pp. 157–58.

121 Harris, *Nights*, p. xiv; Harris, *Life and Letters*, pp. 155–56, 162; Harris, *Uncle Remus*, pp. vii–viii; Joel Chandler Harris, *Uncle Remus and His Friends: Old Plantation Stories, Songs and Ballads with Sketches of Negro Character* (New York: McKinlay, Stone & Mackenzie, 1920 [Boston: Houghton Mifflin Company, 1892]), pp. vi–vii; Thomas Nelson Page, "Immortal Uncle Remus," *Book Buyer* 12 (December 1895):645. For a comparison of the Page and Harris views of the Old South, see Wayne Mixon, "Joel Chandler Harris, the Yeoman Tradition, and the New South Movement," *Georgia Historical Quarterly* 61 (Winter 1977):308–17.

122 Harris, *Uncle Remus*, p. 207.

123 Ibid., pp. 208–10.

124 Ibid., pp. 210–12. For Harris' story of Ananias, a runaway slave who returned to Georgia after serving in the Union army because he "bin brung up right dar, suh — right 'longside er Marster en my young mistiss," see Joel Chandler Harris, *Balaam and His Master and Other Sketches and Stories* (New York: McKinlay, Stone & Mackenzie, 1919 [Boston: Houghton Mifflin Company, 1891]), pp. 113–48.

125 Harris, *Uncle Remus,* pp. xvii, 205, 212; Julia Collier Harris, ed., *Joel Chandler Harris: Editor and Essayist* (Chapel Hill: University of North Carolina Press, 1931), p. 45; Rubin, "Local Color," pp. 1014–15.

126 Robert Bone, *Down Home: A History of Afro-American Short Fiction from Its Beginnings to the End of the Harlem Renaissance* (New York: G. P. Putnam's Sons, 1975), pp. 19–20, 24, 27, 31; Bernard Wolfe, "Uncle Remus and the Malevolent Rabbit," *Commentary* 8 (July 1949):35–36; Paul M. Cousins, *Joel Chandler Harris: A Biography* (Baton Rouge: Louisiana State University Press, 1968), pp. 116–17; Michael Flusche, "Joel Chandler Harris and the Folklore of Slavery," *Journal of American Studies* 9 (December 1975):348–49, 355–56.

127 Rubin, "Local Color," p. 1016; Harris, *Uncle Remus and His Friends,* pp. 222–24, 227, 296–97; Harris, *Uncle Remus,* pp. 229–31. The drawings of Uncle Remus which accompanied Harris's stories portrayed the ex-slave humorously. As drawn by Atlanta artist James H. Moser, Remus had a wrinkled face, white hair, and a short beard. He wore his spectacles pushed back on his forehead and displayed an exaggerated grin. According to Harris, "Moser's conception of the negro is perfect, whatever technical defects there may be about it." Cousins, *Joel Chandler Harris,* p. 113; Beverly R. David, "Visions of the South: Joel Chandler Harris and his Illustrators," *American Literary Realism, 1870–1910* 9 (Summer 1976):189–206; Joel Chandler Harris to Frederick S. Church, 11 June 1880, in Harris, *Life and Letters,* p. 151.

128 Burton J. Hendrick, *The Training of an American: The Earlier Life and Letters of Walter H. Page, 1885–1913* (Boston: Houghton Mifflin Company, 1928), p. 150; Darwin T. Turner, "Daddy Joel Harris and His Old-Time Darkies," *Southern Literary Journal* 1 (December 1968):41; Rubin, "Local Color," p. 1030; Sterling A. Brown, "Negro Character as Seen by White Authors," *Journal of Negro Education* 2 (January 1933):196. For Harris' journalistic commentary on the passing of slavery and the problems of the color line, see Joel Chandler Harris, "The Negro as the South Sees Him: The Old-Time Darky," *Saturday Evening Post* 176 (2 January 1904):1–2, 23; Joel Chandler Harris, "The Negro Problem: Can the South Solve It—And How?," *Saturday Evening Post* 176 (27 February 1904):6–7; Harris, *Editor and Essayist,* pp. 89–92, 110; Joel Chandler Harris, "The Negro of To-Day: His Prospects and His Discouragements," *Saturday Evening Post* 76 (30 January 1904):2–5. For a study that places Harris in the context of southern "progressive conservatism," see Jerry Allen Herndon, "Social Comment in the Writings of Joel Chandler Harris" (Ph.D. diss., Duke University, 1966).

129 Daniel Webster Davis, "Hog Meat," in *The Book of American Negro Poetry,* ed. James Weldon Johnson (New York: Harcourt, Brace & World, Inc., 1959 [1931] [1897]), pp. 83–84; James Edwin Campbell, "Uncle Eph—Epicure," in *Early Black American Poets,* ed. William H. Robinson, Jr. (Dubuque: Wm. C. Brown Company, 1969 [1895]), p. 233; James D. Corrothers, "Sweeten Tatahs," in Robinson, *Early Black American Poets,* [1907], pp. 238–43; Elliott Blaine Henderson, "De Banjo an' De Fiddle," in *The Soliloquy of Satan and Other Poems* (Freeport, New York: Books for Libraries Press, 1972 [Springfield, Ohio, 1907]), p. 30.

130 James Madison Bell, "Admonition," in *The Poetical Works of James Madison Bell* (Lansing, Michigan: Wynkoop Hallenbeck Crawford Co., 1901 [1866]), pp. 20, 25–26; Bell, "The Day and the War," in *Poetical Works*, [1864], pp. 78–79. See also Frances Ellen Watkins Harper, "Home, Sweet Home," in *Atlanta Offering; Poems* (Philadelphia: George S. Ferguson Co., 1895), pp. 26–28. For Harper's optimistic view of the 1863 Emancipation Proclamation, see Frances Ellen Watkins Harper, "President Lincoln's Proclamation of Freedom," in *Poems* (Philadelphia: Merrihew & Son, 1871), p. 34.

131 Arlene A. Elder, *The "Hindered Hand": Cultural Implications of Early African-American Fiction* (Westport: Greenwood Press, 1978), p. 105; Joan R. Sherman, *Invisible Poets: Afro-Americans of the Nineteenth Century* (Urbana: University of Illinois Press, 1974), p. xxviii; Paul Laurence Dunbar, "Mammy Peggy's Pride," in *The Strength of Gideon and Other Stories* (New York: Dodd, Mead & Company, 1903 [1900]), p. 29; Paul Laurence Dunbar, "The Colonel's Awakening," in *Folks From Dixie* (New York: Dodd, Mead and Company, 1898), pp. 69–70, 75; Paul Laurence Dunbar, "The News," in *Lyrics of the Hearthside* (New York: Dodd, Mead and Company, 1899), pp. 147–48.

132 Dunbar, "Mammy Peggy's Pride," p. 38.

133 Paul Laurence Dunbar, "Nelse Hatton's Vengeance," in *Folks From Dixie*, pp. 200–202; Hyder E. Rollins, "The Negro in the Southern Short Story," *Sewanee Review* 24 (January 1916):57. For a similar story, see Victoria Earle, *Aunt Lindy: A Story Founded Upon Real Life* (New York: J. J. Little, 1893).

134 J. Saunders Redding, *To Make a Poet Black* (College Park, Maryland: McGrath Publishing Company, 1968 [Chapel Hill: University of North Carolina Press, 1939]), pp. 59, 62; Paul Laurence Dunbar, "The Poet," in *Lyrics of Love and Laughter* (New York: Dodd, Mead and Company, 1903), p. 82; Paul Laurence Dunbar, "We Wear the Mask," in *Lyrics of Lowly Life* (New York: Dodd, Mead and Company, 1899), p. 167; Paul Laurence Dunbar, "Philosophy," in *Love and Laughter*, pp. 138–39; James Weldon Johnson, *Along This Way: The Autobiography of James Weldon Johnson* (New York: Viking Press, 1968 [1933]), pp. 160–61. For a study which claims that Dunbar was "much more of the protest tradition than his reputation suggests," see Gossie Harold Hudson, "Paul Laurence Dunbar: *Dialect Et La Negritude,*" *Phylon* 34 (September 1973):236–47. See also James A. Emanuel, "Racial Fire in the Poetry of Paul Laurence Dunbar," in *A Singer in the Dawn: Reinterpretations of Paul Laurence Dunbar*, ed. Jay Martin (New York: Dodd, Mead & Company, 1975), pp. 75–93 and Darwin Turner, "Paul Laurence Dunbar: The Rejected Symbol," *Journal of Negro History* 52 (January 1967):1–13.

135 See Paul Laurence Dunbar, "Ode to Ethiopia," in *Lowly Life*, pp. 30–32; Paul Laurence Dunbar, "The Unsung Heroes," in *Love and Laughter*, pp. 94–97; Paul Laurence Dunbar, "The Colored Soldiers," in *Lowly Life*, pp. 114–18.

136 Paul Laurence Dunbar, "The Deserted Plantation," in *Poems of Cabin and Field* (New York: Dodd, Mead & Company, 1894), pp. 13–29. For similar remembrances of the slave quarters community, see Paul Laurence Dunbar, "The Old Cabin," in *Howdy Honey Howdy* (New York: Dodd, Mead and Company,

1905), pp. 117–24; Paul Laurence Dunbar, "To the Eastern Shore," in *Love and Laughter*, pp. 112–14; Sterling M. Means, "The Old Deserted Cabin," in *Negro Poets and Their Poems*, ed. Robert T. Kerlin (Washington, D.C.: Associated Publishers, Inc., 1935 [1915]), p. 239.

137 Charles W. Chesnutt, "Post-Bellum — Pre-Harlem," *Crisis* 38 (June 1931):193; Charles W. Chesnutt to George Washington Cable, 5 June 1890, in Helen M. Chesnutt, *Charles Waddell Chesnutt: Pioneer of the Color Line* (Chapel Hill: University of North Carolina Press, 1952), pp. 57–58.

138 Charles W. Chesnutt, *The Conjure Woman* (Ann Arbor: University of Michigan Press, 1969 [Boston: Houghton Mifflin, 1899]), p. 13; Bone, *Down Home*, p. 81; Richard E. Baldwin, "The Art of *The Conjure Woman*," *American Literature* 43 (November 1971):387; Elder, "Hindered Hand," p. 153. For a study of Chesnutt's use of dialect, see Charles William Foster, "The Representation of Negro Dialect in Charles W. Chesnutt's *The Conjure Woman*" (Ph.D. diss., University of Alabama, 1968).

139 Chesnutt, "Post-Bellum," p. 193; Chesnutt, *Conjure Woman*, pp. 24–25, 70–71, 75, 137, 141–42. Chesnutt claimed that although his *Conjure Woman* stories were "sometimes referred to as folk tales" and did indeed "employ much of the universal machinery of wonder stories," they were, with the exception of "The Goophered Grapevine," "the fruit of my own imagination." Chesnutt, "Post-Bellum," p. 193. For other accounts of white antebellum cruelty, see James H. W. Howard, *Bond and Free; A True Tale of Slave Times* (Harrisburg, Pennsylvania: Edwin K. Myers, 1886), pp. 9, 214–17 and Frances E. W. Harper, *Iola Leroy; or, Shadows Uplifted* (College Park, Maryland: McGrath Publishing Company, 1969 [Boston: James H. Earle, 1892]), p. 115.

140 Chesnutt, *Conjure Woman*, pp. 19, 21, 78. For the story of a sly fugitive slave who returned from Canada, claimed that he missed his Kentucky home and white friends, and then three weeks later led his entire family to freedom, see Charles W. Chesnutt, "The Passing of Grandison," in *The Wife of His Youth and Other Stories of the Color Line* (Boston: Houghton Mifflin Company, 1899).

141 Chesnutt, *Conjure Woman*, pp. 108–9.

142 John Wesley Grant, *Out of the Darkness; or, Diabolism and Destiny* (Freeport, N.Y.: Books for Libraries Press, 1972 [Nashville: National Baptist Publishing Board, 1909]), p. 13; Langston Hughes, "Minstrel Man," in *The Dream Keeper and Other Poems* (New York: Alfred A. Knopf, 1949 [1932]), p. 38; Gwendolyn Bennett, "Heritage," in Johnson, *American Negro Poetry*, p. 245; Johnson, *Along This Way*, pp. 159–61; Countee Cullen, "For Paul Laurence Dunbar," in *Color* (New York: Harper & Brothers, 1925), p. 70; Countee Cullen, ed., *Caroling Dusk: An Anthology of Verse by Negro Poets* (New York: Harper & Brothers, 1927), p. xiv.

143 Alain Locke, "The New Negro," in *The New Negro*, ed. Alain Locke (New York: Atheneum, 1968 [New York: Albert & Charles Boni, Inc., 1925]), p. 4. According to historian August Meier, the term "New Negro" was used at least as early as 1895 to describe feelings of race pride, group solidarity, and independence present within the black community. Among the first authors to

use the term was Booker T. Washington in *A New Negro for a New Century: An Accurate and Up-to-Date Record of the Upward Struggles of the Negro Race* (Chicago: American Publishing House, 1900). August Meier, *Negro Thought in America, 1880–1915: Racial Ideologies in the Age of Booker T. Washington* (Ann Arbor: University of Michigan Press, 1963), pp. 257–60.

144 James Weldon Johnson, "Fifty Years, 1863–1913," in *Fifty Years & Other Poems* (Boston: Cornhill Company, 1917), pp. 2–4. See also Waters Edward Turpin, *These Low Grounds* (College Park, Maryland: McGrath Publishing Company, 1969 [New York: Harper & Brothers, 1937]), pp. 343–44. James Edward McCall, "The New Negro," in Cullen, *Caroling Dusk*, p. 34; Locke, "New Negro," p. 15; James Weldon Johnson, "Race Prejudice and the Negro Artist," *Harper's Monthly Magazine* 157 (November 1928):776; Lewis Alexander, "The Dark Brother," in Cullen, *Caroling Dusk*, p. 124.

145 Georgia Douglas Johnson, "The Passing of the Ex-Slave," in *Bronze: A Book of Verse* (Boston: B. J. Brimmer Company, 1922), p. 35. See also Jean Toomer, "Song of the Son," in *Cane* (New York: Harper & Row, 1969 [New York: Boni & Liveright, Inc., 1923]), p. 21; Langston Hughes, "Aunt Sue's Stories," in *The Weary Blues* (New York: Alfred A. Knopf, 1929 [1926]), p. 57.

146 Langston Hughes, "The Negro Mother," in *The Negro Mother and Other Dramatic Recitations* (New York: Golden Stair Press, 1931), pp. 16–18. For a later incarnation of this compelling figure, see the character "Big Mama" in John O. Killens' novel *Youngblood* (New York: Dial Press, 1954), pp. 6–7.

147 For variations on this theme, see Sterling A. Brown, "Strong Men," in *Southern Road* (New York: Harcourt, Brace and Company, 1932), pp. 51–53; Naomi Long Madgett, "Midway," in *Modern and Contemporary Afro-American Poetry*, ed. Bernard W. Bell (Boston: Allyn and Bacon, Inc., 1972 [1959]), p. 93; Melvin B. Tolson, "Dark Symphony," *Atlantic Monthly* 168 (September 1941): 314–17.

148 Langston Hughes, "The Black Clown," in *Negro Mother*, pp. 8–11; Langston Hughes, "Sharecroppers," in *Proletarian Literature in the United States: An Anthology*, ed. Granville Hicks, Michael Gold, Isidor Schneider, Joseph North, Paul Peters, Alan Calmer (New York: International Publishers, 1935), p. 167; Sterling Brown, "Old King Cotton," in *Southern Road*, pp. 65–66. For a later expression of this theme, see Rolland Snellings [Askia Muhammad Touré], "Floodtide," *Umbra* 1 (Winter 1963):28–31.

149 Sterling Brown, "Children's Children," in *Southern Road*, pp. 107–8.

150 Arna Bontemps, *Black Thunder* (Boston: Beacon Press, 1968 [New York: The Macmillan Company, 1936]), p. 115. For portraits of other rebels and runaways, see Sterling Brown, "Remembering Nat Turner," *Crisis* 46 (February 1939): 48; Robert E. Hayden, "Gabriel," *Opportunity* 17 (October 1939):300; Margaret Walker, "Harriet Tubman," in *The Poetry of the Negro, 1746–1970*, ed. Langston Hughes and Arna Bontemps (Garden City, New York: Doubleday & Company, 1970 [ca. 1942]), pp. 320–25; Isabel M. Thompson, "Masquerade," *Crisis* 42 (July 1935): 201, 217.

151 For literary descriptions of the slave trade, see Robert Hayden, "Middle Pas-

sage," in *Selected Poems* (New York: October House, Inc., 1966), pp. 65–70 and John H. Paynter, *Fugitives of the Pearl* (Washington, D.C.: Associated Publishers, 1930), pp. 132–37. For a black-authored novel which describes the treatment of slaves prior to the end of the "feudal period" in colonial Virginia, see John H. Hill, *Princess Malah* (Washington, D.C.: Associated Publishers, 1933), pp. 17, 47.

152 See, for example, Waters Turpin, *The Rootless* (New York: Vantage Press, 1957) pp. 52, 106, 136–38, 153, 156, 164, 328–30; Claude McKay, "Enslaved," in *Harlem Shadows* (New York: Harcourt, Brace and Company, 1922), p. 32; Margaret Walker, "Ex-Slave," *Opportunity* 16 (November 1938):330.

153 See, for example, Stark Young, *So Red the Rose* (New York: Charles Scribner's Sons, 1934; Joseph Hergesheimer, *Quiet Cities* (New York: Alfred A. Knopf, 1928); T. Bowyer Campbell, *Old Miss* (Boston: Houghton Mifflin Company, 1929); John Charles McNeill, "'Possum Time Again," in *Lyrics from Cotton Land* (Charlotte, North Carolina: Stone Publishing Co., 1922), p. 55; Clement Wood, "Nigger Hebb'n," in *The Earth Turns South* (New York: E. P. Dutton and Company, 1919), p. 18; Benjamin B. Valentine, "Little Mistiss," in *Old Marster and Other Verses* (Richmond: Whittet & Shepperson, 1921), pp. 53–55.

154 Sterling Brown, *The Negro in American Fiction* (Washington, D.C.: Associates in Negro Folk Education, 1937), p. 85. For a study of the continuing literary nationalism of early twentieth-century fiction, see Sheldon Van Auken, "The Southern Historical Novel in the Early Twentieth Century," *Journal of Southern History* 14 (May 1948): 157–91. For an appraisal of the views of black Americans forwarded in the top ten best-selling novels, 1900–1945, see Donald G. Baker, "Black Images: The Afro-American in Popular Novels, 1900–1945," *Journal of Popular Culture* 7 (Fall 1973):327–46.

155 Robert L. Groover, "Margaret Mitchell, The Lady From Atlanta," *Georgia Historical Quarterly* 52 (March 1968):56; Margaret Mitchell to Julia Collier Harris, 28 April 1936, in *Margaret Mitchell's Gone With the Wind Letters, 1936–1949*, ed. Richard Harwell (New York: Macmillan Publishing Co., 1976), p. 3; Finis Farr, *Margaret Mitchell of Atlanta: The Author of Gone with the Wind* (New York: William Morrow & Company, 1965), pp. 29–30, 81, 104, 109. Marian Elder Jones, "Me and My Book," *Georgia Review* 16 (Spring 1962): 186; Margaret Mitchell to Paul Jordan-Smith, 27 May 1936, in Harwell, *Letters*, p. 7–8; Margaret Mitchell to Stephen Vincent Benét, 9 July 1936, in Harwell, *Letters*, p. 36; Margaret Mitchell to Julia Collier Harris, 28 April 1936, in Harwell, *Letters*, p. 5. For Mitchell's literary use of the Civil War era songs, see *Gone With the Wind* (New York: Macmillan Company, 1938 [1936]), pp. 170, 297. For a study of Mitchell's novel as it relates to recent historiography of antebellum Georgia, the Civil War, and Reconstruction, see Robert E. May, "*Gone With the Wind* as Southern History: A Reappraisal," *Southern Quarterly* 17 (Fall 1978):51–64.

156 Groover, "Lady From Atlanta," p. 67; Frank Luther Mott, *Golden Multitudes: The Story of Best Sellers in the United States* (New York: Macmillan Com-

pany, 1947), p. 257; Belle Rosenbaum, "Why Do They Read It?" *Scribner's Magazine* 102 (August 1937): 23. For a study which explains the novel's popularity in terms of its localization of American racial attitudes, see Jerome Stern, "*Gone With the Wind:* The South as America," *Southern Humanities Review* 6 (Winter 1972):5–12.

157 *Gone With the Wind*, pp. 4, 8.

158 Ibid., pp. 24, 31, 38, 62, 68.

159 Ibid., pp. 20, 51, 354, 371, 432.

160 George S. Schuyler, "Not Gone With the Wind," *Crisis* 44 (July 1937):205–6. For a sampling of more recent criticism, see Floyd C. Watkins, *In Time and Place: Some Origins of American Fiction* (Athens: University of Georgia Press, 1977), pp. 35, 37, 39–42, 47.

161 Margaret Mitchell to Susan Myrick, 17 April 1939, in Harwell, *Letters*, pp. 273–74. See also Margaret Mitchell to Herschel Brickell, 8 April 1937, in Harwell, *Letters*, p. 139.

162 For a more thorough examination of these literary trends, see John M. Bradbury, *Renaissance in the South: A Critical History of the Literature, 1920–1960* (Chapel Hill: University of North Carolina Press, 1963). See also Catherine Juanita Starke, *Black Portraiture in American Fiction: Stock Characters, Archetypes, and Individuals* (New York: Basic Books, Inc., 1971), pp. 249–53; Margaret Just Butcher, *The Negro in American Culture* (New York: New American Library, 1971 [New York: Alfred A. Knopf, 1956]), pp. 132–48.

163 T. S. Stribling, *The Forge* (Garden City, New York: Doubleday, Doran & Company, 1933 [1931]), pp. 59–61. See also Stephen Vincent Benét, "Freedom's a Hard-Bought Thing," in *Selected Works of Stephen Vincent Benét*, 2 vols. (New York: Rinehart & Company, 1942 [1940]), 2: 48; Allen Tate, *The Fathers* (Baton Rouge: Louisiana State University Press, 1977 [New York: G. P. Putnam's Sons, 1938]), p. 54. For an interesting twentieth-century interpretation of a famous slaveholding villain, see Vachel Lindsay, "A Negro Sermon: — Simon Legree," in *The Chinese Nightingale and Other Poems* (New York: Macmillan Company, 1917), pp. 104–7.

164 William Faulkner, *Absalom, Absalom!* (New York: Random House, 1951 [1936]), pp. 14–17, 37, 40; Evelyn Scott, *Migrations* (New York: Albert & Charles Boni, 1927), p. 21. For a study which compares the public and critical reception of Margaret Mitchell's and William Faulkner's novels, see James W. Mathews, "The Civil War of 1936: *Gone with the Wind* and *Absalom, Absalom!*" *Georgia Review* 21 (Winter 1967): 462–69.

165 For a similar picture of the slave quarters, see Hamilton Basso, *Cinnamon Seed* (New York: Charles Scribner's Sons, 1934), p. 23.

166 William Faulkner *The Unvanquished* (New York: Random House, 1938), p. 18.

167 Faulkner, *Absalom!*, p. 17; Robert Penn Warren, "Founding Fathers, Nineteenth-Century Style, Southeast U.S.A.," in *Promises: Poems, 1954–1956* (New York: Random House, 1957), pp. 39–41; Scott, *Migrations*, pp. 2–3, 10–11.

168 See, for example, Frances Gaither, *The Red Cock Crows* (New York: The Macmillan Company, 1944), pp. 61, 132, 189, 195, 289; Tate, *Fathers*, pp. 208–9,

245; Stephen Vincent Benét, *John Brown's Body* (Garden City, New York: Doubleday, Doran and Company, 1928), pp. 44–45.

169 George Kibbe Turner, *Hagar's Hoard* (New York: Alfred A. Knopf, 1925 [1920]), p. 20.

170 Scott, *Migrations*, p. 20.

171 Gaither, *Red Cock Crows*, p. 126. Scott, *Migrations*, p. 33; Andrew Nelson Lytle, "Mister McGregor," *Virginia Quarterly Review* 11 (April 1935):227.

172 Katherine Anne Porter, "The Witness," in *The Leaning Tower and Other Stories* (New York: Harcourt, Brace and Company, 1944), pp. 13–14.

173 Ibid., p. 16.

174 Ibid., p. 14.

175 Ibid., p. 15. For the untraditional story of a "grizzled old Negro, with a seamed, cunning, gnomish face" who told tales about "snakes and bugaboos and Raw-Head-and-Bloody-Bones and Jack-muh-Lantum," see Robert Penn Warren, *Band of Angels* (New York: New American Library, 1955 [New York: Random House, 1955]), pp. 14–19.

176 Martin Luther King, Jr., *Why We Can't Wait* (New York: New American Library, 1964 [New York: Harper & Row, 1964]), p. 115. For examples of lingering slave stereotypes, see Basso, *Cinnamon Seed*, pp. 42, 60; John Peale Bishop, *Many Thousands Gone* (New York: Charles Scribner's Sons, 1931 [1930]), pp. 6, 110. For a poetic description of the "wall . . . anciently erected" between black and white Americans, see Donald Davidson, "Geography of the Brain," in *The Tall Men*, (Boston: Houghton Mifflin Company, 1927), p. 39.

177 Hans Nathan, *Dan Emmett and the Rise of Early Negro Minstrelsy* (Norman: University of Oklahoma Press, 1962), pp. 245, 251; Richard B. Harwell, *Confederate Music* (Chapel Hill: University of North Carolina Press, 1950), p. 42.

178 Dan D. Emmett, "I Wish I Was in Dixie's Land" (New York: Firth, Pond & Co., 1860); Nathan, *Dan Emmett*, p. 274; H. S. Stanton, "Dixie War Song" (Augusta: Blackmar & Bro., 1861); A. G. Pike, "Southrons! Hear Your Country Call You," in *A Collection of Southern Patriotic Songs, Made During Confederate Times*, ed. Francis D. Allan (Galveston: J. D. Sawyer, 1874 [ca. 1861]), pp. 29–30. See also "The Star of the West," in *Our War Songs, North & South* (Cleveland: S. Brainard's Sons, 1887 [ca. 1861]), p. 515; "Our Braves in Virginia," in *Southern War Songs*, ed. W. L. Fagan (New York: M. T. Richardson & Co., 1890 [ca. 1861]), pp. 56–57; "Awake! To Arms in Texas!" in Allan, *Patriotic Songs*, [ca. 1861], pp. 8–9. Dan Emmett was a former circus entertainer and founding member of the blackface Virginia Minstrels. His film biography, *Dixie* (1943), starred Bing Crosby and Dorothy Lamour.

179 "Union Dixie," in *Songs of the Civil War*, ed. Irwin Silber (New York: Columbia University Press, 1960 [ca. 1861]), p. 64. See also Frances J. Crosby, "Dixie for the Union," in *Our War Songs*, [ca. 1861], pp. 513–14; "Our Yankee Generals" (New York: H. DeMarsan, 1860). For commentary on the use of "Dixie" and other popular songs for army camp entertainment, see Larzer Ziff, "Songs of the Civil War," *Civil War History* 2 (September 1956):7–28; Bell Irvin Wiley, *The Life of Billy Yank: The Common Soldier of the Union* (In-

dianapolis: Bobbs-Merrill Company, 1952), pp. 157–62; Bell Irvin Wiley, *The Life of Johnny Reb: The Common Soldier of the Confederacy* (Indianapolis: Bobbs-Merrill Company, 1943), pp. 151–57, 185. For Abraham Lincoln's favorable opinion of "Dixie", see Henry Clay Whitney, *Life on the Circuit with Lincoln* (Caldwell, Idaho: Caxton Printers, Ltd., 1940 [Boston: Estes and Lauriat, 1892]), pp. 102–3, 161; Kenneth A. Bernard, *Lincoln and the Music of the Civil War* (Caldwell, Idaho: Caxton Printers, Ltd., 1966), p. 13; Carl Sandburg, *Abraham Lincoln: The War Years*, 4 vols. (New York: Harcourt, Brace & Company, 1939), 4: 207–8.

180 For background on the nothern racism of the era, see V. Jacque Voegeli, *Free but Not Equal: The Midwest and the Negro During the Civil War* (Chicago: University of Chicago Press, 1967); Adrian Cook, *The Armies of the Streets: The New York City Draft Riots of 1863* (Lexington: University Press of Kentucky, 1974); Benjamin Quarles, *Lincoln and the Negro* (New York: Oxford University Press, 1962).

181 "The Beauties of Conscription," reprinted in Alfred M. Williams, "Folk-Songs of the Civil War," *Journal of American Folk-Lore* 5 (October–December, 1892 [ca. 1863]):273; T. W. Crowson, "Run Yanks, or Die!" in Allan, *Patriotic Songs,* [ca. 1861], p. 35; "God Save the South," in *The Army Songster* (Richmond: Geo. L. Bidgood, 1864), p. 65.

182 "Song of Hooker's Picket," in Fagan, *Southern War Songs,* [1863], pp. 219–20.

183 "I Am Fighting for The Nigger" (New York: H. De Marsan, [ca. 1863]). For a recent study of the interconnection between military service and the expansion of black citizenship rights, see Mary Frances Berry, *Military Necessity and Civil Rights Policy: Black Citizenship and the Constitution, 1861–1868* (Port Washington, New York: Kennikat Press, 1977).

184 A. C. D. Sandie, "Ole Uncle Abrum's Comin'," in Willard A. Heaps and Porter W. Heaps, *The Singing Sixties: The Spirit of Civil War Days Drawn from the Music of the Times* (Norman: University of Oklahoma Press, 1960 [ca. 1862]), p. 270; Dan Emmett, "The Black Brigade" (New York: Wm. A. Pond & Co., 1863).

185 "Give Us a Flag," in Silber, *Songs of the Civil War,* [ca. 1863], p. 295. See also J. Mc C. Simpson, "Let the Banner Proudly Wave," in *The Emancipation Car* (Miami: Mnemosyne Publishing Co., 1969 [Zanesville, Ohio: Sullivan & Brown, 1874]), pp. 144–46. Lindley Miller, "Marching Song of the First Arkansas (Negro) Regiment,"in Silber, *Songs of the Civil War* [ca. 1863], p. 38; J. C. Wallace, "We are Coming from the Cotton Fields" (Chicago: Root & Cady, 1864); J. O'Conner and J. P. Jones, "De Darkies' Rallying Song," in Heaps and Heaps, *Singing Sixties,* [ca. 1863], pp. 275–76. For a contrasting image of the black American as an "unreconstructed" southerner who "fit against" the North during the Civil War, see Innes Randolph, "I'm a Good Old Rebel," in Fagan, *Southern War Songs,* (1866), pp. 360–62. For the use of the same song as an instrument of reconciliation during the Spanish-American War, see George H. Callcott, "The Good Old Rebel," *Southern Folklore Quarterly* 18 (September 1954):175–76.

186 Charles Graham Halpine [Miles O'Reilly and S. Lover], "Sambo's Right to Be Kilt" (New York: William Hall & Son, 1864 [1862].

187 For commentary on the minstrels as "raw recruits," see Robert C. Toll, *Blacking Up: The Minstrel Show in Nineteenth-Century America* (New York: Oxford University Press, 1974), pp. 117–24; Alexander Saxton, "Blackface Minstrelsy and Jacksonian Ideology," *American Quarterly* 27 (March 1975): 21–23. For a later use of black soldiers as vehicles for minstrel humor, see the skit entitled "Stupidity and Soldiers" in Frank Dumont, *The Witmark Amateur Minstrel Guide and Burnt Cork Encyclopedia* (Chicago: M. Witmark & Sons, 1905), p. 60.

188 Charles Townsend, *Negro Minstrels with End Men's Jokes, Gags, Speeches, Etc.* (Chicago: T. S. Denison, 1891), p. 33. See also Dan Emmett, "High Daddy" (New York: Wm. A. Pond & Co., 1863); "Good Singing" skit, in Jack Haverly, *Negro Minstrels* (Chicago: Frederick J. Drake & Company, 1902), p. 13.

189 Orville Augustus Roorbach, ed., *Minstrel Gags and End Men's Hand-Book* (New York: Dick & Fitzgerald, 1875), pp. 15–16. For a wartime condemnation of white lawmakers who would support such legislation and thereby attempt to "prove de nigger am superior to de white man," see "De Nigger on de Fence," (New York: H. De Marsan, ca. 1862).

190 Charles White, *Uncle Eph's Dream*, reprinted in Gary D. Engle, ed., *This Grotesque Essence: Plays from the American Minstrel Stage* (Baton Rouge: Louisiana State University Press, 1978 [1874]), p. 57; *Old Zip Coon*, reprinted in Engle, *Grotesque Essence*, [1874], p. 51; Robert M'Kay, "'Way Down in Georgia 'Fo' De Wa','" in Roorbach, *Minstrel Gags*, p. 88; Minnie F. Howard, "Let Me Go Back Chillun" (New York: Hamilton S. Gordon, 1899).

191 For a more extensive listing of black minstrel troupes which performed between 1855 and 1890, see Toll, *Blacking Up*, pp. 275–80. For a study of antebellum Afro-American minstrel dancer William Henry "Master Juba" Lane, see Marian Hannah Winter, "Juba and American Minstrelsy," *Dance Index* 6 (1947):28–47.

192 Toll, *Blacking Up*, pp. 237–48; James McIntyre, "Come To De Gospel Show!" (New York: Willis Woodward & Co., 1884). See also Thomas Sears, "Oh, Glory, Glory, Hallelujah" (St. Louis, Ohio: H. Bollman & Sons, 1881); Harry C. Talbert, "The Gravel Train, or Riding on to Glory" (New York: T. B. Harms & Co., 1884); Theodore W. Johnson, "Black Images in American Popular Song, 1840–1910" (Ph. D. diss., Northwestern University, 1975), pp. 93–96. For examples of black religious music performed by postwar traveling groups such as the Fisk Jubilee Singers, see J. B. T. Marsh, *The Story of the Jubilee Singers; With their Songs* (Boston: Houghton, Mifflin and Co., 1881).

193 For commentary on the white-owned companies and how they "dominated black minstrelsy in most ways," see Toll, *Blacking Up*, pp. 199, 203–11.

194 James A. Bland, "Carry Me Back to Old Virginny," in *The James A. Bland Album of Outstanding Songs*, ed. Charles Haywood (New York: Edward B. Marks Music Corporation, 1946 [1875]), pp. 8–9; Sam Lucas, "Dis Darkey's Growing Old" (Boston: White, Smith & Co., 1881); James S. Putnam, "When

Gabriel Blows His Trumpet, I'll Be Dar" (Boston: John F. Perry, 1881); Gussie L. Davis, "I Long to See Old Massa's Face Again" (n.p.: George Propheter, Jr., 1887); Johnson, "Black Images," p. 87.

195 For a description of Kersands' ability to perform a buck-and-wing while holding two billiard balls in his mouth, see Tom Fletcher, *The Tom Fletcher Story: 100 Years of the Negro in Show Business!* (New York: Burdge & Company, 1954), pp. 61–62. For a sampling of Simond's material, see Ike Simond, *Old Slack's Reminiscence and Pocket History of the Colored Profession from 1865 to 1891* (Chicago, 1892). For a description of black audience response to such performers, see Toll, *Blacking Up,* pp. 226–28.

196 "The Clipper Interviews A Distinguished Amusement Disciple on an Impending and Imposing Enterprise," *New York Clipper* (4 March 1882):836.

197 Ibid.

198 Ibid. For first-hand accounts of the trouble that white racists caused the traveling minstrel troupes, see W. C. Handy, *Father of the Blues* (New York: The Macmillan Company, 1941), pp. 43–45, 58; Fletcher, *100 Years,* p. 57.

199 For a late nineteenth-century black critique of Afro-American minstrelsy, see James M. Trotter, *Music and Some Highly Musical People* (Boston: Lee and Shepard, 1881), pp. 271–75, 282. For Logan's study of the nadir period, see Rayford W. Logan, *The Betrayal of the Negro: From Rutherford B. Hayes to Woodrow Wilson* (New York: Collier Books, 1965).

200 Huber W. Ellingsworth, "The Civil War from the New York Stage," *Southern Speech Journal* 19 (March 1954):233; O. G. Brockett and Lenyth Brockett, "Civil War Theater: Contemporary Treatments," *Civil War History* 1 (September 1955):234–35, 241, 244–45; Iline Fife, "The Confederate Theater in Georgia," *Georgia Review* 9 (Fall 1955):310.

201 Carla Waal, "The First Original Confederate Drama: *The Guerrillas,*" *Virginia Magazine of History and Biography* 70 (October 1962):465.

202 Willard Welsh, "Civil War Theater: The War in Drama," *Civil War History* 1 (September 1955):269, 280; Paul H. Buck, *The Road to Reunion, 1865–1900* (Boston: Little, Brown and Company, 1937), p. 233; Herbert Bergman, "Major Civil War Plays, 1882–1899," *Southern Speech Journal* 19 (March 1954): 224, 226; Clyde Fitch, *Barbara Frietchie, The Frederick Girl* (New York: Life Publishing Company, 1900 [New York: Z & L Rosenfield, 1899]), pp. 37, 41–42, 62–63; William Gillette, *Held by the Enemy* (New York: Samuel French, 1898 [1886]), p. 32; Bronson Howard, *Shenandoah,* in *Representative Plays by American Dramatists, 1856–1911,* ed. Montrose J. Moses, 3 vols. (New York: E. P. Dutton & Company, 1921 [1888]), 3: 397–98, 428.

203 David Belasco, *The Heart of Maryland,* in *The Heart of Maryland & Other Plays,* ed. Glenn Hughes and George Savage (Princeton: Princeton University Press, 1941 [1895]), p. 176.

204 Ibid., pp. 176–77, 186.

205 Augustus Thomas, *Alabama* (New York: R. H. Russell, 1900 [1891]), p. 112.

206 Fitch, *Barbara Frietchie,* p. 87.

207 Dion Boucicault, *Belle Lamar: An Episode of the Civil War,* in *Plays for the*

College Theater, ed. Garrett H. Leverton (New York: Samuel French, 1937 [1874]), p. 138.

208 Gillette, *Held by the Enemy,* pp. 64–65.

209 James A. Herne, "Act III of James A. Herne's *Griffith Davenport,*" *American Literature* 24 (November 1952):348. See also James A. Herne, *The Reverend Griffith Davenport,* in *The Early Plays of James A. Herne,* ed. Arthur Hobson Quinn (Princeton: Princeton University Press, 1940 [1899]), pp. 143, 147.

210 Douglas Gilbert, *American Vaudeville: Its Life and Times* (New York: Whittlesey House, 1940), pp. 3–6, 13–15; Albert F. McLean, Jr., *American Vaudeville as Ritual* (Lexington: University of Kentucky Press, 1965), pp. 1, 18–19, 24; Abel Green and Joe Laurie, Jr., *Show Biz: From Vaude to Video* (New York: Henry Holt and Company, 1951), pp. 269–72.

211 Carl Wittke, *Tambo and Bones: A History of the American Minstrel Stage* (Durham: Duke University Press, 1930), p. 107; Richard Moody, *America Takes the Stage: Romanticism in American Drama and Theatre, 1750–1900* (Bloomington: Indiana University Press, 1955), p. 49; Toll, *Blacking Up,* pp. 134–55. Gilbert, *American Vaudeville,* pp. 37–38, 82–83. For a study of minstrel elements in the related entertainment form known as the burlesque show, see Ralph G. Allen, "Our Native Theatre: Honky-Tonk, Minstrel Shows, Burlesque," in *The American Theatre: A Sum of its Parts,* ed. Henry B. Williams (New York: Samuel French, Inc., 1971), pp. 273–314.

212 Charles Samuels and Louise Samuels, *Once Upon a Stage: The Merry World of Vaudeville* (New York: Dodd, Mead & Company, 1974), p. 197. John E. DiMeglio, *Vaudeville U.S.A.* (Bowling Green, Ohio: Bowling Green University Popular Press, 1973), p. 113; Joe Laurie, Jr., *Vaudeville: From the Honky-Tonks to the Palace* (New York: Henry Holt and Company, 1953), pp. 139–41.

213 Irving Caesar, Sammy Lerner, and Gerald Marks, "Is It True What They Say About Dixie?" (New York: Irving Caesar, 1936). See also Sam Dennison, *Scandalize My Name: Black Imagery in American Popular Music* (New York: Garland Publishing, Inc., 1982), pp. 437–42; Stanley W. White, "The Burnt Cork Illusion of the 1920s in America: A Study in Nostalgia," *Journal of Popular Culture* 5 (Winter 1971): 537–40.

214 White, "Burnt Cork," pp. 535–36, 538, 541, 543, 548; Mc Lean, *Vaudeville as Ritual,* pp. 3, 15.

215 Edith J. R. Isaacs, *The Negro in the American Theatre* (College Park, Maryland: McGrath Publishing Company, 1968 [New York: Theatre Arts Books, 1947]), pp. 35, 39; Ann Charters, *Nobody: The Story of Bert Williams* (New York: The Macmillan Company, 1970), p. 10; Langston Hughes and Milton Meltzer, *Black Magic: A Pictorial History of the Negro in American Entertainment* (Englewood Cliffs, New Jersey: Prentice-Hall, Inc., 1967), p. 47; Alex Rogers and Bert A. Williams, "Nobody" (New York: Attucks Music Publishing Co., 1905). For an interesting evaluation of the "coon songs" ("The Phrenologist Coon" and "The Ghost of the Coon," for example) made popular by Bert Williams, see James Weldon Johnson, *Along This Way: The Autobiography of James Weldon Johnson* (New York: Viking Press, 1968 [1933]), pp. 152–

53. See also Charters, *Nobody*, pp. 49–50; J. Stanley Lemons, "Black Stereotypes as Reflected in Popular Culture, 1880–1920," *American Quarterly* 29 (Spring 1977):106–9.

216 Will Marion Cook, "Bon Bon Buddy," reprinted in Charters, *Nobody*, p. 97.

217 Hughes and Meltzer, *Black Magic*, pp. 46–47; Mabel Rowland, ed., *Bert Williams, Son of Laughter* (New York: English Crafters, 1923), pp. 45, 64; Mitchell, *Black Drama*, p. 84.

218 Charters, *Nobody*, pp. 27, 96; J. B., "Bert Williams," *The Soil* 1 (December 1916):19.

219 Allan Morrison, "One Hundred Years of Negro Entertainment," *Ebony* 18 (September 1963):123; Loften Mitchell, *Black Drama: The Story of the American Negro in the Theatre* (New York: Hawthorn Books, Inc., 1967), p. 46; Orrin Clayton Suthern, II, "Minstrelsy and Popular Culture," *Journal of Popular Culture* 4 (Winter 1971):664–65.

220 Will Marion Cook, "Clorindy, the Origin of the Cakewalk," in *Anthology of the American Negro in the Theatre: A Critical Approach*, ed. Lindsay Patterson (New York: Publishers Company, Inc., 1967), p. 55.

221 Montgomery Gregory, "The Drama of Negro Life," in *The New Negro*, ed. Alain Locke (New York: Atheneum, 1968 [New York: Albert & Charles Boni, Inc., 1925]), p. 159.

222 W. E. B. DuBois, "The National Emancipation Exposition," *Crisis* 7 (November 1913):339–41. For other dramatic portrayals of slave-era struggles, see W. E. B. DuBois, "George Washington and Black Folk: A Pageant for the Bicentenary, 1732–1932," *Crisis* 39 (April 1932):121–24; Willis Richardson, *Attucks, The Martyr*, in *Negro History in Thirteen Plays*, ed. Willis Richardson and May Miller (Washington, D.C.: Associated Publishers, Inc., 1935), pp. 29–61; Randolph Edmonds, *Nat Turner*, in *Six Plays for a Negro Theatre* (Boston: Walter H. Baker Company, 1934), pp. 61–82.

223 May Miller, *Harriet Tubman*, in Richardson and Miller, *Thirteen Plays*, [1935], p. 277. See also Edward J. Mc Coo, *Ethiopia at the Bar of Justice*, in *Plays and Pageants from the Life of the Negro*, ed. Willis Richardson (Washington, D.C.: Associated Publishers, Inc., 1930 [Newport, Kentucky, 1924]), p. 360; Frances Gunner, *The Light of the Women*, in Richardson, *Plays and Pageants*, [1924], pp. 337–39. For depictions of the fierce race pride of antebellum free blacks, see John Matheus, *Ti Yette*, in Richardson, *Plays and Pageants*, [1929], pp. 82, 85, 94, 102–4; May Miller, *Sojourner Truth*, in Richardson and Miller, *Thirteen Plays* [1935], p. 316.

224 Georgia Douglas Johnson, *Frederick Douglass*, in Richardson and Miller, *Thirteen Plays* [1935], p. 152.

225 Dorothy C. Guinn, *Out of the Dark*, in Richardson, *Plays and Pageants*, [1924], pp. 316–17.

226 Langston Hughes, *Don't You Want To Be Free?*, in *Black Theater, U. S. A.: Forty-Five Plays by Black Americans, 1847–1974*, ed. James V. Hatch and Ted Shine (New York: Free Press, 1974 [1937]), p. 263; Randolph Edmonds, "Proclamation for a Negro Theatre," reprinted in Williams, *American Theatre*, [1945],

p. 421. See also Willis Richardson, *The Flight of the Natives*, in *Plays of Negro Life: A Source-Book of Native American Drama*, ed. Alain Locke and Montgomery Gregory (New York: Harper & Brothers, 1927), pp. 103, 106–9; Randolph Edmonds, *Breeders*, in Edmonds, *Six Plays*, p. 99; Georgia Douglas Johnson, *William and Ellen Craft*, in Richardson and Miller, *Thirteen Plays*, [1935], pp. 167–68; Langston Hughes, *The Glory of Negro History*, in *The Langston Hughes Reader* (New York: George Braziller, Inc., 1958 [New York: Folkways Records & Service Corp., 1955]), pp. 466, 469; Lorraine Hansberry, *The Drinking Gourd*, in Hatch and Shine, *Black Theater*, [1960], pp. 718, 728.

227 Dumont, *Minstrel Guide*, p. 1; Sterling Brown, *Negro Poetry and Drama* (New York: Atheneum, 1969 [Washington, D.C.: Associates in Negro Folk Education, 1937]), p. 139.

228 Daniel J. Leab, *From Sambo to Superspade: The Black Experience in Motion Pictures* (Boston: Houghton Mifflin Company, 1975), pp. 8, 11, 14; William K. Everson, *American Silent Film* (New York: Oxford University Press, 1978), pp. 368–69; Thomas Cripps, *Slow Fade to Black: The Negro in American Film, 1900–1942* (New York: Oxford University Press, 1977), pp. 11–13.

229 Thomas Cripps, *Black Film as Genre* (Bloomington: Indiana University Press, 1978), p. 14; Peter Noble, *The Negro in Films* (New York: Arno Press & The New York Times, 1970 [London: Skelton Robinson, 1948]), p. 29.

230 Leab, *Sambo to Superspade*, p. 15; Jack Spears, *The Civil War on the Screen and Other Essays* (New York: A. S. Barnes and Company, 1977), p. 30; Cripps, *Slow Fade*, pp. 28–29. Early Civil War films that showed slaves saving their master's life at the expense of their own were *The Common Enemy* (1910); *The Confederate Spy* (1910); *None Can Do More* (1912); *Domino's Devotion* (1913); *Banty Tim* (1913); *Old Mammy's Secret Code* (1913); *A Black Conspiracy* (1913); *A Slave's Devotion* (1913), and *Dan* (1914).

231 Leab, *Sambo to Superspade*, p. 18. For an account of a rare instance of slave-initiated violence in the 1914 drama, *A Mother of Men*, see Daniel J. Leab, "The Gamut from A to B: The Image of the Black in Pre-1915 Movies," *Political Science Quarterly* 88 (March 1973):61.

232 For a modern study which treats Griffith's film as "the midwife in the rebirth of the most vicious terrorist organization in the history of the United States," the Ku Klux Klan, see John Hope Franklin, "'Birth of a Nation'—Propaganda as History," *Massachusetts Review* 20 (Autumn 1979):417–34.

233 Everson, *American Silent Film*, p. 83; D. W. Griffith and Seymour Stern, "*The Birth of a Nation*: A Reply to Peter Noble," *Sight and Sound* 16 (Spring 1947):32.

234 Raymond A. Cook, "The Man Behind 'The Birth of a Nation,'" *North Carolina Historical Review* 39 (October 1962):535; Leonard C. Archer, *Black Images in the American Theatre: NAACP Protest Campaigns—Stage, Screen, Radio & Television* (Brooklyn: Pageant-Poseidon, Ltd., 1973), p. 192; "Egg Negro Scenes in Liberty Film Play," *New York Times* (15 April 1915), sec. 1, p. 1; Stephen R. Fox, *The Guardian of Boston: William Monroe Trotter* (New

York: Atheneum, 1971), pp. 192–94; "Still Fighting the Film," *Crisis* 12 (June 1916):87. See also Thomas R. Cripps, "The Reaction of the Negro to the Motion Picture *Birth of a Nation*," *Historian* 25 (May 1963):344–62; Cripps, *Slow Fade*, pp. 41–69.

235 Griffith and Stern, "Reply," p. 32; Lillian Gish and Ann Pinchot, *The Movies, Mr. Griffith and Me* (Englewood Cliffs, New Jersey: Prentice-Hall, 1969), p. 162. For accounts of the continuing Afro-American protest against the film, see "'Birth of a Nation' Revived, Draws Protests," *Crisis* 45 (March 1938):84; "Protests Remake of Birth of a Nation," *Crisis* 62 (January 1955):37–38; "NAACP v. 'The Birth of a Nation': The Story of a 50-year Fight," *Crisis* 72 (February 1965):96–97, 102.

236 "The Slanderous Film," *Crisis* 11 (December 1915):76–77.

237 Jim Pines, *Blacks in Films: A Survey of Racial Themes and Images in the American Film* (London: Studio Vista, 1975), pp. 33–34.

238 Donald Bogle, *Toms, Coons, Mulattoes, Mammies, and Bucks: An Interpretive History of Blacks in American Films* (New York: Viking Press, 1973), pp. 107–8; Cripps, *Slow Fade*, pp. 70–89, 170–202; Elmer Anderson Carter, "Of Negro Motion Pictures," *Close Up* 5 (August 1929):119. For commentary on the skin-color caste system which operated in the black-owned film industry, see Daniel J. Leab, "'All Colored'—But Not Much Different: Films Made for Negro Ghetto Audiences, 1913–1928," *Phylon* 36 (September 1975):321–39; James P. Murray, *To Find an Image: Black Films From Uncle Tom to Super Fly* (Indianapolis: Bobbs-Merrill Company, 1973), p. 8.

239 Thomas R. Cripps, "The Myth of the Southern Box Office: A Factor in Racial Stereotyping in American Movies, 1920–1940," in *The Black Experience in America: Selected Essays*, ed. James C. Curtis and Lewis L. Gould (Austin: University of Texas Press, 1970), p. 133; *Variety* 111 (22 August 1933):17.

240 Produced and directed by William Wyler, *Jezebel* was set in the Louisiana of the 1850s. The film romance starred Bette Davis, George Brent, and Henry Fonda.

241 Pines, *Blacks in Films*, p. 48; Spears, *Civil War on the Screen*, p. 60; Bogle, *Toms*, pp. 47–50.

242 Arthur Draper, "Uncle Tom Will Never Die!" reprinted in *Black Films and Film-Makers: A Comprehensive Anthology from Stereotype to Superhero*, ed. Lindsay Patterson (New York: Dodd, Mead & Company, 1975 [1936]), pp. 30–35; Spears, *Civil War on the Screen*, p. 63; Peter A. Soderbergh, "Hollywood and the South, 1930–1960," *Mississippi Quarterly* 19 (Winter 1965–66):4–5.

243 Gavin Lambert, *GWTW: The Making of Gone With the Wind* (Boston: Atlantic Monthly Press/Little, Brown and Company, 1973), pp. 70, 137, 152, 204; Roland Flamini, *Scarlett, Rhett, and a Cast of Thousands: The Filming of Gone With the Wind* (New York: Macmillan Publishing Co., 1975), pp. 185, 210, 333; Margaret Mitchell to Louella Parsons, 29 October 1936, in *Margaret Mitchell's Gone With the Wind Letters, 1936–1949*, ed. Richard Harwell (New York: Macmillan Publishing Co., 1976), p. 84; Robert E. May, "*Gone With*

the Wind as Southern History: A Reappraisal," *Southern Quarterly* 17 (Fall 1978):51–52.

244 Flamini, *Cast of Thousands,* p. 301; Archer, *Black Images,* p. 206. For a summary of the Afro-American response to the film, see John D. Stevens, "The Black Reaction to *Gone With the Wind,*" *Journal of Popular Film* 2 (Fall 1973): 366–71. For Margaret Mitchell's criticism of the film's depiction of life in North Georgia, see Margaret Mitchell to Stephen Vincent Benét, 9 July 1936, in Harwell, *Letters,* p. 36; Margaret Mitchell to Susan Myrick, 10 February 1939, in Harwell, *Letters,* p. 250; Margaret Mitchell to Jere Moore, 16 February 1939, in Harwell, *Letters,* p. 255; Margaret Mitchell to Virginius Dabney, 23 July 1942, in Harwell, *Letters,* pp. 358–59.

245 *Pittsburgh Courier* 31 (6 January 1940):8; Sidney Howard, *GWTW: The Screenplay,* ed. Richard Harwell (New York: Macmillan Publishing Co., 1980 [1939]), pp. 70, 103, 174, 184, 197, 201, 225, 227, 229, 257, 273, 312. For an account of how Maureen O'Hara's husband, Will Price, taught Hattie McDaniel to speak like a "Georgia Negro," see Tom Dyer, "The Making of G-w-t-W," *Films in Review* 8 (May 1957):208.

246 *Amsterdam News* (6 January 1940):16. For black critiques of *Song of the South,* see "Rebuke," *Crisis* 54 (February 1947):52; "Needed: A Negro Legion of Decency," *Ebony* 2 (February 1947):36.

247 For a study of the faithful natives seen in films set in African locales, see Alfred E. Opubur and Adebayo Ogunbi, "Ooga Booga: the African Image in American Films," in *Other Voices, Other Views: An International Collection of Essays from the Bicentennial,* ed. Robin W. Winks (Westport: Greenwood Press, 1978), pp. 343–75.

248 John Oliver Killens, "Hollywood in Black and White," in *The State of the Nation,* ed. David Boroff (Englewood Cliffs, New Jersey: Prentice-Hall, Inc., 1965), p. 102–3.

249 Ibid., pp. 102, 107.

250 Ibid., p. 107.

CHAPTER 5. *The Debate Continues, 1965–1980*

1 For a general introduction to the spirit of the era during which "New Left" academicians believed that historians should initiate change so that "coming generations will have a new history," see Howard Zinn, *The Politics of History* (Boston: Beacon Press, 1970); Staughton Lynd, "A Profession of History," in *New American Review #2* (New York: New American Library, 1968) pp. 192–205; Irwin Unger, "The 'New Left' and American History: Some Recent Trends in United States Historiography," *American Historical Review* 72 (July 1967):1237–63.

2 For useful sociocultural studies which reveal the interconnections of the various "protest ethics," see Milton Viorst, *Fire in the Streets: America in the 1960s* (New York: Simon and Schuster, 1979); James McEvoy and Abraham Miller,

eds., *Black Power and Student Rebellion* (Belmont, California: Wadsworth Publishing Company, 1969); Joseph Boskin and Robert A. Rosenstone, eds., *Seasons of Rebellion: Protest and Radicalism in Recent America* (New York: Holt, Rinehart and Winston, Inc., 1972). John W. Blassingame, ed., *New Perspectives on Black Studies* (Urbana: University of Illinois Press, 1971) is a good companion volume of contemporary essays.

3 For additional commentary on these issues, see Armstead L. Robinson, Craig C. Foster, and Donald H. Ogilvie, eds., *Black Studies in the University: A Symposium* (New Haven: Yale University Press, 1969); Margaret Walker Alexander, "Black Studies: Some Personal Observations," *Afro-American Studies* 1 (May 1970):41–43; Alex Poinsett, "The Metamorphosis of Howard University," *Ebony* 27 (December 1971):110–22.

4 For a summary of the objectives of Black Studies programs in the early 1970s, see William D. Smith, "Black Studies: A Survey of Models and Curricula," *Journal of Black Studies* 1 (March 1971):259–72.

5 For charges that traditional histories had tended to promote "race belittlement," see Kelly Miller, "Negro History,"*Opportunity* 4 (March 1926): 86; Herman Dreer, "The Education of the Negro with Respect to His Background," *Journal of Negro History* 19 (January 1934): 45–47; L. Lemar Thompson, "A College Student Looks at the Problem of Teaching Negro History to Negro College Students," *Negro History Bulletin* 6 (December 1942): 62–63; "Negro History and the Advancement of Negro Masses," *Negro History Bulletin* 22 (December 1958): 72. For commentary on the general utility of black history, see Merl R. Eppse, *A Guide to the Study of the Negro in American History* (Nashville: National Educational Publishing Company, 1937), p. vii; Mary McLeod Bethune, "Clarifying Our Vision with the Facts," *Journal of Negro History* 23 (January 1938): 12–14; W. F. Savoy, "What Does the History of the Negro Mean to You?" *Journal of Negro History* 25 (October 1940): 464–68; W. M. Brewer, "Acquainting the Negro with History," *Negro History Bulletin* 8 (December 1944): 54, 68; John Hope Franklin, "The New Negro History," *Crisis* 64 (February 1957): 73–75. On using black history to help solve the "problems of the color line," see J. W. Bell, "The Teaching of Negro History," *Journal of Negro History* 8 (April 1923): 123–24; Albert N. D. Brooks, "Negro History—A Foundation for Integration," *Negro History Bulletin* 17 (January 1954): 94, 96; Charles V. Hamilton, "Negro History: An Approach to Awareness," *Negro History Bulletin* 21 (April 1958): 168. For the use of black history in solidifying a nationwide black "brotherhood," see W. Edward Farrison, "Negro Scholarship," *Crisis* 41 (February 1934): 34; Walter L. Daykin, "Nationalism as Expressed in Negro History," *Social Forces* 13 (December 1934): 257–63. On cross-cultural approaches to black history, see Grace Hays Johnson, "Phases of Cultural History of Significance for Negro Students," *Journal of Negro History* 22 (January 1937): 35–36; Ora Mae Lewis, "The Historian and Negro History," *Negro History Bulletin* 6 (March 1943): 134–39; Melville J. Herskovits, "The Present Status and Needs of Afroamerican Research,"*Journal of Negro History* 36 (April 1951): 123–47.

6 James G. Spady, "The Afro-American Historical Society: The Nucleus of Black Bibliophilies, 1897–1923," *Negro History Bulletin* 37 (June–July 1974): 254–57; Charles H. Wesley, "Racial Historical Societies and the American Heritage," *Journal of Negro History* 37 (January 1952): 27–29; Alfred A. Moss, Jr., *The American Negro Academy: Voice of the Talented Tenth* (Baton Rouge: Louisiana State University Press, 1981).

7 Carter G. Woodson, "Ten Years of Collecting and Publishing the Records of the Negro," *Journal of Negro History* 10 (October 1925): 599–600.

8 Charles H. Wesley, "Carter G. Woodson—As a Scholar," *Journal of Negro History* 36 (January 1951): 20.

9 For Woodson's personal account of his many accomplishments, see "An Accounting for Twenty-Five Years," *Journal of Negro History* 25 (October 1940): 422–31.

10 Benjamin Brawley, *A Social History of the American Negro* (New York: Collier Books, 1970 [New York: Macmillan Company, 1921]), p. 341.

11 Frank Bowles and Frank A. De Costa, *Between Two Worlds: A Profile of Negro Higher Education* (New York: McGraw-Hill Book Company, 1971), p. 83; Herbert Aptheker, "The Negro College Student in the 1920's—Years of Preparation and Protest: An Introduction," *Science & Society* 33 (Spring 1969): 152.

12 W. E. Burghardt DuBois and Augustus Granville Dill, eds., *The College-Bred Negro American* (Atlanta: Atlanta University Press, 1910), p. 23.

13 Up until 1938 fewer than a half dozen Afro-Americans had ever held regular staff appointments at predominantly white colleges. By 1940 at least 330 doctorates had been conferred upon black Americans but none taught at a white college in that year. Black representation increased to about eighty by the end of the war years, but many of these individuals were part-time lecturers or instructors. By 1960 some 200 black faculty members were employed at predominantly white colleges. James Allen Moss, "Negro Teachers in Predominantly White Colleges," *Journal of Negro Education* 27 (Fall 1958): 451–58; Allen B. Ballard, *The Education of Black Folk: The Afro-American Struggle for Knowledge in White America* (New York: Harper & Row, 1973), pp. 43–44.

14 C. G. Woodson, "Negro Life and History in Our Schools," *Journal of Negro History* 4 (July 1919): 278. Woodson's survey reported Black Studies offerings in eight northern universities. A 1932 study of 580 white colleges revealed that 95 were offering courses in race relations. George Longe, "The Study of the Negro," *Crisis* 43 (October 1936): 304. For an interesting account of how one such course came to be incorporated into the curriculum of the University of Toledo, see Constance Ridley Heslip, "The Study of the Negro in College and University Curricula," *Negro History Bulletin* 7 (December 1943): 59–60, 67–70.

15 Woodson, "Negro Life and History," p. 277.

16 Henry Allen Bullock, *A History of Negro Education in the South: From 1619 to the Present* (Cambridge: Harvard University Press, 1967), pp. 77–78, 162–66; W. E. Burghardt DuBois, *The College-Bred Negro* (Atlanta: Atlanta University Press, 1900), pp. 18–25.

17 Raymond Wolters, *The New Negro on Campus: Black College Rebellions of the 1920s* (Princeton: Princeton University Press, 1975), pp. vii, 18, 77, 192.

18 Ibid., pp. 341–43; Langston Hughes, "Cowards from the Colleges," *Crisis* 40 (August 1934): 226–28.

19 Kelly Miller, "The Function of the Negro College," *Dial* 32 (16 April 1902): 269–70; Kelly Miller, "Howard: The National Negro University," in *The New Negro*, ed. Alain Locke (New York: Atheneum, 1968 [New York: Albert & Charles Boni, Inc., 1925]), p. 321. See also Thomas Jesse Jones, ed., *Negro Education: A Study of the Private and Higher Schools for Colored People in the United States*, 2 vols. (Washington, D.C.: Government Printing Office, 1917), 1:56; Alain Locke, "Negro Education Bids for Par," *Survey* 54 (1 September 1925): 569–70; R. R. Moton, "Negro Higher and Professional Education in 1943," *Journal of Negro Education*, 2 (July 1933): 397–402.

20 James M. McPherson, "White Liberals and Black Power in Negro Education, 1865–1915," *American Historical Review* 75 (June 1970):1377. John Hope Franklin, "Courses Concerning the Negro in Negro Colleges," *Quarterly Review of Higher Education Among Negroes* 8 (July 1940): 138; Michael R. Winston, *The Howard University Department of History: 1913–1973* (Washington, D.C.: Department of History, Howard University, 1973), p. 23; Joe M. Richardson, *A History of Fisk University, 1865–1946* (University, Alabama: University of Alabama Press, 1980), pp. 84–100; Nick Aaron Ford, *Black Studies: Threat-or-Challenge* (Port Washington: Kennikat Press, 1973), pp. 48–49, 52; Thomas L. Dabney, "The Study of the Negro," *Journal of Negro History* 19 (July 1934): 279–80.

21 Charles S. Johnson, *The Negro College Graduate* (Chapel Hill: University of North Carolina Press, 1938), p. 359.

22 Lawrence Crouchett, "Early Black Studies Movements," *Journal of Black Studies* 2 (December 1971): 198–99; Franklin, "Courses Concerning the Negro," pp. 138–42; E. M. Coleman, "The Teaching of Negro History in Negro Colleges," *Negro History Bulletin* 12 (December 1948): 54, 66–67; Daniel C. Thompson, *Private Black Colleges at the Crossroads* (Westport: Greenwood Press, 1973), pp. 189, 206–7; Robert D. Reid, "Curricular Changes in Colleges and Universities for Negroes," *Journal of Higher Education* 38 (March 1967):159.

23 Harry Washington Greene, *Holders of Doctorates Among American Negroes* (Boston: Meador Publishing Company, 1946), pp. 47–48; Earl E. Thorpe, *Black Historians: A Critique* (New York: William Morrow and Company, 1971), p. 196.

24 William B. Hesseltine and Louis Kaplan, "Negro Doctors of Philosophy in History," *Negro History Bulletin* 6 (December 1942): 67.

25 Kenneth M. Stampp, *The Peculiar Institution: Slavery in the Ante-Bellum South* (New York: Alfred A. Knopf, 1956), pp. 86–191. The picture was made even more complex by the appearance of studies that focused upon the industrial and urban aspects of slavery. See, for example, Robert S. Starobin, *Industrial Slavery in the Old South* (New York: Oxford University Press, 1970); James E. Newton and Ronald L. Lewis, eds., *The Other Slaves: Mechanics, Artisans,*

and Craftsmen (Boston: G. K. Hall, 1978); Ronald L. Lewis, *Coal, Iron, and Slaves: Industrial Slavery in Maryland and Virginia, 1715–1865* (Westport: Greenwood Press, 1979); Richard C. Wade, *Slavery in the Cities: The South 1820–1860* (New York: Oxford University Press, 1964); Claudia Dale Goldin, *Urban Slavery in the American South, 1820–1860: A Quantitative History* (Chicago: University of Chicago Press, 1976).

26 "Stanley M. Elkins: Slavery," in *Interpreting American History: Conversations with Historians,* ed. John A. Garraty, 2 vols. (New York: Macmillan Company, 1970), 1:198; Stanley M. Elkins, "Slavery and Ideology," in *The Debate Over Slavery: Stanley Elkins and His Critics,* ed. Ann J. Lane (Urbana: University of Illinois Press, 1971), p. 325; "The Question of 'Sambo'," *Newberry Library Bulletin* 5 (December 1958): 36; Stanley M. Elkins, *Slavery: A Problem in American Institutional and Intellectual Life* (New York: Grosset & Dunlap, 1963 [Chicago: University of Chicago Press, 1959]), p. 84.

27 "Stanley M. Elkins," p. 198; Elkins, *Slavery,* pp. 81–87. For a discussion of the counterproposal which stated that Sambo was not a uniquely American product, that he had existed "wherever slavery has existed," and that he "could suddenly turn fierce," see Eugene D. Genovese, "Rebelliousness and Docility in the Negro Slave: A Critique of the Elkins Thesis," *Civil War History* 13 (December 1967): 293–314; Orlando Patterson, "Quashee," in Lane, *Debate,* pp. 210–19; Elkins, "Slavery and Ideology," pp. 349–53. For collections of essays that critique *Slavery* from a comparative history perspective, see Robert Brent Toplin, ed., *Slavery and Race Relations in Latin America* (Westport: Greenwood Press, 1974) and Laura Foner and Eugene D. Genovese, eds., *Slavery in the New World: A Reader in Comparative History* (Englewood Cliffs, Prentice-Hall, 1969).

28 "Question of 'Sambo'," pp. 24, 29; Genovese, "Rebelliousness and Docility," pp. 308–9, 311; George M. Fredrickson and Christopher Lasch, "Resistance to Slavery," *Civil War History* 13 (December 1967): 320–22, 326–27; Earl E. Thorpe, "Chattel Slavery & Concentration Camps," *Negro History Bulletin* 25 (May 1962): 172–75. Vincent P. Franklin, "Slavery, Personality, and Black Culture — Some Theoretical Issues," *Phylon* 35 (March 1974): 61–62; Elkins, "Slavery and Ideology," p. 359; Elkins, *Slavery,* p. 94. In seeking to identify psychologically corrosive features of the concentration camps, Elkins relied heavily upon the writings of Dachau and Buchenwald survivor Bruno Bettelheim. For these materials as well as those which more recently have asserted that Nazi camp inmates may actually have suffered "infantilization" to a much less critical degree than Bettelheim and Elkins assumed, see Bruno Bettelheim, "Individual and Mass Behavior in Extreme Situations," *Journal of Abnormal and Social Psychology* 38 (October 1943): 417–52; Bruno Bettelheim, *The Informed Heart: Autonomy in a Mass Age* (New York: The Free Press, 1960); Elie A. Cohen, *Human Behavior in The Concentration Camp* (New York: W. W. Norton & Company, 1953); Terrence Des Pres, *The Survivor: An Anatomy of Life in the Death Camps* (New York: Oxford University Press, 1976). For a defense of Elkins against charges of determinism, see Norman R. Yet-

man, "Slavery and Personality: A Problem in the Study of Modal Personality in Historical Populations," in *American Character and Culture in a Changing World: Some Twentieth-Century Perspectives,* ed. John A. Hague (Westport: Greenwood Press, 1979), pp. 350–54.

29 For late 1960s and early 1970s commentary on the contributions of African and Afro-American folk culture to the psychological survival of the slaves, see Sterling Stuckey, "Through the Prism of Folklore: The Black Ethos in Slavery," *Massachusetts Review* 9 (Summer 1968):417–37; Lawrence W. Levine, "Slave Songs and Slave Consciousness: An Exploration in Neglected Sources," in *Anonymous Americans: Explorations in Nineteenth-Century Social History,* ed. Tamara K. Hareven (Englewood Cliffs: Prentice-Hall, 1971), pp. 99–130. For commentary on the strength and viability of a separate Afro-American culture, see Mina Davis Caulfield, "Slavery and the Origins of Black Culture: Elkins Revisited," in *Americans From Africa,* vol. 1: *Slavery and Its Aftermath,* ed. Peter I. Rose (New York: Atherton Press, 1970), pp. 171–93; Robert Blauner, "Black Culture: Myth or Reality?" in *Americans From Africa,* vol. 2: *Old Memories, New Moods,* ed. Peter I. Rose (New York: Atherton Press, 1970), pp. 417–41; Houston A. Baker, Jr., "Completely Well: One View of Black American Culture," in *Key Issues in the Afro-American Experience,* ed. Nathan I. Huggins, Martin Kilson, Daniel M. Fox, 2 vols. (New York: Harcourt Brace Jovanovich, Inc., 1971), 1:20–33. For Elkins' response to the concept of culture as a form of slave resistance, see "The Slavery Debate," *Commentary* 60 (December 1975): 40–54.

30 Walter B. Weare, review of *The Slave Community,* in *Civil War History* 19 (June 1973): 177. For a study contrasting the works of Elkins and Blassingame, see William Issel, "History, Social Science, and Ideology: Elkins and Blassingame on Ante-Bellum American Slavery," *History Teacher* 9 (November 1975): 56–72.

31 John W. Blassingame, *The Slave Community: Plantation Life in the Antebellum South* (New York: Oxford University Press, 1972), p. 216.

32 Blassingame, *Slave Community,* pp. viii, 150, 153, 207–8, 213; Elkins, "Slavery Debate," p. 45.

33 Blassingame, *Slave Community,* pp. 28–29, 41–42, 76, 78–79, 99–100, 154, 172, 201, 203–4, 206–7, 214–15, 226. For a later Blassingame study of the status and role model structure of the slave community, see "Status and Social Structure in the Slave Community: Evidence from New Sources," in *Perspectives and Irony in American Slavery,* ed. Harry P. Owens (Jackson: University Press of Mississippi, 1976), pp. 137–51. For late sixties narrative-based commentary supporting Blassingame's claims regarding black "significant others," see Gilbert Osofsky, ed., *Puttin' On Ole Massa: The Slave Narratives of Henry Bibb, William Wells Brown, and Solomon Northup* (New York: Harper Torchbooks, 1969), pp. 38–39.

34 Blassingame, *Slave Community,* pp. vii, 227–35; John W. Blassingame, "Black Autobiographies as History and Literature," *Black Scholar* 5 (December 1973–January 1974): 3. John W. Blassingame, "Redefining *The Slave Community:*

A Response to the Critics," in *Revisiting Blassingame's The Slave Community: The Scholars Respond*, ed. Al-Tony Gilmore (Westport: Greenwood Press, 1978), pp. 162–63. See also John W. Blassingame, "Using the Testimony of Ex-Slaves: Approaches and Problems," *Journal of Southern History* 41 (November 1975): 473–92. For commentary on the slave narrative as literary genre and historical source, see Frances Smith Foster, *Witnessing Slavery: The Development of Ante-bellum Slave Narratives* (Westport: Greenwood Press, 1979); Charles H. Nichols, "Slave Narratives and the Plantation Legend," *Phylon* 10 (Fall 1949): 201–10; William W. Nichols, "Slave Narratives: Dismissed Evidence in the Writing of Southern History," *Phylon* 32 (Winter 1971): 403–9; Edward Margolies, "Ante-Bellum Slave Narratives: Their Place in American Literary History," *Studies in Black Literature* 4 (Autumn 1973): 1–8; David Thomas Bailey, "A Divided Prism: Two Sources of Black Testimony on Slavery," *Journal of Southern History* 46 (August 1980): 381–404. John Sekora and Darwin T. Turner, eds., *The Art of Slave Narrative: Original Essays in Criticism and Theory* (Macomb, Illinois: Western Illinois University, 1982).

35 Blassingame, "Response," p. 147; Earle E. Thorpe, "*The Slave Community:* Studies of Slavery Need Freud and Marx," in Gilmore, *Revisiting*, p. 49. See also George P. Rawick, "Some Notes on a Social Analysis of Slavery: A Critique and Assessment of *The Slave Community*," in Gilmore, *Revisiting*, pp. 22–24; Stanley Engerman, "Reconsidering *The Slave Community*," in Gilmore, *Revisiting*, pp. 98, 100–103; Ralph D. Carter, "Slavery and the Climate of Opinion," in Gilmore, *Revisiting*, p. 89–92; Leslie Howard Owens, "Blacks in *The Slave Community*," in Gilmore, *Revisiting*, pp. 62, 64–65. For a more detailed summary of the reviews generated by Blassingame's book, see Mary Frances Berry, "*The Slave Community*: A Review of Reviews," in Gilmore, *Revisiting*, pp. 3–16. Blassingame incorporated some of the reviewers' suggestions in a revised and enlarged edition of the book published in 1979.

36 Albert J. Raboteau, *Slave Religion: The "Invisible Institution" in the Antebellum South* (New York: Oxford University Press, 1978); Thomas L. Webber, *Deep Like the Rivers: Education in the Slave Quarter Community, 1831–1865* (New York: W. W. Norton & Company, 1978). In addition to George Rawick's forty-one volume collection of reprinted Federal Writers' Project interviews, *The American Slave: A Composite Autobiography* (Westport: Greenwood Press, 1972–1979), various other examples of primary research materials on slaves were collected and published during the 1970s. See especially Robert S. Starobin, ed., *Blacks in Bondage: Letters of American Slaves* (New York: New Viewpoints, 1974); Charles L. Perdue, Jr., Thomas E. Barden, Robert K. Phillips, eds., *Weevils in the Wheat: Interviews with Virginia Ex-Slaves* (Charlottesville: University Press of Virginia, 1976); John W. Blassingame, ed., *Slave Testimony: Two Centuries of Letters, Speeches, Interviews, and Autobiographies* (Baton Rouge: Louisiana State University Press, 1977); Randall M. Miller, ed. *"Dear Master": Letters of a Slave Family* (Ithaca: Cornell University Press, 1978).

37 Lawrence W. Levine, *Black Culture and Black Consciousness: Afro-American Folk Thought from Slavery to Freedom* (New York: Oxford University Press,

1977); Dena J. Epstein, *Sinful Tunes and Spirituals: Black Folk Music to the Civil War* (Urbana: University of Illinois Press, 1977).

38 Eugene D. Genovese, *Roll, Jordan, Roll: The World the Slaves Made* (New York: Pantheon Books, 1974).

39 William L. Van Deburg, *The Slave Drivers: Black Agricultural Labor Supervisors in the Antebellum South* (Westport: Greenwood Press, 1979); Herbert G. Gutman, *The Black Family in Slavery and Freedom, 1750–1925* (New York: Pantheon Books, 1976).

40 Leslie Howard Owens, *This Species of Property: Slave Life and Culture in the Old South* (New York: Oxford University Press, 1976); Nathan Irvin Huggins, *Black Odyssey: The Afro-American Ordeal in Slavery* (New York: Pantheon Books, 1977); Levine, *Black Culture*, p. xi.

41 For an evaluation of Blassingame's versus Fogel's and Engerman's concentration upon one particular type of evidence, see Thomas J. Pressly and Harvey H. Chamberlin, "Slavery and Scholarship, Some Problems of Evidence," *Pacific Northwest Quarterly* 66 (April 1975): 79–84.

42 Robert William Fogel and Stanley L. Engerman, *Time on the Cross*, vol. 1: *The Economics of American Negro Slavery* (Boston: Little, Brown and Company, 1974), p. 258. Fogel and Engerman became interested in the economic analysis of the slave system following the publication of Alfred H. Conrad's and John R. Meyer's revisionist study on plantation profitability, "The Economics of Slavery in the Ante-Bellum South," *Journal of Political Economy* 66 (April 1958): 95–130. For commentary on Conrad's and Meyer's importance to recent economic history trends, see Raymond Dacey, "A Historiography of Negro Slavery, 1918–1976," in *Issues and Ideas in America*, ed. Benjamin J. Taylor and Thurman J. White (Norman : University of Oklahoma Press, 1976), pp. 116–21. See also Hugh G. J. Aitken, ed., *Did Slavery Pay?: Readings in the Economics of Black Slavery in the United States* (Boston: Houghton Mifflin Company, 1971). For a detailed account of the progressive development of Fogel's and Engerman's methodology and findings, see Robert William Fogel, "From the Marxists to the Mormons," *The* (London) *Times Literary Supplement* (13 June 1975): 667–70. See also Fogel's and Engerman's "The Economics of Slavery," in *The Reinterpretation of American Economic History*, ed. Robert William Fogel and Stanley L. Engerman (New York: Harper & Row, 1971), pp. 311–41.

43 Charles Crowe, "Time on the Cross: The Historical Monograph as a Pop Event," *History Teacher* 9 (August 1976): 588, 594–602, 626; Sterling Plumpp, review of *Time on the Cross*, in *Black Books Bulletin* 3 (Spring 1975): 57; Winthrop D. Jordan, "The Tone of Snake-Root Salesmen," *Psychology Today* 24 (September 1974): 119; Herbert Aptheker, "Heavenly Days in Dixie: Or, the Time of Their Lives [II]," *Political Affairs* 53 (July 1974): 57; Fred Siegel, "Time on the Cross: A First Appraisal," *Historical Methods Newsletter* 7 (September 1974): 299–301.

44 Fogel and Engerman, *Time on the Cross*, 1: 4–6, 129–30, 135–37, 141–43, 147, 153, 156–57, 229–32. For a critique of the cliometricians' conceptualization

of the traditional interpretation of slavery, see Peter Kolchin, "Toward a Reinterpretation of Slavery," *Journal of Social History* 9 (Fall 1975): 101–2.

45 Aptheker, "Heavenly Days," p. 54; Kenneth M. Stampp, "A Humanistic Perspective," in *Reckoning with Slavery: A Critical Study in the Quantitative History of American Negro Slavery*, ed. Paul A. David, Herbert G. Gutman, Richard Sutch, Peter Temin, Gavin Wright (New York: Oxford University Press, 1976), pp. 17–19; Crowe, "Pop Event," pp. 626–27; Allan Kulikoff, "Black Society and the Economics of Slavery," *Maryland Historical Magazine* 70 (Summer 1975): 204; John W. Blassingame, "The Mathematics of Slavery," *Atlantic* 234 (August 1974): 82; Herbert G. Gutman, *Slavery and the Numbers Game: A Critique of Time on the Cross* (Urbana: University of Illinois Press, 1975), pp. 168, 176.

46 Paul A. David and Peter Temin, "Slavery: The Progressive Institution?" *Journal of Economic History* 34 (September 1974): 740, 748; Richard Sutch, "The Treatment Received by American Slaves: A Critical Review of the Evidence Presented in *Time on the Cross*," *Explorations in Economic History* 12 (October 1975): 427; Roger L. Ransom, "Was It Really All That Great To Be a Slave?" *Agricultural History* 48 (October 1974): 581–82; Thomas Holt, "On the Cross: The Role of Quantitative Methods in the Reconstruction of the Afro-American Experience," *Journal of Negro History* 61 (April 1976): 160, 165; Gutman, *Numbers Game*, p. 173. For enlightening tabulations of Fogel's and Engerman's measurements and methodology as compiled by two traditional historians, see Stampp, "Humanistic Perspective," p. 9; Blassingame, "Mathematics," p. 79.

47 For an account of the "Today" show appearance, see Soma Golden, "New Slavery Book Kindles a Dispute," *New York Times* (2 May 1974), sec. 1, pp. 49, 57.

48 August Meier, "Old Wine in New Bottles: A Review of *Time on the Cross*," *Civil War History* 20 (September 1974): 251; Charles Crowe, "Slavery, Ideology, and 'Cliometrics'," *Technology and Culture* 17 (April 1976): 279. See also David and Temin, "Progressive Institution," pp. 745–46. For Robert Fogel's response to the critics, see Robert William Fogel, "The Limits of Quantitative Methods in History," *American Historical Review* 80 (April 1975): 342–43, 349; Kenneth L. Woodward, "History by the Numbers," *Newsweek* (20 October 1975): 70; Robert W. Fogel, "Reply to Oscar Handlin," *Perspectives in American History* 9 (1975): 29–32; Robert William Fogel, "Cliometrics and Culture: Some Recent Developments in the Historiography of Slavery," *Journal of Social History* 11 (Fall 1977): 45, 47.

49 For an able expression of this historiographical mood, see Huggins, *Black Odyssey*, pp. xi, xv–xvi, 203–4.

50 Martin Duberman, "Historical Fictions," *New York Times Book Review* (11 August 1968): 26–27; C. Vann Woodward, "Confessions of a Rebel: 1831," *New Republic* 157 (7 October 1967): 25–28. See also Anna Mary Wells, Vincent Harding, Mike Thelwell, Eugene D. Genovese, "An Exchange on 'Nat Turner'," *New York Review of Books* 11 (7 November 1968): 35; Shaun O'Connell, "Styron's Nat Turner," *Nation* 205 (16 October 1967): 373–74. Although

he predicted that both blacks and whites would be critical, Afro-American novelist and longtime friend, James Baldwin, gave Styron's book a sympathetic review. For this and other complimentary black-authored estimations of *Nat Turner,* see Raymond A. Sokolov, "Into the Mind of Nat Turner," *Newsweek* 70 (16 October 1967): 67, 69; Saunders Redding, et al., "Recommended Summer Reading," *American Scholar* 37 (Summer 1968): 542; Benjamin Quarles, review of *The Confessions of Nat Turner,* in *Social Studies* 59 (November 1968): 280.

51 Charles H. Rowell, "Poetry, History and Humanism: An Interview with Margaret Walker," *Black World* 25 (December 1975): 11; Lerone Bennett, Jr., "Nat's Last White Man," in *William Styron's Nat Turner: Ten Black Writers Respond,* ed. John Henrik Clarke (Boston: Beacon Press, 1968), p. 4; Ernest Kaiser, "The Failure of William Styron," in Clarke, *Ten Black Writers,* pp. 57, 65. For a transcript of the heated exchange between Styron and assorted critics at a 1968 Southern Historical Association session, see Ralph Ellison, William Styron, Robert Penn Warren, C. Vann Woodward, "The Uses of History in Fiction," *Southern Literary Journal* 1 (Spring 1969): 57–90. For critiques of Styron's critics, see Stephen B. Oates, "Styron & the Blacks—Another View," *Nation* 220 (31 May 1975): 662–64; Jervis Anderson, "Styron and His Black Critics," *Dissent* 16 (March–April 1969): 157–66; Eugene D. Genovese, "The Nat Turner Case," *New York Review of Books* 11 (12 September 1968): 34–37.

52 William Styron, *The Confessions of Nat Turner* (New York: Random House, 1967), pp. 70, 322, 410.

53 Ibid., pp. 176–78, 183, 258, 264–65, 347, 426; Bennett, "Last White Man," p. 6; Alvin F. Poussaint, "*The Confessions of Nat Turner* and the Dilemma of William Styron," in Clarke, *Ten Black Writers,* p. 21.

54 Styron, *Nat Turner,* pp. 27, 53, 56, 224, 232, 396.

55 Robert Canzoneri and Page Stegner, "An Interview with William Styron," *Per/Se* 1 (Summer 1966): 39; William Styron, *Sophie's Choice* (New York: Random House, 1979), pp. 420–22. For opinions as to the degree to which Styron mastered the sources pertaining to the 1831 insurrection, see Henry Irving Tragle, "Styron and His Sources," *Massachusetts Review* 11 (Winter 1970): 135–53; Herbert Aptheker, "A Note on the History," *Nation* 205 (16 October 1967): 375–76. For a critique of the literary quality of *Nat Turner,* see Richard Gilman, "Nat Turner Revisited," *New Republic* 158 (27 April 1968): 23–32. For a study of the novel in relation to earlier Styron themes and characters, see Marc L. Ratner, "Styron's Rebel," *American Quarterly* 21 (Fall 1969): 595–608. For the original *Confessions,* antebellum commentary on the insurrection, and a selection of modern-day appraisals of the revolt and of Styron's Turner, see John B. Duff and Peter M. Mitchell, eds., *The Nat Turner Rebellion: The Historical Event and the Modern Controversy* (New York: Harper & Row, 1971).

56 William Styron, review of *American Negro Slave Revolts,* in *New York Review of Books* 1 (26 September 1963):19; James Jones and William Styron, "Two Writers Talk it Over," *Esquire* 60 (July 1963):58; William Styron, "This Quiet Dust," *Harper's Magazine* 230 (April 1965):138.

57 Daniel Panger, *Ol' Prophet Nat* (Greenwich, Connecticut: Fawcett Publications, Inc., 1967 [Winston-Salem: John F. Blair, 1967]), pp. 17–18, 31–32, 51–52, 79–80, 105, 114–17, 153–55.

58 Ibid., pp. 56–57, 64.

59 Ibid., p. 63.

60 Ibid., pp. 59–61, 99, 137, 143, 150.

61 A. X. Nicholas, "(For Lee)," in *We Speak as Liberators: Young Black Poets,* ed. Orde Coombs (New York: Dodd, Mead & Company, 1970), p. 116; Abena Walker, "Washington, D.C.—Ain't It a Mess,"in *Synergy: An Anthology of Washington, D.C. Blackpoetry,* ed. Ahmos Zu-Bolton II and E. Ethelbert Miller (Washington, D.C.: Energy Blacksouth Press, 1975 [1970]), p. 30; Mae Jackson, "reincarnation," *Black World* 19 (September 1970): 35; Jon Eckels, "Hell, Mary," in *Home Is Where the Soul Is* (Detroit: Broadside Press, 1969), pp. 13–14; Conrad Kent Rivers, "Watts," in *The Still Voice of Harlem* (London, England: Paul Breman, 1968), p. 15; Sylvia Young, "Three Thoughts," in *Black Poets Write On!: An Anthology of Black Philadelphia Poets* (Philadelphia: Black History Museum Committee, 1970), p. 24. See also Angelo Lewis, "America Bleeds," *Motive* 31 (November 1970): 29; Rob Penny, "and we conquered," in *The Poetry of Black America: Anthology of the 20th Century,* ed. Arnold Adoff (New York: Harper & Row, 1973 [1970], p. 391.

62 S. E. Anderson, "The Red The Black & The Green," *Black World* 20 (August 1971): 60; Arnold Kemp, "The End of the World," in Coombs, *Liberators,* p. 89; Jayne Cortez, "How Long Has Trane Been Gone," in *Pisstained Stairs and the Monkey Man's Wares* (New York: Phrase Text, 1969), p. 42; Mari Evans, "Vive Noir!," in *I Am a Black Woman* (New York: William Morrow and Company, 1970), pp. 72–73: Don L. Lee, "A Message All Blackpeople Can Dig (& a few negroes too)," in *Don't Cry, Scream* (Detroit: Broadside Press, 1969), p. 64.

63 Robert A. Gross, "The Black Novelists: 'Our Turn,'" *Newsweek* 73 (16 June 1969): 94; Ernest J. Gaines, *The Autobiography of Miss Jane Pittman* (New York: Bantam Books, 1972 [New York: Dial Press, 1971]), p. 9; Margaret Walker, *Jubilee* (New York: Bantam Books, 1967 [Boston: Houghton Mifflin Company, 1966]), p. 54; John O. Killens, *Slaves* (New York: Pyramid Books, 1969), pp. 8, 24, 26, 47, 69–70, 122.

64 Fred Beauford, "A Conversation with Ernest J. Gaines," *Black Creation* 4 (Fall 1972): 16; John O'Brien, ed., *Interviews with Black Writers* (New York: Liveright, 1973), p. 82; Ruth Laney, "A Conversation with Ernest Gaines," *Southern Review* 10 (January 1974): 3, 13–14.

65 Margaret Walker, *How I Wrote Jubilee* (Chicago: Third World Press, 1972), pp. 12, 18; Charles H. Rowell, "Poetry, History and Humanism: An Interview with Margaret Walker," *Black World* 25 (December 1975): 7, 10; Nikki Giovanni and Margaret Walker, *A Poetic Equation: Conversations Between Nikki Giovanni and Margaret Walker* (Washington, D.C.: Howard University Press, 1974), p. 1.

66 Alex Haley, "My Furthest-Back Person —The African,'" *New York Times Maga-*

zine (16 July 1972): 13; Alex Haley, *Roots*, (Garden City, New York: Double-day & Company, 1976), pp. 664–67, 670–79, 681; Hans J. Massaquoi, "Alex Haley: The Man Behind *Roots*," *Ebony* 32 (April 1977): 41; Jessica Harris, "An Interview with Alex Haley, Author of *Roots*," *Essence* 7 (October 1976): 27; Alex Haley, "What *Roots* Means to Me," *Reader's Digest* 110 (May 1977): 74. For Senegalese President Leopold S. Senghor's complimentary view that Haley's book "revealed us to ourselves," sees Hans J. Massaquoi, "Alex Haley in Juffure," *Ebony* 32 (July 1977): 40.

67 Merrill Maguire Skaggs, "*Roots*: A New Black Myth," *Southern Quarterly* 17 (Fall 1978): 49; Joan Wixen, "Bridging an Ocean and Two Centuries," Madison (Wisc.) *Capitol Times* (17 January 1977): 15; Mel Watkins, "A Talk With Alex Haley," *New York Times Book Review* (26 September 1976): 2.

68 David Herbert Donald, "Family Chronicle," *Commentary* 62 (December 1976): 72–73; Willie Lee Rose, "An American Family," *New York Review of Books* 23 (11 November 1976): 4; Lewis H. Lapham, "The Black Man's Burden: Serving the Captive's Need," *Harper's* 254 (June 1977): 16; Mark Ottaway, "Tangled Roots," *Sunday Times* (London), (10 April 1977): 17. See also Gary B. and Elizabeth Shown Mills, "*Roots* and the New 'Faction': A Legitimate Tool for Clio?" *Virginia Magazine of History and Biography* 89 (January 1981): 3–26.

69 John Darnton, "Haley, Assailing Critic, Says 'Roots' Is Sound," *New York Times* (19 April 1977), sec. 1, p. 3; Ottaway, "Tangled Roots," p. 21; Malcolm R. West, "Black Historians Reflect on Criticisms of *Roots*," *Jet* 52 (28 April 1977): 16–17. For accounts of the plagiarism suits filed by novelists Harold Courlander and Margaret Walker, see "The 'Roots' Cases," *New York* 11 (20 November 1978): 126–27; "Uprooted," *Newsweek* 93 (22 January 1979): 10; "View from the Whirlpool," *Time* 113 (19 February 1979): 88; Herb Boyd, "Plagiarism and the Roots Suits," *First World* 2 (no. 3, 1979): 31–33.

70 Frank Yerby, *The Foxes of Harrow* (New York: Dial Press, 1946), pp. 244, 318, 405; Frank Yerby, *Floodtide* (New York: Dell Publishing Co., 1976 [New York: Dial Press, 1950]), p. 64; Frank Yerby, *Fairoaks* (New York: Dell Publishing Co., 1969 [New York: Dial Press, 1957]), pp. 49, 69–71; Darwin T. Turner, "Frank Yerby as Debunker," *Massachusetts Review* 9 (Summer 1968): 574; Hugh M. Gloster, "The Significance of Frank Yerby," *Crisis* 55 (January 1948): 13.

71 Maryemma Graham, "Frank Yerby, King of the Costume Novel," *Essence* 6 (October 1975): 70; Jack B. Moore, "The Guilt of the Victim: Racial Themes in Some Frank Yerby Novels," *Journal of Popular Culture* 8 (Spring 1975): 747.

72 "Mystery Man of Letters," *Ebony* 10 (February 1955): 31–32; Frank Yerby, "How and Why I Write the Costume Novel," *Harper's Magazine* 219 (October 1959): 145, 148–49; Graham, "King," pp. 70, 88; Blyden Jackson, "Silver Foxes," *Journal of Negro Education* 15 (Fall 1946): 652.

73 Graham, "King," p. 88; Frank Yerby, *The Dahomean* (New York: Dial Press, 1971), p. vii; Frank Yerby, *Benton's Row* (New York: Dell Publishing Co., 1977

[New York: Dial Press, 1954]), p. 6; Yerby, *Foxes*, pp. 18, 51–52, 57, 95; Yerby, *Floodtide*, pp. 9, 12, 27, 36, 185, 260; Yerby, *Fairoaks*, pp. 7–9, 263.

74 For portrayals of proud, deceptive slaves, see Yerby, *Foxes*, pp. 118–19, 308–09; Yerby, *Floodtide*, pp. 63–64, 89, 273; Yerby, *Fairoaks*, p. 43.

75 Yerby, *Dahomean*, p. vii; Graham, "King," pp. 71, 88, 92.

76 Frank Yerby, *A Darkness at Ingraham's Crest* (New York: Dell Publishing Co., 1980 [New York: Dial Press, 1979]), pp. 78, 95, 178–79, 682, 701.

77 Ibid., pp. 75–76, 128–29, 192, 199–200, 271, 331, 339, 374, 463, 573–75, 595, 609, 613, 723, 734, 755–56.

78 For other examples of this genre, see the Sabrehill series written by Raymond Giles, Marie De Jourlet's Windhaven books, the Bondmaster series penned by Richard Tresillian, and titles such as Hugo Paul, *Plantation Breed* (New York: Prestige Books, 1969) and George McNeill, *The Plantation* (New York: Bantam Books, 1975). For a clever satire on the sex and slavery novels, see Ishmael Reed, *Flight to Canada* (New York: Random House, 1976), pp. 99–103, 108, 127–28, 153.

79 "The Best-Seller Breed," *Newsweek* 49 (13 May 1957): 122; Earl F. Bargainnier, "The Falconhurst Series: A New Popular Image of the Old South," *Journal of Popular Culture* 10 (Fall 1976): 298–99.

80 Rudy Maxa, "The Master of Mandingo," *Washington Post/Potomac* 7 (13 July 1975): 20.

81 Bargainnier, "Falconhurst Series," pp. 298–99.

82 In Whittington's first contribution to the series, *Taproots of Falconhurst* (1978), it was noted that "Ashley Carter" could trace his southern ancestry back at least nine generations to an eighteenth-century James River settler. A great-great-uncle was said to have been a Confederate general during the Civil War.

83 Kyle Onstott, *Mandingo* (Greenwich, Conn.: Fawcett Publications, 1963 [Richmond: Denlinger, 1957]), pp. 71, 181; Lance Horner and Kyle Onstott, *Falconhurst Fancy* (Greenwich, Conn.: Fawcett Publications, 1966), pp. 80, 427; Lance Horner, *The Mustee* (Greenwich, Conn.: Fawcett Publications, 1967), pp. 24, 39, 99, 100, 212, 280; Lance Horner, *Flight to Falconhurst* (Greenwich, Conn.: Fawcett Publications, 1971), p. 78; Lance Horner, *Mistress of Falconhurst* (Greenwich, Conn.: Fawcett Publications, 1973), pp. 8, 32, 150, 171–72, 234; Harry Whittington [Ashley Carter], *Scandal of Falconhurst* (New York: Fawcett Gold Medal Books, 1980), p. 409; Harry Whittington [Ashley Carter], *Taproots of Falconhurst* (New York: Fawcett Gold Medal Books, 1978), p. 60; Kyle Onstott, *Drum* (Greenwich, Conn.: Fawcett Publications, 1966 [New York: Dial Press, 1962]), p. 323.

84 Onstott, *Drum*, p. 257; Horner and Onstott, *Fancy*, pp. 57, 134–35; Onstott, *Master*, pp. 9, 48, 277, 332; Horner, *Flight*, pp. 93, 247.

85 Randolph Edmonds, "Proclamation for a Negro Theatre," reprinted in *The American Theatre: A Sum of its Parts*, ed. Henry B. Williams (New York: Samuel French, Inc., 1971 [1945]), p. 421.

86 Herbert Stokes, *The Uncle Toms*, in *Drama Review* 12 (Summer 1968): 58–60.

During the twentieth century, variations of the original Uncle Tom were seen in a variety of theatrical contexts. For *Uncle Tom's Cabin* on the turn-of-the-century minstrel stage, see Frank Dumont, *The Witmark Amateur Minstrel Guide and Burnt Cork Encyclopedia* (Chicago: M. Witmark & Sons, 1905), pp. 36-37. For Uncle Tom in vaudeville and musical comedy, see Harry Birdoff, *The World's Greatest Hit: Uncle Tom's Cabin* (New York: S. F. Vanni, 1947), pp. 369-72, 375, 379, 384. For accounts of more formal theater versions, see Frank Rahill, "America's Number One Hit," *Theatre Arts* 36 (October 1952): 23-24 and Richard Moody, "Uncle Tom, The Theater and Mrs. Stowe," *American Heritage* 6 (October 1955): 103. For *Uncle Tom's Cabin* as an inspiration for modern ballet, see Richard Rodgers and Oscar Hammerstein, *The King and I* (New York: Random House, 1951), pp. 98-109 and E. E. Cummings, *Tom: A Ballet*, in *Three Plays & A Ballet*, ed. by George J. Firmage (New York: October House, Inc., 1967 [1935]), pp. 141-70. For Uncle Tom in song, see Birdoff, *World's Greatest Hit*, p. 407 and Howard Sackler, *The Great White Hope* (New York: Dial Press, 1968), pp. 183-85. For story lines and descriptions of motion pictures featuring everyone from Ben Turpin (*Uncle Tom Without the Cabin*, 1919) to Barbra Streisand (*Funny Lady*, 1975) in the Harriet Beecher Stowe roles, see Kalton C. Lahue, *World of Laughter: The Motion Picture Comedy Short, 1910-1930* (Norman: University of Oklahoma Press, 1966), p. 178; Kenneth W. Munden, ed., *The American Film Institute Catalog of Motion Pictures Produced in the United States: Feature Films, 1921-1930* (New York: R. R. Bowker, 1971), p. 822; Birdoff, *World's Greatest Hit*, pp. 396-410; William L. Slout, "*Uncle Tom's Cabin* in American Film History," *Journal of Popular Film* 2 (Spring 1973): 142-50; Thomas Cripps, *Slow Fade to Black: The Negro in American Film, 1900-1942* (New York: Oxford University Press, 1977), pp. 15-16, 150-52, 157, 159-65; Donald Bogle, *Toms, Coons, Mulattoes, Mammies, and Bucks: An Interpretive History of Blacks in American Films* (New York: Viking Press, 1973), pp. 6-8, 17.

87 LeRoi Jones, *Home: Social Essays* (New York: William Morrow & Co., Inc., 1966), pp. 210-15.

88 Clifford Mason, *Gabriel: The Story of a Slave Rebellion*, in *Black Drama Anthology*, ed. Woodie King and Ron Milner (New York: New American Library, 1972 [1968]), p. 222; Amiri Baraka, *Slave Ship*, in *The Motion of History and Other Plays* (New York: William Morrow and Company, Inc., 1978 [1967]), pp. 135, 138, 139, 143, 145.

89 Baraka, *Slave Ship*, p. 143; Mason, *Gabriel*, pp. 172, 176. See also Val Ferdinand, *Blk Love Song #1*, in *Black Theater, U.S.A.: Forty-Five Plays by Black Americans, 1847-1974*, ed. James V. Hatch and Ted Shine (New York: Free Press, 1974 [1969]), p. 868.

90 Loften Mitchell, *Tell Pharaoh*, in *The Black Teacher and the Dramatic Arts: A Dialogue, Bibliography, and Anthology*, ed. William R. Reardon and Thomas D. Pawley (Westport: Negro Universities Press, 1970 [1967]), pp. 262, 269, 273; Mason, *Gabriel*, p. 179.

91 Mitchell, *Tell Pharaoh*, p. 263; Mason, *Gabriel*, pp. 179, 186, 193-95; Amiri

Baraka, *The Motion of History,* in *The Motion of History and Other Plays,* [1976], pp. 21, 75.

92 Baraka, *Motion of History,* p. 75; Mason, *Gabriel,* pp. 195, 220; Joseph A. Walker, *Ododo,* in King and Milner, *Black Drama Anthology,* [1968], pp. 362, 364.

93 Mason, *Gabriel,* p. 226; Baraka, *Motion of History,* pp. 71–72.

94 *New York Times* reviewer Vincent Canby referred to Lee as "a slave with a 1968 black awareness." For Canby's review of *The Scalphunters,* see *New York Times* (3 April 1968), sec. 1, p. 40.

95 For further commentary on *The Scalphunters,* see Edward Mapp, *Blacks in American Films: Today and Yesterday* (Metuchen, New Jersey: Scarecrow Press, Inc., 1972), pp. 180–81.

96 Herbert Biberman, "We Never Say Nigger in Front of Them," *New York Times* (19 January 1969), sec. 2, pp. 1, 11. For the storyline of *Slaves,* see Richard P. Krafsur, ed., *The American Film Institute Catalog of Motion Pictures: Feature Films, 1961–1970* (New York: R. R. Bowker Co., 1976), p. 1000.

97 Clarence Waldron, "Dionne Warwick: A Singer's Singer," *Black Collegian* 9 (March–April 1979): 212; Bob Kessler and Bobby Scott, "Another Mornin'" (New York: Walter Reade Music Corp., 1969); Bob Kessler and Bobby Scott, "Slaves" (New York: Walter Reade Music Corp., 1969); Herbert J. Biberman and Alida Sherman, "Black Lullabye" (New York: Walter Reade Music Corp., 1969).

98 For commentary on the first three films, see Phyllis Rauch Klotman, *Frame by Frame: A Black Filmography* (Bloomington: Indiana University Press, 1979), pp. 304, 483; James P. Murray, *To Find an Image: Black Films From Uncle Tom to Super Fly* (Indianapolis: Bobbs-Merrill Company, 1973), pp. 142–43. For evaluations of *Mandingo* as a play and as a film that has "less interest in slavery than 'Deep Throat' has in sexual therapy," see John McCarten, "The Laddie's Not for Boiling," *New Yorker* 37 (3 June 1961): 90; Louis Kronenberger, ed., *The Best Plays of 1960–61* (New York: Dodd, Mead & Company, 1961), pp. 341–42; Vincent Canby, review of *Mandingo,* in *New York Times* (8 May 1975), sec. 1, p. 49; Vincent Canby, "What Makes a Movie Immoral?" *New York Times* (18 May 1975), sec. 2, p. 19. See also Vincent Canby, review of *Drum, in New York Times* (31 July 1976), sec. 1, p. 11.

99 Marilyn Diane Fife, "Black Image in American TV: The First Two Decades," *Black Scholar* 6 (November 1974): 8–11; Robert Lewis Shayon, "Living Color on Television," *Saturday Review* 45 (24 November 1962): 25; Martin Maloney, "Black is the Color of Our New TV," *TV Guide* 16 (16 November 1968): 8. For studies of nonwhite representation in television programming of the 1970s, see United States Commission on Civil Rights, *Window Dressing on the Set: Women and Minorities in Television* (Washington, D.C.: U.S. Government Printing Office, 1977); United States Commission on Civil Rights, *Window Dressing on the Set: An Update* (Washington, D.C.: U.S. Government Printing Office, 1979); John F. Seggar and Penny Wheeler, "World of Work on TV: Ethnic and Sex Representation in TV Drama," *Journal of Broadcasting* 17 (Spring 1973): 201–14.

100 *Report of the National Advisory Commission on Civil Disorders* (New York: Bantam Books, 1968), pp. 1, 383, 386; Thomas Cripps, "The Noble Black Savage: A Problem in the Politics of Television Art," *Journal of Popular Culture* 8 (Spring 1975): 690–91; Richard Lemon, "Black is the Color of TV's Newest Stars," *Saturday Evening Post* 241 (30 November 1968): 42–43. For a study of the increase in black television commercial appearances during the late sixties, see J. R. Dominick and B. S. Greenberg, "Three Seasons of Blacks on Television," *Journal of Advertising Research* 10 (#2, 1970): 21–27.

101 Fife, "Black Image," p. 14; Knolly Moses, "The Black Image on Television: Who Controls It?" *Black Enterprise* 10 (September 1979): 33.

102 Ben Stein, *The View from Sunset Boulevard* (New York: Basic Books, 1979), pp. 105–116; Benjamin Stein, "Welcome to the Land of Shiny Cars, Fake Waterfalls and Happy Endings," *TV Guide* 27 (20 January 1979): 5–6, 8, 10.

103 "Pluria Marshall: Watchdog for Communications," *Black Enterprise* 10 (September 1979): 37; Moses, "Black Image," pp. 34–35, 38, 40.

104 Michele Wallace, "Tyson as Tubman: Pure, Narrow, and From Above," *Ms.* 7 (December 1978): 35, 38; Harry F. Waters, "Reading Beyond 'Roots,'" *Newsweek* 92 (11 December 1978): 108. Black criticism of the actual content of the teleplay may have been muted by the fact that Afro-American playwright Lonne Elder III adapted the screenplay from Marcy Heidish's 1976 novel. Charles L. Sanders, "Cicely Tyson: She Can Smile Again After a Three-Year Ordeal," *Ebony* 34 (January 1979): 34.

105 Eugenia Collier, "A House of Twisted Mirrors: The Black Reflection in the Media," *Current History* 67 (November 1974): 231, 234; Alvin Ramsey, "Through a Glass Whitely: The Televised Rape of *Miss Jane Pittman*," *Black World* 23 (August 1974): 31–36. For other opinions, see Stephanie Harrington, "Did 'Jane Pittman' Really Show Us Black History?" *New York Times* (10 February 1974), sec. 2, p. 17; Richard A. Blake, "Miss Jane, You Died Too Soon," *America* 130 (2 March 1974): 155; Nikki Giovanni, "'Jane Pittman' Fulfilled My Deepest Expectations," *New York Times* (3 March 1974), sec. 2, p. 17. Part of the alleged whitewashing of Gaines' novel may have been the result of financial backers' and network programmers' initial lack of interest in the project. Gaines had no control over the final product: "I hope people will credit me or damn me for the book, not for the film. . . . Professionally its another man's work." Tom Carter, "Ernest Gaines," *Essence* 6 (July 1975): 52.

106 Ramsey, "Through a Glass Whitely," p. 31; David L. Wolper and Quincy Troupe, *The Inside Story of TV's "Roots"* (New York: Warner Books, 1978), pp. 69–70, 92, 129–30, 143–44, 154; Harry F. Waters, "After Haley's Comet," *Newsweek* 89 (14 February 1977): 97; Harry F. Waters and Vern E. Smith, "One Man's Family," *Newsweek* 87 (21 June 1976): 73. The final episode had a Nielsen rating of 51.1 and a 71% share of all television sets in use at broadcast time. These figures were unsurpassed until November 21, 1980, when a key episode of the prime-time CBS soap opera "Dallas" achieved a 53.3 rating and a 76% share of the audience. "J. R. Helps 'Dallas' Set a TV Record," *Wisconsin State Journal* (26 November 1980): 12.

107 Richard M. Levine, "Roots and Branches," *New Times* 11 (4 September 1978):

54; Sandra Rattley, "The Impact of *Roots:* Real or Imagined?" *Africa Report* 22 (May-June 1977): 15; John Merritt and Carolyn Merritt, "Run Kunta Kinte" (Oklahoma City: Merico Publishing, 1977); Gerald Fried, "Roots Mural Theme Bridge (Plantation Life)" (Beverly Hills: DLW Music, Inc., 1977).

108 Wolper and Troupe, *Inside Story,* p. 149; Levine, "Roots and Branches," p. 56.

109 "Why 'Roots' Hit Home," *Time* 109 (14 February 1977): 70; "Everybody's Search for Roots," *Newsweek* 90 (4 July 1977): 24, 30, 35; David A. Gerber, "Haley's *Roots* and Our Own: An Inquiry Into the Nature of a Popular Phenomenon," *Journal of Ethnic Studies* 5 (#3, 1977): 103–7; Ali A. Mazrui, "Roots: The End of America's Amnesia?" *Africa Report* 22 (May-June 1977): 7–8. A 1977 Harris survey indicated that Americans gave the series a positive rating by an 83%–15% majority. A second poll revealed that 95% of those queried felt that the series was a realistic depiction of history. Kenneth K. Hur and John P. Robinson, "The Social Impact of 'Roots'," *Journalism Quarterly* 55 (Spring 1978): 19; Wolper and Troupe, *Inside Story,* p. 158.

110 Wolper and Troupe, *Inside Story,* p. 158.

111 Rattley, "Impact of Roots," pp. 13–14; Lance Morrow, "Living with the 'Peculiar Institution,'" *Time* 109 (14 February 1977): 76; "*Roots* Grows Into a Winner," *Time* 109 (7 February 1977): 96; Wolper and Troupe, *Inside Story,* pp. 56–58, 148, 169, 173; Herb Boyd, "'Roots.' 'Naw, Rutz, Dummy,'" *Essence* 8 (August 1977): 48. The 1979 sequel, "Roots: The Next Generations" also met with black criticism. See especially, Eugenia Collier, "A Distortion of Our History and Culture," *First World* 2 (#3, 1979): 29–30.

112 Rattley, "Impact of Roots," p. 13.

113 Although it was claimed that "Roots" employed "the largest number of black actors and technicians ever assembled to make a movie," no black screenwriters were used because those in charge felt that they had to have the "top experienced television drama writers" working on the project. Wolper and Troupe, *Inside Story,* pp. 54, 163.

114 Richard Schickel, "Viewpoint: Middlebrow *Mandingo,*" *Time* 109 (24 January 1977): 56; Howard F. Stein, "In Search of 'Roots': An Epic of Origins and Destiny," *Journal of Popular Culture* 11 (Summer 1977): 14; Hur and Robinson, "Social Impact," p. 19; Michael J. Arlen: "The Prisoner of the Golden Dream," *New Yorker* 55 (26 March 1979): 115.

115 "Why 'Roots' Hit Home," p. 69; Wolper and Troupe, *Inside Story,* pp. 254, 259; "*Roots* Grows into a Winner," p. 96; Morrow, "'Peculiar Institution,'" p. 76.

116 The later portions of the series were based upon a sequel, *Look Away, Beulah Land* (Garden City, New York: Doubleday & Company, 1977).

117 Adrienne Lanier Seward, "Editor's Comment," *Voices in Black Studies* 4 (March-April 1980): 2.

118 John J. O'Connor, "'Beulah Land'—Pure Corn Pone," *New York Times* (5 October 1980), sec. 4, p. 35; Peter J. Boyer, "Troubled 'Beulah Land' Succeeds as Soap Opera," *Wisconsin State Journal* (4 September 1980): 7; "'Beulah Land' Controversy," *Voices in Black Studies* 4 (September-October 1980): 2; Frank

Emerson, "In Beulah Land," *Black Enterprise* 10 (July 1980): 14–15; Marilyn Beck, "'Beulah Land' Protested," *Wisconsin State Journal* (8 March 1980): 3.

119 One way in which the filmmakers attempted to deal with brutality of this sort was to introduce each night's show with the warning that although "Beulah Land" centered upon the lives of three generations of white masters, it also dealt with certain aspects of the "cruel, indefensible, complex institution of slavery."

120 Boyer, "Soap Opera," p. 7.

CHAPTER 6: *Conclusion*

1 Kenneth M. Stampp, Winthrop D. Jordan, Lawrence W. Levine, Robert L. Middlekauff, Charles G. Sellers, George W. Stocking, Jr., "The Negro in American History Textbooks," *Negro History Bulletin* 31 (October 1968): 14.

2 Benjamin Solomon and Beatrice Young, "Racism in U.S. History: Unweaving the Threads," *Changing Education* 2 (Winter-Spring 1968): 7–13; Marilyn Gittell and Bruce Dollar, "Cultural Pluralism: Traditional and Alternative Models in Higher Education," in *Badges and Indicia of Slavery: Cultural Pluralism Redefined*, ed. Antonia Pantoja, Barbara Blourock, James Bowman (Lincoln, Nebraska: Cultural Pluralism Committee, Study Commission on Undergraduate Education and the Education of Teachers, 1975), pp. 42–44; James A. Banks, "Teaching Black Studies for Social Change," in *Teaching Ethnic Studies: Concepts and Strategies*, ed. James A. Banks (Washington, D.C.: National Council for the Social Studies, 1973), pp. 149–80; Robert B. Howsam, Dean C. Corrigan, George W. Denemark, Robert J. Nash, *Educating a Profession* (Washington, D.C.: American Association of Colleges for Teacher Education, 1976), pp. 96–97, 105. For a study comparing high school and college history texts of the early sixties with those of the early seventies, see Floyd Hilding Pearson, "A Content Analysis of the Treatment of Black People and Race Relations in United States History Textbooks," (Ph.D. diss., University of Minnesota, 1976). See also Frances FitzGerald, *America Revised: History Schoolbooks in the Twentieth Century* (Boston: Atlantic Monthly Press/Little, Brown and Company, 1979). On the question of whether academic histories have initiated or reflected more popular forms of cultural expression, see Jack Temple Kirby, *Media-Made Dixie: The South in the American Imagination* (Baton Rouge: Louisiana State University Press, 1978), pp. xv–xvii, 76, 78.

3 On this point, see John David Smith, "A Different View of Slavery: Black Historians Attack the Proslavery Argument, 1890–1920," *Journal of Negro History* 65 (Fall 1980): 304–5. For representative texts, see Allen Weinstein and R. Jackson Wilson, *Freedom and Crisis: An American History*, 2 vols. (New York: Random House, 1974), 1: 302–6; Bernard Bailyn, David Brion Davis, David Herbert Donald, John L. Thomas, Robert H. Wiebe, Gordon S. Wood, *The Great Republic: A History of the American People* (Lexington, Mass.: D. C. Heath and Company, 1977), pp. 169, 506, 568–72; Peter N. Carroll and

David W. Noble, *The Free and the Unfree: A New History of the United States* (New York: Penguin Books, 1977), pp. 86, 158–59.

4 Gerald Baydo, *A Topical History of the United States* (Englewood Cliffs: Prentice-Hall, Inc., 1974), p. 299. For slave unrest as portrayed in monographs of the 1970s, see especially Gerald W. Mullin, *Flight and Rebellion: Slave Resistance in Eighteenth-Century Virginia* (New York: Oxford University Press, 1972); Peter H. Wood, *Black Majority: Negroes in Colonial South Carolina from 1670 through the Stono Rebellion* (New York: W. W. Norton, 1974); Stephen B. Oates, *The Fires of Jubilee: Nat Turner's Fierce Rebellion* (New York: Harper & Row, 1975); Eugene D. Genovese, *From Rebellion to Revolution: Afro-American Slave Revolts in the Making of the Modern World* (Baton Rouge: Louisiana State University Press, 1979).

5 For pessimistic commentary on the impact and the future of Black Studies, see Eugene D. Genovese, "The Influence of the Black Power Movement on Historical Scholarship: Reflections of a White Historian," *Daedalus* 99 (Spring 1970): 473–94; Marvin W. Peterson, Robert T. Blackburn, Zelda F. Gamson, Carlos H. Arce, Roselle W. Davenport, James R. Mingle, *Black Students on White Campuses: The Impacts of Increased Black Enrollments* (Ann Arbor: Institute for Social Research, The University of Michigan, 1978), pp. 181–93; Kenny J. Williams, "The Black Studies Syndrome," *Change* 13 (October 1981): 30–37. For a case study of one long-troubled Black Studies program, see George Howe Colt, "Will the Huggins Approach Save Afro-American Studies?" *Harvard Magazine* 84 (September–October 1981): 38–46, 62, 70.

6 For statistical data and commentary on the continuing separate and unequal position of black America during the late 1970s, see U.S. Department of Commerce, *Social Indicators III: Selected Data on Social Conditions and Trends in the United States* (Washington, D.C.; U.S. Government Printing Office, 1980), pp. 297, 311–12, 358, 495–96; Richard Polenberg, *One Nation Divisible: Class, Race, and Ethnicity in the United States Since 1938* (New York: Viking Press, 1980), pp. 250, 274–75; Dorothy K. Newman, Nancy J. Amidei, Barbara L. Carter, Dawn Day, William J. Kruvant, Jack S. Russell, *Protest, Politics, and Prosperity: Black Americans and White Institutions, 1940–75* (New York: Pantheon Books, 1978), pp. 27, 285–86; Joel Dreyfuss, "'Black Progress' Myth and Ghetto Reality," *Progressive* 41 (November 1977): 21–25; Reynolds Farley, "Trends in Racial Inequalities: Have the Gains of the 1960s Disappeared in the 1970s?" *American Sociological Review* 42 (April 1977): 189–208; Harvard Sitkoff, *The Struggle for Black Equality, 1954–1980* (New York: Hill and Wang, 1981), pp. 228–37.

SELECTED BIBLIOGRAPHY

The selected bibliography is designed to guide interested readers to the reference works, secondary books and articles, dissertations and theses found to be most useful in researching and writing *Slavery and Race in American Popular Culture.* Since primary works in this study have been treated as source materials on popular culture, they are not included in the selected bibliography. The most important primary works are discussed in the text and listed in the notes.

REFERENCE

Arata, Esther Spring. *More Black American Playwrights: A Bibliography.* Metuchen, N.J.: Scarecrow Press, 1978.

Arata, Esther Spring and Rotoli, Nicholas John. *Black American Playwrights, 1800 to the Present: A Bibliography.* Metuchen, N.J.: Scarecrow Press, 1976.

Chapman, Dorothy H. *Index to Black Poetry.* Boston: G. K. Hall & Co., 1974.

Crandall, Marjorie Lyle. *Confederate Imprints: A Check List Based Principally on the Collection of the Boston Athenaeum.* 2 vols. Boston: Boston Athenaeum, 1955.

Dickinson, A. T., Jr. *American Historical Fiction.* Metuchen, N.J.: Scarecrow Press, 1971.

Dumond, Dwight Lowell. *A Bibliography of Antislavery in America.* Ann Arbor: University of Michigan Press, 1961.

Ellis, Jack C., Derry, Charles, and Kern, Sharon. *The Film Book Bibliography, 1940–1975.* Metuchen, N.J.: Scarecrow Press, 1979.

Fairbanks, Carol and Engeldinger, Eugene A. *Black American Fiction: A Bibliography.* Metuchen, N.J.: Scarecrow Press, 1978.

French, William P.; Fabre, Michel J.; Singh, Amritjit; and Fabre, Geneviève E. *Afro-American Poetry and Drama, 1760–1975: A Guide to Information Sources.* Detroit: Gale Research Company, 1979.

Green, Fletcher M. and Copeland, J. Isaac. *The Old South.* Arlington Heights, Illinois: AHM Publishing Corporation, 1980.

Halliwell, Leslie. *Halliwell's Film Guide: A Survey of 8,000 English-Language Movies.* London: Granada Publishing, 1977.

Harwell, Richard. *More Confederate Imprints.* 2 vols. Richmond: Virginia State Library, 1957.

Hatch, James V. *Black Image on the American Stage: A Bibliography of Plays and Musicals, 1770–1970.* New York: DBS Publications, Inc., 1970.

Hatch, James V. and Abdullah, Omanii, eds. *Black Playwrights, 1823–1977: An Annotated Bibliography of Plays.* New York: R. R. Bowker Company, 1977.

Hogg, Peter C. *The African Slave Trade and its Suppression: A Classified and Annotated Bibliography of Books, Pamphlets and Periodical Articles.* London: Frank Cass, 1973.

Houston, Helen Ruth. *The Afro-American Novel, 1965–1975: A Descriptive Bibliography of Primary and Secondary Material.* Troy, New York: Whitston Publishing Company, 1977.

Hyatt, Marshall. *The Afro-American Cinematic Experience.* Wilmington, Delaware: Scholarly Resources Inc., 1983.

Inge, M. Thomas; Duke, Maurice; and Bryer, Jackson R., eds. *Black American Writers: Bibliographical Essays.* 2 vols. New York: St. Martin's Press, 1978.

Jackson, Irene V. *Afro-American Religious Music: A Bibliography and A Catalogue of Gospel Music.* Westport: Greenwood Press, 1979.

Kallenbach, Jessamine S. *Index to Black American Literary Anthologies.* Boston: G. K. Hall & Co., 1979.

Kirby, David K. *American Fiction to 1900: A Guide to Information Sources.* Detroit: Gale Research Company, 1975.

Klotman, Phyllis Rauch. *Frame by Frame: A Black Filmography.* Bloomington: Indiana University Press, 1979.

McPherson, James M.; Holland, Laurence B.; Banner, James M., Jr.; Weiss, Nancy J.; and Bell, Michael D. *Blacks in America: Bibliographical Essays.* Garden City, N.Y.: Doubleday & Company, Inc., 1971.

Margolies, Edward and Bakish, David. *Afro-American Fiction, 1853–1976: A Guide to Information Sources.* Detroit: Gale Research Company, 1979.

Meserve, Walter J. *American Drama to 1900: A Guide to Information Sources.* Detroit: Gale Research Company, 1980.

Miller, Joseph C. *Slavery: A Comparative Teaching Bibliography.* Waltham, Massachusetts: Crossroads Press/African Studies Association, 1977.

Miller, Joseph C. "Slavery: A Further Supplementary Bibliography." *Slavery & Abolition: A Journal of Comparative Studies* 1 (September 1980): 199–258.

Miller, Joseph C. and Borus, Daniel H. "Slavery: A Supplementary Teaching Bibliography." *Slavery & Abolition: A Journal of Comparative Studies* 1 (May 1980): 65–110.

Nevins, Allan; Robertson, James I., Jr.; and Wiley, Bell I. *Civil War Books: A Critical Bibliography.* 2 vols. Baton Rouge: Louisiana State University Press, 1967, 1969.

Obudho, Constance E. *Black-White Racial Attitudes: An Annotated Bibliography.* Westport: Greenwood Press, 1976.

Peavy, Charles D. *Afro-American Literature and Culture Since World War II: A Guide to Information Sources.* Detroit: Gale Research Company, 1979.

Perry, Margaret. *The Harlem Renaissance: An Annotated Bibliography.* New York: Garland Publishing, Inc., 1982.

Poteet, G. Howard. *Published Radio, Television, and Film Scripts: A Bibliography.* Troy, N.Y.: Whitston Publishing Company, 1975.

Powers, Anne, ed. *Blacks in American Movies: A Selected Bibliography.* Metuchen, N.J.: Scarecrow Press, 1974.

Rubin, Louis D., Jr. *A Bibliographic Guide to the Study of Southern Literature.* Baton Rouge: Louisiana State University Press, 1969.

Rush, Theressa Gunnels; Myers, Carol Fairbanks; and Arata, Esther Spring. *Black*

American Writers, Past and Present: A Biographical and Bibliographical Dictionary. 2 vols. Metuchen, N.J.: Scarecrow Press, 1975.

Sampson, Henry T. *Blacks in Black and White: A Source Book on Black Films.* Metuchen, N.J.: Scarecrow Press, 1977.

Sampson, Henry T. *Blacks in Blackface: A Source Book on Early Black Musical Shows.* Metuchen, N.J.: Scarecrow Press, 1980.

Smith, Dwight L., ed. *Afro-American History: A Bibliography.* Santa Barbara: ABC-Clio, Inc., 1974.

Smith, Rebecca W. "Catalogue of the Chief Novels and Short Stories by American Authors Dealing with the Civil War and its Effects, 1861–1899." *Bulletin of Bibliography* 16 (September-December 1939): 193–94; 17 (January-April 1940): 10–12; 17 (May-August, 1940): 33–35; 17 (September-December, 1940): 53–55; 17 (January-April, 1941): 72–75.

Stephens, Lester D., ed. *Historiography: A Bibliography.* Metuchen, N.J.: Scarecrow Press, 1975.

Szwed, John F. and Abrahams, Roger D. *Afro-American Folk Culture: An Annotated Bibliography of Materials from North, Central and South America and the West Indies.* 2 vols. Philadelphia: Institute for the Study of Human Issues, 1978.

Turner, Darwin T. *Afro-American Writers.* New York: Appleton-Century-Crofts, 1970.

SECONDARY SOURCES: BOOKS

Abramson, Doris E. *Negro Playwrights in the American Theatre, 1925–1959.* New York: Columbia University Press, 1969.

Andrews, Hannah Page Wheeler. "Theme and Variations: 'Uncle Tom's Cabin' as Book, Play, and Film." Ph.D. diss., University of North Carolina, Chapel Hill, 1979.

Archer, Leonard C. *Black Images in the American Theatre: NAACP Protest Campaigns — Stage, Screen, Radio & Television.* Brooklyn: Pageant-Poseidon, Ltd., 1973.

Bassett, John Spencer. *The Middle Group of American Historians.* New York: The Macmillan Company, 1917.

Beaty, John O. *John Esten Cooke, Virginian.* New York: Columbia University Press, 1922.

Berghahn, Marion. *Images of Africa in Black American Literature.* Totowa, N.J.: Rowman and Littlefield, 1977.

Berzon, Judith R. *Neither White Nor Black: The Mulatto Character in American Fiction.* New York: New York University Press, 1978.

Birdoff, Harry. *The World's Greatest Hit: Uncle Tom's Cabin.* New York: S. F. Vanni, 1947.

Blassingame, John W., ed. *New Perspectives on Black Studies.* Urbana: University of Illinois Press, 1971.

Bode, Carl. *The Anatomy of American Popular Culture, 1840–1861*. Berkeley: University of California Press, 1959.

Bogle, Donald. *Toms, Coons, Mulattoes, Mammies, and Bucks: An Interpretive History of Blacks in American Films*. New York: Viking Press, 1973.

Bond, Frederick W. *The Negro and the Drama*. Washington, D.C.: Associated Publishers, Inc., 1940.

Bone, Robert. *Down Home: A History of Afro-American Short Fiction from Its Beginnings to the End of the Harlem Renaissance*. New York: G. P. Putnam's Sons, 1975.

Bone, Robert. *The Negro Novel in America*. New Haven: Yale University Press, 1958.

Bradbury, John M. *Renaissance in the South: A Critical History of the Literature, 1920–1960*. Chapel Hill: University of North Carolina Press, 1963.

Brookes, Stella Brewer. *Joel Chandler Harris — Folklorist*. Athens: University of Georgia Press, 1950.

Brown, Herbert Ross. *The Sentimental Novel in America, 1789–1860*. Durham, N.C.: Duke University Press, 1940.

Brown, Sterling. *The Negro in American Fiction*. Washington, D.C.: Associates in Negro Folk Education, 1937.

Brown, Sterling. *Negro Poetry and Drama*. Washington, D.C.: Associates in Negro Folk Education, 1937.

Buck, Paul H. *The Road to Reunion, 1865–1900*. Boston: Little, Brown and Company, 1937.

Butcher, Margaret Just. *The Negro in American Culture*. New York: Alfred A. Knopf, 1956.

Callcott, George H. *History in the United States, 1800–1860: Its Practice and Purpose*. Baltimore: Johns Hopkins Press, 1970.

Campbell, Edward D. C., Jr. *The Celluloid South: Hollywood and the Southern Myth*. Knoxville: University of Tennessee Press, 1981.

Canary, Robert H. *George Bancroft*. New York: Twayne Publishers, Inc., 1974.

Charters, Ann. *Nobody: The Story of Bert Williams*. New York: The Macmillan Company, 1970.

Charvat, William. *Literary Publishing in America, 1790–1850*. Philadelphia: University of Pennsylvania Press, 1959.

Clarke, John Henrik, ed. *William Styron's Nat Turner: Ten Black Writers Respond*. Boston: Beacon Press, 1968.

Collins, John Daniel. "American Drama in Antislavery Agitation, 1792–1861." Ph.D. diss., State University of Iowa, 1963.

Connelly, Thomas L. and Bellows, Barbara L. *God and General Longstreet: The Lost Cause and the Southern Mind*. Baton Rouge: Louisiana State University Press, 1982.

Cook, Mercer, and Henderson, Stephen E. *The Militant Black Writer in Africa and the United States*. Madison: University of Wisconsin Press, 1969.

Cousins, Paul M. *Joel Chandler Harris: A Biography*. Baton Rouge: Louisiana State University Press, 1968.

Craig, E. Quita. *Black Drama of the Federal Theatre Era: Beyond the Formal Horizons*. Amherst: University of Massachusetts Press, 1980.

Cripps, Thomas. *Black Film as Genre.* Bloomington: Indiana University Press, 1978.

Cripps, Thomas. *Slow Fade to Black: The Negro in American Film, 1900–1942.* New York: Oxford University Press, 1977.

Crozier, Alice C. *The Novels of Harriet Beecher Stowe.* New York: Oxford University Press, 1969.

Cunliffe, Marcus. *Chattel Slavery and Wage Slavery: The Anglo-American Context, 1830–1860.* Athens: University of Georgia Press, 1979.

David, Paul A.; Gutman, Herbert G.; Sutch, Richard; Temin, Peter; and Wright, Gavin, eds. *Reckoning with Slavery: A Critical Study in the Quantitative History of American Negro Slavery.* New York: Oxford University Press, 1976.

Davidson, Frank Costellow. "The Rise, Development, Decline and Influence of the American Minstrel Show." Ph.D. diss., New York University, 1952.

Dennison, Sam. *Scandalize My Name: Black Imagery in American Popular Music.* New York: Garland Publishing, Inc., 1982.

DiMeglio, John E. *Vaudeville U.S.A.* Bowling Green, Ohio: Bowling Green University Popular Press, 1973.

Dormon, James H., Jr. *Theater in the Ante Bellum South, 1815–1861.* Chapel Hill: University of North Carolina Press, 1967.

Duff, John B., and Mitchell, Peter M., eds. *The Nat Turner Rebellion: The Historical Event and the Modern Controversy.* New York: Harper & Row, 1971.

Eaklor, Vicki L. "Music in the American Antislavery Movement, 1830–1860." M.A. thesis, Washington University, 1979.

Elder, Arlene A. The "Hindered Hand": Cultural Implications of Early African-American Fiction. Westport: Greenwood Press, 1978.

Epstein, Dena J. *Sinful Tunes and Spirituals: Black Folk Music to the Civil War.* Urbana: University of Illinois Press, 1977.

Everson, William K. *American Silent Film.* New York: Oxford University Press, 1978.

Farr, Finis. *Margaret Mitchell of Atlanta: The Author of Gone With the Wind.* New York: William Morrow & Company, 1965.

Farrison, William Edward. *William Wells Brown, Author & Reformer.* Chicago: University of Chicago Press, 1969.

Faust, Drew Gilpin. *A Sacred Circle: The Dilemma of the Intellectual in the Old South, 1840–1860.* Baltimore: Johns Hopkins University Press, 1977.

Fiedler, Leslie A. *The Inadvertent Epic: From Uncle Tom's Cabin to Roots.* Toronto: Canadian Broadcasting Corporation, 1979.

Flamini, Roland. *Scarlett, Rhett, and a Cast of Thousands: The Filming of Gone With the Wind.* New York: Macmillan Publishing Co., 1975.

Floan, Howard R. *The South in Northern Eyes, 1831 to 1861.* Austin: University of Texas Press, 1958.

Ford, Nick Aaron. *Black Studies: Threat-or-Challenge.* Port Washington: Kennikat Press, 1973.

Fredrickson, George M. *The Black Image in the White Mind: The Debate on Afro-American Character and Destiny, 1817–1914.* New York: Harper & Row, 1971.

French, Warren, ed. *The South and Film*. Jackson: University Press of Mississippi, 1981.

Friedman, Lawrence J. *The White Savage: Racial Fantasies in the Postbellum South*. Englewood Cliffs, N.J.: Prentice-Hall, Inc., 1970.

Furnas, J. C. *Goodbye to Uncle Tom*. New York: William Sloane Associates, 1956.

Gaines, Francis Pendleton. *The Southern Plantation: A Study in the Development and the Accuracy of a Tradition*. New York: Columbia University Press, 1924.

Gans, Herbert J. *Popular Culture and High Culture: An Analysis and Evaluation of Taste*. New York: Basic Books, Inc., 1974.

Gay, Peter. *A Loss of Mastery: Puritan Historians in Colonial America*. Berkeley: University of California Press, 1966.

Gayle, Addison Jr. *The Way of the New World: The Black Novel in America*. Garden City, N.Y.: Anchor Press/Doubleday, 1975.

Gilbert, Douglas. *American Vaudeville: Its Life and Times*. New York: Whittlesey House, 1940.

Gilmore, Al-Tony, ed. *Revisiting Blassingame's* The Slave Community: *The Scholars Respond*. Westport: Greenwood Press, 1978.

Gossett, Thomas F. *Race: The History of an Idea in America*. Dallas: Southern Methodist University Press, 1963.

Graham, Philip. *Showboats: The History of an American Institution*. Austin: University of Texas Press, 1951.

Gray, Richard. *The Literature of Memory: Modern Writers of the American South*. Baltimore: The Johns Hopkins University Press, 1977.

Grimsted, David. *Melodrama Unveiled: American Theater and Culture, 1800–1850*. Chicago: University of Chicago Press, 1968.

Gutman, Herbert G. *Slavery and the Numbers Game: A Critique of Time on the Cross*. Urbana: University of Illinois Press, 1975.

Hart, James D. *The Popular Book: A History of America's Literary Taste*. New York: Oxford University Press, 1950.

Harwell, Richard B. *Confederate Music*. Chapel Hill: University of North Carolina Press, 1950.

Heaps, Willard A., and Heaps, Porter W. *The Singing Sixties: The Spirit of Civil War Days Drawn from the Music of the Times*. Norman: University of Oklahoma Press, 1960.

Herndon, Jerry Allen. "Social Comment in the Writings of Joel Chandler Harris." Ph.D. diss., Duke University, 1966.

Higham, John. *History: The Development of Historical Studies in the United States*. Englewood Cliffs, N.J.: Prentice-Hall, Inc., 1965.

Hofstadter, Richard. *The Progressive Historians: Turner, Beard, Parrington*. New York: Alfred A. Knopf, 1968.

Horsman, Reginald. *Race and Manifest Destiny: The Origins of American Racial Anglo-Saxonism*. Cambridge: Harvard University Press, 1981.

Hubbell, Jay B. *The South in American Literature, 1607–1900*. Durham: Duke University Press, 1954.

Hubbell, Jay B. *Virginia Life in Fiction*. Dallas: Southern Methodist University Press, 1922.

Huggins, Nathan Irvin. *Harlem Renaissance.* New York: Oxford University Press, 1971.

Hughes, Langston and Meltzer, Milton. *Black Magic: A Pictorial History of the Negro in American Entertainment.* Englewood Cliffs, N.J.: Prentice-Hall, Inc., 1967.

Isaacs, Edith J.R. *The Negro in the American Theatre.* New York: Theatre Arts Books, 1947.

Johnson, Theodore W. "Black Images in American Popular Song, 1840-1910." Ph.D. diss., Northwestern University, 1975.

Jordan, Winthrop D. *White Over Black: American Attitudes Toward the Negro, 1550-1812.* Chapel Hill: University of North Carolina Press, 1968.

Kimball, William Joseph. "The Civil War in American Novels: 1920-1939." Ph.D. diss., Pennsylvania State University, 1957.

King, Richard H. *A Southern Renaissance: The Cultural Awakening of the American South, 1930-1955.* New York: Oxford University Press, 1980.

Kirby, Jack Temple. *Darkness at the Dawning: Race and Reform in the Progressive South.* Philadelphia: J.B. Lippincott Company, 1972.

Kirby, Jack Temple. *Media-Made Dixie: The South in the American Imagination.* Baton Rouge: Louisiana State University Press, 1978.

Kirkham, E. Bruce. *The Building of Uncle Tom's Cabin.* Knoxville: University of Tennessee Press, 1977.

Kraus, Michael. *The Writing of American History.* Norman: University of Oklahoma Press, 1953.

Lahue, Kalton C. *World of Laughter: The Motion Picture Comedy Short, 1910-1930.* Norman: University of Oklahoma Press, 1966.

Lambert, Gavin. *GWTW: The Making of Gone With the Wind.* Boston: Atlantic Monthly Press/Little, Brown and Company, 1973.

Lane, Anne J., ed. *The Debate Over Slavery: Stanley Elkins and His Critics.* Urbana: University of Illinois Press, 1971.

Laurie, Joe, Jr. *Vaudeville: From the Honky-Tonks to the Palace.* New York: Henry Holt and Company, 1953.

Leab, Daniel J. *From Sambo to Superspade: The Black Experience in Motion Pictures.* Boston: Houghton Mifflin Company, 1975.

Lentz, Perry. "Our Missing Epic: A Study in Novels About the American Civil War." Ph.D. diss., Vanderbilt University, 1970.

Levin, David. *History as Romantic Art: Bancroft, Prescott, Motley, and Parkman.* Stanford: Stanford University Press, 1959.

Levine, Lawrence W. *Black Culture and Black Consciousness: Afro-American Folk Thought from Slavery to Freedom.* New York: Oxford University Press, 1977.

Lively, Robert A. *Fiction Fights the Civil War: An Unfinished Chapter in the Literary History of the American People.* Chapel Hill: University of North Carolina Press, 1957.

Loewenberg, Bert James. *American History in American Thought: Christopher Columbus to Henry Adams.* New York: Simon and Schuster, 1972.

Logan, Rayford W. *The Betrayal of the Negro: From Rutherford B. Hayes to Woodrow Wilson.* New York: Collier Books, 1965.

Loggins, Vernon. *The Negro Author: His Development in America.* New York: Columbia University Press, 1931.

MacDonald, J. Fred. *Blacks and White TV: Afro-Americans in Television since 1948.* Chicago: Nelson-Hall Publishers, 1983.

McLean, Albert F., Jr. *American Vaudeville as Ritual.* Lexington: University of Kentucky Press, 1965.

McLean, Robert Colin. *George Tucker: Moral Philosopher and Man of Letters.* Chapel Hill: University of North Carolina Press, 1961.

Mapp, Edward. *Blacks in American Films: Today and Yesterday.* Metuchen, N.J.: Scarecrow Press, Inc., 1972.

Mitchell, Loften. *Black Drama: The Story of the American Negro in the Theatre.* New York: Hawthorn Books, Inc., 1967.

Moody, Richard. *America Takes the Stage: Romanticism in American Drama and Theatre, 1750–1900.* Bloomington: Indiana University Press, 1955.

Morison, Samuel Eliot. *The Intellectual Life of Colonial New England.* New York: New York University Press, 1956.

Most, Ralph C. "Civil War Fiction: 1890–1920." Ph.D. diss., University of Pennsylvania, 1951.

Mott, Frank Luther. *Golden Multitudes: The Story of Best Sellers in the United States.* New York: Macmillan Company, 1947.

Murdock, Kenneth B. *Literature & Theology in Colonial New England.* Cambridge: Harvard University Press, 1949.

Murray, James P. *To Find an Image: Black Films From Uncle Tom to Super Fly.* Indianapolis: Bobbs-Merrill Company, 1973.

Nathan, Hans. *Dan Emmett and the Rise of Early Negro Minstrelsy.* Norman: University of Oklahoma Press, 1962.

Nelson, John Herbert. *The Negro Character in American Literature.* Lawrence, Kansas: University of Kansas, Department of Journalism Press, 1926.

Nesteby, James R. *Black Images in American Films, 1896–1954: The Interplay Between Civil Rights and Film Culture.* Washington, D.C.: University Press of America, 1982.

Newby, I. A. *Jim Crow's Defense: Anti-Negro Thought in America, 1900–1930.* Baton Rouge: Louisiana State University Press, 1965.

Nilon, Charles Hampton. "Some Aspects of the Treatment of Negro Characters by Five Representative American Novelists: Cooper, Melville, Tourgee, Glasgow, Faulkner." Ph.D. diss., University of Wisconsin, 1952.

Noble, Peter. *The Negro in Films.* London: Skelton Robinson, 1948.

Nye, Russel B. *George Bancroft: Brahmin Rebel.* New York: Alfred A. Knopf, 1944.

Nye, Russel B. *The Unembarrassed Muse: The Popular Arts in America.* New York: The Dial Press, 1970.

Osterweis, Rollin G. *Romanticism and Nationalism in the Old South.* New Haven: Yale University Press, 1949.

Osterweis, Rollin G. *The Myth of the Lost Cause, 1865–1900.* Hamden, Conn.: Archon Books, 1973.

Patterson, Cecil Lloyd. "A Different Drum: The Image of the Negro in the Nineteenth Century Popular Song Books." Ph.D. diss., University of Pennsylvania, 1961.

Patterson, Lindsay, ed. *Anthology of the American Negro in the Theatre: A Critical Approach.* New York: Publishers Company, Inc., 1967.

Patterson, Lindsay, ed. *Black Films and Film-Makers: A Comprehensive Anthology from Stereotype to Superhero.* New York: Dodd, Mead & Company, 1975.

Pearson, Floyd Hilding. "A Content Analysis of the Treatment of Black People and Race Relations in United States History Textbooks." Ph.D. diss., University of Minnesota, 1976.

Petter, Henri. *The Early American Novel.* Columbus: Ohio State University Press, 1971.

Pines, Jim. *Blacks in Films: A Survey of Racial Themes and Images in the American Film* London: Studio Vista, 1975.

Pressly, Thomas J. *Americans Interpret Their Civil War.* Princeton: Princeton University Press, 1954.

Quinn, Arthur Hobson. *A History of the American Drama: From the Beginning to the Civil War.* New York: Harper & Brothers, 1923.

Rankin, Hugh F. *The Theater in Colonial America.* Chapel Hill: University of North Carolina Press, 1965.

Redding, J. Saunders. *To Make a Poet Black.* Chapel Hill: University of North Carolina Press, 1939.

Redmond, Eugene B. *Drumvoices: The Mission of Afro-American Poetry.* Garden City, N.Y.: Anchor Press/Doubleday, 1976.

Richmond, M.A. *Bid the Vassal Soar: Interpretive Essays on the Life and Poetry of Phillis Wheatley and George Moses Horton.* Washington, D.C.: Howard University Press, 1974.

Ridgely, J. V. *Nineteenth-Century Southern Literature.* Lexington: University Press of Kentucky, 1980.

Robinson, William H. *Phillis Wheatley in the Black American Beginnings.* Detroit: Broadside Press, 1975.

Rose, Alan Henry. *Demonic Vision: Racial Fantasy and Southern Fiction.* Hamden, Conn.: Archon Books, 1976.

Schuster, Richard. "American Civil War Novels to 1880." Ph.D. diss., Columbia University, 1961.

Seidman, Benedict S. "Historical Writing in the United States, 1775–1830." M.A. thesis, University of Wisconsin, 1941.

Sherman, Alfonso. "The Diversity of Treatment of the Negro Character in American Drama Prior to 1860." Ph.D. diss., Indiana University, 1964.

Sherman, Joan R. *Invisible Poets: Afro-Americans of the Nineteenth Century.* Urbana: University of Illinois Press, 1974.

Skaggs, Merrill Maguire. *The Folk of Southern Fiction.* Athens: University of Georgia Press, 1972.

Sklar, Robert. *Movie-Made America: A Social History of American Movies.* New York: Random House, 1975.

Smith, Burton H. "A Study of American Historians and Their Interpretation of Negro Slavery in the United States." Ph.D. diss., Washington State University, 1970.

Smith, John David. "The Formative Period of American Slave Historiography, 1890–1920." Ph.D. diss., University of Kentucky, 1977.

Southern, Eileen. *The Music of Black Americans: A History.* New York: W. W. Norton & Company, 1971.

Spears, Jack. *The Civil War on the Screen and Other Essays.* New York: A. S. Barnes and Company, 1977.

Starke, Catherine Juanita. *Black Portraiture in American Fiction: Stock Characters, Archetypes, and Individuals.* New York: Basic Books, Inc., 1971.

Stein, Ben. *The View from Sunset Boulevard.* New York: Basic Books, 1979.

Stephenson, Wendell Holmes. *The South Lives in History: Southern Historians and Their Legacy.* Baton Rouge: Louisiana State University Press, 1955.

Sweet, Leonard I. *Black Images of America, 1784–1870.* New York: W. W. Norton & Company, Inc., 1976.

Takaki, Ronald T. *Iron Cages: Race and Culture in Nineteenth-Century America.* New York: Alfred A. Knopf, 1979.

Taylor, William R. *Cavalier and Yankee: The Old South and American National Character.* New York: George Braziller, Inc., 1961.

Thorpe, Earl E. *Black Historians: A Critique.* New York: William Morrow and Company, 1971.

Tischler, Nancy M. *Black Masks: Negro Characters in Modern Southern Fiction.* University Park: Pennsylvania State University Press, 1969.

Toll, Robert C. *Blacking Up: The Minstrel Show in Nineteenth-Century America.* New York: Oxford University Press, 1974.

Tudor, Andrew. *Image and Influence: Studies in the Sociology of Film.* New York: St. Martin's Press, 1975.

Turner, Lorenzo Dow. *Anti-Slavery Sentiment in American Literature Prior to 1865.* Washington, D.C.: Association for the Study of Negro Life and History, 1929.

United States Commission on Civil Rights. *Window Dressing on the Set: An Update.* Washington, D.C.: U.S. Government Printing Office, 1979.

United States Commission on Civil Rights. *Window Dressing on the Set: Women and Minorities in Television.* Washington, D.C.: U.S. Government Printing Office, 1977.

Wagner, Jean. *Black Poets of the United States: From Paul Laurence Dunbar to Langston Hughes.* Translated by Kenneth Douglas. Urbana: University of Illinois Press, 1973. [Paris: Librairie Istra, 1962.]

Weber, John Sherwood. "The American War Novel Dealing With the Revolutionary and Civil Wars." Ph.D. diss., University of Wisconsin, 1947.

Wilson, Edmund. *Patriotic Gore: Studies in the Literature of the American Civil War.* New York: Oxford University Press, 1962.

Wish, Harvey. *The American Historian: A Social-Intellectual History of the Writing of the American Past.* New York: Oxford University Press, 1960.

Wittke, Carl. *Tambo and Bones: A History of the American Minstrel Stage.* Durham: Duke University Press, 1930.

Wolters, Raymond. *The New Negro on Campus: Black College Rebellions of the 1920s.* Princeton: Princeton University Press, 1975.

Yellin, Jean Fagan. *The Intricate Knot: Black Figures in American Literature, 1776–1863.* New York: New York University Press, 1972.

Zinn, Howard. *The Politics of History.* Boston: Beacon Press, 1970.

SECONDARY SOURCES: ARTICLES

Akers, Charles W. "'Our Modern Egyptians': Phillis Wheatley and the Whig Campaign Against Slavery in Revolutionary Boston." *Journal of Negro History* 60 (July 1975): 397–410.

Albrecht, Milton C. "The Relationship of Literature and Society." *American Journal of Sociology* 59 (March 1954): 425–36.

Allen, Ralph G. "Our Native Theatre: Honky-Tonk, Minstrel Shows, Burlesque." In *The American Theatre: A Sum of its Parts,* pp. 273–314. Edited by Henry B. Williams. New York: Samuel French, Inc., 1971.

Anderson, Jervis. "Styron and His Black Critics." *Dissent* 16 (March-April 1969): 157–66.

Aptheker, Herbert. "The Negro College Student in the 1920s — Years of Preparation and Protest: An Introduction." *Science & Society* 33 (Spring 1969): 150–67.

Bailey, David Thomas. "A Divided Prism: Two Sources of Black Testimony on Slavery." *Journal of Southern History* 46 (August 1980): 381–404.

Baker, Donald G. "Black Images: The Afro-American in Popular Novels, 1900–1945." *Journal of Popular Culture* 7 (Fall 1973): 327–46.

Baker, Houston A., Jr. "Completely Well: One View of Black American Culture." In *Key Issues in the Afro-American Experience,* pp. 20–33. Edited by Nathan I. Huggins, Martin Kilson, and Daniel M. Fox. 2 vols. New York: Harcourt Brace Jovanovich, Inc., 1971.

Baldwin, Richard E. "The Art of *The Conjure Woman.*" *American Literature* 43 (November 1971): 385–98.

Bargainnier, Earl F. "The Falconhurst Series: A New Popular Image of the Old South." *Journal of Popular Culture* 10 (Fall 1976): 298–314.

Blauner, Robert. "Black Culture: Myth or Reality?" In *Americans From Africa.* Vol. 2: *Old Memories, New Moods,* pp. 417–41. Edited by Peter I. Rose. New York: Atherton Press, 1970.

Boardman, Helen. "The Rise of the Negro Historian." *Negro History Bulletin* 8 (April 1945): 148–54, 166.

Boskin, Joseph. "Sambo: The National Jester in the Popular Culture." In *The Great Fear: Race in the Mind of America,* pp. 165–85. Edited by Gary B. Nash and Richard Weiss. New York: Holt, Rinehart and Winston, Inc., 1970.

Brockett, O. G., and Brockett, Lenyth. "Civil War Theater: Contemporary Treatments." *Civil War History* 1 (September 1955): 229–50.

Brown, Sterling A. "Negro Character as Seen by White Authors." *Journal of Negro Education* 2 (January 1933): 179–203.

Burns, Edward McNall. "The Philosophy of History of the Founding Fathers." *Historian* 16 (Spring 1954): 142–68.

Canaday, Nicholas, Jr. "The Antislavery Novel Prior to 1852 and Hildreth's *The Slave* (1836)." *CLA Journal* 17 (December 1973): 175–91.

Cantor, Milton. "The Image of the Negro in Colonial Literature." *New England Quarterly* 36 (December 1963): 452–77.

Carsel, Wilfred. "The Slaveholder's Indictment of Northern Wage Slavery." *Journal of Southern History* 6 (November 1940): 504–20.

Cassara, Ernest. "The Rehabilitation of Uncle Tom: Significant Themes in Mrs. Stowe's Antislavery Novel." *CLA Journal* 17 (December 1973): 230–40.

Caulfield, Mina Davis. "Slavery and the Origins of Black Culture: Elkins Revisited." In *Americans From Africa*. Vol. 1: *Slavery and Its Aftermath*, pp. 171–93. Edited by Peter I. Rose. New York: Atherton Press, 1970.

Cohn, Jan. "The Civil War in Magazine Fiction of the 1860s." *Journal of Popular Culture* 4 (Fall 1970): 355–82.

Cohn, Jan. "The Negro Character in Northern Magazine Fiction of the 1860s." *New England Quarterly* 43 (December 1970): 572–92.

Collier, Eugenia. "A House of Twisted Mirrors: The Black Reflection in the Media." *Current History* 67 (November 1974): 228–31, 234.

Cripps, Thomas R. "The Myth of the Southern Box Office: A Factor in Racial Stereotyping in American Movies, 1920–1940." In *The Black Experience in America: Selected Essays*, pp. 116–44. Edited by James C. Curtis and Lewis L. Gould. Austin: University of Texas Press, 1970.

Cripps, Thomas R. "The Noble Black Savage: A Problem in the Politics of Television Art." *Journal of Popular Culture* 8 (Spring 1975): 687–95.

Cripps, Thomas R. "The Reaction of the Negro to the Motion Picture *Birth of a Nation.*" *Historian* 25 (May 1963): 344–62.

Crocker, Ruth Hutchinson."Ulrich Phillips: A Southern Historian Reconsidered." *Louisiana Studies* 15 (Summer 1976): 113–30.

Crouchett, Lawrence. "Early Black Studies Movements." *Journal of Black Studies* 2 (December 1971): 189–200.

Crowe, Charles. "Slavery, Ideology, and 'Cliometrics'." *Technology and Culture* 17 (April 1976): 271–85.

Crowe, Charles. "The Emergence of Progressive History." *Journal of the History of Ideas* 27 (January-March 1966): 109–24.

Crowe, Charles. "Time on the Cross: The Historical Monograph as a Pop Event." *History Teacher* 9 (August 1976): 588–630.

Cruden, Robert. "James Ford Rhodes and the Negro: A Study in the Problem of Objectivity." *Ohio History* 71 (July 1962): 129–37.

Dacey, Raymond. "A Historiography of Negro Slavery, 1918–1976." In *Issues and Ideas in America*, pp. 113–28. Edited by Benjamin J. Taylor and Thurman J. White. Norman: University of Oklahoma Press, 1976.

Damon, S. Foster. "The Negro in Early American Songsters." *Papers of the Bibliographical Society of America* 28 (1934): 132–63.

David, Beverly R. "Visions of the South: Joel Chandler Harris and his Illustrators." *American Literary Realism, 1870–1910* 9 (Summer 1976): 189–206.

Davis, Arthur P. "Personal Elements in the Poetry of Phillis Wheatley." *Phylon* 14 (June 1953): 191–98.

Davis, Arthur P. "*The Garies and Their Friends:* A Neglected Pioneer Novel." *CLA Journal* 13 (September 1969): 27–34.

Davis, David Brion. "Slavery and the Post-World War II Historians." In *Slavery, Colonialism, and Racism*, pp. 1–16. Edited by Sidney W. Mintz. New York: W. W. Norton & Company, 1974.

Davis, Leona King. "Literary Opinions on Slavery in American Literature from After the American Revolution to the Civil War." *Negro History Bulletin* 23 (February 1960): 99–101, 104.

Davis, Richard Beale. "The 'Virginia Novel' Before *Swallow Barn*." *Virginia Magazine of History and Biography* 71 (July 1963): 278–93.

Daykin, Walter L. "Negro Types in American White Fiction." *Sociology and Social Research* 22 (September-October 1937): 45–52.

Degler, Carl N. "Why Historians Change Their Minds." *Pacific Historical Review* 45 (May 1976): 167–84.

DeVries, James H. "The Tradition of the Sentimental Novel in *The Garies and Their Friends*." *CLA Journal* 17 (December 1973): 241–49.

Dowty, Alan. "Urban Slavery in Pro-Southern Fiction of the 1850's." *Journal of Southern History* 32 (February 1966): 25–41.

Duvall, Severn. "*Uncle Tom's Cabin:* The Sinister Side of the Patriarchy." *New England Quarterly* 36 (March 1963): 3–22.

Edmonds, Randolph. "Black Drama in the American Theatre: 1700–1970." In *The American Theatre: A Sum of its Parts*, pp. 379–426. Edited by Henry B. Williams. New York: Samuel French, Inc., 1971.

Emanuel, James A. "Racial Fire in the Poetry of Paul Laurence Dunbar." In *A Singer in the Dawn: Reinterpretations of Paul Laurence Dunbar*, pp. 75–93. Edited by Jay Martin. New York: Dodd, Mead & Company, 1975.

English, Thomas H. "The Other Uncle Remus." *Georgia Review* 21 (Summer 1967): 210–17.

Farrison, W. Edward. "George Moses Horton: Poet for Freedom." *CLA Journal* 14 (March 1971): 227–41.

Ferguson, Alfred R. "The Abolition of Blacks in Abolitionist Fiction, 1830–1860." *Journal of Black Studies* 5 (December 1974): 134–56.

Fife, Iline. "The Confederate Theatre." *Southern Speech Journal* 20 (Spring 1955): 224–31.

Fife, Marilyn Diane. "Black Image in American TV: The First Two Decades." *Black Scholar* 6 (November 1974): 7–15.

Fleming, Robert E. "Black, White, and Mulatto in Martin R. Delany's *Blake*." *Negro History Bulletin* 36 (February 1973): 37–39.

Flusche, Michael. "Joel Chandler Harris and the Folklore of Slavery." *Journal of American Studies* 9 (December 1975): 347–63.

Fogel, Robert William. "Cliometrics and Culture: Some Recent Developments in the Historiography of Slavery." *Journal of Social History* 11 (Fall 1977): 34–51.

Franklin, John Hope. "'Birth of a Nation'—Propaganda as History." *Massachusetts Review* 20 (Autumn 1979): 417–34.

Franklin, John Hope. "The New Negro History." *Crisis* 64 (February 1957): 69–75.

Franklin, Vincent P. "Slavery, Personality, and Black Culture—Some Theoretical Issues." *Phylon* 35 (March 1974): 54–63.

Gayle, Addison, Jr. "Cultural Hegemony: The Southern White Writer and American Letters." In *Amistad 1*, pp. 3–24. Edited by John A. Williams and Charles F. Harris. New York: Vintage Books. 1970.

Genovese, Eugene D. "The Influence of the Black Power Movement on Historical Scholarship: Reflections of a White Historian." *Daedalus* 99 (Spring 1970): 473–94.

George, Katherine. "The Civilized West Looks at Primitive Africa, 1400–1800: A Study in Ethnocentrism." *Isis* 49 (March 1958): 62–72.

Gerber, David A. "Haley's *Roots* and Our Own: An Inquiry Into the Nature of a Popular Phenomenon." *Journal of Ethnic Studies* 5 (no. 3, 1977): 87–111.

Glenn, Stanley. "The Development of the Negro Character in American Comedy Before the Civil War." *Southern Speech Journal* 26 (Winter 1960): 133–48.

Glicksberg, Charles I. "Bias, Fiction, and the Negro." *Phylon* 13 (June 1952): 127–35.

Graham, Maryemma. "Frank Yerby, King of the Costume Novel." *Essence* 6 (October 1975): 70–1, 88–89, 91–92.

Green, Alan W. C. "'Jim Crow', 'Zip Coon': The Northern Origins of Negro Minstrelsy." *Massachusetts Review* 11 (Spring 1970): 385–97.

Griffin, Max L. "Cooper's Attitude Toward the South." *Studies in Philology* 48 (January 1951): 67–76.

Gross, Seymour L., and Bender, Eileen. "History, Politics and Literature: The Myth of Nat Turner." *American Quarterly* 23 (October 1971): 487–518.

Haines, Deborah L. "Scientific History as a Teaching Method: The Formative Years." *Journal of American History* 63 (March 1977): 892–912.

Hall, L. A. "Some Early Black-Face Performers and the First Minstrel Troupe." *Harvard Library Notes* 1 (October 1920): 39–45.

Handlin, Oscar. "The Capacity of Quantitative History." *Perspectives in American History* 9 (1975): 7–26.

Harris, Robert L., Jr. "Coming of Age: The Transformation of Afro-American Historiography." *Journal of Negro History* 67 (Summer 1982): 107–121.

Harwell, Richard B. "Gone with Miss Ravenel's Courage; or Bugles Blow So Red: A Note on the Civil War Novel." *New England Quarterly* 35 (June 1962): 253–61.

Hill, Herbert. "'Uncle Tom': An Enduring American Myth." *Crisis* 72 (May 1965): 289–95.

Hite, Roger W. "'Stand Still and See the Salvation': The Rhetorical Design of Martin Delany's *Blake*." *Journal of Black Studies* 5 (December 1974): 192–202.

Hofstadter, Richard. "U.B. Phillips and the Plantation Legend." *Journal of Negro History* 29 (April 1944): 109–24.

Holt, Thomas. "On the Cross: The Role of Quantitative Methods in the Reconstruction of the Afro-American Experience." *Journal of Negro History* 61 (April 1976): 158–72.

Holt, W. Stull. "The Idea of Scientific History in America." *Journal of the History of Ideas* 1 (June 1940): 352–62.

Hovet, Theodore R. "Modernization and the American Fall into Slavery in *Uncle Tom's Cabin.*" *New England Quarterly* 54 (December 1981):499–518.

Hudson, Benjamin F. "Another View of 'Uncle Tom'." *Phylon* 24 (Spring 1963): 79–87.

Hudson, Gossie Harold. "Paul Laurence Dunbar: *Dialect Et La Negritude.*" *Phylon* 34 (September 1973): 236–47.

Hur, Kenneth K., and Robinson, John P. "The Social Impact of 'Roots.'" *Journalism Quarterly* 55 (Spring 1978): 19–24, 83.

Isani, Mukhtar Ali. "Far from 'Gambia's Golden Shore': The Black in Late Eighteenth-Century American Imaginative Literature." *William and Mary Quarterly* 36 (July 1979): 353–72.

Issel, William. "History, Social Science, and Ideology: Elkins and Blassingame on Ante-Bellum American Slavery." *History Teacher* 9 (November 1975): 56–72.

Johnson, Edwin D. "Aphra Behn's 'Oroonoko'." *Journal of Negro History* 10 (July 1925): 334–42.

Johnson, James Weldon. "Race Prejudice and the Negro Artist." *Harper's Monthly Magazine* 157 (November 1928): 769–76.

Kaplan, Sidney. "*The Octoroon:* Early History of the Drama of Miscegenation." *Journal of Negro Education* 20 (Fall 1951): 547–57.

Killens, John Oliver. "Hollywood in Black and White." In *The State of the Nation,* pp. 100–07. Edited by David Boroff. Englewood Cliffs, N.J.: Prentice-Hall, Inc., 1965.

Kugler, Ruben F. "U. B. Phillips' Use of Sources." *Journal of Negro History* 47 (July 1962): 153–68.

Lamplugh, George R. "The Image of the Negro in Popular Magazine Fiction, 1875–1900." *Journal of Negro History* 57 (April 1972): 177–89.

Leab, Daniel J. "'All-Colored' – But Not Much Different: Films Made for Negro Ghetto Audiences, 1913–1928." *Phylon* 36 (September 1975): 321–39.

Leab, Daniel J. "The Gamut from A to B: The Image of the Black in Pre-1915 Movies." *Political Science Quarterly* 88 (March 1973): 53–70.

Leary, Lewis: "Thomas Branagan: Republican Rhetoric and Romanticism in America." *Pennsylvania Magazine of History and Biography* 77 (July 1953): 332–52.

Lemons, Stanley. "Black Stereotypes as Reflected in Popular Culture, 1880–1920." *American Quarterly* 29 (Spring 1977): 102–16.

Levy, David W. "Racial Stereotypes in Antislavery Fiction." *Phylon* 31 (Fall 1970): 265–79.

McDowell, Tremaine. "The Negro in the Southern Novel Prior to 1850." *Journal of English and Germanic Philology* 25 (1926): 455–73.

Martin, Terence. "Social Institutions in the Early American Novel." *American Quarterly* 9 (Spring 1957): 72–84.

Mathews, James W. "The Civil War of 1936: *Gone with the Wind* and *Absalom, Absalom!*" *Georgia Review* 21 (Winter 1967): 462–69.

May, Robert E. "*Gone With the Wind* as Southern History: A Reappraisal." *Southern Quarterly* 17 (Fall 1978): 51–64.

Mazrui, Ali A. "Roots: The End of America's Amnesia?" *Africa Report* 22 (May–June 1977): 6–11.

Miller, Randall M. "Mrs. Stowe's Negro: George Harris' Negritude in *Uncle Tom's Cabin.*" *Colby Library Quarterly* 10 (December 1974): 521–26.

Mills, Gary B., and Mills, Elizabeth Shown. "*Roots* and the New 'Faction': A Legitimate Tool for Clio?" *Virginia Magazine of History and Biography* 89 (January 1981): 3–26.

Mixon, Wayne. "Joel Chandler Harris, the Yeoman Tradition, and the New South Movement." *Georgia Historical Quarterly* 61 (Winter 1977): 308–17.

Mohr, Clarence L. "Southern Blacks in the Civil War: A Century of Historiography." *Journal of Negro History* 59 (April 1974): 177–95.

Moore, Jack B. "Images of the Negro in Early American Short Fiction." *Mississippi Quarterly* 22 (Winter 1968–69): 47–57.

Moore, Jack B. "The Guilt of the Victim: Racial Themes in Some Frank Yerby Novels." *Journal of Popular Culture* 8 (Spring 1975): 746–56.

Moody, Richard. "Uncle Tom, the Theater and Mrs. Stowe." *American Heritage* 6 (October 1955): 29–103.

Mugleston, William F. "Southern Literature as History: Slavery in the Antebellum Novel." *History Teacher* 8 (November 1974): 17–30.

Murdock, Kenneth B. "Clio in the Wilderness: History and Biography in Puritan New England." *Church History* 24 (September 1955): 221–38.

Newby, I.A. "Historians and Negroes." *Journal of Negro History* 54 (January 1969): 32–47.

Nicholas, H. G. "Uncle Tom's Cabin, 1852–1952." *American Heritage* 4 (Winter 1953): 20–3, 72.

Nichols, Charles. "Slave Narratives and the Plantation Legend." *Phylon* 10 (Fall 1949): 201–10.

Nichols, Charles. "The Origins of Uncle Tom's Cabin." *Phylon* 19 (Fall 1958): 328–34.

Nichols, William W. "Slave Narratives: Dismissed Evidence in the Writing of Southern History." *Phylon* 32 (Winter 1971): 403–9.

O'Daniel, Therman B. "Cooper's Treatment of the Negro." *Phylon* 8 (June 1947): 164–76.

Orton, Richard, "Black Folk Entertainments and the Evolution of American Minstrelsy." *Negro History Bulletin* 41 (September-October 1978): 885–87.

Palmer, Jaclyn C. "Images of Slavery: Black and White Writers." *Negro History Bulletin* 41 (September-October 1978): 888–89.

Patterson, Cecil L. "A Different Drum: The Image of the Negro in the Nineteenth Century Songster." *CLA Journal* 8 (September 1964): 44–50.

Pawley, Thomas D. "The First Black Playwrights." *Black World* 21 (April 1972): 16–24.

Pease, William H., and Pease, Jane H. "Antislavery Ambivalence: Immediatism, Expediency, Race." *American Quarterly* 17 (Winter 1965): 682–95.

Peeples, Ken, Jr. "The Paradox of the 'Good Gray Poet' (Walt Whitman on Slavery and the Black Man)." *Phylon* 35 (March 1974): 22–32.

Peters, Erskine. "Jupiter Hammon: His Engagement with Interpretation." *Journal of Ethnic Studies* 8 (Winter 1981): 1–12.

Porter, Dorothy B. "The Organized Educational Activities of Negro Literary Societies, 1828–1846." *Journal of Negro Education* 5 (October 1936): 555–76.

Pressly, Thomas J., and Chamberlin, Harvey H. "Slavery and Scholarship, Some Problems of Evidence." *Pacific Northwest Quarterly* 66 (April 1975): 79–84.

Rattley, Sandra. "The Impact of *Roots:* Real or Imagined?" *Africa Report* 22 (May–June 1977): 12–16.

Ridgely, Joseph V. "*Woodcraft:* Simms's First Answer to *Uncle Tom's Cabin.*" *American Literature* 31 (January 1960): 421–33.

Riggio, Thomas P. "*Uncle Tom* Reconstructed: A Neglected Chapter in the History of a Book." *American Quarterly* 28 (Spring 1976): 56–70.

Roper, John Herbert. "A Case of Forgotten Identity: Ulrich B. Phillips as a Young Progressive." *Georgia Historical Quarterly* 60 (Summer 1976): 165–75.

Roppolo, Joseph P. "Harriet Beecher Stowe and New Orleans: A Study in Hate." *New England Quarterly* 30 (September 1957): 346–62.

Roppolo, Joseph P. "Uncle Tom in New Orleans: Three Lost Plays." *New England Quarterly* 27 (June 1954): 213–26.

Rose, Alan Henry. "The Image of the Negro in the Pre-Civil War Novels of John Pendleton Kennedy and William Gilmore Simms." *Journal of American Studies* 4 (1970): 217–26.

Rose, Willie Lee. "Race and Region in American Historical Fiction: Four Episodes in Popular Culture." In *Region, Race, and Reconstruction: Essays in Honor of C. Vann Woodward*, pp. 113–39. Edited by J. Morgan Kousser and James M. McPherson. New York: Oxford University Press, 1982.

Rubin, Louis D., Jr. "The Image of an Army: The Civil War in Southern Fiction." In *Southern Writers: Appraisals in Our Time*, pp. 50–70. Edited by R. C. Simonini, Jr. Charlottesville: University Press of Virginia, 1964.

Rubin, Louis D., Jr. "Southern Local Color and the Black Man." *Southern Review* 6 (October 1970): 1011–30.

Salem, Sam E. "U.B. Phillips and the Scientific Tradition." *Georgia Historical Quarterly* 44 (June 1960): 172–85.

Saveth, Edward N. "A Science of American History," *Diogenes* 26 (Summer 1959): 107–22.

Saxton, Alexander. "Blackface Minstrelsy and Jacksonian Ideology." *American Quarterly* 27 (March 1975): 3–28.

Scheiber, Harry N. "Black Is Computable: The Controversy over *Time on the Cross* and the History of American Slavery." *American Scholar* 44 (Autumn 1975): 656–73.

Sherman, Joan R. "James Monroe Whitfield, Poet and Emigrationist: A Voice of Protest and Despair." *Journal of Negro History* 57 (April 1972): 169–76.

Singal, Daniel Joseph. "Ulrich B. Phillips: The Old South as the New." *Journal of American History* 63 (March 1977): 871–91.

Skaggs, Merrill Maguire. "*Roots:* A New Black Myth." *Southern Quarterly* 17 (Fall 1978): 42–50.

Slout, William L. "*Uncle Tom's Cabin* in American Film History." *Journal of Popular Film* 2 (Spring 1973): 137–51.

Smallwood, Osborn T. "The Historical Significance of Whittier's Anti-Slavery Poems as Reflected by Their Political and Social Background." *Journal of Negro History* 35 (April 1950): 150–73.

Smith, John David. "A Different View of Slavery: Black Historians Attack the Pro-slavery Argument, 1890–1920." *Journal of Negro History* 65 (Fall 1980): 298–311.

Smith, John David. "The Historiographic Rise, Fall, and Resurrection of Ulrich Bonnell Phillips." *Georgia Historical Quarterly* 65 (Summer 1981): 138–53.

Soderbergh, Peter A. "Hollywood and the South, 1930–1960." *Mississippi Quarterly* 19 (Winter 1965–66): 1–19.

Spiller, Robert E. "Fenimore Cooper's Defense of Slave-Owning America." *American Historical Review* 35 (April 1930): 575–82.

Stampp, Kenneth M. "Rebels and Sambos: The Search for the Negro's Personality in Slavery." *Journal of Southern History* 37 (August 1971): 367–92.

Stampp, Kenneth M. "Slavery—The Historian's Burden." In *Perspectives and Irony in American Slavery*, pp. 153–70. Edited by Harry P. Owens. Jackson: University Press of Mississippi, 1976.

Stampp, Kenneth M. "The Historian and Southern Negro Slavery." *American Historical Review* 57 (April 1952): 613–24.

Starr, Raymond. "Historians and the Origins of British North American Slavery." *Historian* 36 (November 1973): 1–18.

Stein, Howard F. "In Search of 'Roots': An Epic of Origins and Destiny." *Journal of Popular Culture* 11 (Summer 1977): 11–17.

Stern, Jerome. "*Gone With the Wind:* The South as America." *Southern Humanities Review* 6 (Winter 1972): 5–12.

Stevens, John D. "The Black Reaction to *Gone With the Wind.*" *Journal of Popular Film* 2 (Fall 1973): 366–71.

Stuckey, Sterling. "Twilight of Our Past: Reflections on the Origins of Black History." In *Amistad 2*, pp. 261–95. Edited by John A. Williams and Charles F. Harris. New York: Vintage Books, 1971.

Suthern, Orrin Clayton II. "Minstrelsy and Popular Culture." *Journal of Popular Culture* 4 (Winter 1971): 658–73.

Tandy, Jeannette Reid. "Pro-Slavery Propaganda in American Fiction of the Fifties —Part I." *South Atlantic Quarterly* 21 (January 1922): 41–50.

Tandy, Jeannette Reid. "Pro-Slavery Propaganda in American Fiction of the Fifties —Part II." *South Atlantic Quarterly* 21 (April 1922): 170–78.

Thompson, Lawrence S. "The Civil War in Fiction." *Civil War History* 2 (March 1956): 83–95.

Toll, Robert C. "Behind the Blackface: Minstrel Men and Minstrel Myths." *American Heritage* 29 (April-May, 1978): 93–105.

Tragle, Henry Irving. "Styron and His Sources." *Massachusetts Review* 11 (Winter 1970): 135–53.

Trent, Toni. "Stratification Among Blacks by Black Authors." *Negro History Bulletin* 34 (December 1971): 179–81.

Turner, Darwin T. "Daddy Joel Harris and His Old-Time Darkies." *Southern Literary Journal* 1 (December 1968): 20–41.

Turner, Darwin T. "Frank Yerby as Debunker." *Massachusetts Review* 9 (Summer 1968): 569–77.

Turner, Darwin T. "Paul Laurence Dunbar: The Rejected Symbol." *Journal of Negro History* 52 (January 1967): 1–13.

Unger, Irwin. "The 'New Left' and American History: Some Recent Trends in United States Historiography." *American Historical Review* 72 (July 1967): 1237–63.

Uya, Okon E. "The Culture of Slavery: Black Experience Through a White Filter." *Afro-American Studies* 1 (January 1971): 1–7.

Van Auken, Sheldon. "The Southern Historical Novel in the Early Twentieth Century." *Journal of Southern History* 14 (May 1948): 157–91.

Waal, Carla. "The First Original Confederate Drama: *The Guerrillas.*" *Virginia Magazine of History and Biography* 70 (October 1962): 459–67.

Wall, Bennett H. "African Slavery." In *Writing Southern History: Essays in Historiography in Honor of Fletcher M. Green*, pp. 175–97. Edited by Arthur S. Link and Rembert W. Patrick. Baton Rouge: Louisiana State University Press, 1965.

Walser, Richard. "Negro Dialect in Eighteenth-Century American Drama." *American Speech* 30 (December 1955): 269–76.

Ward, John William. "*Uncle Tom's Cabin*, As a Matter of Historical Fact." *Columbia University Forum* 9 (Winter 1966): 42–47.

Welsh, Willard. "Civil War Theater: The War in Drama." *Civil War History* 1 (September 1955): 251–80.

Wermuth, Paul C. "Swallow Barn: A Virginia Idyll." *Virginia Cavalcade* 9 (Summer 1959): 30–34.

Wesley, Charles H. "Racial Historical Societies and the American Heritage." *Journal of Negro History* 37 (January 1952): 11–35.

White, John. "The Novelist as Historian: William Styron and American Negro Slavery." *Journal of American Studies* 4 (no. 2, 1970): 233–45.

White, Stanley W. "The Burnt Cork Illusion of the 1920s in America: A Study in Nostalgia." *Journal of Popular Culture* 5 (Winter 1971): 530–50.

Williams, Ernest P. "William Styron and His Ten Black Critics: A Belated Mediation." *Phylon* 37 (Summer 1976): 189–95.

Wilson, Charles R. "Racial Reservations: Indians and Blacks in American Magazines, 1865–1900." *Journal of Popular Culture* 10 (Summer 1976): 70–79.

Winter, Marian Hannah. "Juba and American Minstrelsy." *Dance Index* 6 (1947): 28–47.

Wolfe, Bernard. "Uncle Remus and the Malevolent Rabbit." *Commentary* 8 (July 1949): 31–41.

Wood, Peter. "'I Did the Best I Could for My Day': The Study of Early Black History during the Second Reconstruction, 1960 to 1976." *William and Mary Quarterly* 35 (April 1978): 185–225.

Woodward, C. Vann. "Clio With Soul." *Journal of American History* 5 (June 1969): 5–20.

Woodward, C. Vann. "History from Slave Sources." *American Historical Review* 79 (April 1974): 470–81.

Yetman, Norman R. "Slavery and Personality: A Problem in the Study of Modal Personality in Historical Populations." In *American Character and Culture in a Changing World: Some Twentieth-Century Perspectives,* pp. 349–66. Edited by John A. Hague. Westport: Greenwood Press, 1979.

Zanger, Jules. "The 'Tragic Octoroon' in Pre-Civil War Fiction." *American Quarterly* 18 (Spring 1966): 63–70.

Zeugner, John. "A Note on Martin Delany's *Blake,* and Black Militancy." *Phylon* 32 (Spring 1971): 98–105.

Ziff, Larzer, "Songs of the Civil War." *Civil War History* 2 (September 1956): 7–28.

INDEX

Hallam, Lewis, 22
Hamilton, Aunt "Pittypat" (character in *Gone With the Wind*), 126
Hammon, Jupiter, 55–56, 57
Hannah (character in *The Escape*), 63
"Happy Are We, Darkies So Gay," 48
Happy Uncle Tom's Cabin (Sanford), 47
Harlem Renaissance, 102, 120, 121, 132, 202–3
Harris, Eliza (character in *Uncle Tom's Cabin*), 34
Harris, George (character in *Uncle Tom's Cabin*), 34, 48
Harris, Joel Chandler: creates Uncle Remus, 96, 200; as folklorist, 96–97; contributions to American literature, 97, 98, 101
Harris, William T., 133–34
Harry (character in *Love and Friendship*), 20–21
Hayes, Rutherford B., 77
Heart of Maryland, The (Belasco), 116
Held by the Enemy (Gillette), 115, 117
Hentz, Caroline Lee, 25, 38
Heroes: Founding Fathers as, 8, 13; slaves as, 50, 58–59, 60–61, 90–91, 120–21, 142, 147–48, 151–52; fugitive slaves as, 59–60, 76–77; slaveholders as, 72–74; abolitionists as, 74–75; Underground Railroad conductors as, 75–76; of Civil War, 92–93
"Heroic Slave, The" (Douglass), 60–61
Hildreth, Richard, 31
Hill, Daniel H., 92
Hilt to Hilt (Cooke), 92
Hireling and the Slave, The (Grayson), 36
Historians: in early America, 5–9; in antebellum era, 26, 30, 169; use of reminiscences, 72, 188; use of slave sources, 89, 136, 137–38, 140; use of oral history, 144–45; "New Left," 214
History: interpretations of slavery in, 4–9, 26–31, 51–54, 67–89, 131–40; writing in early America, 5–8; in college curriculum, 6, 26, 132–35, 164; publishing, 6, 26, 89–90, 132; writing in antebellum era, 26; organizations, 51–52, 131–32; writing in late nineteenth-century, 77–78; writing in early twentieth-century, 82; oral, 138, 144–45. *See also* Slaves, education
History and Remarkable Life of the Truly Honourable Col. Jacque, The (Defoe), 10

History of Georgia, The (McCall), 8–9
History of Great Britain, The (Hume), 6
History of Scotland, The (Robertson), 6
History of the United States (Bancroft), 27–30
History of the United States (Ramsay), 9
History of the United States from the Compromise of 1850 (Rhodes), 78–79
His Trust, 122
His Trust Fulfilled, 122
Hofstadter, Richard, 87
Holiday, Billie, 67
Holland, Henry (character in *Blake*), 183
Holly, James Theodore, 52
Holly, Joseph C., 59
Home of the Brave, 127
Horner, Lance, 148
Horseshoe Robinson (Tayleure), 46
Horton, George Moses, 59
Howard, Bronson, 115
Hughes, Langston: creates black role model, 103; on black colleges, 134
Hume, David, 6
Hwesu. *See* Parks, Wesley

"I Am Monarch of Nought I Survey," 45
"I Long to See Old Massa's Face Again," 113
Imoinda (character in *Oroonoko*), 10
In Dahomey, 118
Insurrections. *See* Slaves, personality traits—rebellious
Introduction to the History of America (McCulloch), 26
Intruder in the Dust, 127

Jack (character in *Clotel*), 62
Jackson, Mae, 143
Jerry (character in *The Guerrillas*), 115
Jezebel, 124–25
Johnson, Edward, 5–6
Johnson, Georgia Douglass, 120
Johnson, James Weldon, 102
Jolson, Al, 118
Jonathan (character in *The Forest Rose*), 22
Jones, LeRoi, 150
Jordan, Vernon, 156–57
Jordan, Winthrop, 5
Josair (minstrel character), 112
Journal of Negro History, 132
Jubilee (Walker), 144

DESIGNED BY ED FRANK PRODUCTIONS
COMPOSED BY METRICOMP
GRUNDY CENTER, IOWA
MANUFACTURED BY THOMSON-SHORE, INC.
DEXTER, MICHIGAN
TEXT AND DISPLAY LINES ARE SET IN PALATINO

Library of Congress Cataloging in Publication Data
Van Deburg, William L.
Slavery & race in American popular culture.
Bibliography: pp. 233–252.
Includes index.
1. Slavery — United States — Historiography. 2. Afro-
Americans — Historiography. 3. Slavery and slaves in
literature. 4. Afro-Americans in literature. 5. Afro-
Americans in motion pictures. 6. United States — Popular
culture. I. Title. II. Title: Slavery and race in
American popular culture.
E441.V23 1984   305.8'96073'072   83-40272
ISBN 0-299-09630-0
ISBN 0-299-09634-3 (pbk.)